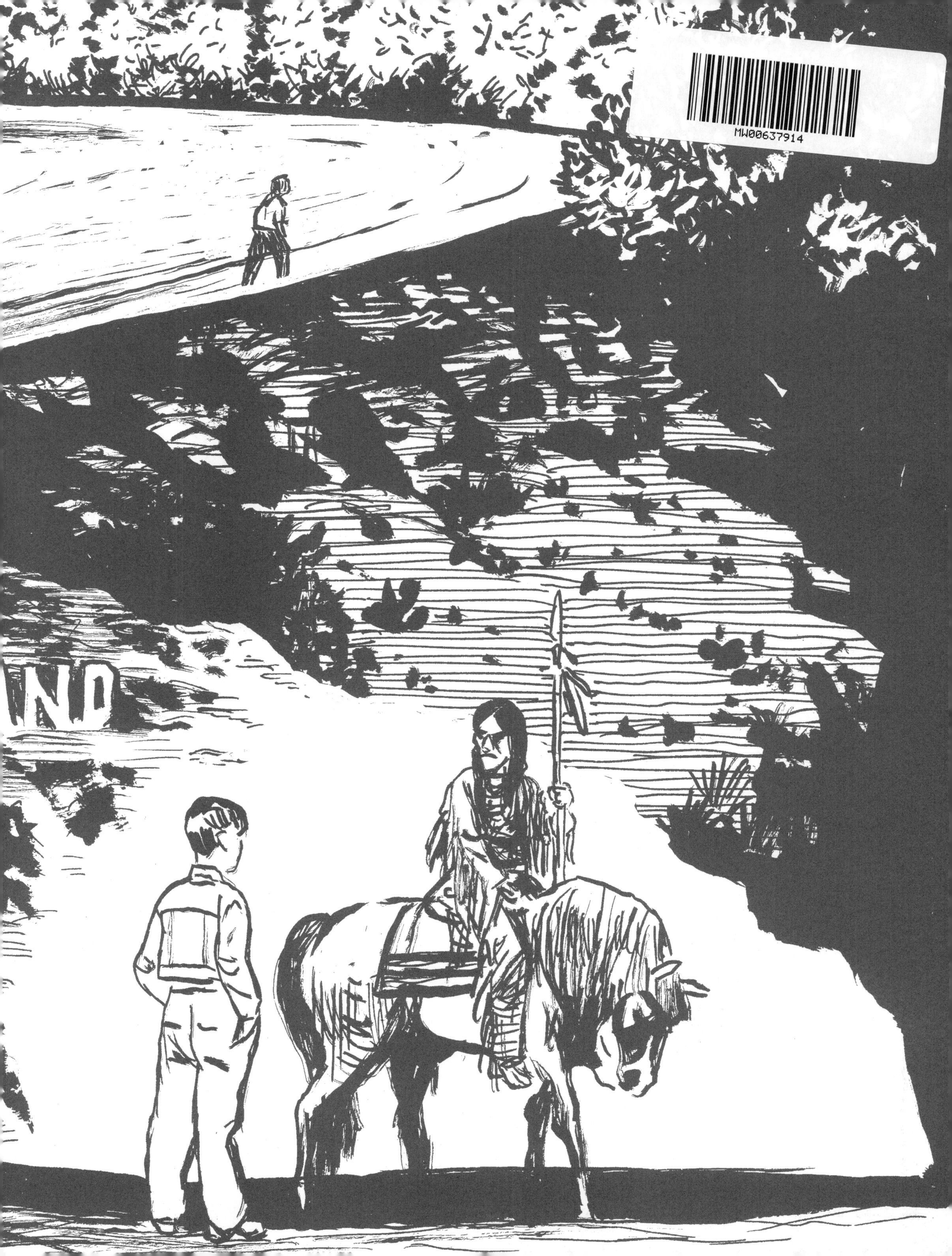

# Erased

**An Actor of Color's Journey Through the Heyday of Hollywood**

Written by Loo Hui Phang
Art by Hugues Micol
Translation by Edward Gauvin

nbm GRAPHIC
NOVELS
Nantier · Beall · Minoustchine
NEW YORK

Thanks to Raoul Peck, Helena Gonçalves, Viviana Andriani, Nick Nguyen, Karine Virengue.
Loo Hui Phang

*This work was awarded the Grand Prize in non-fiction for excellence in publication and translation as part of Albertine Translation, formerly French Voices, a program created by Villa Albertine, funded by Albertine Foundation and the Albertine Books Foundation with the support of Van Cleef & Arpels.*

*For the French edition by Futuropolis, Loo Hui Phang was awarded the Prix René Goscinny 2021, for her work as a writer, at the Angouleme International Comics Festival.*

ISBN 9781681123387
© Futuropolis / 2020
All rights reserved
Rights arranged in collaboration with One Rev Ltd.
© 2024 NBM for the English translation
Library of Congress Control Number: 2024930524
Lettering by Ortho
Printed in China
First printing July 2024

**This title is also available in e-book (ISBN 9781681123394)**

# Preface

## Raoul Peck

March 6, 2020

"So while we still can, let's stamp our faces and bodies on the white man's images... These faces, these bodies are real. Let us occupy their terrain every way we can," utters an Indigenous American extra to the citizen Maximus Ohanzee Wildhorse, hero of the bold, powerful, and unbridled work before you.

That's exactly what I feel like I've been doing all my life, just like billions of other children of the othered "third" world: subverting what the "first" world presented to me as bedrock fact.

Like them, I loved Hollywood. Like them, I projected myself onto its cowboys, wiping out Indians, then "civilizing" Blacks, exterminating Arabs, decimating Asians (according to the war of the moment).

My own heroic aspirations had to be found elsewhere. They had to be made from scratch. For with time, one tires of supplying logical explanations for the absurd "reality" on every screen that bore no relation to one's own. In my reality, I made the covert discovery that the "Indians"— well, they were us. An "us" that, far from being a minority, comprised a good ¾ of the world's population.

These figures demonstrate film's fearsomely subversive capacity to produce images capable of neutralizing the very reality of lived experience! Cultural alienation through popcorn and Coca-Cola.

Escaping the Dream Factory is no easy task, for it is seductive, comforting, soothing... and annihilating,

especially for those on the "right" side. Much later, I learned to decipher this language and find my own. I had to assert myself or else be made a mindless fool. But how to go about it when images we can call "ours" are rare, if not nonexistent? Quite simply, by giving ourselves permission to deconstruct, reconstruct, reclaim, pirate. Swipe anything your hand happens to fall on. In my filmmaking practice—both fictive and documentary— I've often used images shot by others. No one asked my opinion beforehand, so I take the liberty of doing as I please. Such liberty is essential, even a matter of life and death. And it is from such liberty, conquered and claimed, that our two creators, Loo Hui Phang and Hugues Micol, proceed.

It is this liberated imagination that creates new, hitherto unsuspected spaces. It enables us to recalibrate what no longer works, realign what is out of joint, uncouple what was previously conflated, reveal what was once obscured. And all in all, such imagination becomes a source of joy and pleasure.

"Hollywood is a fiction. And like all fictions, it is myriad, changing, sincere, deceitful," writes Loo Hui Phang.

In Hollywood's Dream Factory, we sometimes come across, in the interstices, another story consigned to the background. Through these disguises and distortions, stories, images, bodies, emotions—in short, life—are also printed on celluloid. And here, we begin to make out what isn't just a movie anymore. At least, not for everyone.

Other artists, writers, and musicians before us have, each in their own way, tried to fulfill this quest for meaning, for roots, for history—all that buried memory. From James Baldwin to Toni Morrison, Paul Robeson to Jacques Stephen Alexis, Chinua Achebe to Wole Soyinka. Work as exhausting as it is exalting. On one hand, the sheer joy of discovery and invention; on the other, the crushingly intimidating task that lies before you. Such that the entire undertaking can seem at times as desperate as it is suicidal (or sacrificial, for the more mystically-minded).

How, indeed, to remedy centuries of denial so swiftly replaced by contemporary ignorance, by an often total suppression of whole swaths of history, even entire civilizations interred beneath twisted sediments and pseudoscientific discourses? For science, too, drifted into these genocidal byways—take, for instance, the great racist theories of the late 19th century, made up from whole cloth. A lethal straying that cost entire peoples their lives on every continent, including Europe. Victims have donned various denominations over the ages, from Jew to Muslim (as early as the 17th century!) to Arab (indifferently applied today) to "Black," to Indian (or the compound Native American, as we now put it) to Asian and everyone every era has labeled as "different," "foreign," "heathen," "barbarian," "invader"—or simply "migrant," as at the gates of today's Europe.

It is understandable, then, why some of us can seem "angry" at times when faced with the denial of a reality so painful and seemingly with no end in sight. Yes, we are "impatient" to have true history understood. Its meaning, its omissions, its disfigurement. For without this, no future can be negotiated. For any of us.

But in order to recreate another less tainted history, how to find the words, concepts, images, how to rename feelings? And then, how to share them with others? It isn't about winning anyone over, but rather simply facilitating an openness of mind, however modest, and a minimal capacity for taking in something new. Naturally, it isn't at all about attacking the average citizen of the West, quick to anger when their goodwill, their benevolence, is questioned. At the slightest suspicion seen as unjustified, they throw it all back in our faces. These days, for instance, you're not supposed to say "White," even though the n-word was once tossed around at the drop of a hat. How can you help but smile (after all, we're not going to weep) at the recent coinage "reverse racism"? The height of oxymoronity.

And so, without swerving from our stated goal of deconstruction, we must be even smarter than our adversaries. At any rate, we cannot do otherwise, so potent is the knot in our stomachs. Untameable, and indomitable. Let us press on, then, through pedagogy, in bringing the "other" along with us on this new adventure. In the end, their own future is also at stake, since we all depend on one another. The poverty of some influences the wealth of others—and in our times, even more so.

Let us then share our findings with those who have never spared us a glance. Those unaware of our very existence and ignorant of the fancy that everyone is someone else's "other" somewhere. The heartbreak of otherness.

As James Baldwin put it in his "Pin-Drop Speech" at Cambridge: "There is scarcely any hope for the American dream, because the people who are denied participation in it, by their very presence, will wreck it."

Finding other creative paths and voices would be more or less viable, if we didn't have to gather memories at the same time. For we are terribly deprived of them, so thoroughly have our legacies been looted, devastated, despoiled, plundered. Rare are the vestiges—be they material, intellectual, cultural, or intangible—that have survived the ravages of each successive genocide.

How to create, from next to nothing, critical and independent thought, a burgeoning philosophy in the making? Not "instead of" Western contributions, since such contributions do not come from "nowhere" either, ignoring as they do others' contributions, but rather as a complement to the West's dogmas. And these new "creations," by virtue of their agile and multifarious origins, utterly self-possessed, inclusive, secular, declare a "world philosophy" with their universalist vision. A philosophy, let us hope, able to rejuvenate an exhausted West, short on inspiration, gorged, complacent in its clear Eurocentric conscience. Another side effect of this way of apprehending the world is an even rarer phenomenon: these creations produce humanity. A commodity hard to copy.

Revisiting the grand tapestry of the Hollywoodian dream from a different angle also lets us revisit the myths and ghosts invented in era after era for the well-being of a reassuring vision in which those in charge of contracts and budgets could create a celluloid world in keeping with their own image and dreams, saving for themselves the starring role. But now we know what that dream conceals. And we know the dream world has never been the real world, neither in front of or behind the camera. A concocted vision that invaded everything else with its ideology and its merchandise.

In this sense, Loo Hui Phang and Hugues Micol already occupy a more advanced stage, and they have a field day with their unbridled inventions, anchoring them firmly in research. And better yet, they're funny!

In embarking on this mind-blowing journey, we find a tale that defies imagination, reversing customary roles, shaking up the world as we know it, even upending clichés with formidable jujitsu moves, so unlike the efforts of intellectual idlers.

It makes us want to see a thousand other stories in the same vein blossom. All those worlds to catch up with. All that lost time. Words and pictures here teem with liberating creativity, explosions of ideas and images each wilder than the last. Rich and unrepressed, they sweep us far away from this inhibited world. The subtext and the unsaid are just as effective and multiply tenfold the power of this story, or rather stories. For in real life, we are indeed born of a multitude of stories.

Revisiting the Dream Factory, seeing it through this new lens, is an occasion of incredible rapture. I feel at home. And should John Wayne, along the way, get publicly roasted at last, well—that's priceless!

Raoul Peck
("I Am Not Your Negro")

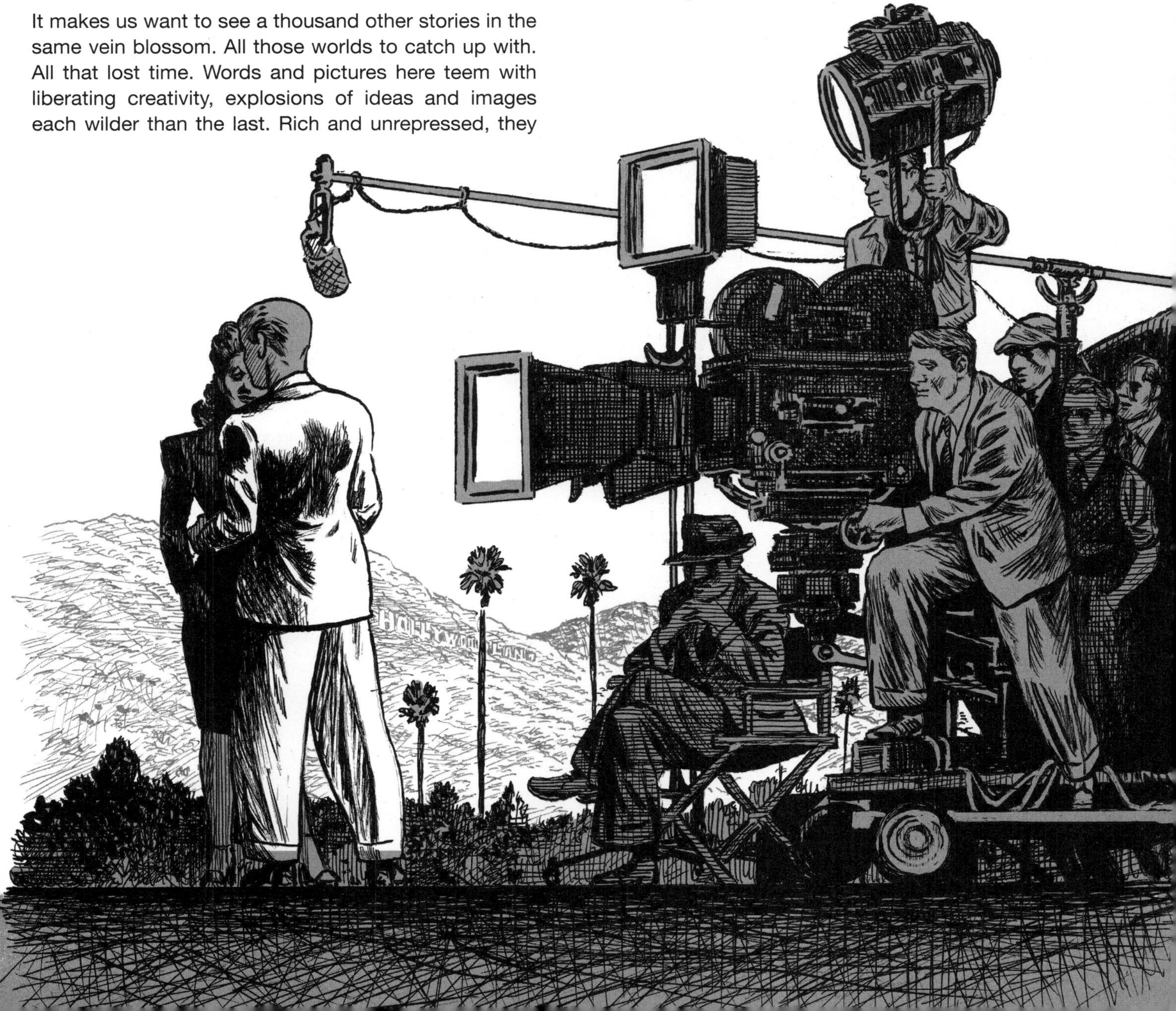

## Maximus Wyld: A Bibliography

Kenneth Anger, *Hollywood Babylon,* Arrow, 1975.
Kenneth Anger, *Hollywood Babylon II*, Arrow, 1984.

Anne-Marie Bidaud, *Hollywood et le rêve américain, cinéma et idéologie aux États-Unis* [Hollywood and the American Dream: Cinema and Ideology in the U.S.], Armand Colin, 2017.

Arnaud Balvay, *John Ford et les Indiens* [John Ford and the Indians], Séguier, 2015.

Whitney Battle-Baptiste & Britt Rusert, eds. *W.E.B. Du Bois's Data Portraits: Visualizing Black America*, Princeton Architectural Press, 2018.

Stéphane Benaïm, *Les Visions d'Orient de Josef von Sternberg* [Josef Von Sternberg's Oriental Visions], LettMotif, 2016.

Frank Capra, *The Name Above the Title: An Autobiography*, Bantam, 1971.

Florence Colombani, *Les Indomptables* [The Untameables], Fayard, 2017.

Yann-Brice Dherbier, *Cary Grant: A Life in Pictures*, Pavilion, 2011.

Régis Dubois, *Le cinéma des Noirs américains entre intégration et contestation* [African American Cinema: From Integration to Protest], Cerf-Corlet, 2005.

Régis Dubois, *Hollywood, cinéma et idéologie* [Hollywood, Cinema, and Ideology], Sulliver éditions, 2008.

Paul Gilroy, *The Black Atlantic: Modernity and Double Consciousness*, Verso, 1993.

Élizabeth Gouslan, *Ava, la femme qui aimait les hommes* [Ava: The Woman Who Loved Men], Robert Laffont, 2012.

Gerald Horne, *Paul Robeson: The Artist as Revolutionary*, Pluto Press, 2016.

Pap Ndiaye & Louise Madinier, *Le modèle Noir, de Géricault à Matisse* [The Black Model: From Géricault to Matisse], Musée d'Orsay & Flammarion, 2019.

Kenneth Bancroft Clark, *The Negro Protest: James Baldwin, Malcolm X, Martin Luther King talk with Kenneth B. Clark*, Beacon Press, 1963.

HOLLYWOOD IS A FICTION. AND LIKE ALL FICTIONS, IT IS MYRIAD, CHANGING, SINCERE, DECEITFUL.
AN UNBRIDLED ENGINE OF PREDATORY FLUIDITY, IT CONCEALS
WITHIN ITS DEPTHS CHASMS, FRACTURES, STUTTERS.
BETWEEN ITS GLITTERING LAYERS FESTER MAIMED APPETITES, VISCID BOGS
WHERE MARTYRS TO SUCCESS GROW MIRED. STRUCK DOWN MID-FLIGHT
FROM THE HEAVENS, THEY SINK INTO THE BITTEREST OF DAMNATIONS:
OBSCURITY.

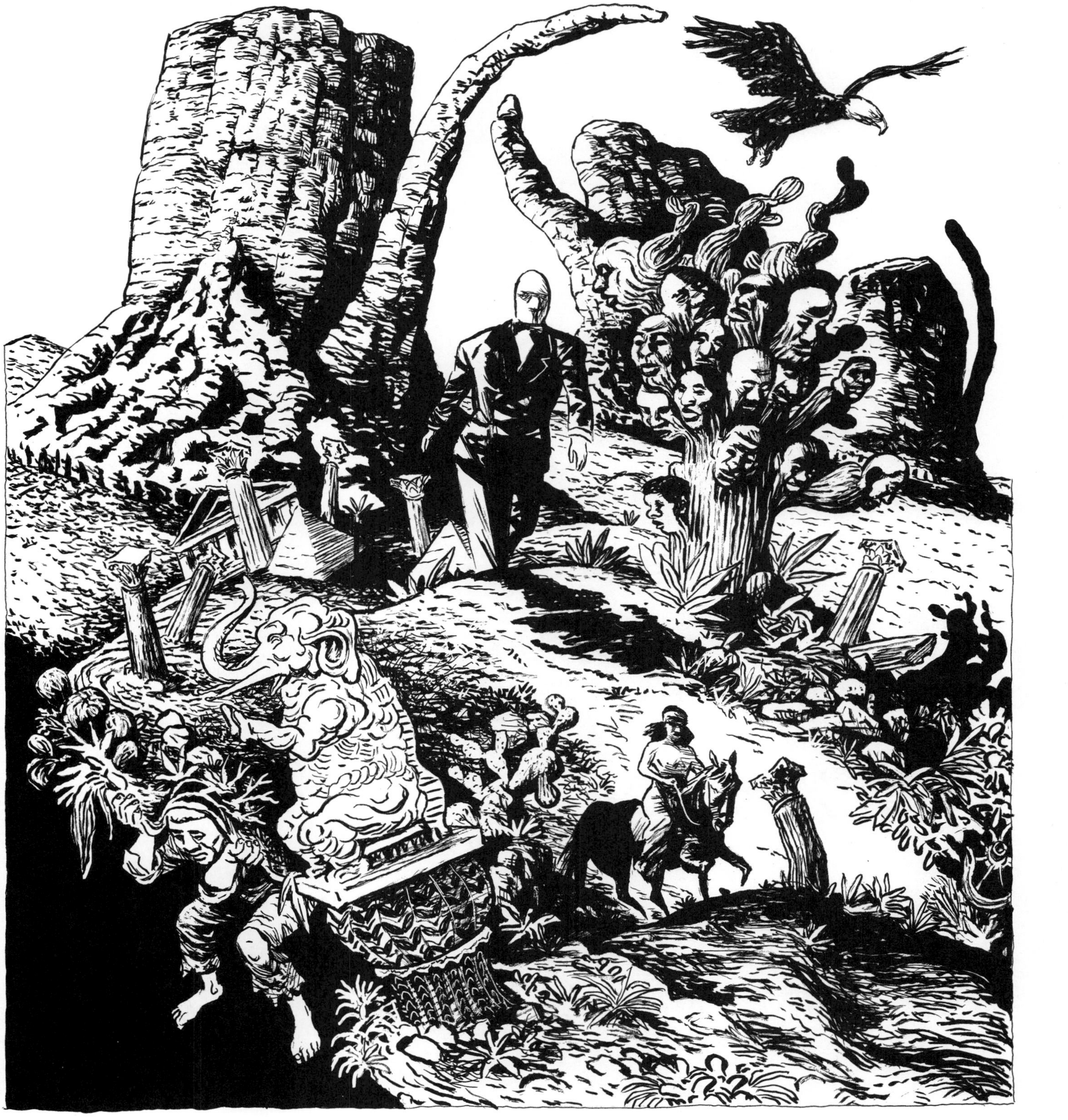

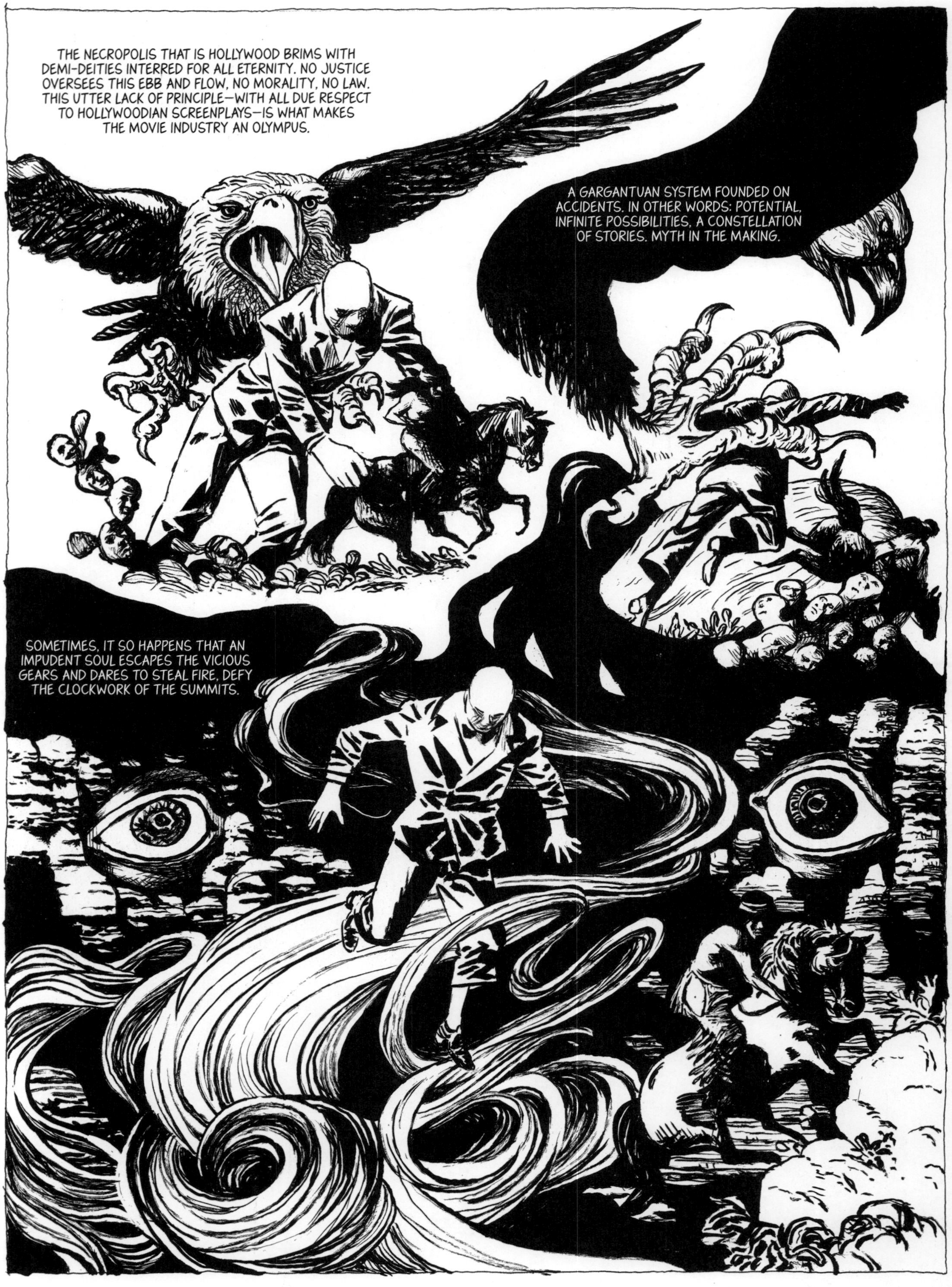
THE NECROPOLIS THAT IS HOLLYWOOD BRIMS WITH DEMI-DEITIES INTERRED FOR ALL ETERNITY. NO JUSTICE OVERSEES THIS EBB AND FLOW, NO MORALITY, NO LAW. THIS UTTER LACK OF PRINCIPLE—WITH ALL DUE RESPECT TO HOLLYWOODIAN SCREENPLAYS—IS WHAT MAKES THE MOVIE INDUSTRY AN OLYMPUS.
A GARGANTUAN SYSTEM FOUNDED ON ACCIDENTS. IN OTHER WORDS: POTENTIAL, INFINITE POSSIBILITIES, A CONSTELLATION OF STORIES. MYTH IN THE MAKING.
SOMETIMES, IT SO HAPPENS THAT AN IMPUDENT SOUL ESCAPES THE VICIOUS GEARS AND DARES TO STEAL FIRE, DEFY THE CLOCKWORK OF THE SUMMITS.

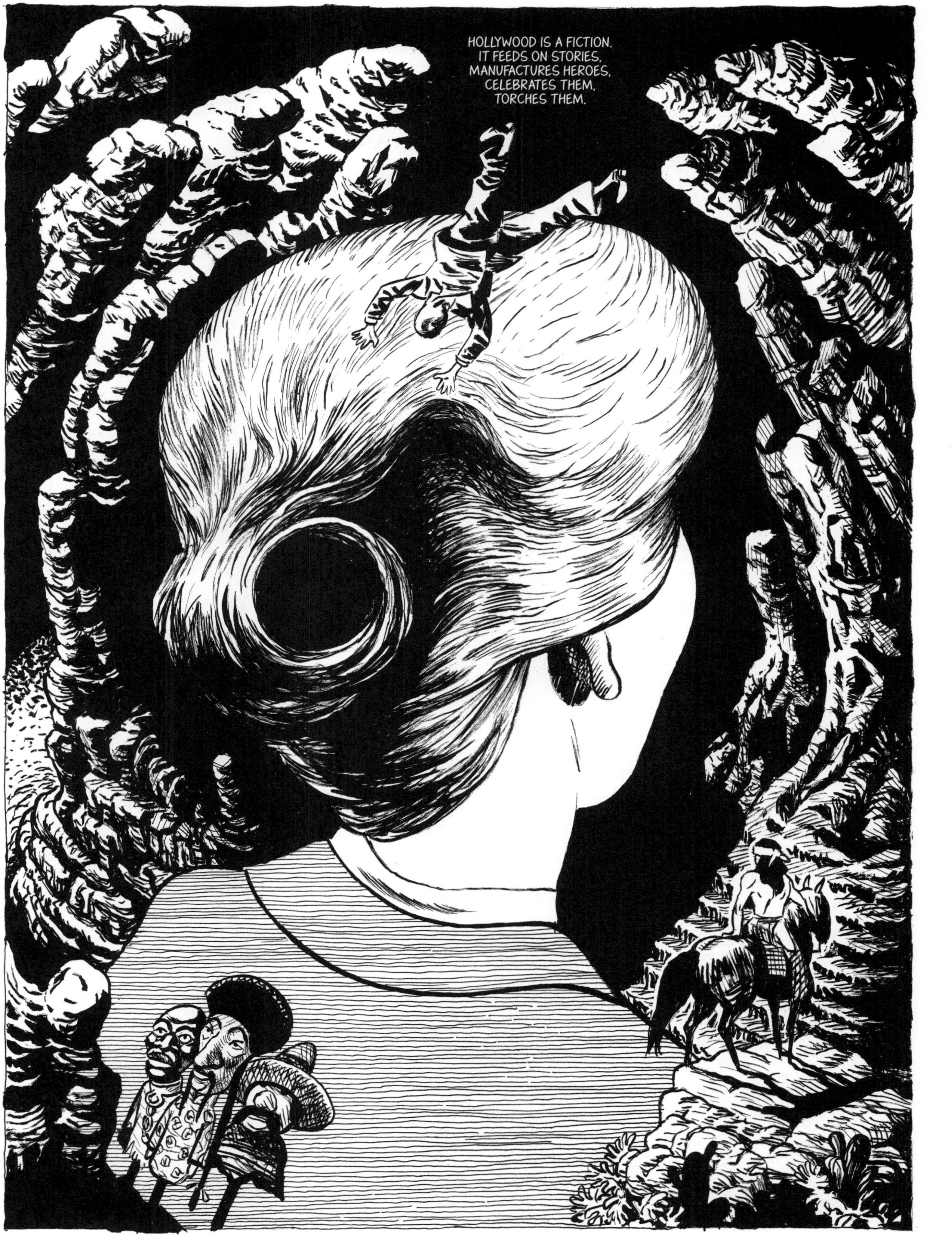
HOLLYWOOD IS A FICTION.
IT FEEDS ON STORIES,
MANUFACTURES HEROES,
CELEBRATES THEM,
TORCHES THEM.

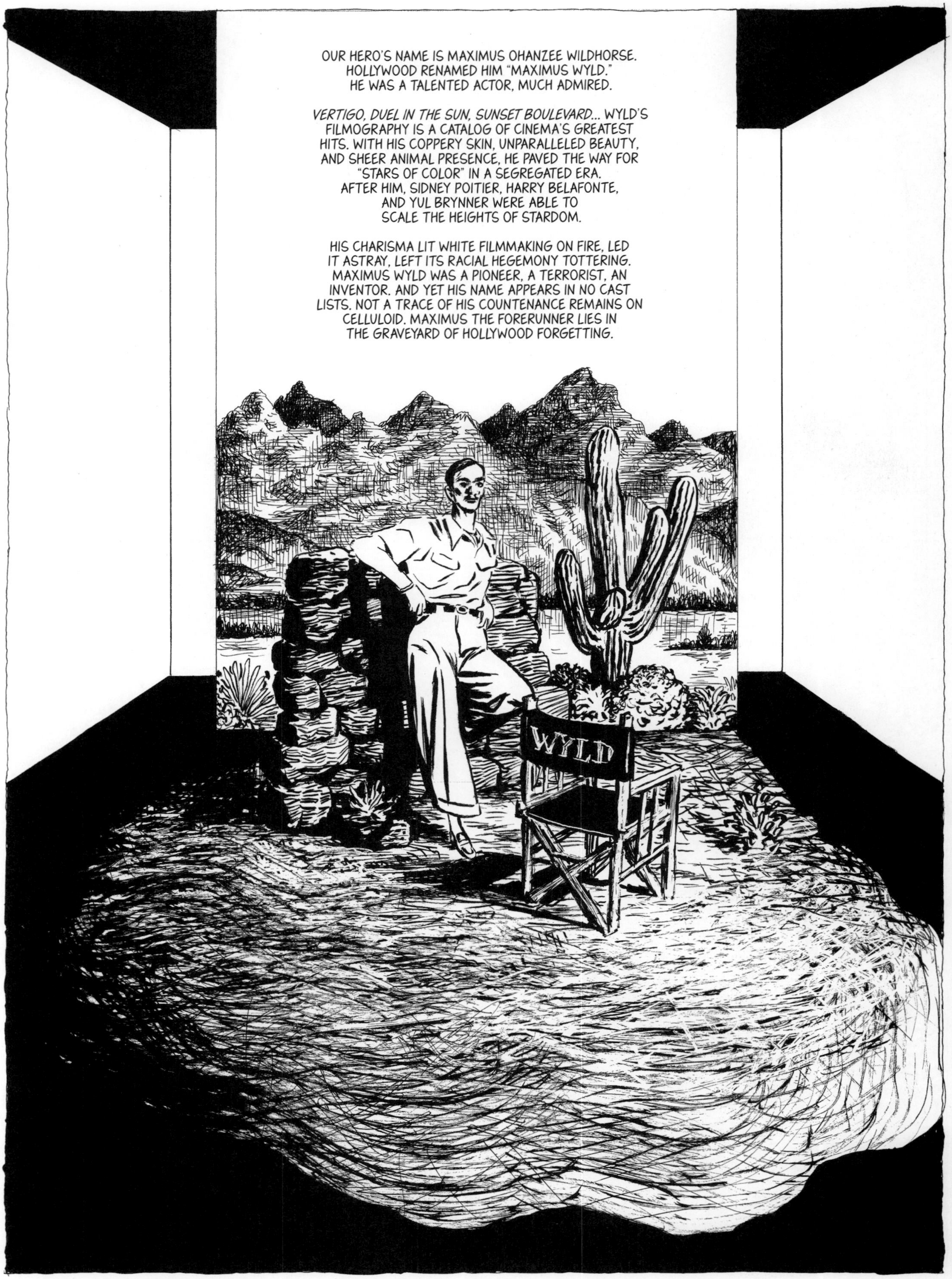
OUR HERO'S NAME IS MAXIMUS OHANZEE WILDHORSE. HOLLYWOOD RENAMED HIM "MAXIMUS WYLD." HE WAS A TALENTED ACTOR, MUCH ADMIRED.
*VERTIGO, DUEL IN THE SUN, SUNSET BOULEVARD*... WYLD'S FILMOGRAPHY IS A CATALOG OF CINEMA'S GREATEST HITS. WITH HIS COPPERY SKIN, UNPARALLELED BEAUTY, AND SHEER ANIMAL PRESENCE, HE PAVED THE WAY FOR "STARS OF COLOR" IN A SEGREGATED ERA. AFTER HIM, SIDNEY POITIER, HARRY BELAFONTE, AND YUL BRYNNER WERE ABLE TO SCALE THE HEIGHTS OF STARDOM.
HIS CHARISMA LIT WHITE FILMMAKING ON FIRE, LED IT ASTRAY, LEFT ITS RACIAL HEGEMONY TOTTERING. MAXIMUS WYLD WAS A PIONEER, A TERRORIST, AN INVENTOR. AND YET HIS NAME APPEARS IN NO CAST LISTS. NOT A TRACE OF HIS COUNTENANCE REMAINS ON CELLULOID. MAXIMUS THE FORERUNNER LIES IN THE GRAVEYARD OF HOLLYWOOD FORGETTING.
WYLD

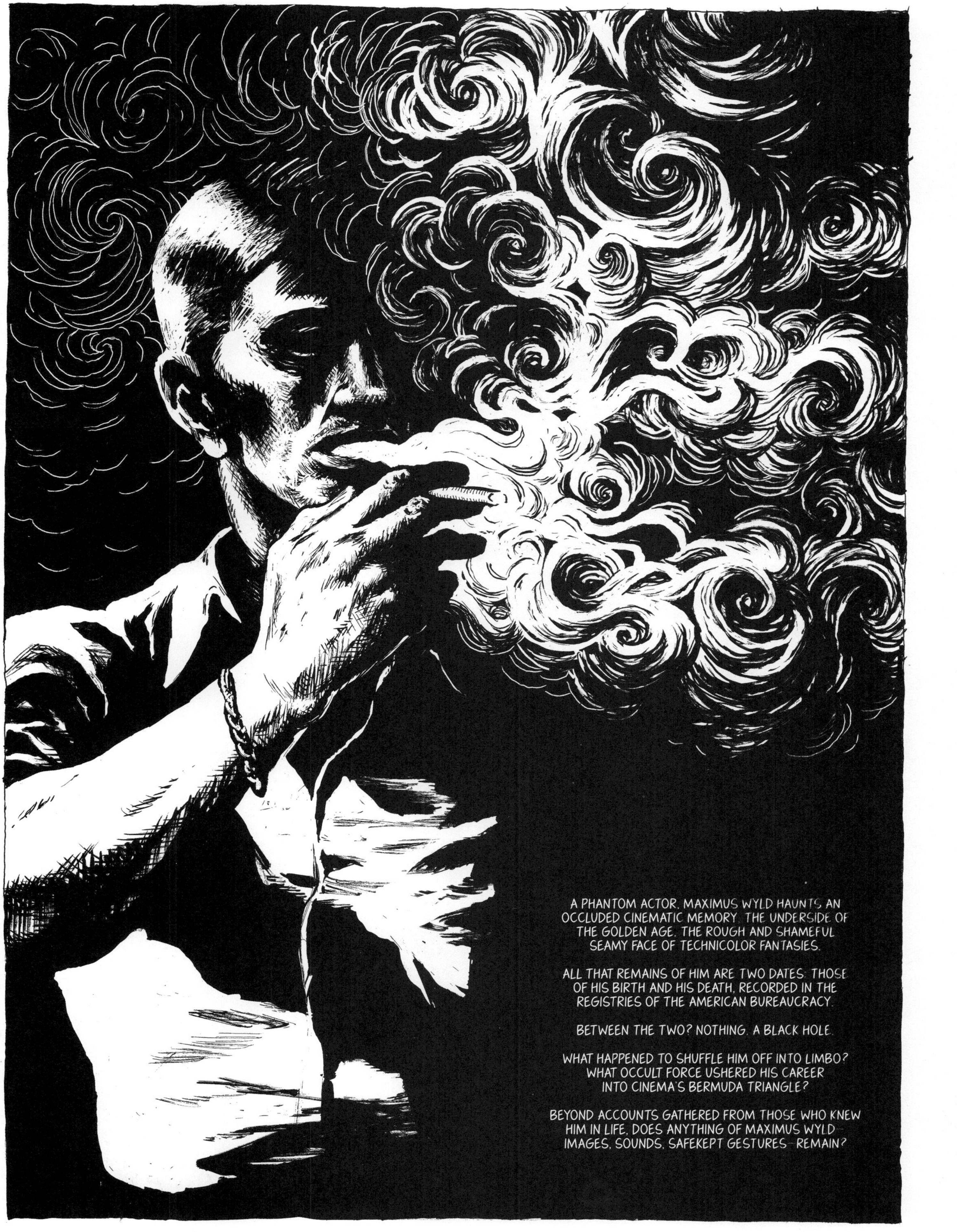
A PHANTOM ACTOR, MAXIMUS WYLD HAUNTS AN OCCLUDED CINEMATIC MEMORY. THE UNDERSIDE OF THE GOLDEN AGE. THE ROUGH AND SHAMEFUL SEAMY FACE OF TECHNICOLOR FANTASIES.
ALL THAT REMAINS OF HIM ARE TWO DATES: THOSE OF HIS BIRTH AND HIS DEATH, RECORDED IN THE REGISTRIES OF THE AMERICAN BUREAUCRACY.
BETWEEN THE TWO? NOTHING. A BLACK HOLE.
WHAT HAPPENED TO SHUFFLE HIM OFF INTO LIMBO? WHAT OCCULT FORCE USHERED HIS CAREER INTO CINEMA'S BERMUDA TRIANGLE?
BEYOND ACCOUNTS GATHERED FROM THOSE WHO KNEW HIM IN LIFE, DOES ANYTHING OF MAXIMUS WYLD—IMAGES, SOUNDS, SAFEKEPT GESTURES—REMAIN?

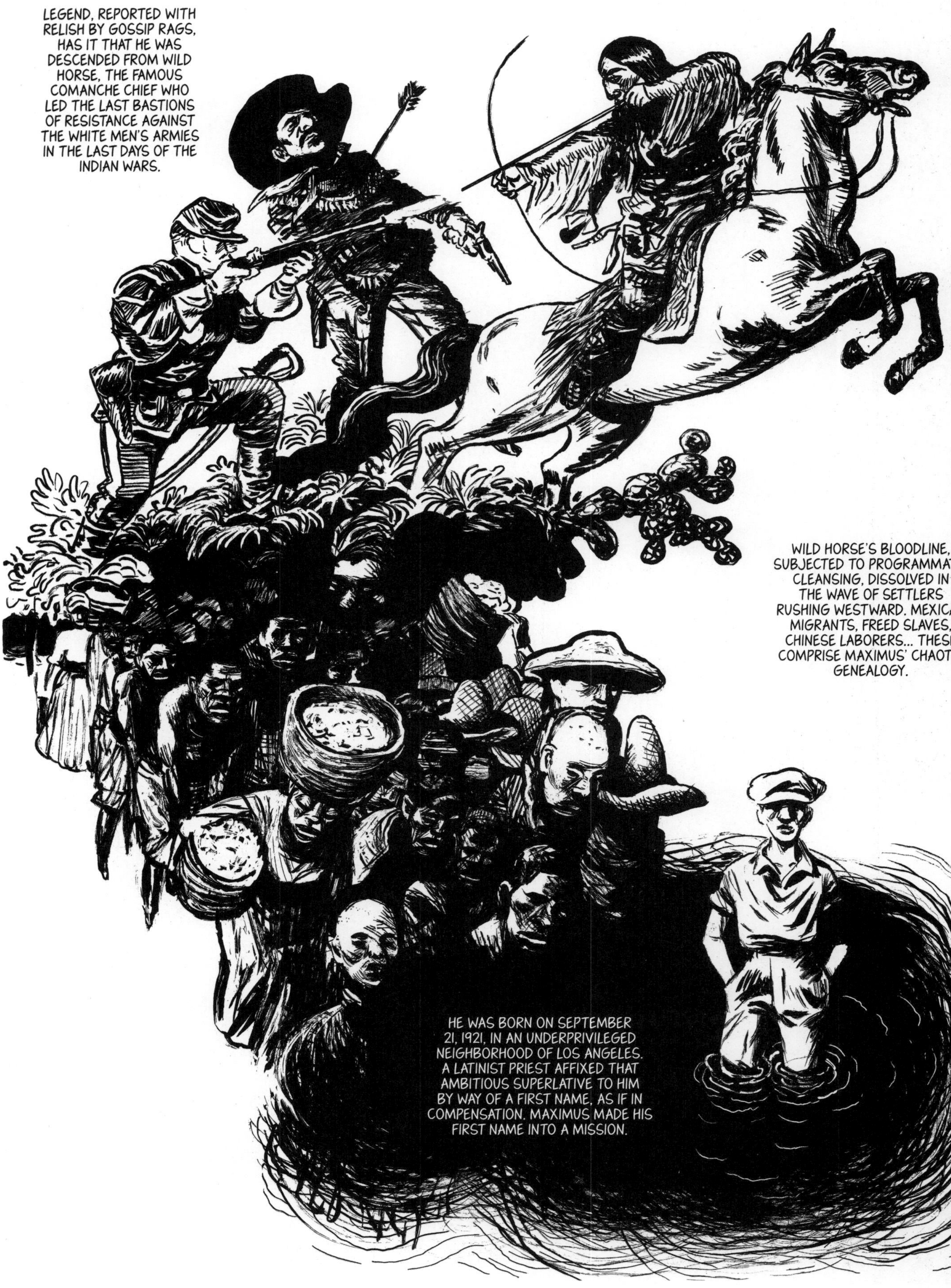
LEGEND, REPORTED WITH RELISH BY GOSSIP RAGS, HAS IT THAT HE WAS DESCENDED FROM WILD HORSE, THE FAMOUS COMANCHE CHIEF WHO LED THE LAST BASTIONS OF RESISTANCE AGAINST THE WHITE MEN'S ARMIES IN THE LAST DAYS OF THE INDIAN WARS.
WILD HORSE'S BLOODLINE, SUBJECTED TO PROGRAMMATIC CLEANSING, DISSOLVED IN THE WAVE OF SETTLERS RUSHING WESTWARD. MEXICAN MIGRANTS, FREED SLAVES, CHINESE LABORERS... THESE COMPRISE MAXIMUS' CHAOTIC GENEALOGY.
HE WAS BORN ON SEPTEMBER 21, 1921, IN AN UNDERPRIVILEGED NEIGHBORHOOD OF LOS ANGELES. A LATINIST PRIEST AFFIXED THAT AMBITIOUS SUPERLATIVE TO HIM BY WAY OF A FIRST NAME, AS IF IN COMPENSATION. MAXIMUS MADE HIS FIRST NAME INTO A MISSION.

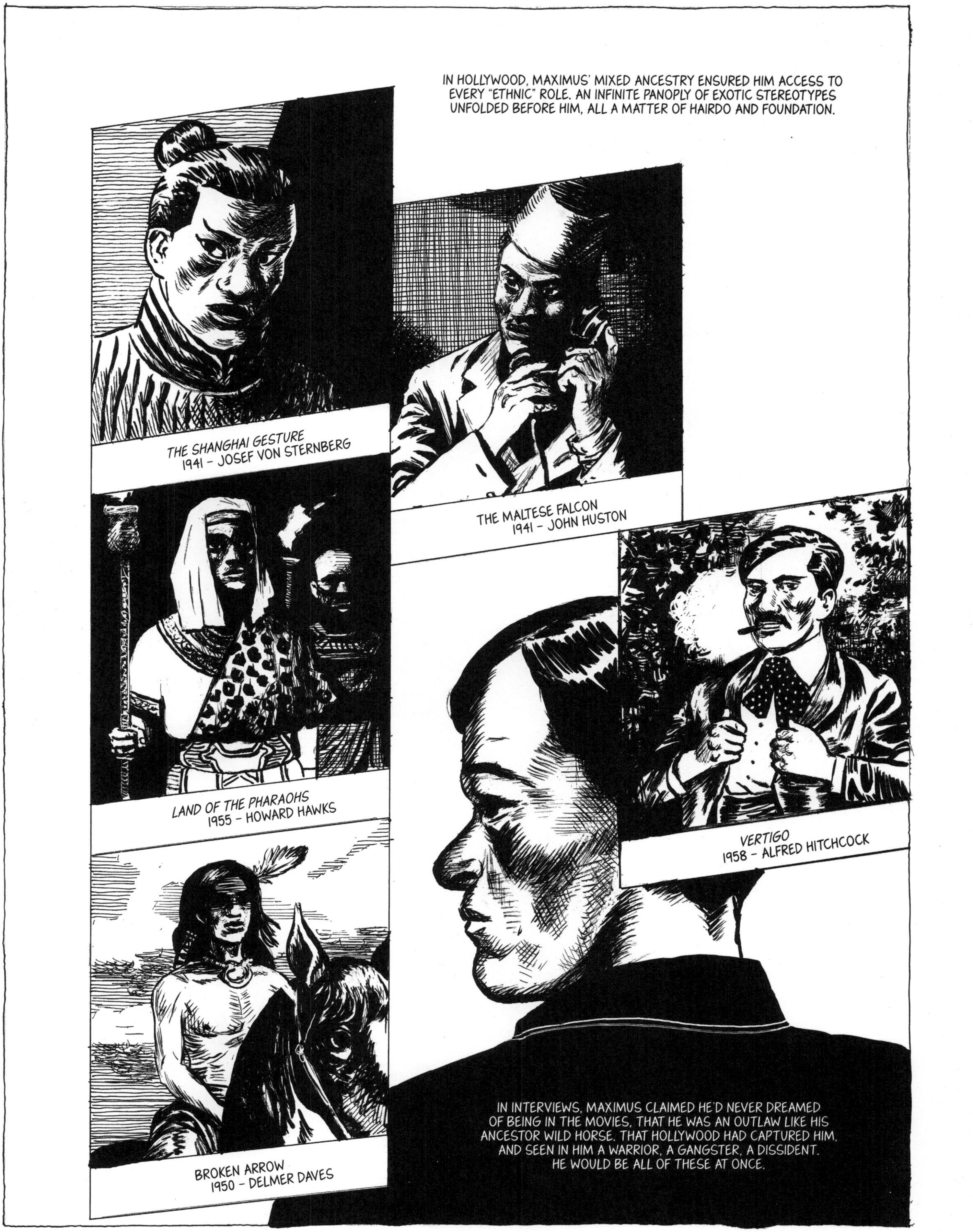
IN HOLLYWOOD, MAXIMUS' MIXED ANCESTRY ENSURED HIM ACCESS TO EVERY "ETHNIC" ROLE. AN INFINITE PANOPLY OF EXOTIC STEREOTYPES UNFOLDED BEFORE HIM, ALL A MATTER OF HAIRDO AND FOUNDATION.
THE SHANGHAI GESTURE 1941 – JOSEF VON STERNBERG
THE MALTESE FALCON 1941 – JOHN HUSTON
LAND OF THE PHARAOHS 1955 – HOWARD HAWKS
VERTIGO 1958 – ALFRED HITCHCOCK
BROKEN ARROW 1950 – DELMER DAVES
IN INTERVIEWS, MAXIMUS CLAIMED HE'D NEVER DREAMED OF BEING IN THE MOVIES, THAT HE WAS AN OUTLAW LIKE HIS ANCESTOR WILD HORSE. THAT HOLLYWOOD HAD CAPTURED HIM, AND SEEN IN HIM A WARRIOR, A GANGSTER, A DISSIDENT. HE WOULD BE ALL OF THESE AT ONCE.

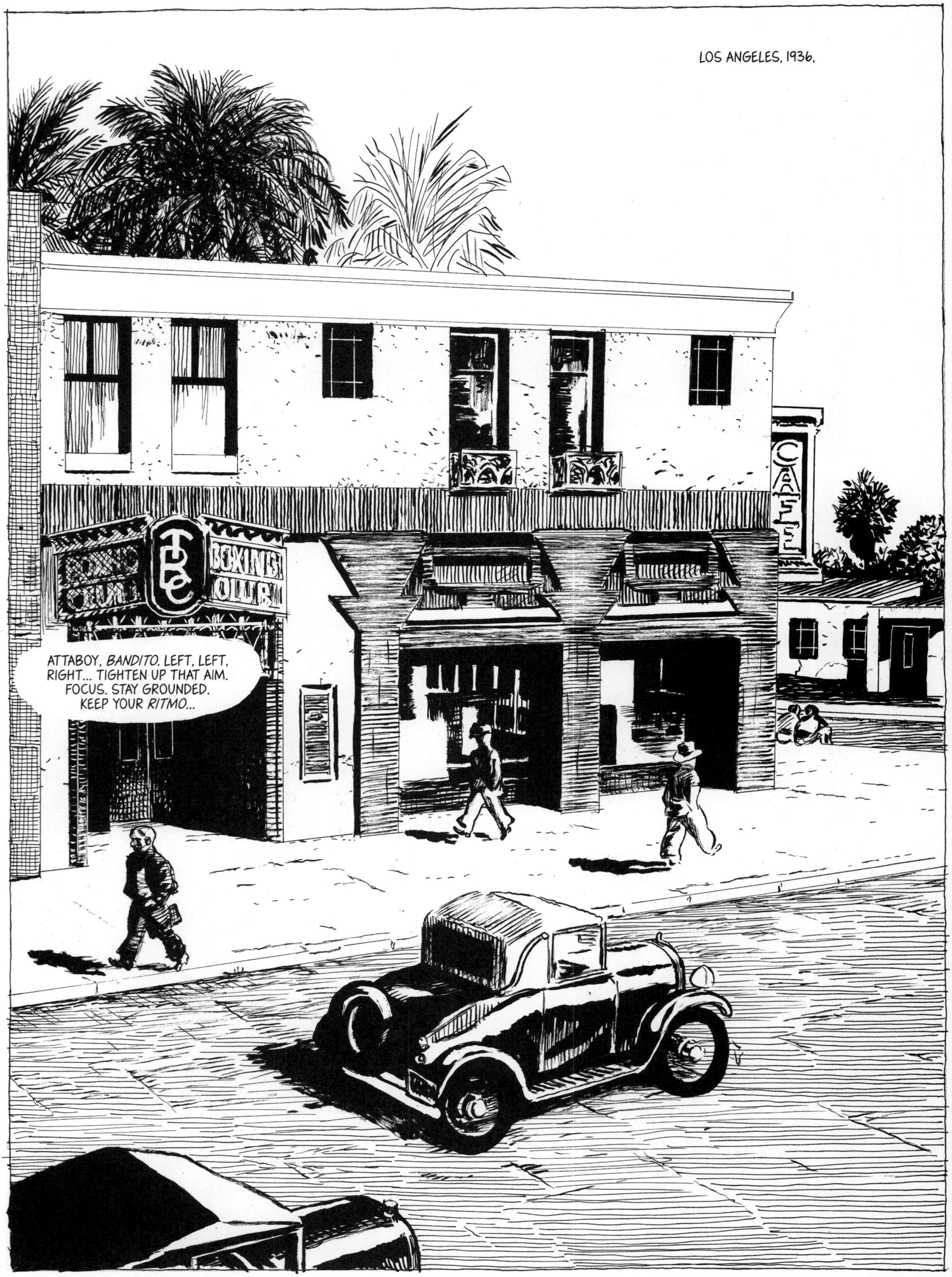
LOS ANGELES, 1936.
BOXING CLUB
CAFE
ATTABOY, *BANDITO*. LEFT, LEFT, RIGHT... TIGHTEN UP THAT AIM. FOCUS. STAY GROUNDED. KEEP YOUR *RITMO*...

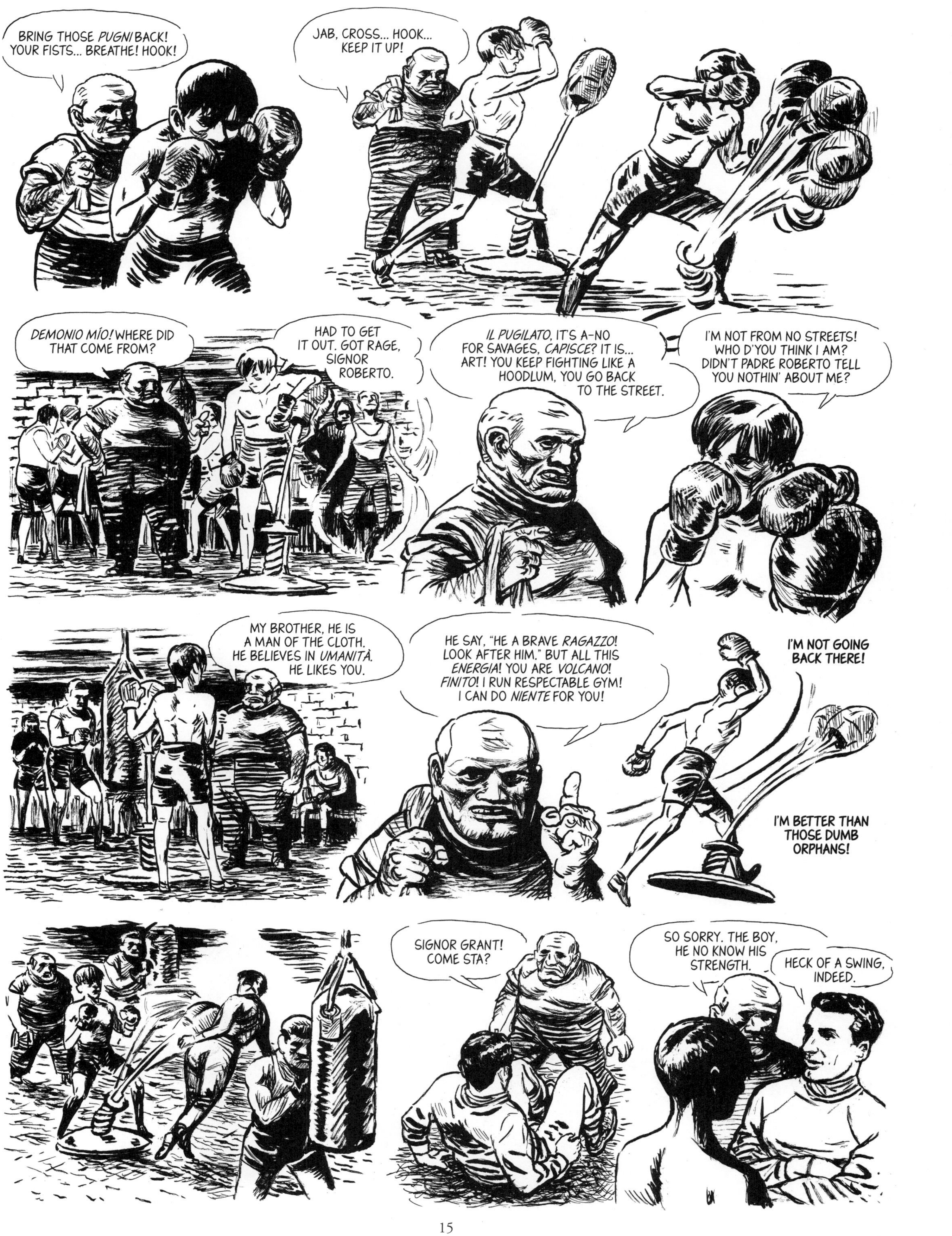
BRING THOSE *PUGNI* BACK! YOUR FISTS... BREATHE! HOOK!
JAB, CROSS... HOOK... KEEP IT UP!
*DEMONIO MÍO!* WHERE DID THAT COME FROM?
HAD TO GET IT OUT. GOT RAGE, SIGNOR ROBERTO.
*IL PUGILATO*, IT'S A-NO FOR SAVAGES, *CAPISCE?* IT IS... ART! YOU KEEP FIGHTING LIKE A HOODLUM, YOU GO BACK TO THE STREET.
I'M NOT FROM NO STREETS! WHO D'YOU THINK I AM? DIDN'T PADRE ROBERTO TELL YOU NOTHIN' ABOUT ME?
MY BROTHER, HE IS A MAN OF THE CLOTH. HE BELIEVES IN *UMANITÀ*. HE LIKES YOU.
HE SAY, "HE A BRAVE *RAGAZZO*! LOOK AFTER HIM." BUT ALL THIS *ENERGIA*! YOU ARE *VOLCANO*! *FINITO*! I RUN RESPECTABLE GYM! I CAN DO *NIENTE* FOR YOU!
**I'M NOT GOING BACK THERE!**
**I'M BETTER THAN THOSE DUMB ORPHANS!**
SIGNOR GRANT! COME STA?
SO SORRY. THE BOY, HE NO KNOW HIS STRENGTH.
HECK OF A SWING, INDEED.

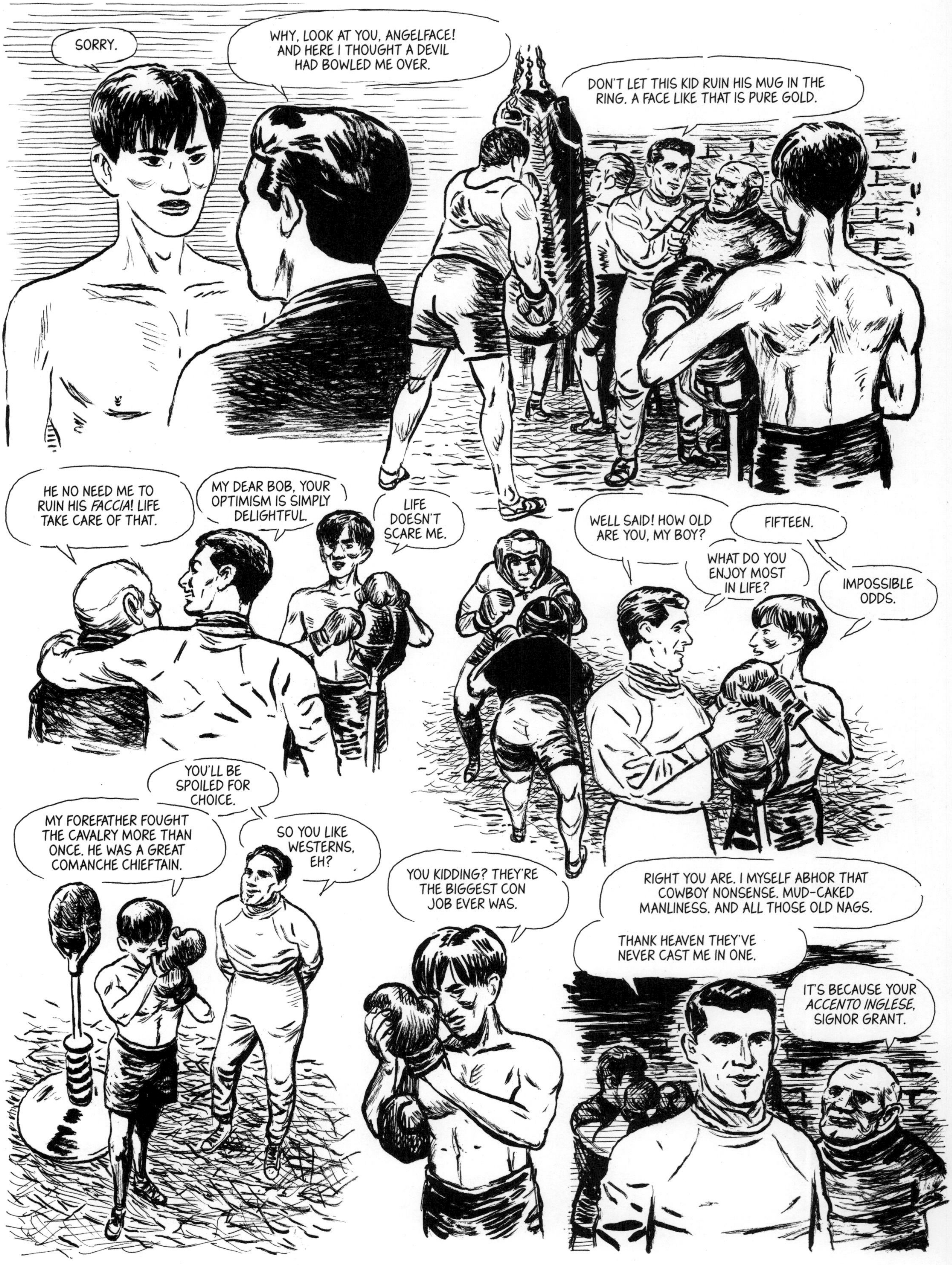
SORRY.
WHY, LOOK AT YOU, ANGELFACE! AND HERE I THOUGHT A DEVIL HAD BOWLED ME OVER.
DON'T LET THIS KID RUIN HIS MUG IN THE RING. A FACE LIKE THAT IS PURE GOLD.
HE NO NEED ME TO RUIN HIS *FACCIA*! LIFE TAKE CARE OF THAT.
MY DEAR BOB, YOUR OPTIMISM IS SIMPLY DELIGHTFUL.
LIFE DOESN'T SCARE ME.
WELL SAID! HOW OLD ARE YOU, MY BOY?
FIFTEEN.
WHAT DO YOU ENJOY MOST IN LIFE?
IMPOSSIBLE ODDS.
YOU'LL BE SPOILED FOR CHOICE.
MY FOREFATHER FOUGHT THE CAVALRY MORE THAN ONCE. HE WAS A GREAT COMANCHE CHIEFTAIN.
SO YOU LIKE WESTERNS, EH?
YOU KIDDING? THEY'RE THE BIGGEST CON JOB EVER WAS.
RIGHT YOU ARE. I MYSELF ABHOR THAT COWBOY NONSENSE. MUD-CAKED MANLINESS. AND ALL THOSE OLD NAGS.
THANK HEAVEN THEY'VE NEVER CAST ME IN ONE.
IT'S BECAUSE YOUR *ACCENTO INGLESE*, SIGNOR GRANT.

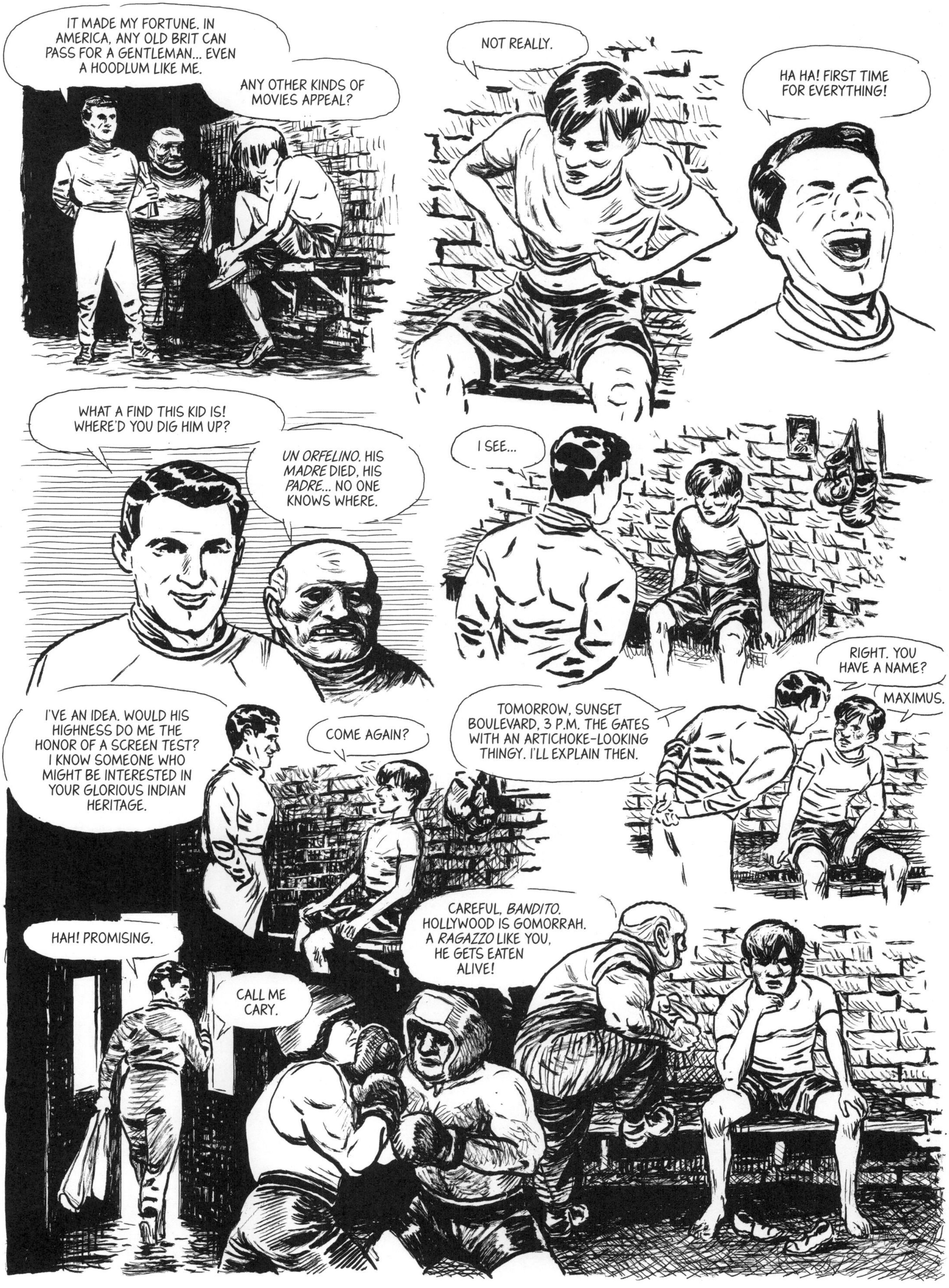
IT MADE MY FORTUNE. IN AMERICA, ANY OLD BRIT CAN PASS FOR A GENTLEMAN... EVEN A HOODLUM LIKE ME.
ANY OTHER KINDS OF MOVIES APPEAL?
NOT REALLY.
HA HA! FIRST TIME FOR EVERYTHING!
WHAT A FIND THIS KID IS! WHERE'D YOU DIG HIM UP?
*UN ORFELINO*. HIS *MADRE* DIED, HIS *PADRE*... NO ONE KNOWS WHERE.
I SEE...
RIGHT. YOU HAVE A NAME?
MAXIMUS.
I'VE AN IDEA. WOULD HIS HIGHNESS DO ME THE HONOR OF A SCREEN TEST? I KNOW SOMEONE WHO MIGHT BE INTERESTED IN YOUR GLORIOUS INDIAN HERITAGE.
COME AGAIN?
TOMORROW, SUNSET BOULEVARD, 3 P.M. THE GATES WITH AN ARTICHOKE-LOOKING THINGY. I'LL EXPLAIN THEN.
HAH! PROMISING.
CALL ME CARY.
CAREFUL, *BANDITO*. HOLLYWOOD IS GOMORRAH. A *RAGAZZO* LIKE YOU, HE GETS EATEN ALIVE!

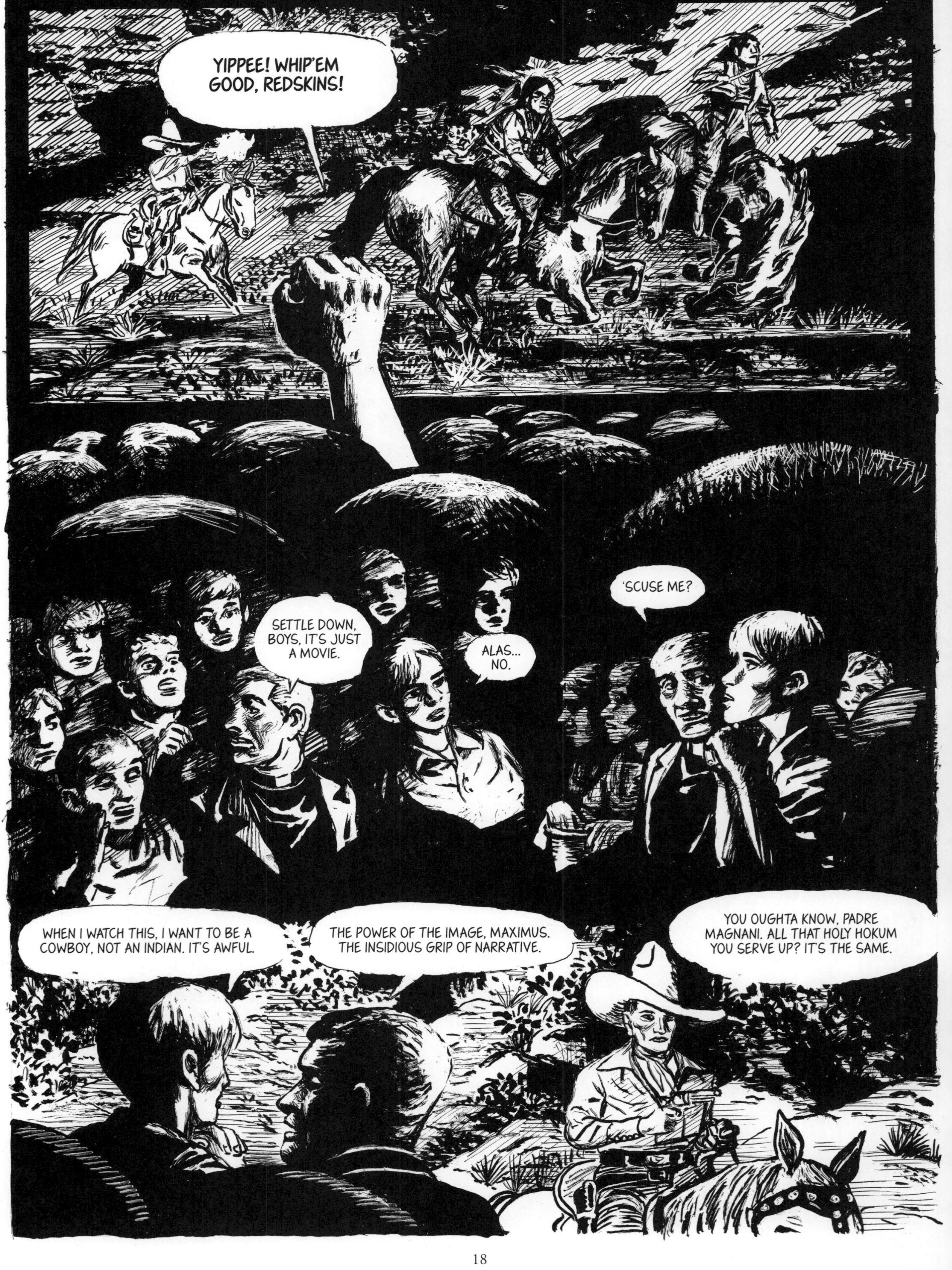
YIPPEE! WHIP'EM GOOD, REDSKINS!
SETTLE DOWN, BOYS, IT'S JUST A MOVIE.
ALAS... NO.
'SCUSE ME?
WHEN I WATCH THIS, I WANT TO BE A COWBOY, NOT AN INDIAN. IT'S AWFUL.
THE POWER OF THE IMAGE, MAXIMUS. THE INSIDIOUS GRIP OF NARRATIVE.
YOU OUGHTA KNOW, PADRE MAGNANI. ALL THAT HOLY HOKUM YOU SERVE UP? IT'S THE SAME.

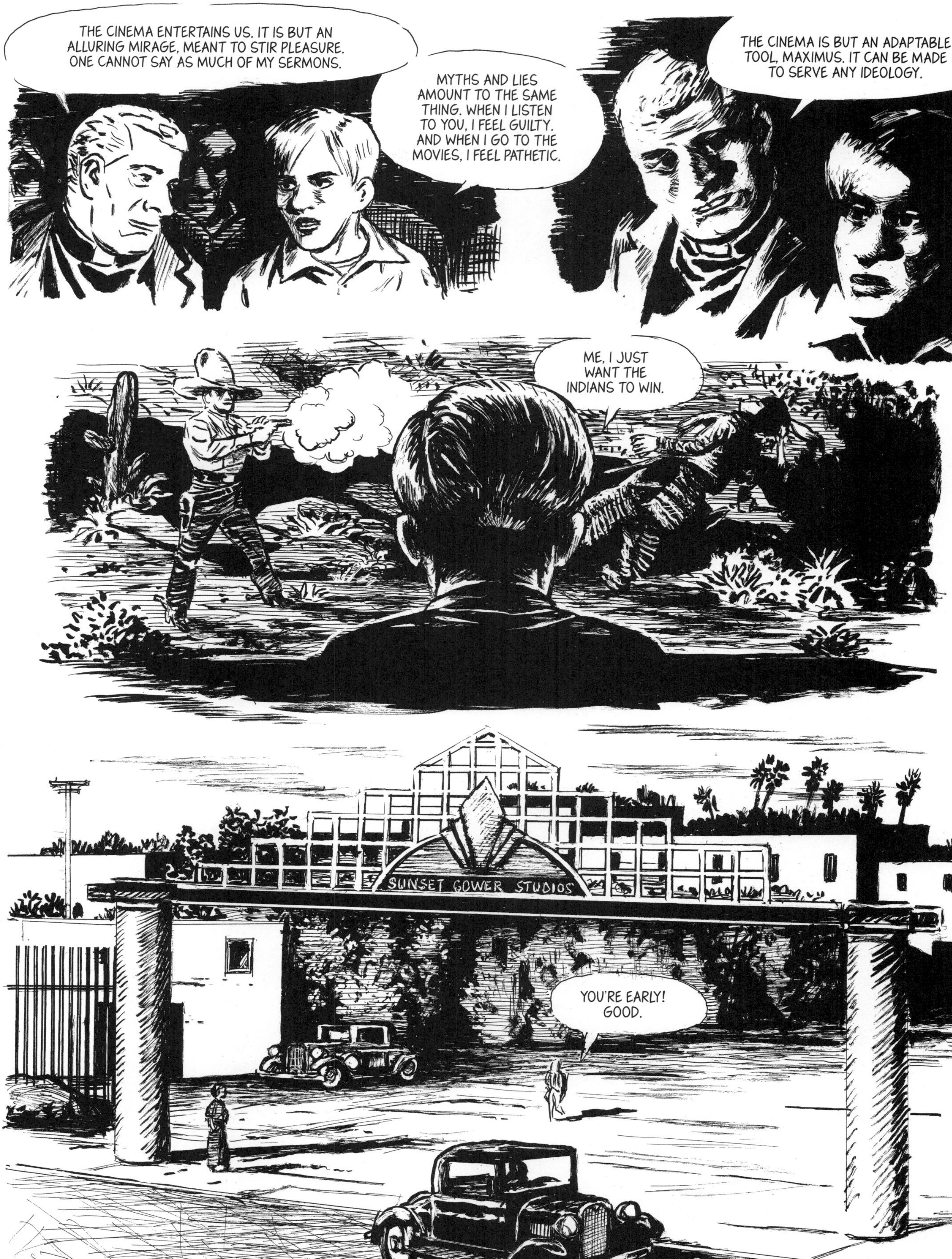
THE CINEMA ENTERTAINS US. IT IS BUT AN ALLURING MIRAGE, MEANT TO STIR PLEASURE. ONE CANNOT SAY AS MUCH OF MY SERMONS.
MYTHS AND LIES AMOUNT TO THE SAME THING. WHEN I LISTEN TO YOU, I FEEL GUILTY. AND WHEN I GO TO THE MOVIES, I FEEL PATHETIC.
THE CINEMA IS BUT AN ADAPTABLE TOOL, MAXIMUS. IT CAN BE MADE TO SERVE ANY IDEOLOGY.
ME, I JUST WANT THE INDIANS TO WIN.
SUNSET GOWER STUDIOS
YOU'RE EARLY! GOOD.

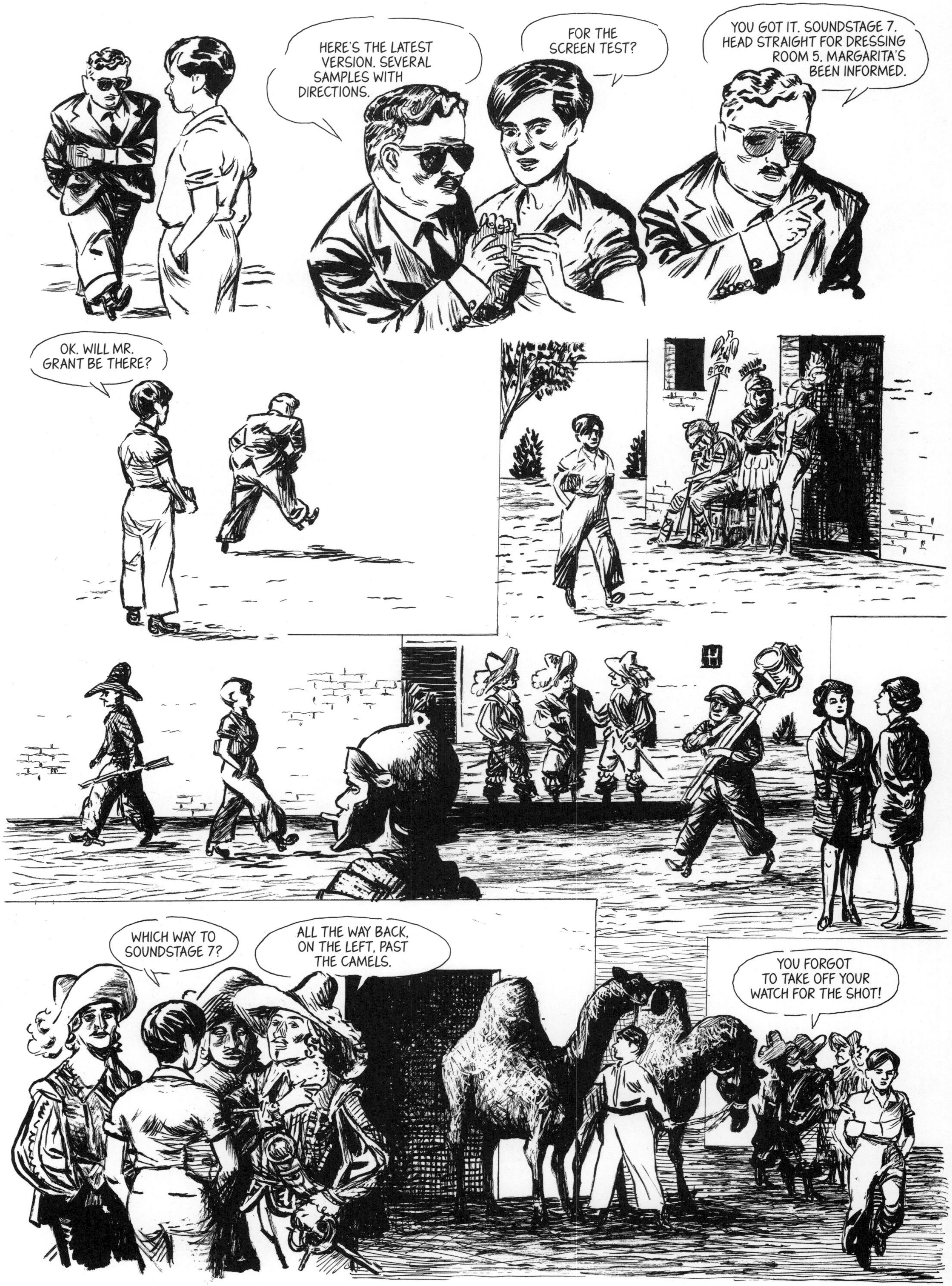
HERE'S THE LATEST VERSION. SEVERAL SAMPLES WITH DIRECTIONS.
FOR THE SCREEN TEST?
YOU GOT IT. SOUNDSTAGE 7. HEAD STRAIGHT FOR DRESSING ROOM 5. MARGARITA'S BEEN INFORMED.
OK. WILL MR. GRANT BE THERE?
WHICH WAY TO SOUNDSTAGE 7?
ALL THE WAY BACK, ON THE LEFT, PAST THE CAMELS.
YOU FORGOT TO TAKE OFF YOUR WATCH FOR THE SHOT!

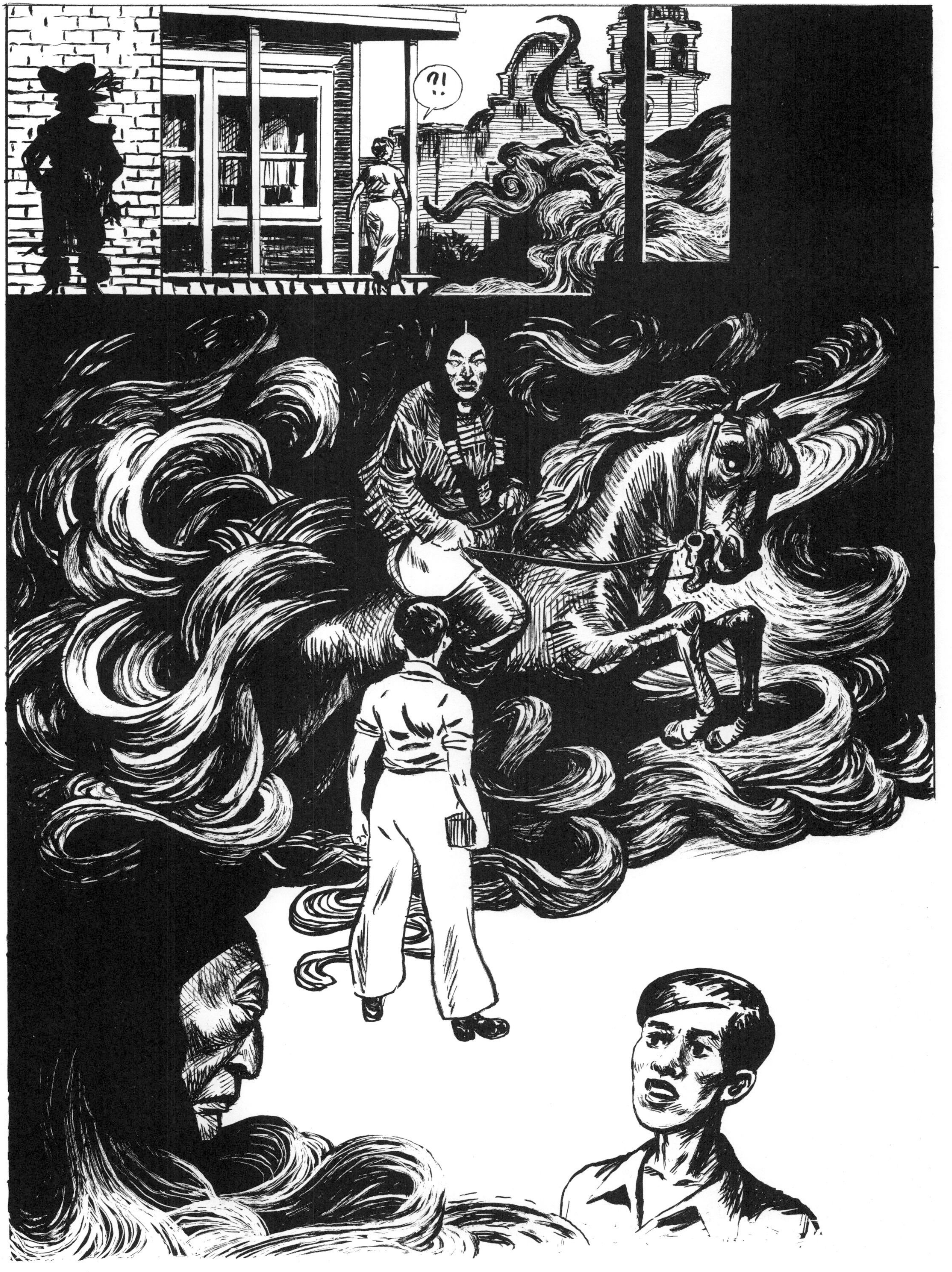
?!

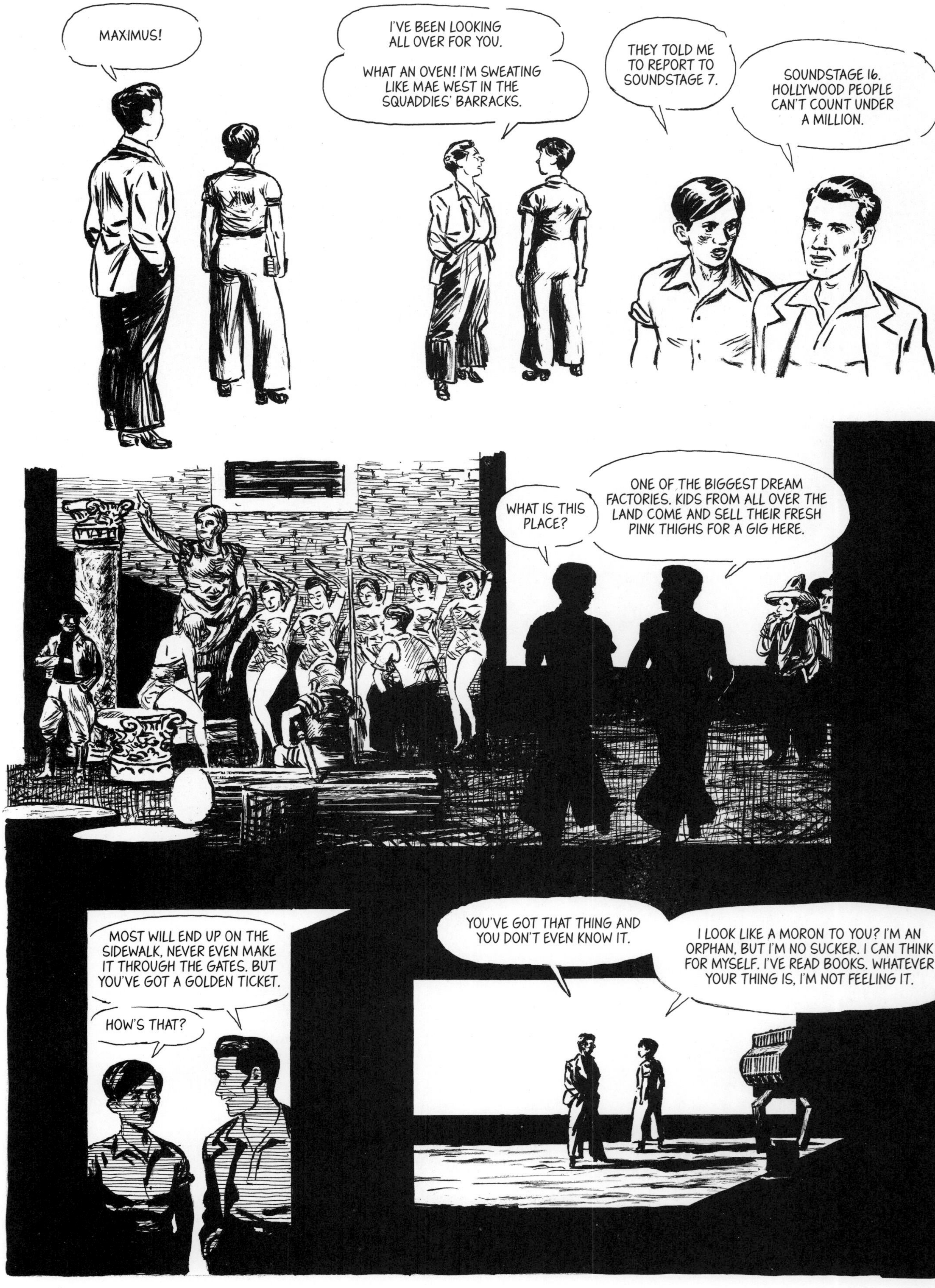
MAXIMUS!
I'VE BEEN LOOKING ALL OVER FOR YOU.
WHAT AN OVEN! I'M SWEATING LIKE MAE WEST IN THE SQUADDIES' BARRACKS.
THEY TOLD ME TO REPORT TO SOUNDSTAGE 7.
SOUNDSTAGE 16. HOLLYWOOD PEOPLE CAN'T COUNT UNDER A MILLION.
WHAT IS THIS PLACE?
ONE OF THE BIGGEST DREAM FACTORIES. KIDS FROM ALL OVER THE LAND COME AND SELL THEIR FRESH PINK THIGHS FOR A GIG HERE.
MOST WILL END UP ON THE SIDEWALK, NEVER EVEN MAKE IT THROUGH THE GATES. BUT YOU'VE GOT A GOLDEN TICKET.
HOW'S THAT?
YOU'VE GOT THAT THING AND YOU DON'T EVEN KNOW IT.
I LOOK LIKE A MORON TO YOU? I'M AN ORPHAN, BUT I'M NO SUCKER. I CAN THINK FOR MYSELF. I'VE READ BOOKS. WHATEVER YOUR THING IS, I'M NOT FEELING IT.

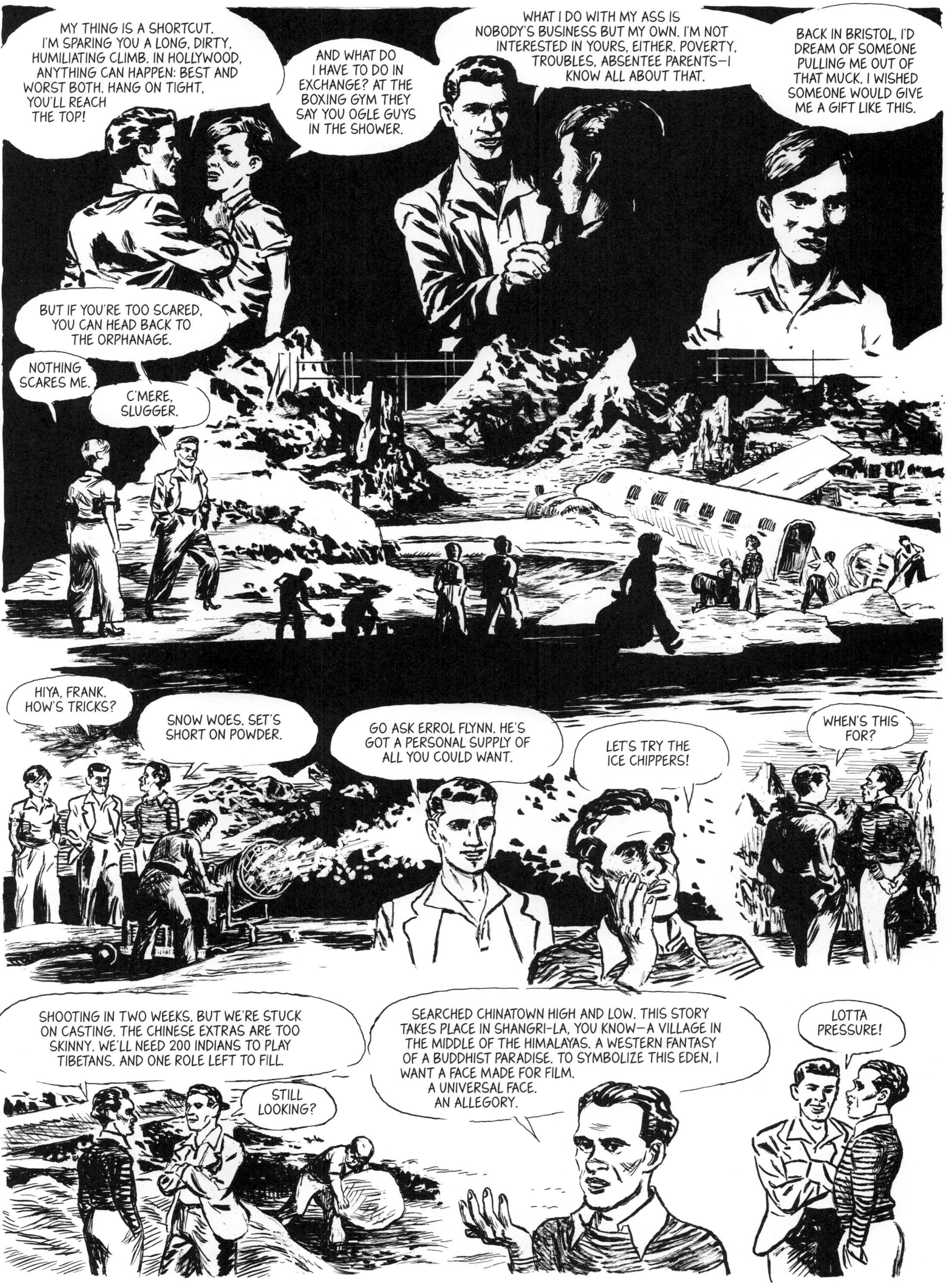
MY THING IS A SHORTCUT. I'M SPARING YOU A LONG, DIRTY, HUMILIATING CLIMB. IN HOLLYWOOD, ANYTHING CAN HAPPEN: BEST AND WORST BOTH. HANG ON TIGHT, YOU'LL REACH THE TOP!
AND WHAT DO I HAVE TO DO IN EXCHANGE? AT THE BOXING GYM THEY SAY YOU OGLE GUYS IN THE SHOWER.
WHAT I DO WITH MY ASS IS NOBODY'S BUSINESS BUT MY OWN. I'M NOT INTERESTED IN YOURS, EITHER. POVERTY, TROUBLES, ABSENTEE PARENTS—I KNOW ALL ABOUT THAT.
BACK IN BRISTOL, I'D DREAM OF SOMEONE PULLING ME OUT OF THAT MUCK. I WISHED SOMEONE WOULD GIVE ME A GIFT LIKE THIS.
BUT IF YOU'RE TOO SCARED, YOU CAN HEAD BACK TO THE ORPHANAGE.
NOTHING SCARES ME.
C'MERE, SLUGGER.
HIYA, FRANK. HOW'S TRICKS?
SNOW WOES. SET'S SHORT ON POWDER.
GO ASK ERROL FLYNN. HE'S GOT A PERSONAL SUPPLY OF ALL YOU COULD WANT.
LET'S TRY THE ICE CHIPPERS!
WHEN'S THIS FOR?
SHOOTING IN TWO WEEKS. BUT WE'RE STUCK ON CASTING. THE CHINESE EXTRAS ARE TOO SKINNY. WE'LL NEED 200 INDIANS TO PLAY TIBETANS. AND ONE ROLE LEFT TO FILL.
STILL LOOKING?
SEARCHED CHINATOWN HIGH AND LOW. THIS STORY TAKES PLACE IN SHANGRI-LA, YOU KNOW—A VILLAGE IN THE MIDDLE OF THE HIMALAYAS. A WESTERN FANTASY OF A BUDDHIST PARADISE. TO SYMBOLIZE THIS EDEN, I WANT A FACE MADE FOR FILM. A UNIVERSAL FACE. AN ALLEGORY.
LOTTA PRESSURE!

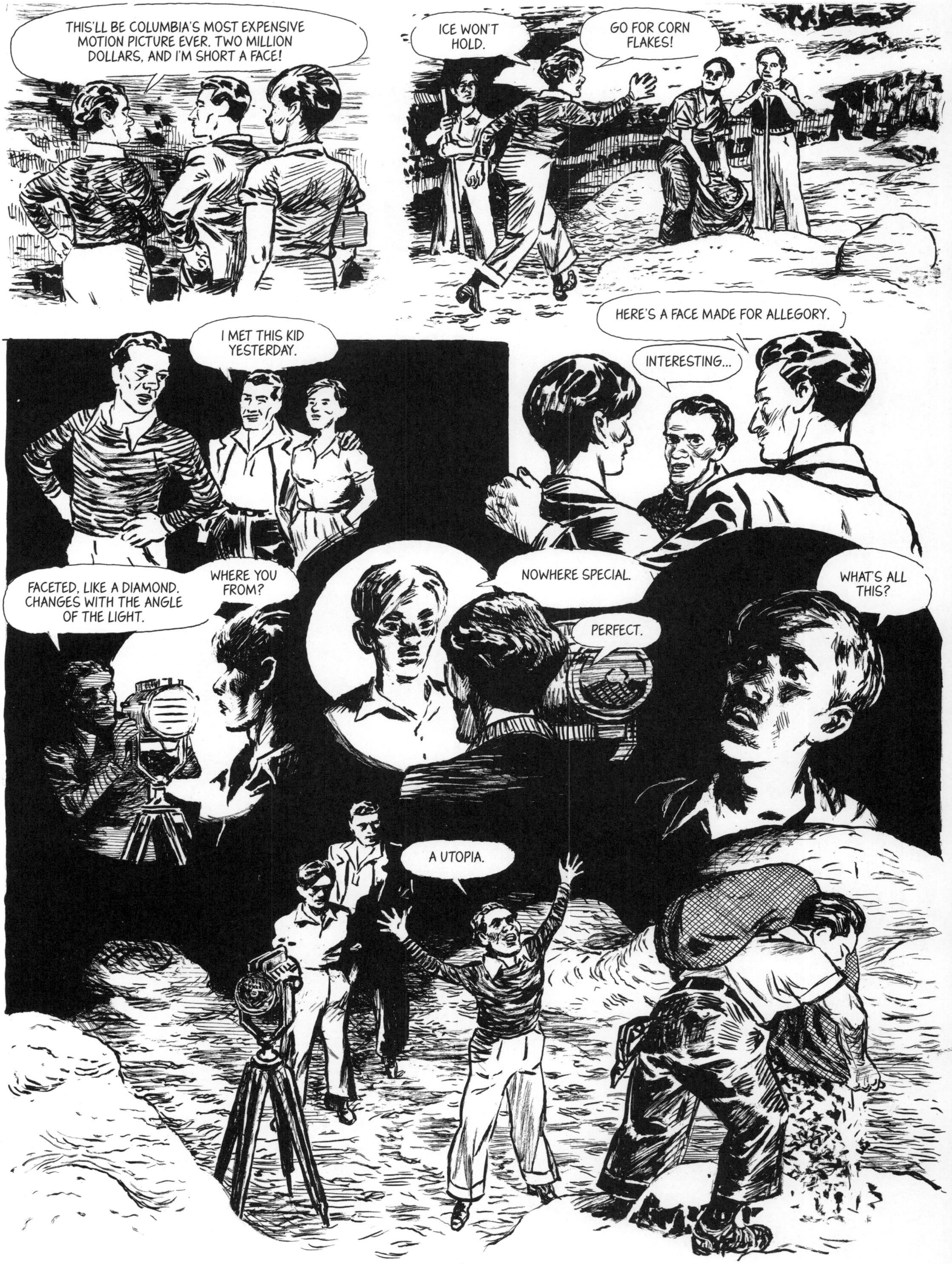
THIS'LL BE COLUMBIA'S MOST EXPENSIVE MOTION PICTURE EVER. TWO MILLION DOLLARS, AND I'M SHORT A FACE!
ICE WON'T HOLD.
GO FOR CORN FLAKES!
I MET THIS KID YESTERDAY.
HERE'S A FACE MADE FOR ALLEGORY.
INTERESTING...
FACETED, LIKE A DIAMOND. CHANGES WITH THE ANGLE OF THE LIGHT.
WHERE YOU FROM?
NOWHERE SPECIAL.
PERFECT.
WHAT'S ALL THIS?
A UTOPIA.

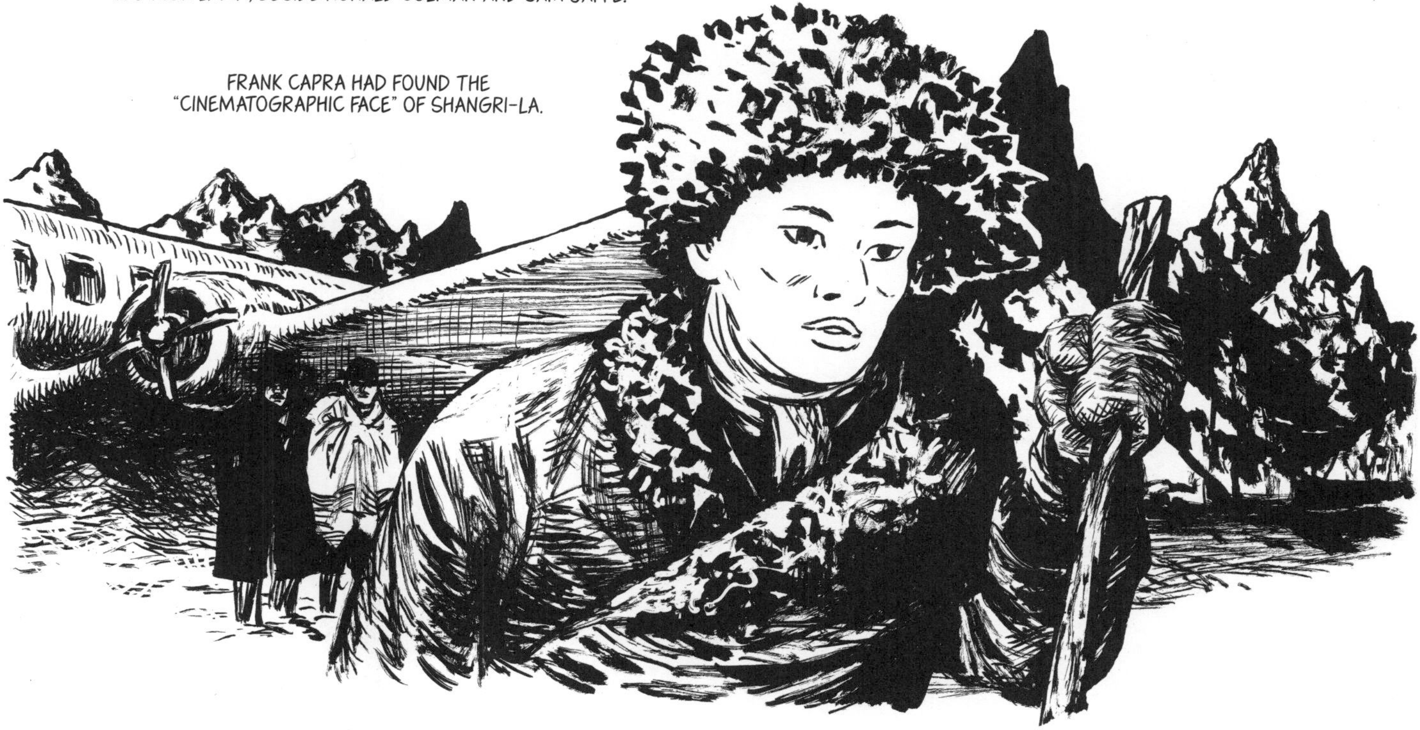
TWO WEEKS LATER, IN A REFRIGERATED HANGAR ON THE INDUSTRIAL OUTSKIRTS OF LOS ANGELES, SHOOTING FOR *LOST HORIZON* BEGAN. MAXIMUS WAS PLAYING THE ROLE OF DAHOE, A YOUNG DISCIPLE OF THE HIGH LAMA, BESIDE RONALD COLMAN AND SAM JAFFE.
RELEASED ON SEPTEMBER 1, 1937, *LOST HORIZON* WAS A WORLDWIDE HIT.
FRANK CAPRA HAD FOUND THE "CINEMATOGRAPHIC FACE" OF SHANGRI-LA.
FOR THIS FIRST AND SILENT ROLE, MAXIMUS HAD 5 MINUTES, 7 SECONDS OF SCREEN TIME.
BUT AT THE PREVIEW SCREENING IN SANTA BARBARA, AUDIENCE RESPONSE WAS DISASTROUS. THREE DAYS LATER, CAPRA ASKED HIS EDITOR GENE HAVLICK TO CUT THE FIRST TWO REELS OF THE FILM.

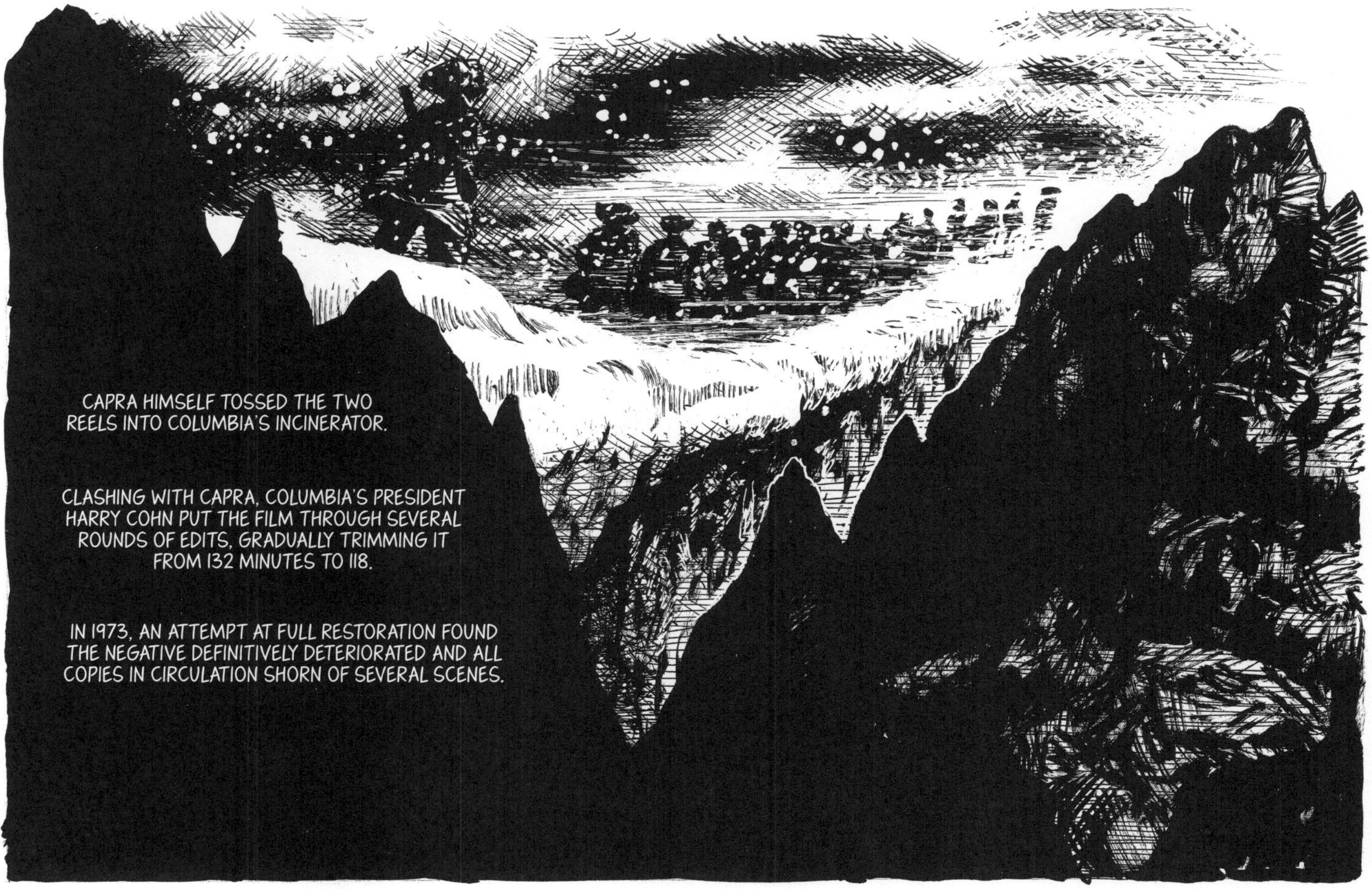
CAPRA HIMSELF TOSSED THE TWO REELS INTO COLUMBIA'S INCINERATOR.
CLASHING WITH CAPRA, COLUMBIA'S PRESIDENT HARRY COHN PUT THE FILM THROUGH SEVERAL ROUNDS OF EDITS, GRADUALLY TRIMMING IT FROM 132 MINUTES TO 118.
IN 1973, AN ATTEMPT AT FULL RESTORATION FOUND THE NEGATIVE DEFINITIVELY DETERIORATED AND ALL COPIES IN CIRCULATION SHORN OF SEVERAL SCENES.

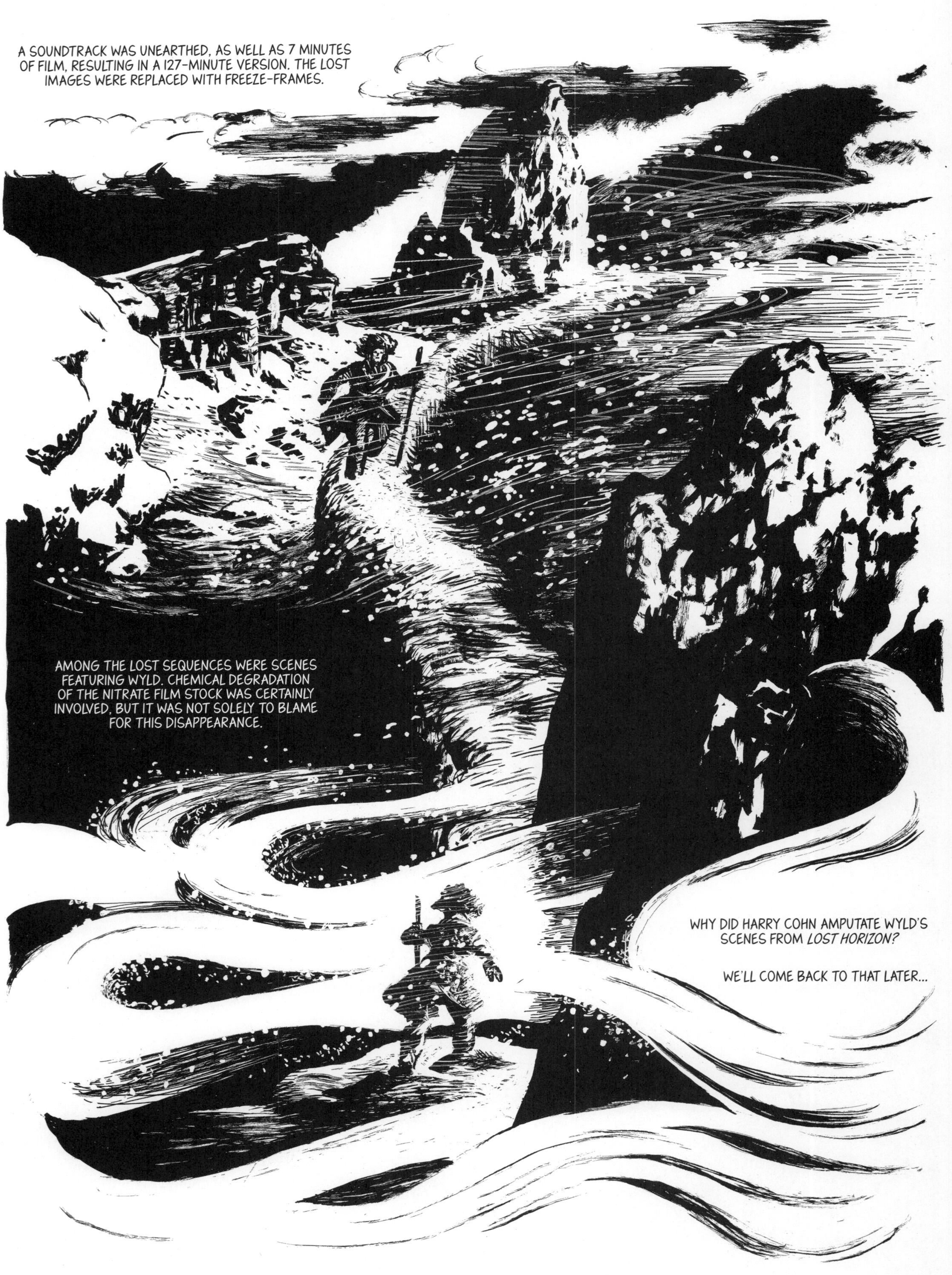
A SOUNDTRACK WAS UNEARTHED, AS WELL AS 7 MINUTES OF FILM, RESULTING IN A 127-MINUTE VERSION. THE LOST IMAGES WERE REPLACED WITH FREEZE-FRAMES.
AMONG THE LOST SEQUENCES WERE SCENES FEATURING WYLD. CHEMICAL DEGRADATION OF THE NITRATE FILM STOCK WAS CERTAINLY INVOLVED, BUT IT WAS NOT SOLELY TO BLAME FOR THIS DISAPPEARANCE.
WHY DID HARRY COHN AMPUTATE WYLD'S SCENES FROM *LOST HORIZON?*
WE'LL COME BACK TO THAT LATER...

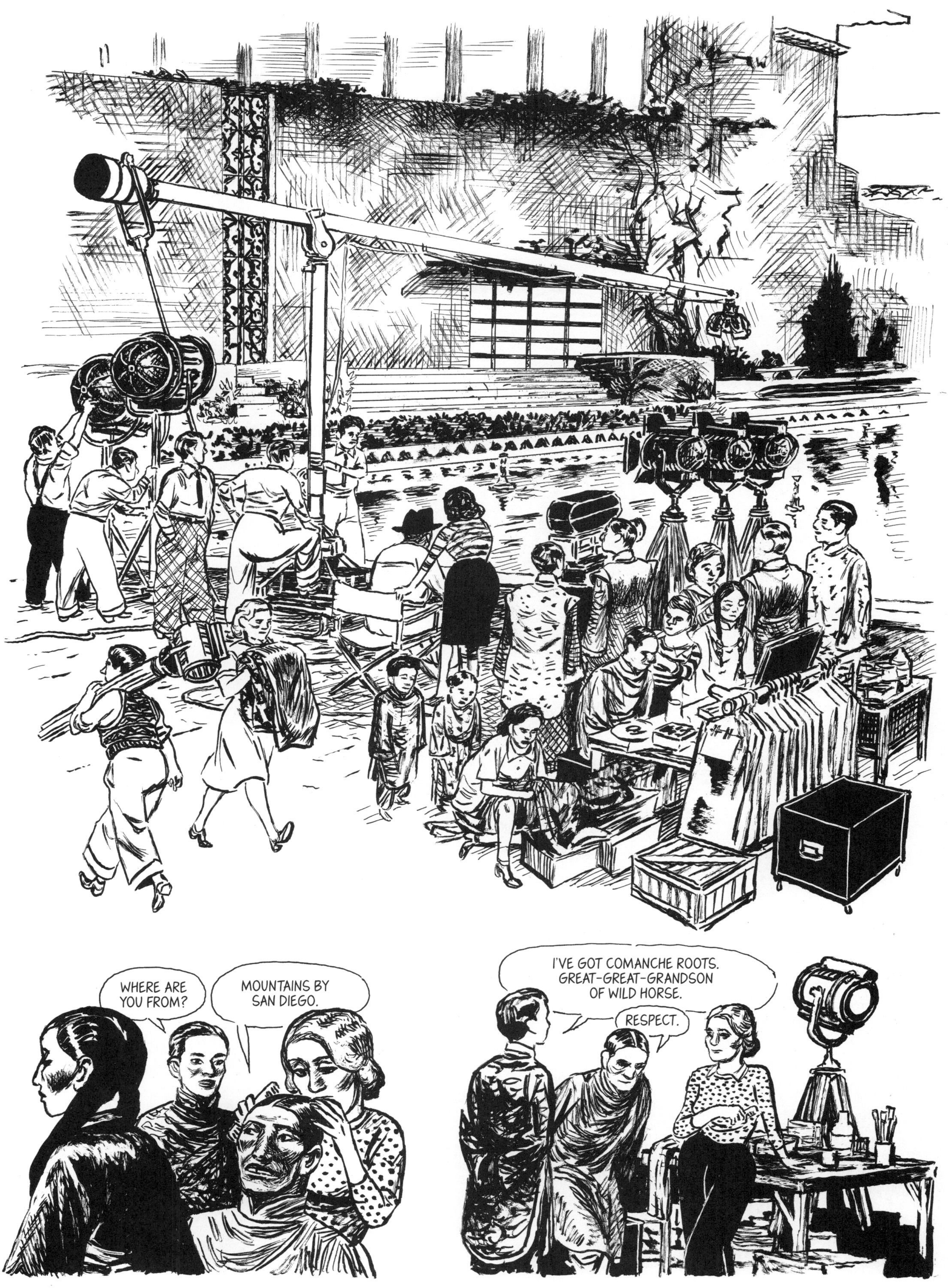
WHERE ARE YOU FROM?
MOUNTAINS BY SAN DIEGO.
I'VE GOT COMANCHE ROOTS. GREAT-GREAT-GRANDSON OF WILD HORSE.
RESPECT.

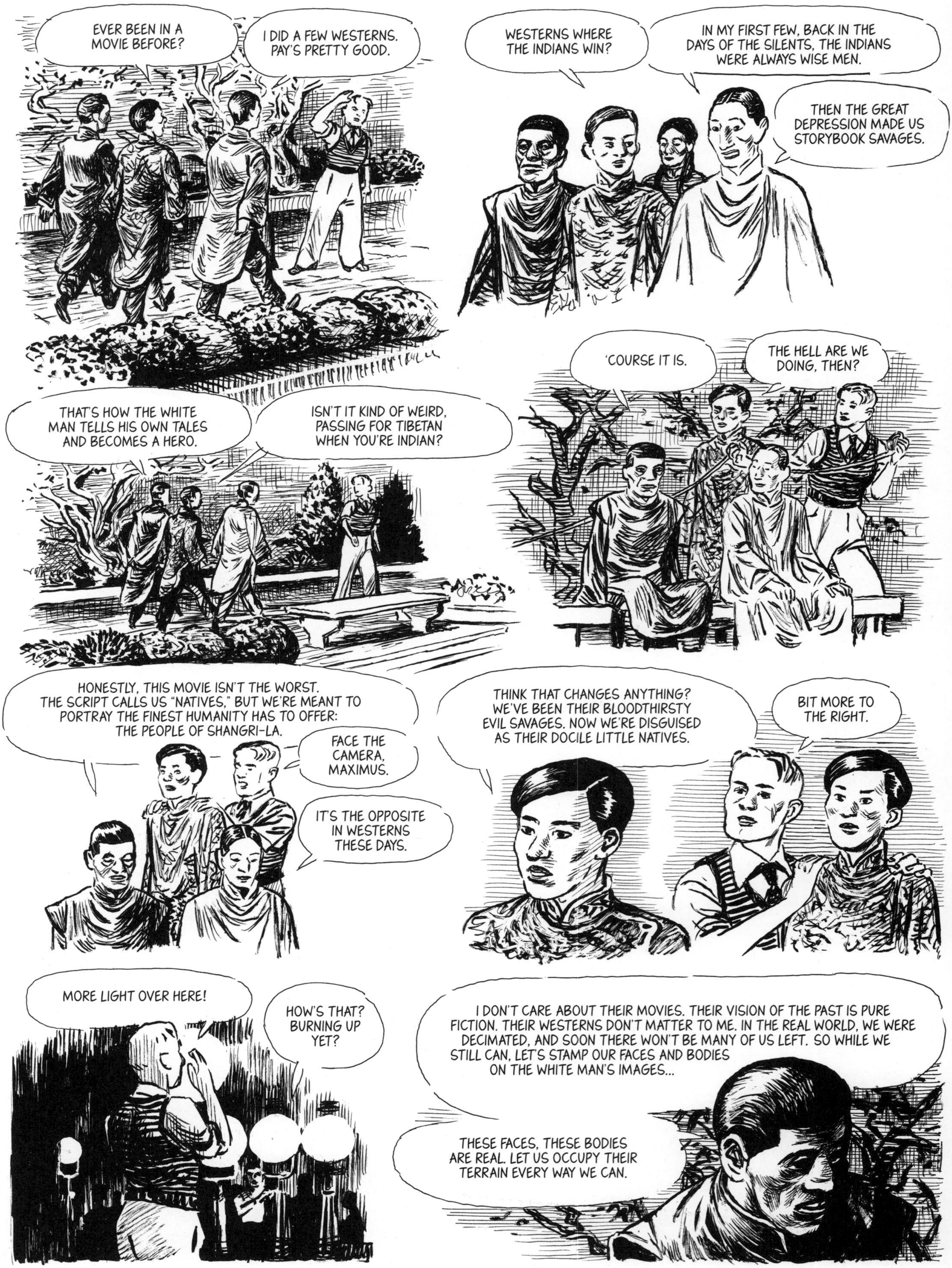
EVER BEEN IN A MOVIE BEFORE?
I DID A FEW WESTERNS. PAY'S PRETTY GOOD.
WESTERNS WHERE THE INDIANS WIN?
IN MY FIRST FEW, BACK IN THE DAYS OF THE SILENTS, THE INDIANS WERE ALWAYS WISE MEN.
THEN THE GREAT DEPRESSION MADE US STORYBOOK SAVAGES.
THAT'S HOW THE WHITE MAN TELLS HIS OWN TALES AND BECOMES A HERO.
ISN'T IT KIND OF WEIRD, PASSING FOR TIBETAN WHEN YOU'RE INDIAN?
'COURSE IT IS.
THE HELL ARE WE DOING, THEN?
HONESTLY, THIS MOVIE ISN'T THE WORST. THE SCRIPT CALLS US "NATIVES," BUT WE'RE MEANT TO PORTRAY THE FINEST HUMANITY HAS TO OFFER: THE PEOPLE OF SHANGRI-LA.
FACE THE CAMERA, MAXIMUS.
IT'S THE OPPOSITE IN WESTERNS THESE DAYS.
THINK THAT CHANGES ANYTHING? WE'VE BEEN THEIR BLOODTHIRSTY EVIL SAVAGES. NOW WE'RE DISGUISED AS THEIR DOCILE LITTLE NATIVES.
BIT MORE TO THE RIGHT.
MORE LIGHT OVER HERE!
HOW'S THAT? BURNING UP YET?
I DON'T CARE ABOUT THEIR MOVIES. THEIR VISION OF THE PAST IS PURE FICTION. THEIR WESTERNS DON'T MATTER TO ME. IN THE REAL WORLD, WE WERE DECIMATED, AND SOON THERE WON'T BE MANY OF US LEFT. SO WHILE WE STILL CAN, LET'S STAMP OUR FACES AND BODIES ON THE WHITE MAN'S IMAGES...
THESE FACES, THESE BODIES ARE REAL. LET US OCCUPY THEIR TERRAIN EVERY WAY WE CAN.

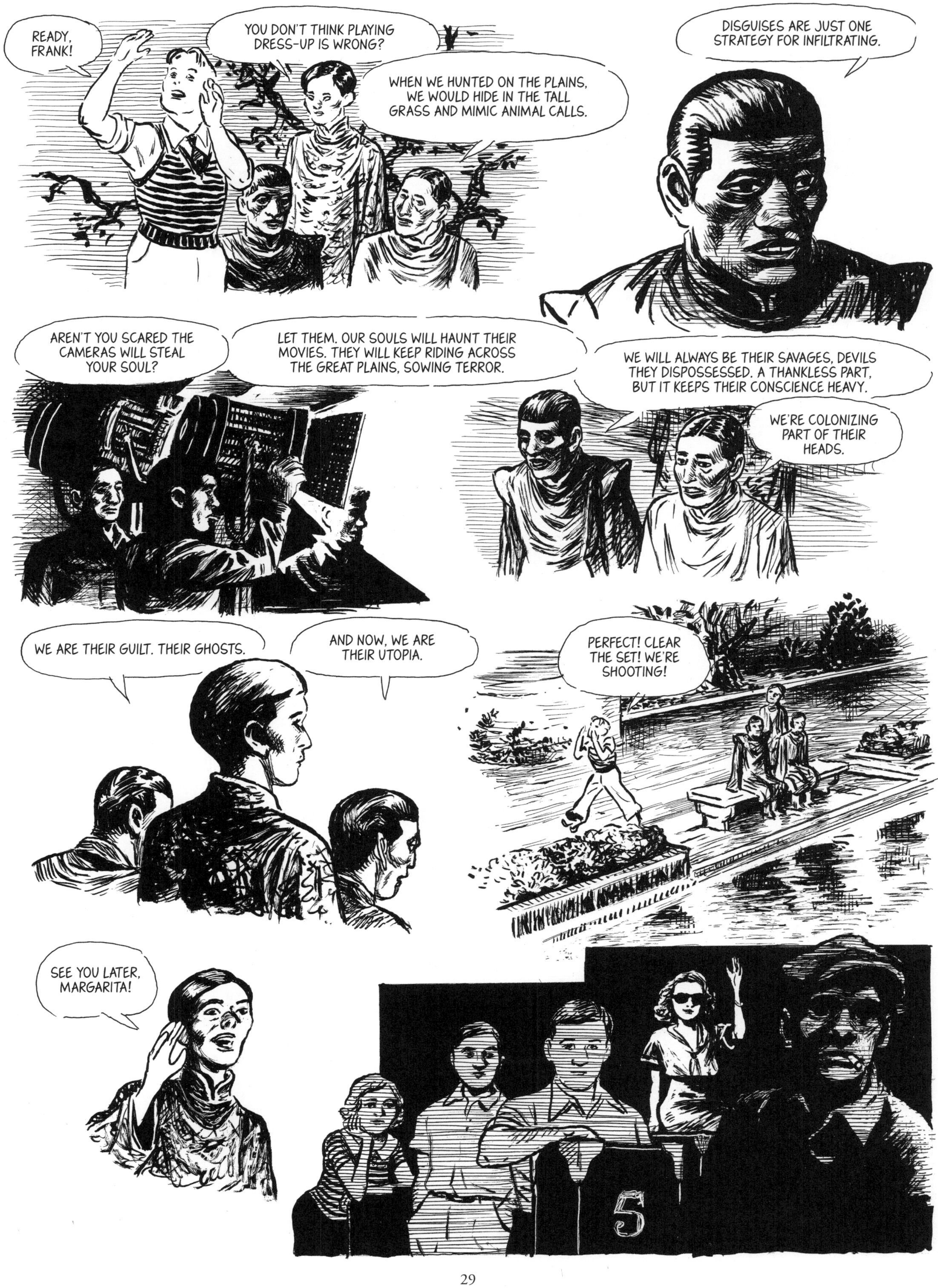
READY, FRANK!
YOU DON'T THINK PLAYING DRESS-UP IS WRONG?
WHEN WE HUNTED ON THE PLAINS, WE WOULD HIDE IN THE TALL GRASS AND MIMIC ANIMAL CALLS.
DISGUISES ARE JUST ONE STRATEGY FOR INFILTRATING.
AREN'T YOU SCARED THE CAMERAS WILL STEAL YOUR SOUL?
LET THEM. OUR SOULS WILL HAUNT THEIR MOVIES. THEY WILL KEEP RIDING ACROSS THE GREAT PLAINS, SOWING TERROR.
WE WILL ALWAYS BE THEIR SAVAGES, DEVILS THEY DISPOSSESSED. A THANKLESS PART, BUT IT KEEPS THEIR CONSCIENCE HEAVY.
WE'RE COLONIZING PART OF THEIR HEADS.
WE ARE THEIR GUILT. THEIR GHOSTS.
AND NOW, WE ARE THEIR UTOPIA.
PERFECT! CLEAR THE SET! WE'RE SHOOTING!
SEE YOU LATER, MARGARITA!
5

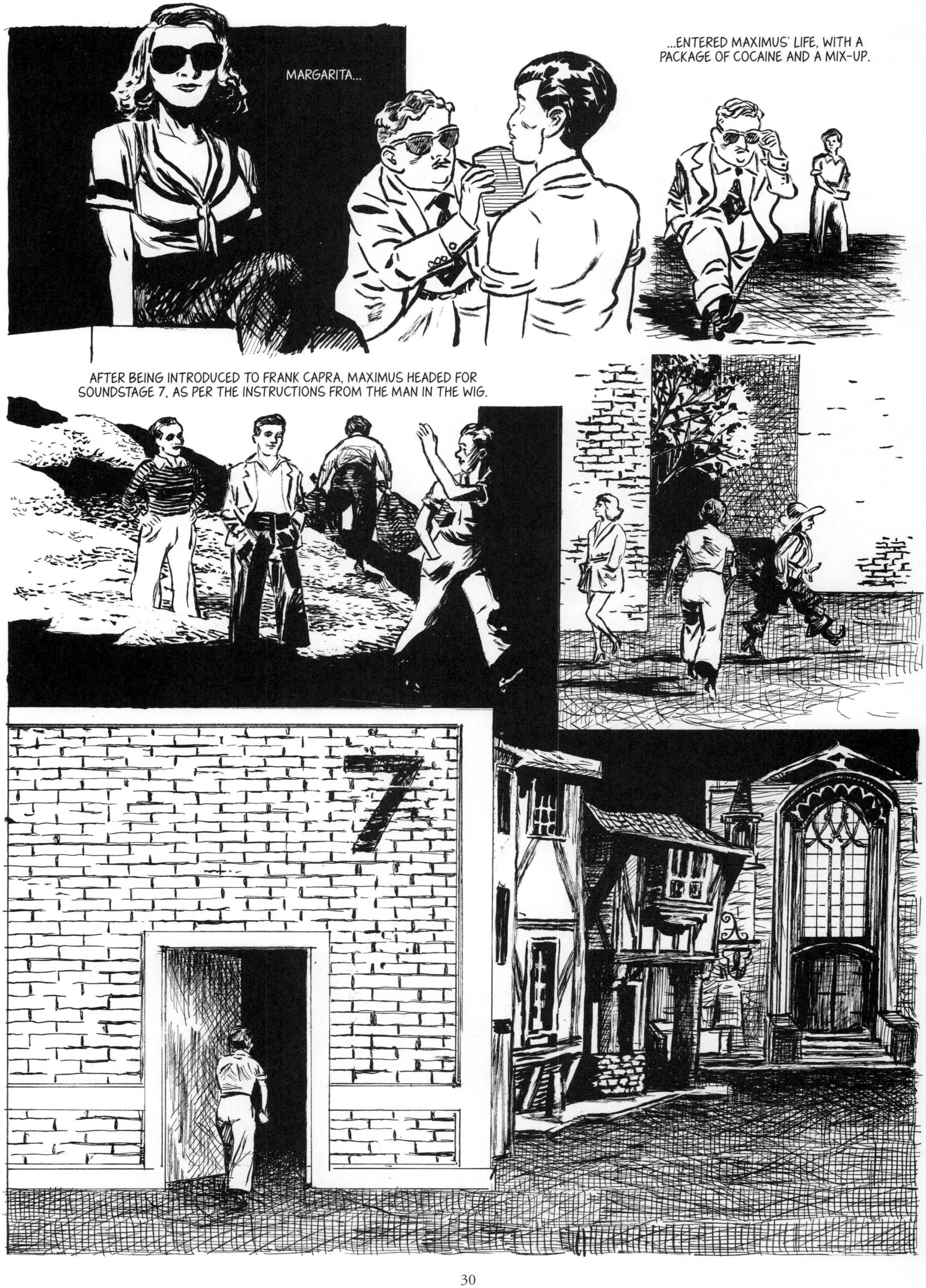
MARGARITA...
...ENTERED MAXIMUS' LIFE, WITH A PACKAGE OF COCAINE AND A MIX-UP.
AFTER BEING INTRODUCED TO FRANK CAPRA, MAXIMUS HEADED FOR SOUNDSTAGE 7, AS PER THE INSTRUCTIONS FROM THE MAN IN THE WIG.
7

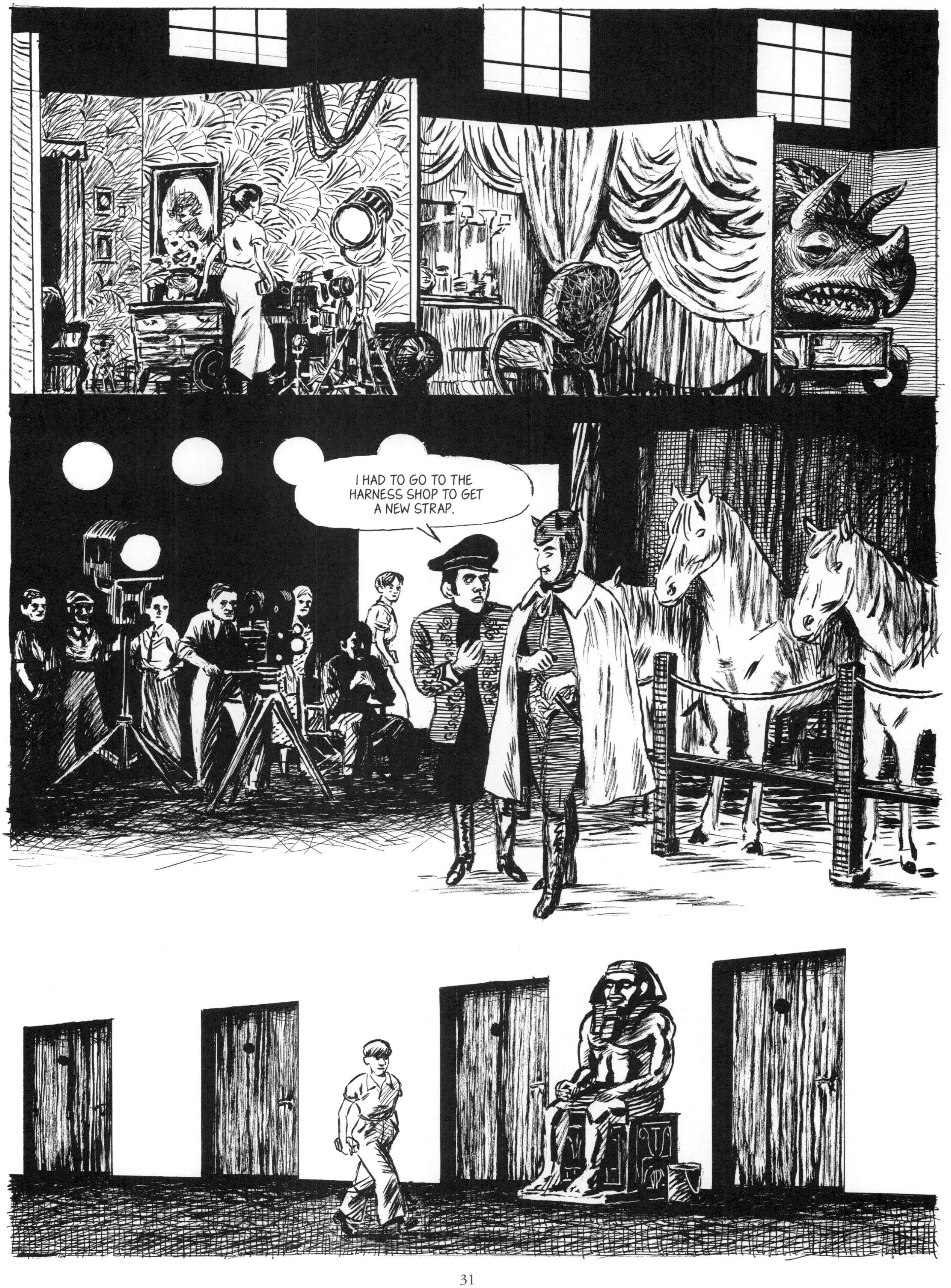
I HAD TO GO TO THE HARNESS SHOP TO GET A NEW STRAP.

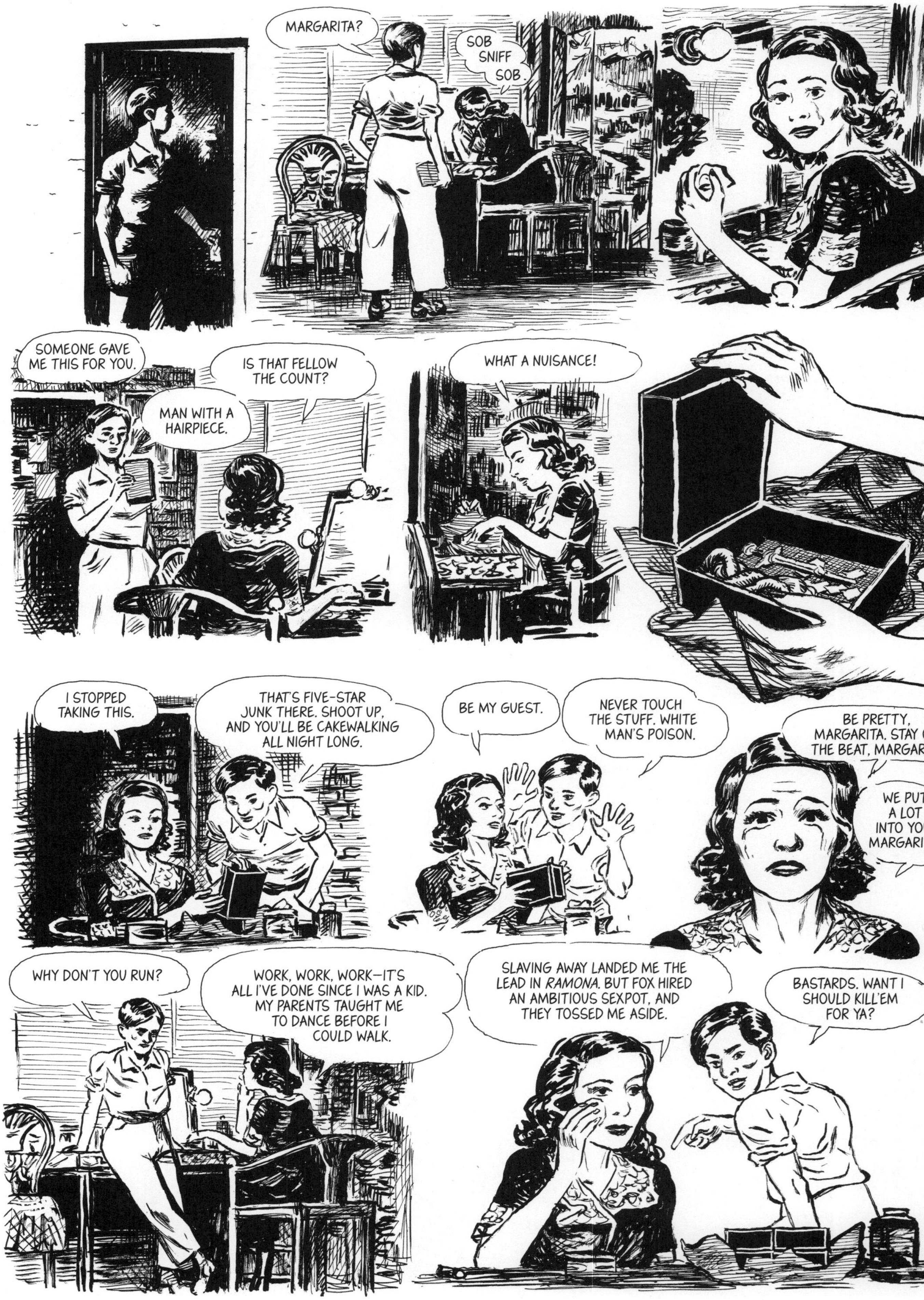
MARGARITA?
SOB SNIFF SOB.
SOMEONE GAVE ME THIS FOR YOU.
IS THAT FELLOW THE COUNT?
MAN WITH A HAIRPIECE.
WHAT A NUISANCE!
I STOPPED TAKING THIS.
THAT'S FIVE-STAR JUNK THERE. SHOOT UP, AND YOU'LL BE CAKEWALKING ALL NIGHT LONG.
BE MY GUEST.
NEVER TOUCH THE STUFF. WHITE MAN'S POISON.
BE PRETTY, MARGARITA. STAY ON THE BEAT, MARGARITA.
WE PUT A LOT INTO YOU, MARGARITA.
WHY DON'T YOU RUN?
WORK, WORK, WORK—IT'S ALL I'VE DONE SINCE I WAS A KID. MY PARENTS TAUGHT ME TO DANCE BEFORE I COULD WALK.
SLAVING AWAY LANDED ME THE LEAD IN *RAMONA*. BUT FOX HIRED AN AMBITIOUS SEXPOT, AND THEY TOSSED ME ASIDE.
BASTARDS. WANT I SHOULD KILL'EM FOR YA?

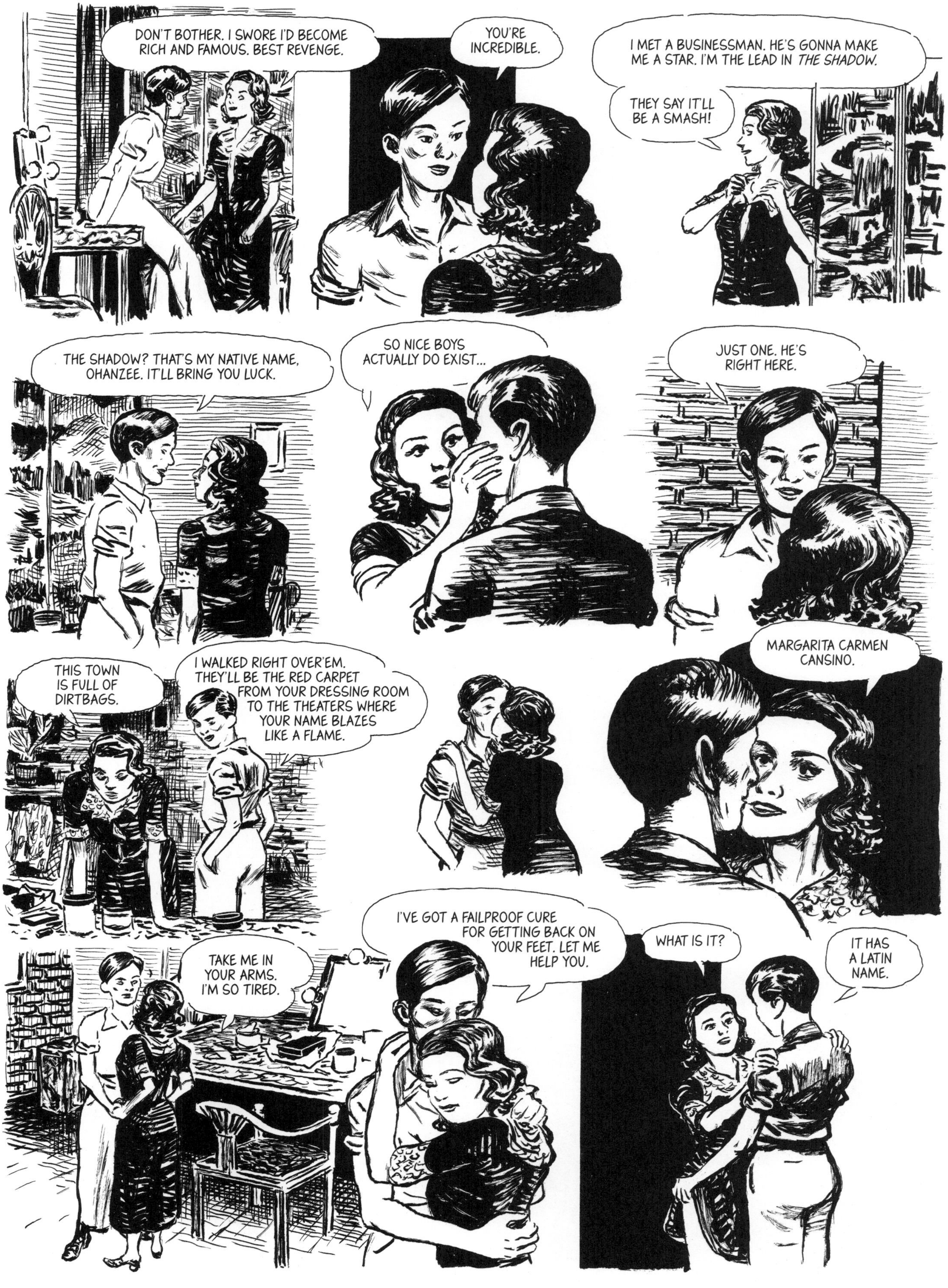
DON'T BOTHER. I SWORE I'D BECOME RICH AND FAMOUS. BEST REVENGE.
YOU'RE INCREDIBLE.
I MET A BUSINESSMAN. HE'S GONNA MAKE ME A STAR. I'M THE LEAD IN *THE SHADOW*.
THEY SAY IT'LL BE A SMASH!
THE SHADOW? THAT'S MY NATIVE NAME, OHANZEE. IT'LL BRING YOU LUCK.
SO NICE BOYS ACTUALLY DO EXIST...
JUST ONE. HE'S RIGHT HERE.
THIS TOWN IS FULL OF DIRTBAGS.
I WALKED RIGHT OVER'EM. THEY'LL BE THE RED CARPET FROM YOUR DRESSING ROOM TO THE THEATERS WHERE YOUR NAME BLAZES LIKE A FLAME.
MARGARITA CARMEN CANSINO.
TAKE ME IN YOUR ARMS. I'M SO TIRED.
I'VE GOT A FAILPROOF CURE FOR GETTING BACK ON YOUR FEET. LET ME HELP YOU.
WHAT IS IT?
IT HAS A LATIN NAME.

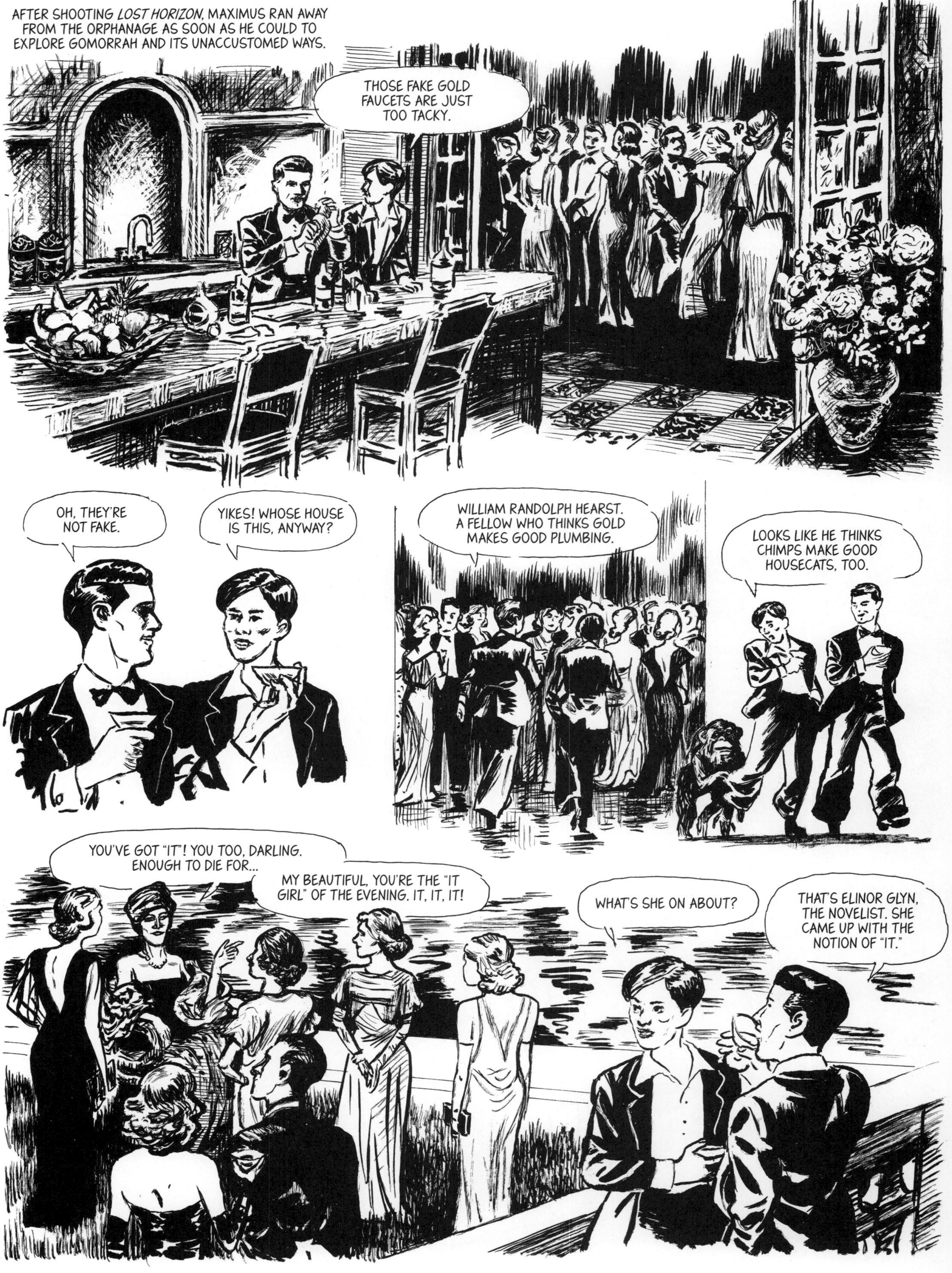
AFTER SHOOTING *LOST HORIZON*, MAXIMUS RAN AWAY FROM THE ORPHANAGE AS SOON AS HE COULD TO EXPLORE GOMORRAH AND ITS UNACCUSTOMED WAYS.
THOSE FAKE GOLD FAUCETS ARE JUST TOO TACKY.
OH, THEY'RE NOT FAKE.
YIKES! WHOSE HOUSE IS THIS, ANYWAY?
WILLIAM RANDOLPH HEARST. A FELLOW WHO THINKS GOLD MAKES GOOD PLUMBING.
LOOKS LIKE HE THINKS CHIMPS MAKE GOOD HOUSECATS, TOO.
YOU'VE GOT "IT"! YOU TOO, DARLING. ENOUGH TO DIE FOR...
MY BEAUTIFUL, YOU'RE THE "IT GIRL" OF THE EVENING. IT, IT, IT!
WHAT'S SHE ON ABOUT?
THAT'S ELINOR GLYN, THE NOVELIST. SHE CAME UP WITH THE NOTION OF "IT."

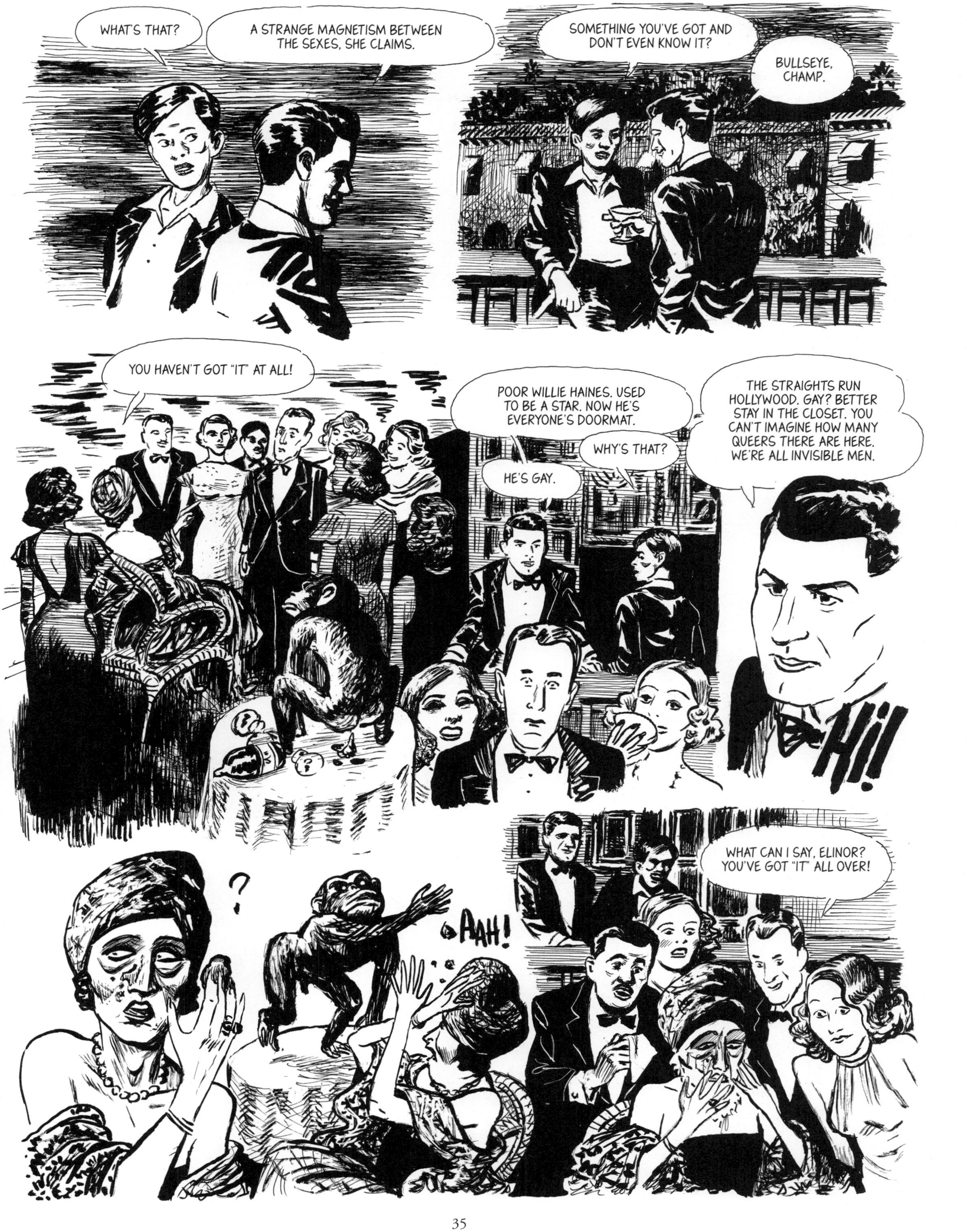
WHAT'S THAT?
A STRANGE MAGNETISM BETWEEN THE SEXES, SHE CLAIMS.
SOMETHING YOU'VE GOT AND DON'T EVEN KNOW IT?
BULLSEYE, CHAMP.
YOU HAVEN'T GOT "IT" AT ALL!
POOR WILLIE HAINES. USED TO BE A STAR. NOW HE'S EVERYONE'S DOORMAT.
WHY'S THAT?
HE'S GAY.
THE STRAIGHTS RUN HOLLYWOOD. GAY? BETTER STAY IN THE CLOSET. YOU CAN'T IMAGINE HOW MANY QUEERS THERE ARE HERE. WE'RE ALL INVISIBLE MEN.
HI!
?
AAH!
WHAT CAN I SAY, ELINOR? YOU'VE GOT "IT" ALL OVER!

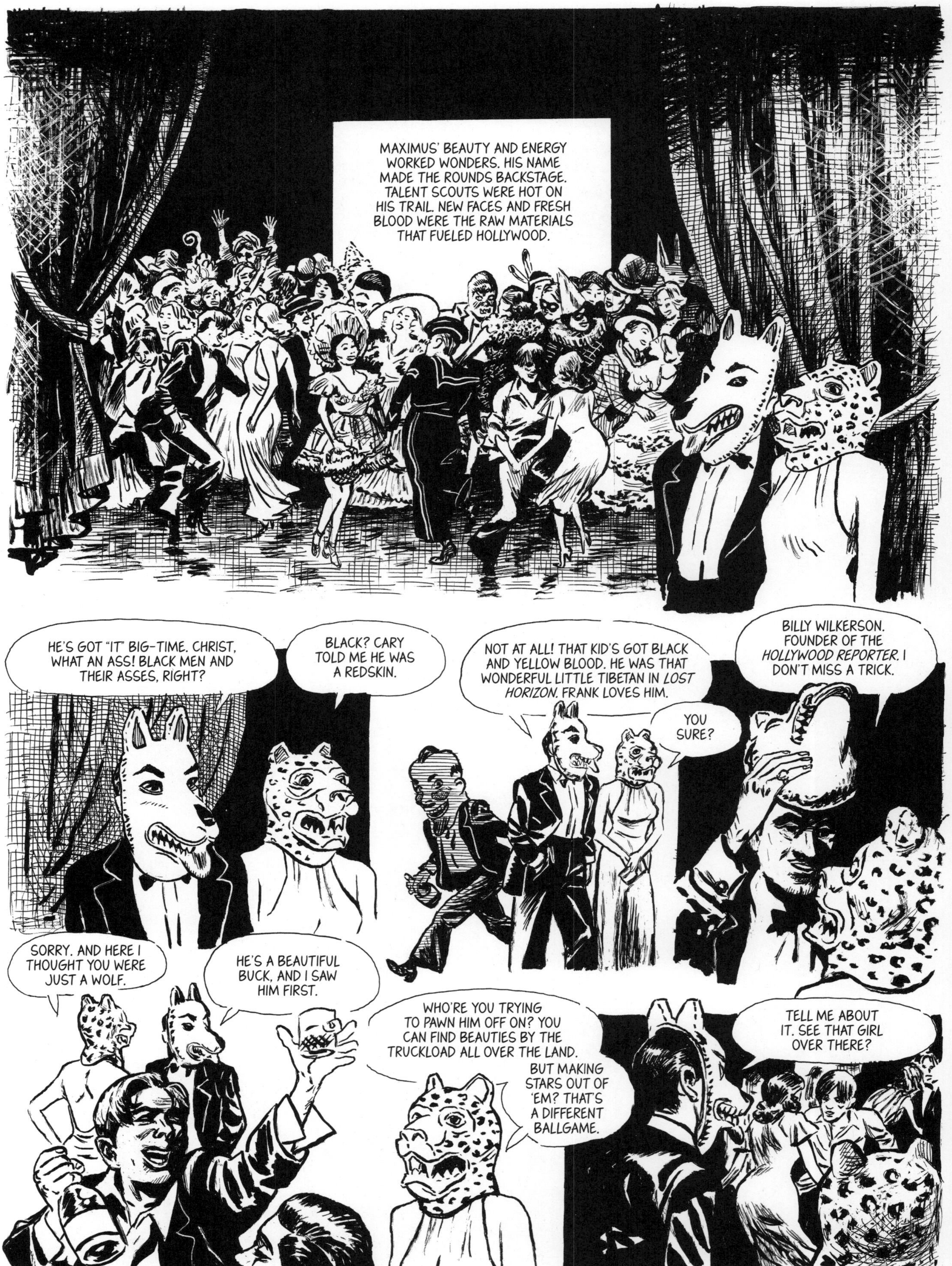
MAXIMUS' BEAUTY AND ENERGY WORKED WONDERS. HIS NAME MADE THE ROUNDS BACKSTAGE. TALENT SCOUTS WERE HOT ON HIS TRAIL. NEW FACES AND FRESH BLOOD WERE THE RAW MATERIALS THAT FUELED HOLLYWOOD.
HE'S GOT "IT" BIG-TIME. CHRIST, WHAT AN ASS! BLACK MEN AND THEIR ASSES, RIGHT?
BLACK? CARY TOLD ME HE WAS A REDSKIN.
NOT AT ALL! THAT KID'S GOT BLACK AND YELLOW BLOOD. HE WAS THAT WONDERFUL LITTLE TIBETAN IN *LOST HORIZON*. FRANK LOVES HIM.
YOU SURE?
BILLY WILKERSON. FOUNDER OF THE *HOLLYWOOD REPORTER*. I DON'T MISS A TRICK.
SORRY. AND HERE I THOUGHT YOU WERE JUST A WOLF.
HE'S A BEAUTIFUL BUCK, AND I SAW HIM FIRST.
WHO'RE YOU TRYING TO PAWN HIM OFF ON? YOU CAN FIND BEAUTIES BY THE TRUCKLOAD ALL OVER THE LAND.
BUT MAKING STARS OUT OF 'EM? THAT'S A DIFFERENT BALLGAME.
TELL ME ABOUT IT. SEE THAT GIRL OVER THERE?

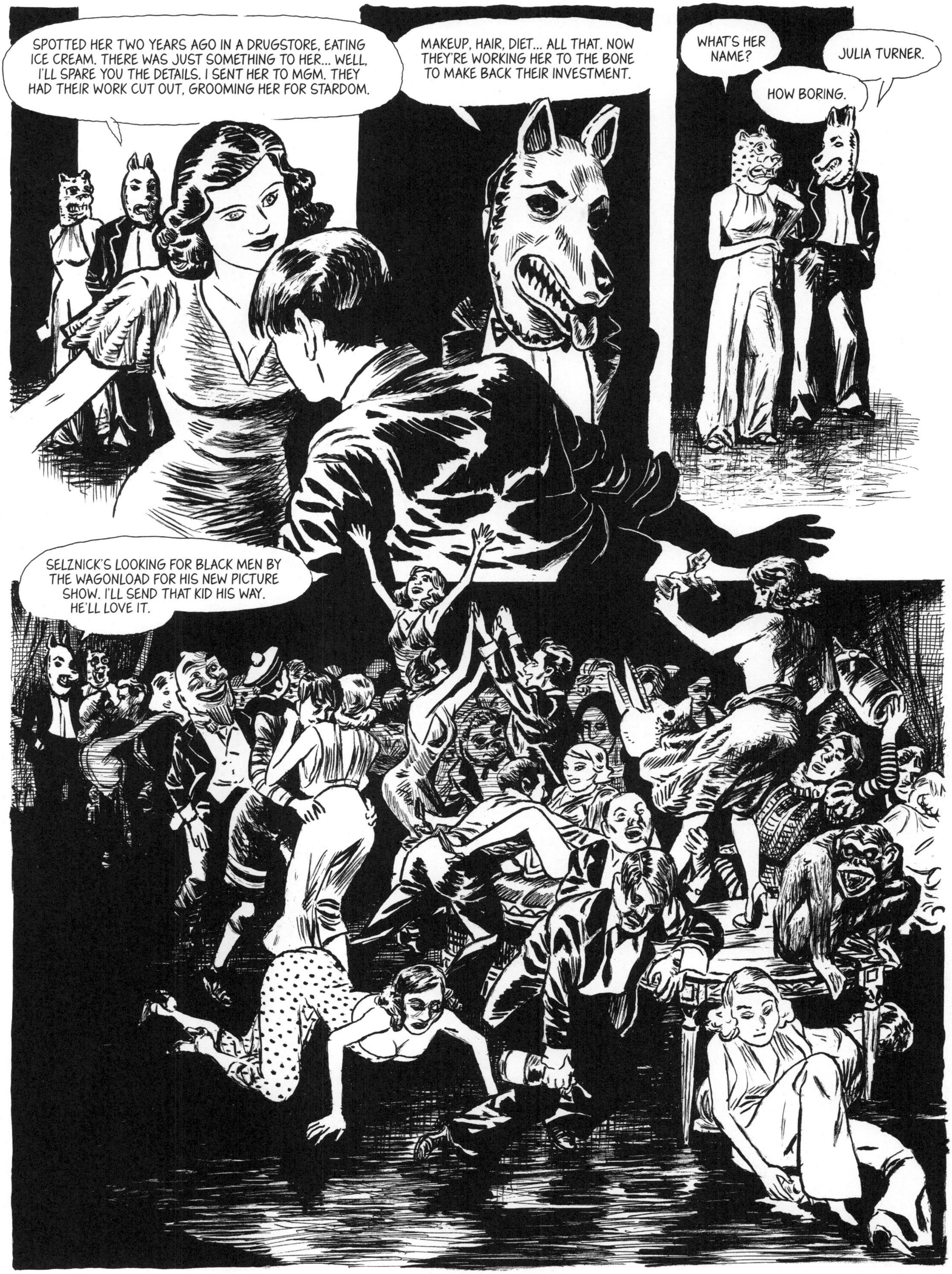
SPOTTED HER TWO YEARS AGO IN A DRUGSTORE, EATING ICE CREAM. THERE WAS JUST SOMETHING TO HER... WELL, I'LL SPARE YOU THE DETAILS. I SENT HER TO MGM. THEY HAD THEIR WORK CUT OUT, GROOMING HER FOR STARDOM.
MAKEUP, HAIR, DIET... ALL THAT. NOW THEY'RE WORKING HER TO THE BONE TO MAKE BACK THEIR INVESTMENT.
WHAT'S HER NAME?
JULIA TURNER.
HOW BORING.
SELZNICK'S LOOKING FOR BLACK MEN BY THE WAGONLOAD FOR HIS NEW PICTURE SHOW. I'LL SEND THAT KID HIS WAY. HE'LL LOVE IT.

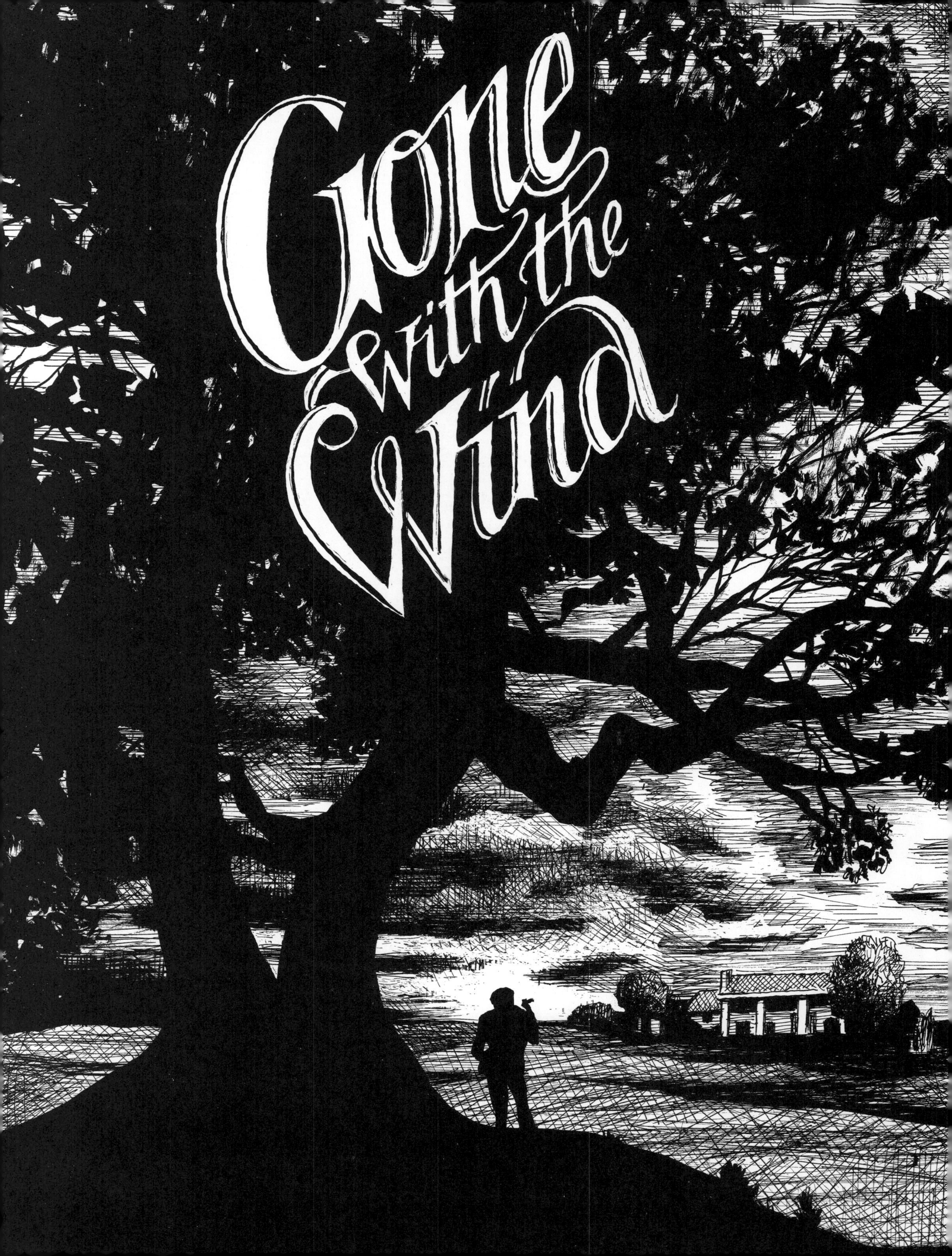
Gone with the Wind

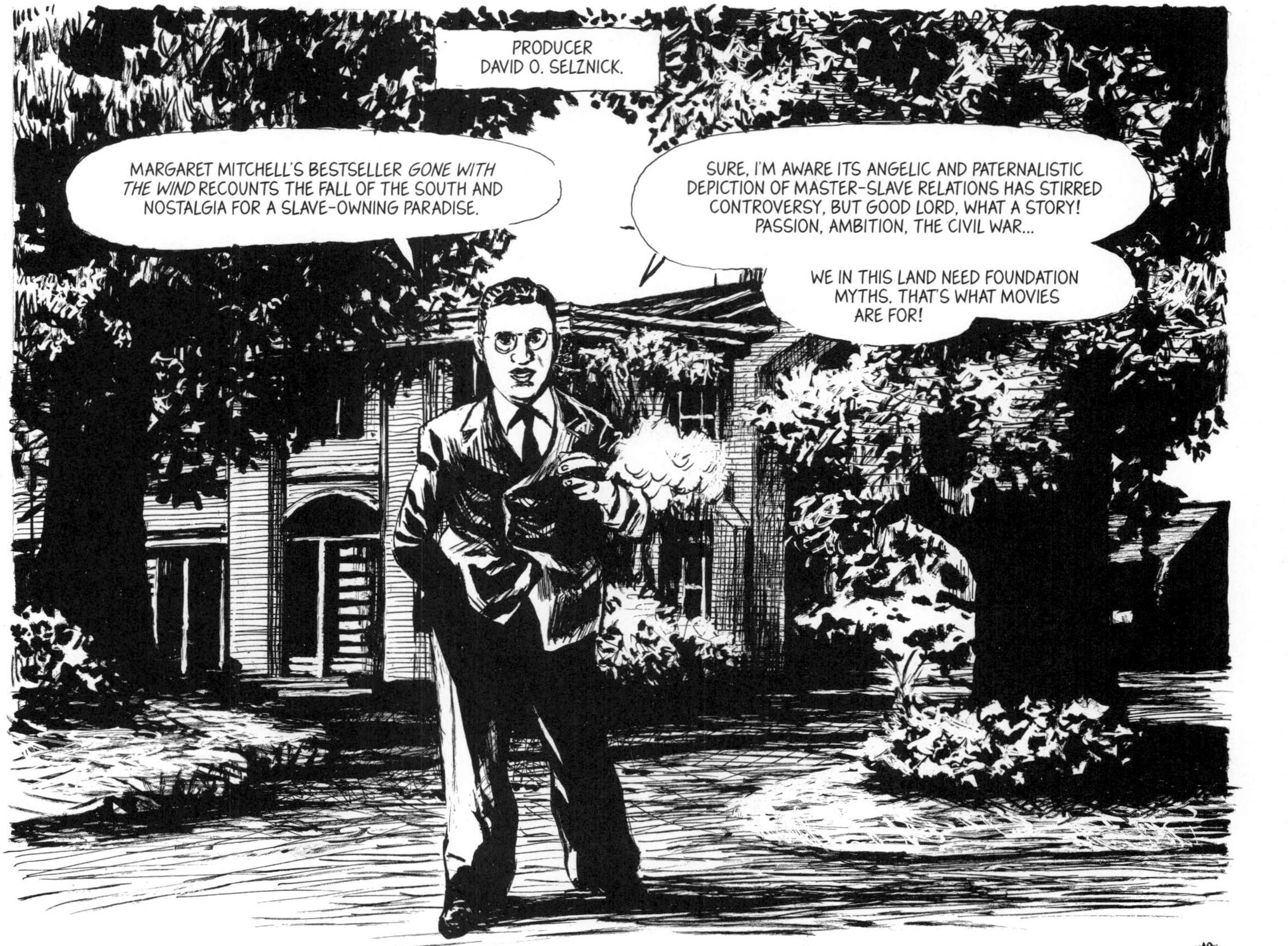
PRODUCER DAVID O. SELZNICK.
MARGARET MITCHELL'S BESTSELLER *GONE WITH THE WIND* RECOUNTS THE FALL OF THE SOUTH AND NOSTALGIA FOR A SLAVE-OWNING PARADISE.
SURE, I'M AWARE ITS ANGELIC AND PATERNALISTIC DEPICTION OF MASTER-SLAVE RELATIONS HAS STIRRED CONTROVERSY, BUT GOOD LORD, WHAT A STORY! PASSION, AMBITION, THE CIVIL WAR...
WE IN THIS LAND NEED FOUNDATION MYTHS. THAT'S WHAT MOVIES ARE FOR!

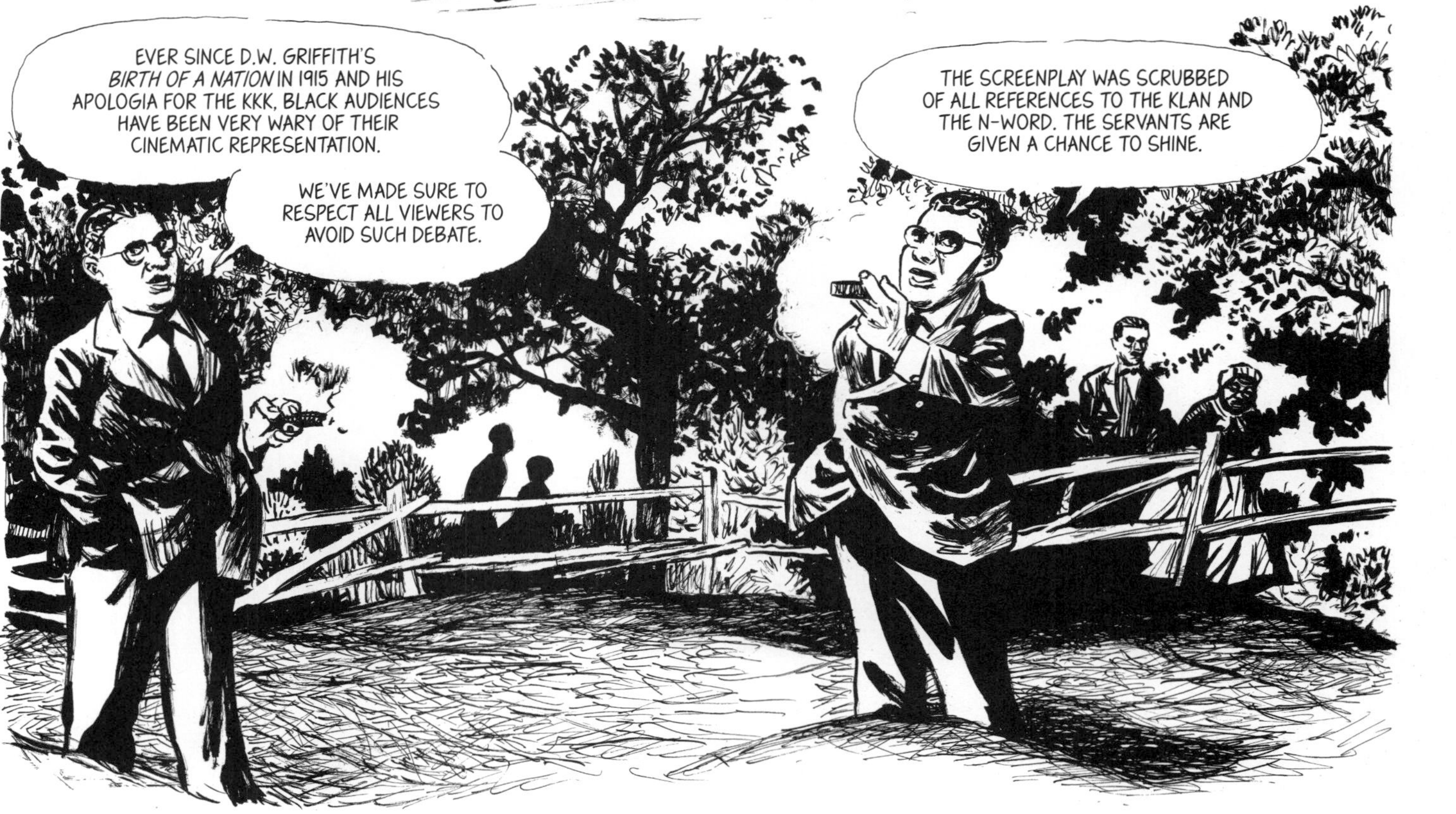
EVER SINCE D.W. GRIFFITH'S *BIRTH OF A NATION* IN 1915 AND HIS APOLOGIA FOR THE KKK, BLACK AUDIENCES HAVE BEEN VERY WARY OF THEIR CINEMATIC REPRESENTATION.
WE'VE MADE SURE TO RESPECT ALL VIEWERS TO AVOID SUCH DEBATE.
THE SCREENPLAY WAS SCRUBBED OF ALL REFERENCES TO THE KLAN AND THE N-WORD. THE SERVANTS ARE GIVEN A CHANCE TO SHINE.

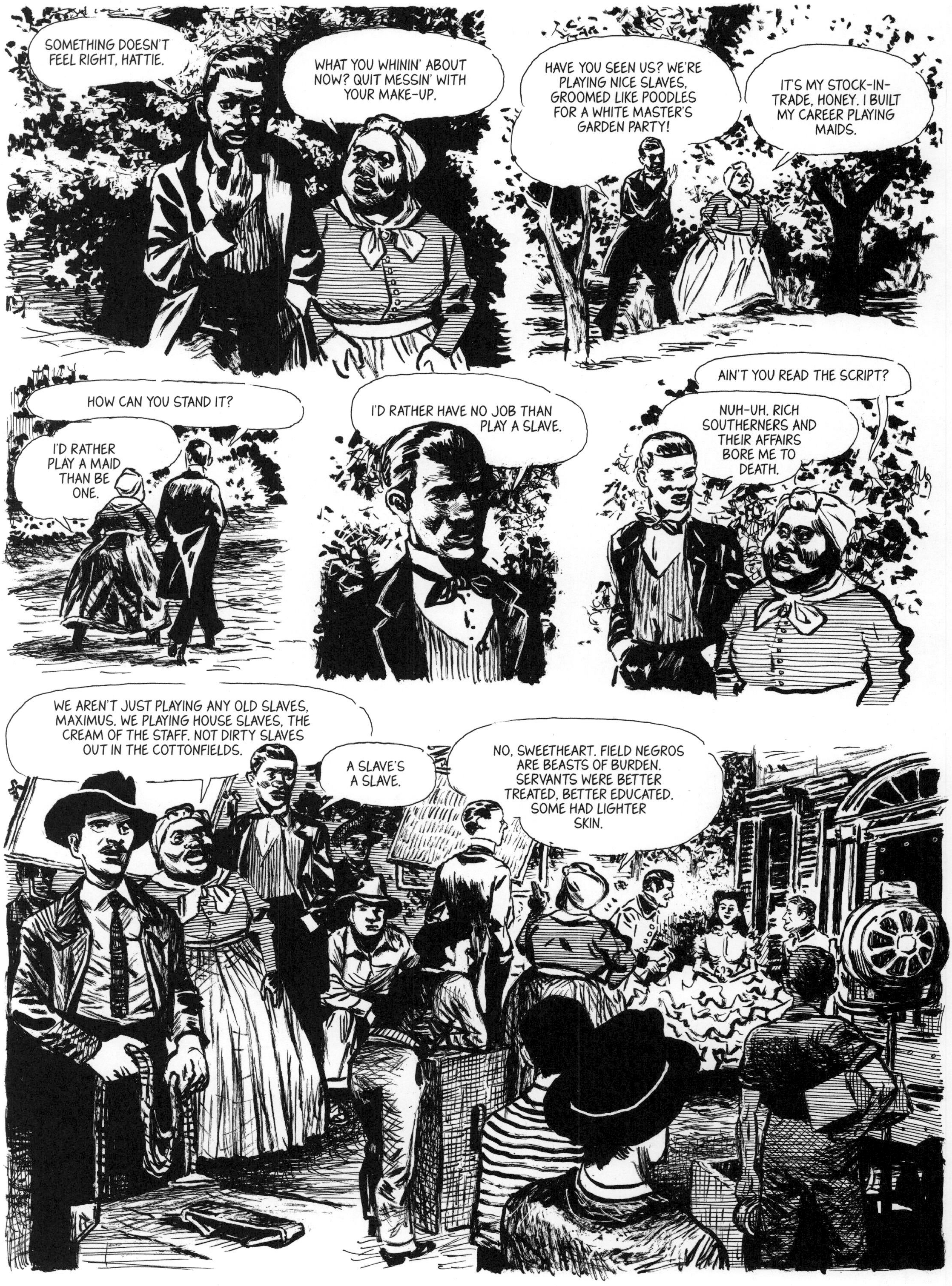
SOMETHING DOESN'T FEEL RIGHT, HATTIE.
WHAT YOU WHININ' ABOUT NOW? QUIT MESSIN' WITH YOUR MAKE-UP.
HAVE YOU SEEN US? WE'RE PLAYING NICE SLAVES, GROOMED LIKE POODLES FOR A WHITE MASTER'S GARDEN PARTY!
IT'S MY STOCK-IN-TRADE, HONEY. I BUILT MY CAREER PLAYING MAIDS.
HOW CAN YOU STAND IT?
I'D RATHER PLAY A MAID THAN BE ONE.
I'D RATHER HAVE NO JOB THAN PLAY A SLAVE.
AIN'T YOU READ THE SCRIPT?
NUH-UH. RICH SOUTHERNERS AND THEIR AFFAIRS BORE ME TO DEATH.
WE AREN'T JUST PLAYING ANY OLD SLAVES, MAXIMUS. WE PLAYING HOUSE SLAVES, THE CREAM OF THE STAFF. NOT DIRTY SLAVES OUT IN THE COTTONFIELDS.
A SLAVE'S A SLAVE.
NO, SWEETHEART. FIELD NEGROS ARE BEASTS OF BURDEN. SERVANTS WERE BETTER TREATED, BETTER EDUCATED. SOME HAD LIGHTER SKIN.

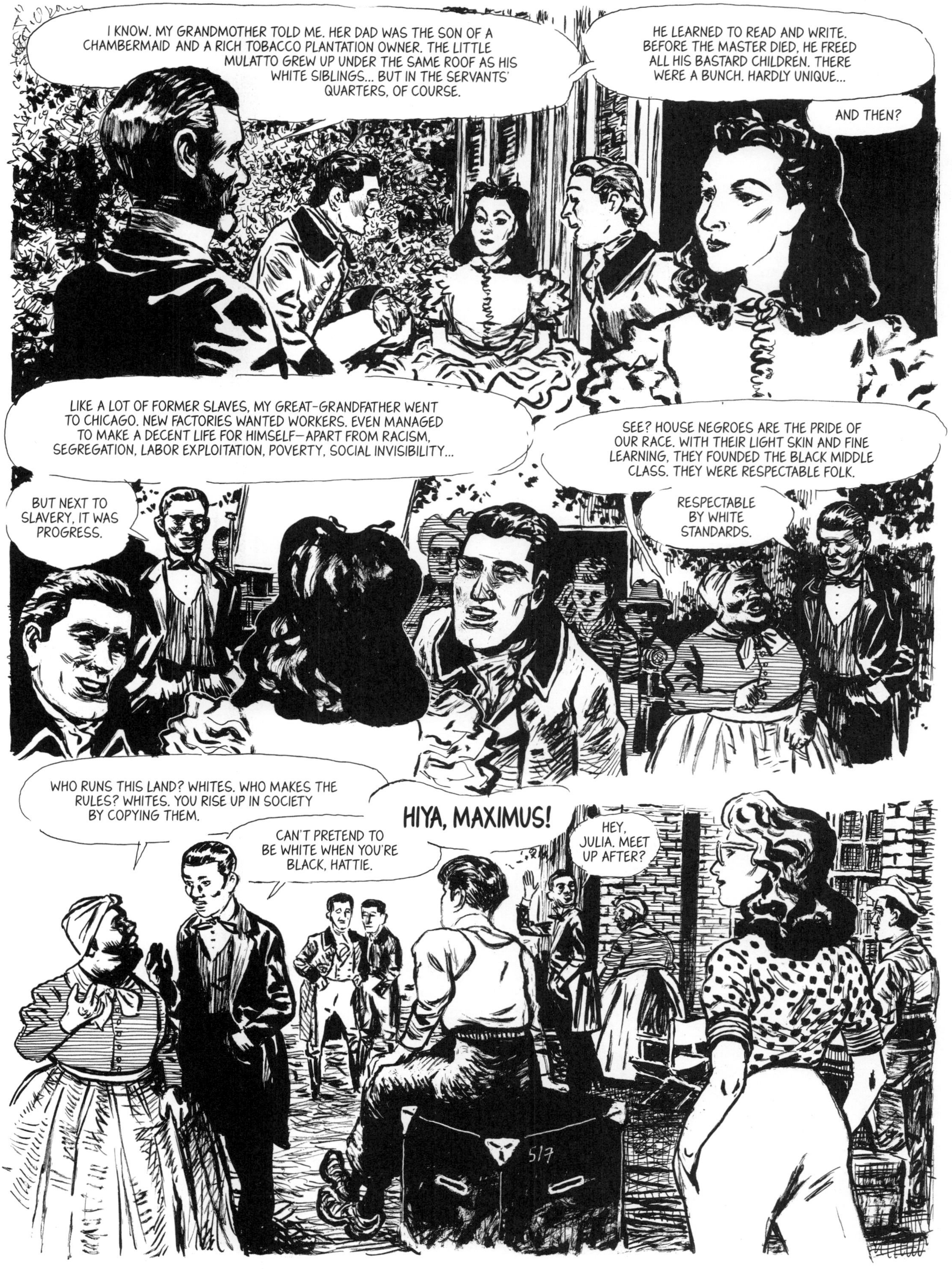
I KNOW. MY GRANDMOTHER TOLD ME. HER DAD WAS THE SON OF A CHAMBERMAID AND A RICH TOBACCO PLANTATION OWNER. THE LITTLE MULATTO GREW UP UNDER THE SAME ROOF AS HIS WHITE SIBLINGS... BUT IN THE SERVANTS' QUARTERS, OF COURSE.
HE LEARNED TO READ AND WRITE. BEFORE THE MASTER DIED, HE FREED ALL HIS BASTARD CHILDREN. THERE WERE A BUNCH. HARDLY UNIQUE...
AND THEN?
LIKE A LOT OF FORMER SLAVES, MY GREAT-GRANDFATHER WENT TO CHICAGO. NEW FACTORIES WANTED WORKERS. EVEN MANAGED TO MAKE A DECENT LIFE FOR HIMSELF—APART FROM RACISM, SEGREGATION, LABOR EXPLOITATION, POVERTY, SOCIAL INVISIBILITY...
BUT NEXT TO SLAVERY, IT WAS PROGRESS.
SEE? HOUSE NEGROES ARE THE PRIDE OF OUR RACE. WITH THEIR LIGHT SKIN AND FINE LEARNING, THEY FOUNDED THE BLACK MIDDLE CLASS. THEY WERE RESPECTABLE FOLK.
RESPECTABLE BY WHITE STANDARDS.
WHO RUNS THIS LAND? WHITES. WHO MAKES THE RULES? WHITES. YOU RISE UP IN SOCIETY BY COPYING THEM.
CAN'T PRETEND TO BE WHITE WHEN YOU'RE BLACK, HATTIE.
HIYA, MAXIMUS!
HEY, JULIA. MEET UP AFTER?

MOVIES AND SEGREGATION : TWO INTEGRAL ELEMENTS OF AMERICA THAT AROSE AND SPREAD SIMULTANEOUSLY IN THE LATE 19TH CENTURY.

ON APRIL 23, 1896, THOMAS EDISON INAUGURATED PUBLIC SCREENINGS, PREMIERING A FILM ON A BIG SCREEN IN A NEW YORK THEATER. ON MAY 18, LESS THAN A MONTH LATER, THE SUPREME COURT MADE SEGREGATION OFFICIAL BY UPHOLDING "JIM CROW" LAWS AND LAYING OUT THE ANTI-BLACK "SEPARATE BUT EQUAL" DOCTRINE.

FROM THEN ON, SOCIAL SYSTEMS PURSUED TWO GOALS: KEEPING RACES APART AND CONVINCING PEOPLE OF COLOR THAT THEY WERE INFERIOR.

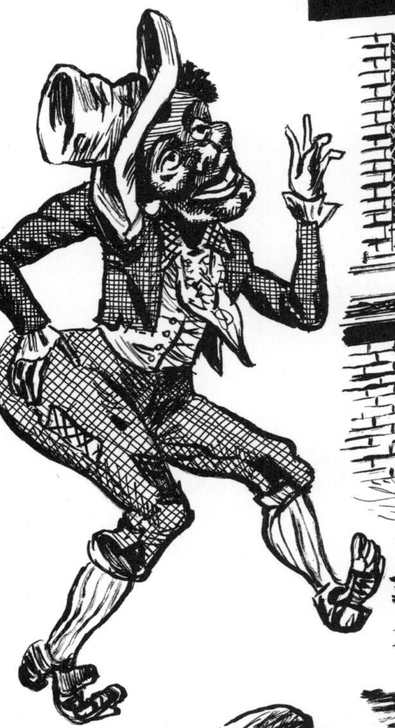

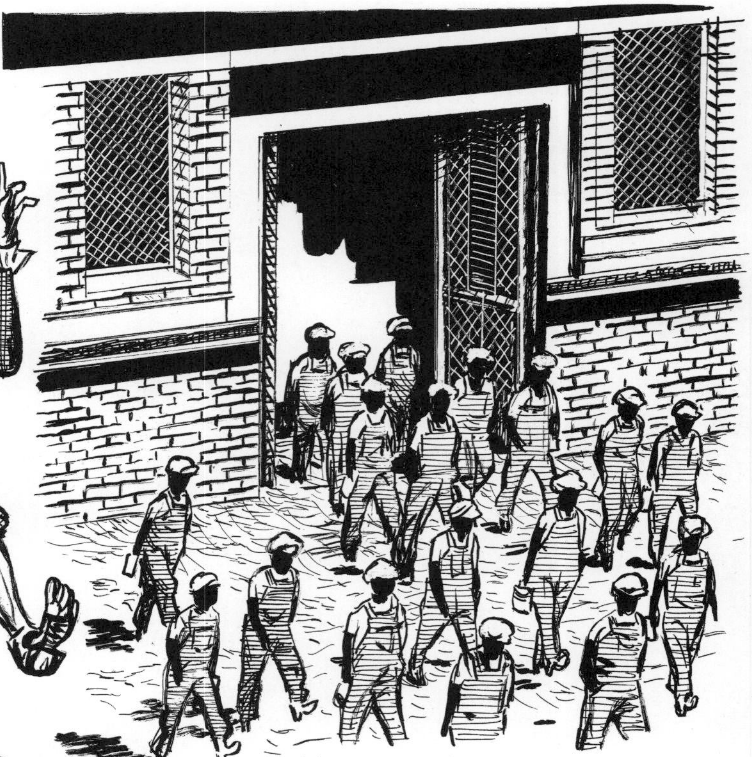

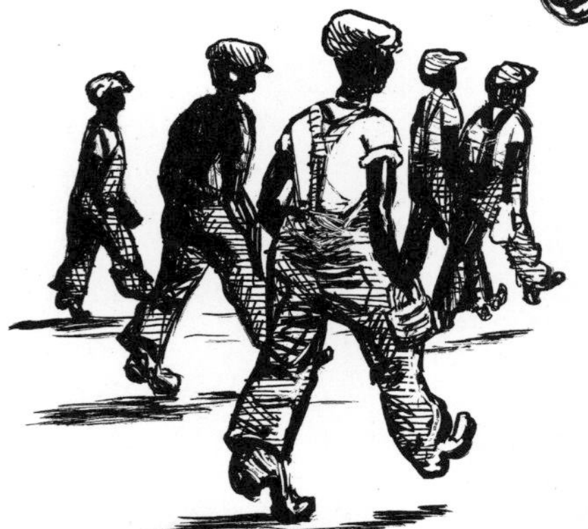

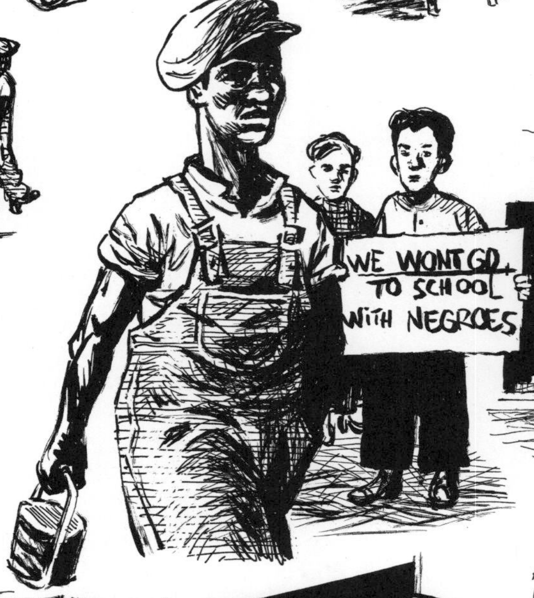
WE WONT GO TO SCHOOL WITH NEGROES

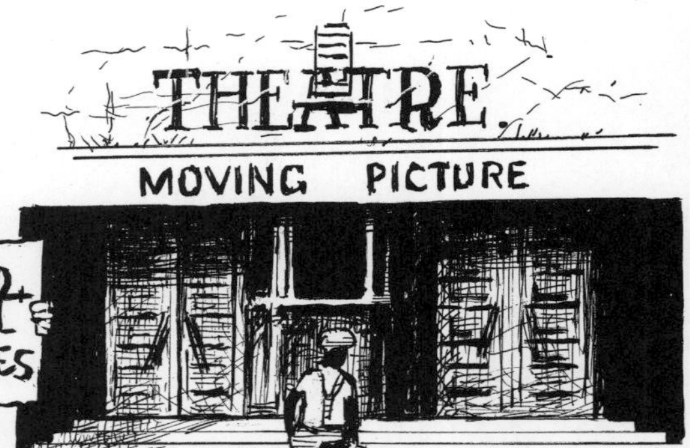
THEATRE.
MOVING PICTURE

SOON, FILM PIONEERS EDISON, PORTER, AND GRIFFITH WERE IMMORTALIZING BLACK FIGURES FROM "NEGRO" FOLKLORE.

IN 1903, EDWIN S. PORTER MADE A 19-MINUTE ADAPTATION OF HARRIET BEECHER STOWE'S NOVEL, *UNCLE TOM'S CABIN*. THE FIRST BLACK CHARACTER IN FILM, THE TITULAR TOM WAS PLAYED BY A WHITE ACTOR IN BLACKFACE, OVERPLAYING THE "GOOD NEGRO."

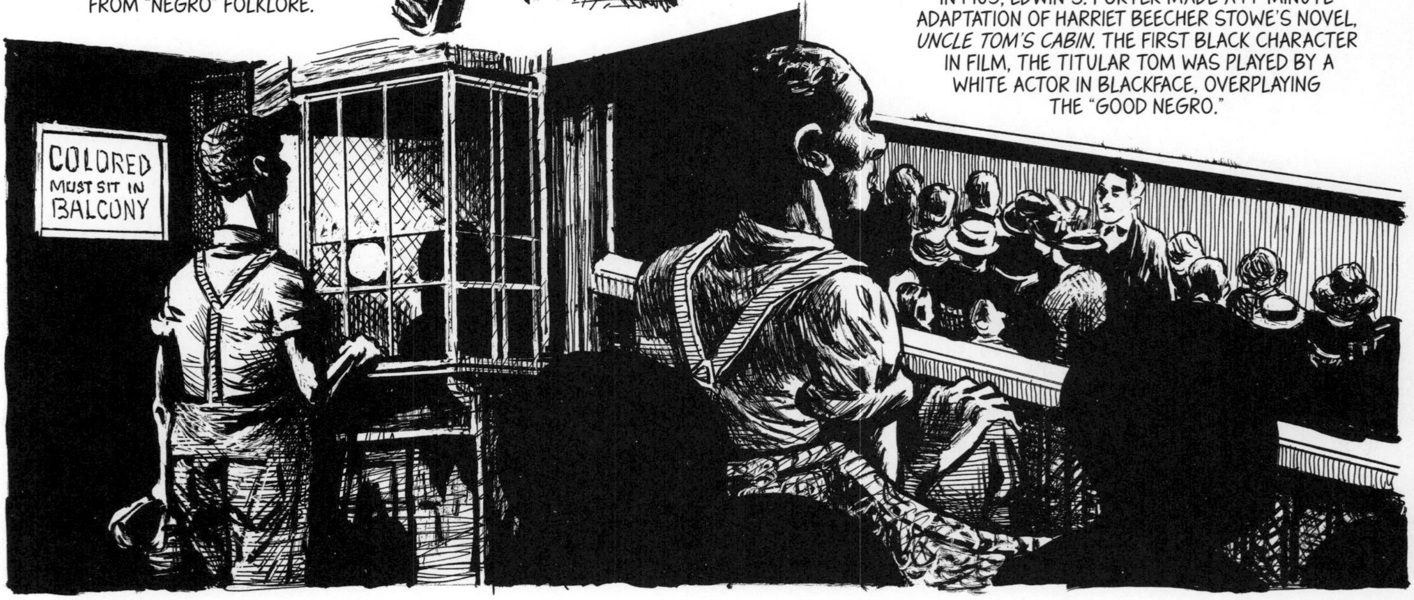
COLORED MUST SIT IN BALCONY

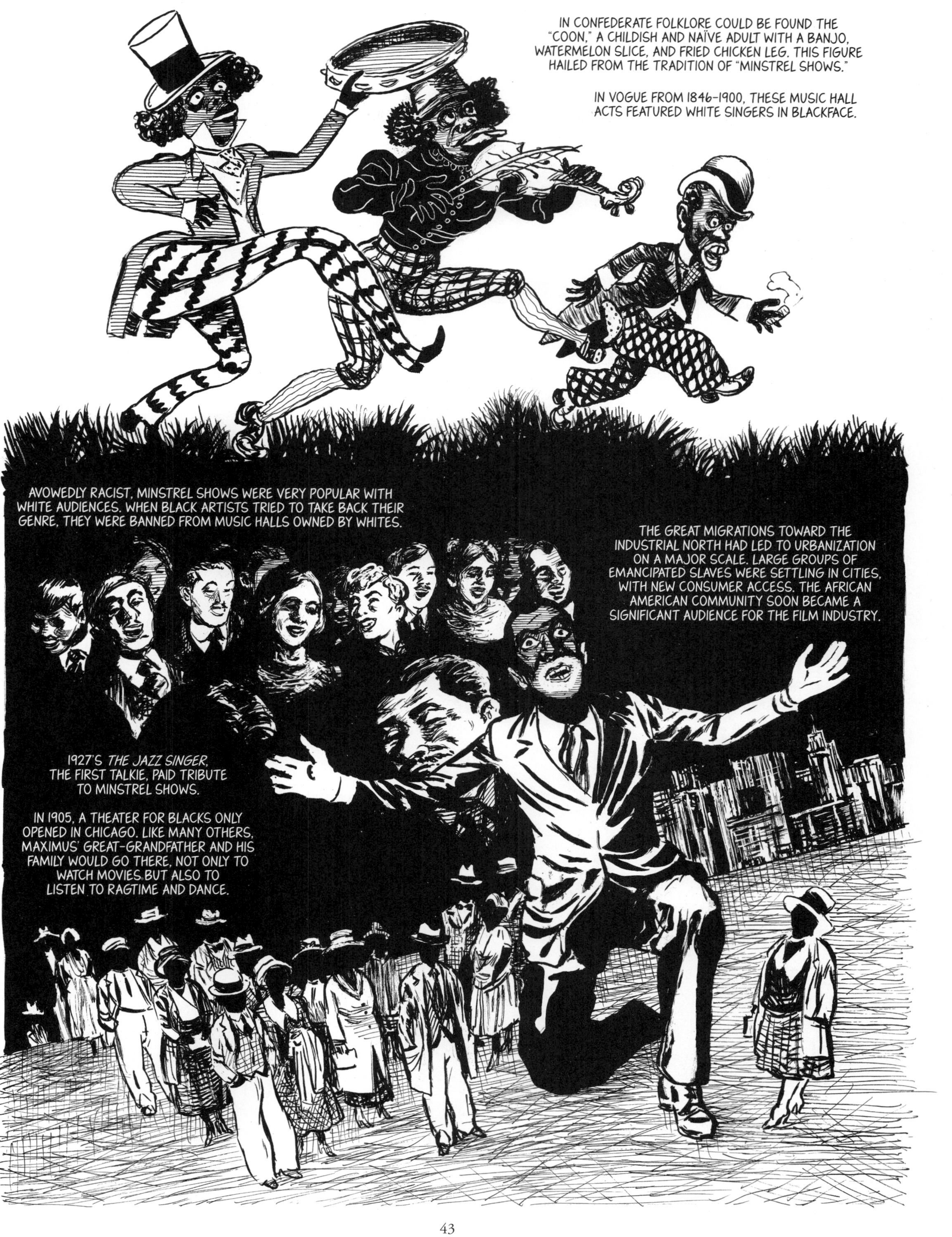
IN CONFEDERATE FOLKLORE COULD BE FOUND THE "COON," A CHILDISH AND NAÏVE ADULT WITH A BANJO, WATERMELON SLICE, AND FRIED CHICKEN LEG. THIS FIGURE HAILED FROM THE TRADITION OF "MINSTREL SHOWS."
IN VOGUE FROM 1846–1900, THESE MUSIC HALL ACTS FEATURED WHITE SINGERS IN BLACKFACE.
AVOWEDLY RACIST, MINSTREL SHOWS WERE VERY POPULAR WITH WHITE AUDIENCES. WHEN BLACK ARTISTS TRIED TO TAKE BACK THEIR GENRE, THEY WERE BANNED FROM MUSIC HALLS OWNED BY WHITES.
THE GREAT MIGRATIONS TOWARD THE INDUSTRIAL NORTH HAD LED TO URBANIZATION ON A MAJOR SCALE. LARGE GROUPS OF EMANCIPATED SLAVES WERE SETTLING IN CITIES, WITH NEW CONSUMER ACCESS. THE AFRICAN AMERICAN COMMUNITY SOON BECAME A SIGNIFICANT AUDIENCE FOR THE FILM INDUSTRY.
1927'S *THE JAZZ SINGER*, THE FIRST TALKIE, PAID TRIBUTE TO MINSTREL SHOWS.
IN 1905, A THEATER FOR BLACKS ONLY OPENED IN CHICAGO. LIKE MANY OTHERS, MAXIMUS' GREAT-GRANDFATHER AND HIS FAMILY WOULD GO THERE, NOT ONLY TO WATCH MOVIES BUT ALSO TO LISTEN TO RAGTIME AND DANCE.

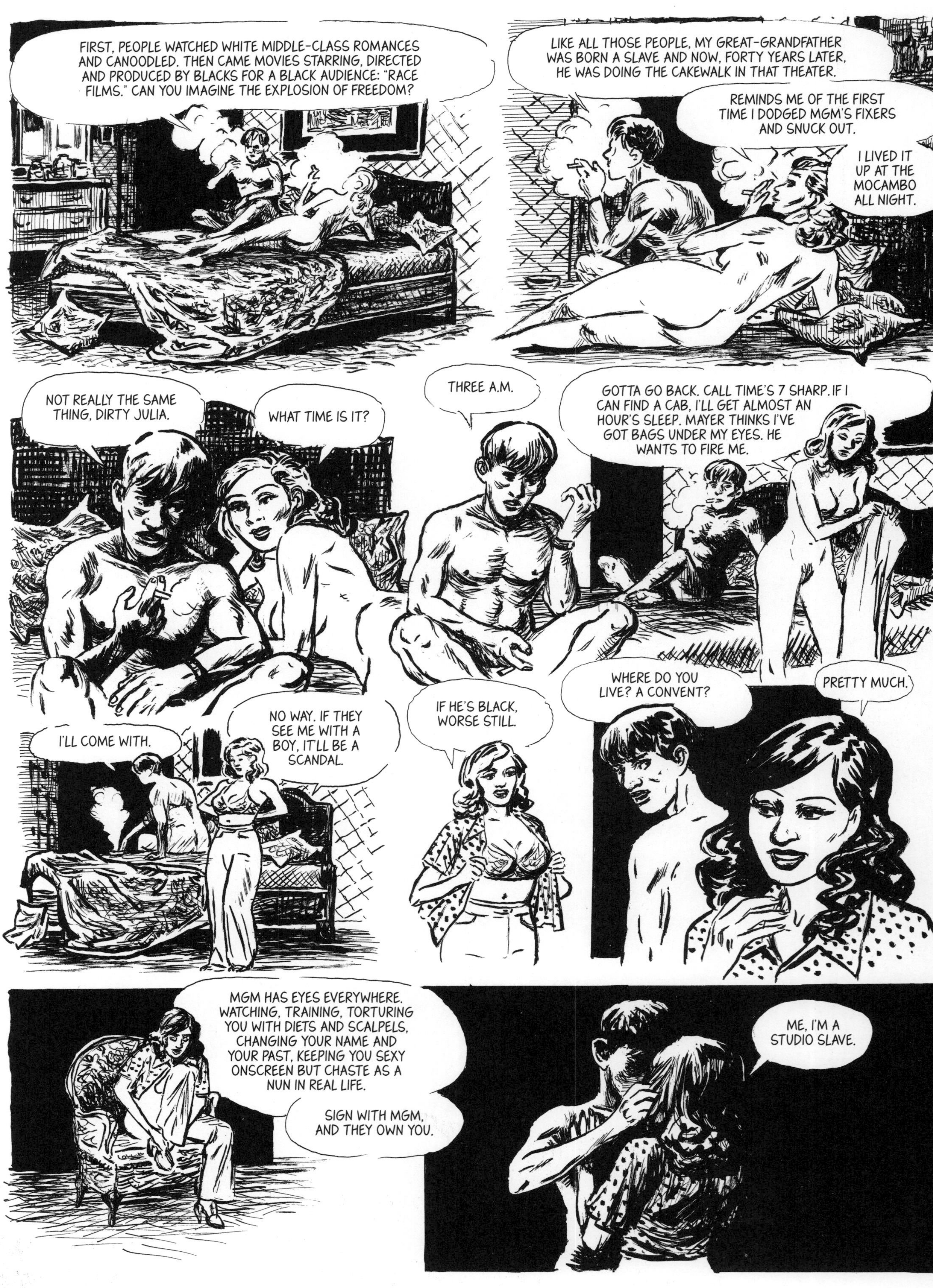
FIRST, PEOPLE WATCHED WHITE MIDDLE-CLASS ROMANCES AND CANOODLED. THEN CAME MOVIES STARRING, DIRECTED AND PRODUCED BY BLACKS FOR A BLACK AUDIENCE: "RACE FILMS." CAN YOU IMAGINE THE EXPLOSION OF FREEDOM?
LIKE ALL THOSE PEOPLE, MY GREAT-GRANDFATHER WAS BORN A SLAVE AND NOW, FORTY YEARS LATER, HE WAS DOING THE CAKEWALK IN THAT THEATER.
REMINDS ME OF THE FIRST TIME I DODGED MGM'S FIXERS AND SNUCK OUT.
I LIVED IT UP AT THE MOCAMBO ALL NIGHT.
NOT REALLY THE SAME THING, DIRTY JULIA.
WHAT TIME IS IT?
THREE A.M.
GOTTA GO BACK. CALL TIME'S 7 SHARP. IF I CAN FIND A CAB, I'LL GET ALMOST AN HOUR'S SLEEP. MAYER THINKS I'VE GOT BAGS UNDER MY EYES. HE WANTS TO FIRE ME.
I'LL COME WITH.
NO WAY. IF THEY SEE ME WITH A BOY, IT'LL BE A SCANDAL.
IF HE'S BLACK, WORSE STILL.
WHERE DO YOU LIVE? A CONVENT?
PRETTY MUCH.
MGM HAS EYES EVERYWHERE. WATCHING, TRAINING, TORTURING YOU WITH DIETS AND SCALPELS, CHANGING YOUR NAME AND YOUR PAST, KEEPING YOU SEXY ONSCREEN BUT CHASTE AS A NUN IN REAL LIFE.
SIGN WITH MGM, AND THEY OWN YOU.
ME, I'M A STUDIO SLAVE.

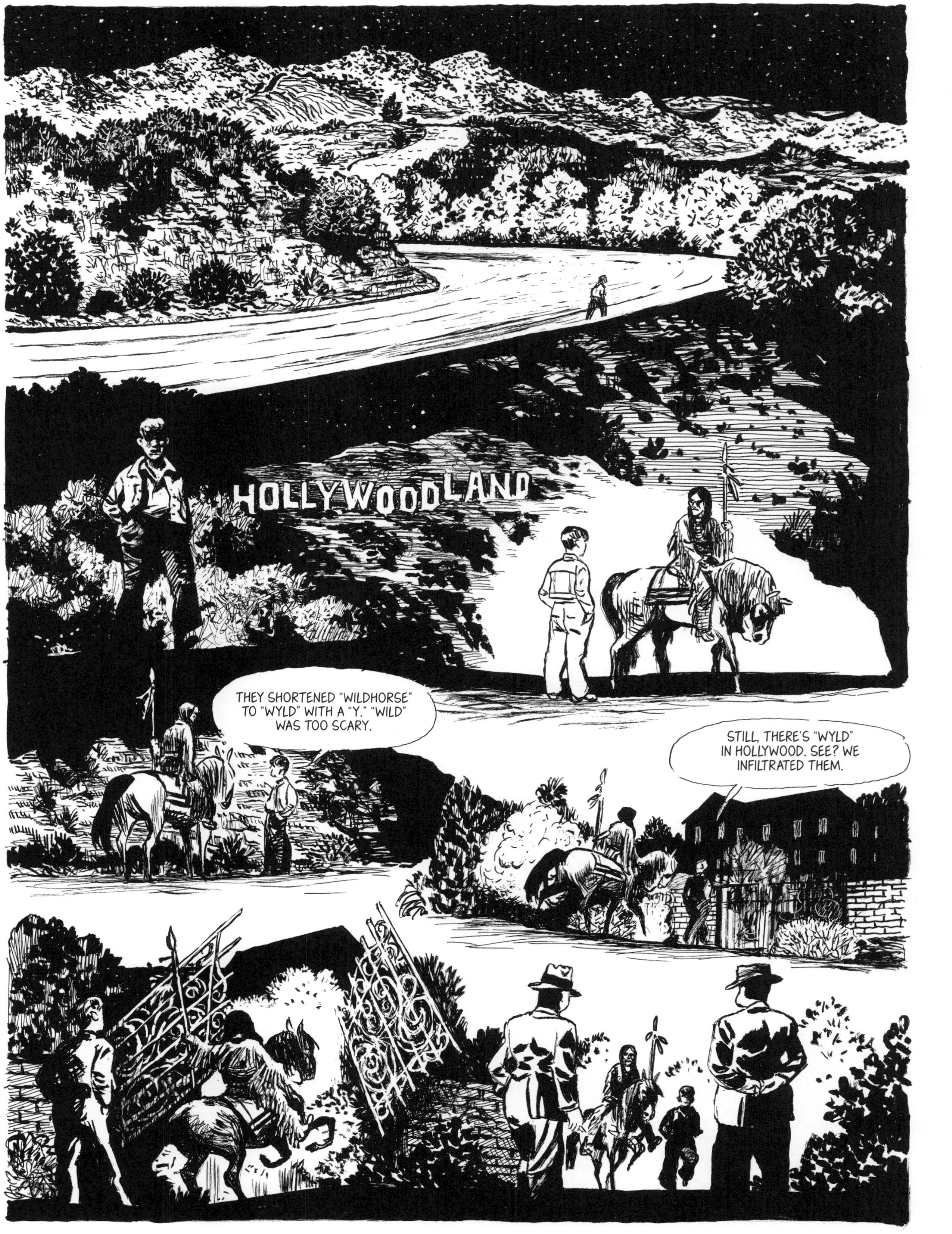
HOLLYWOODLAND
THEY SHORTENED "WILDHORSE" TO "WYLD" WITH A "Y." "WILD" WAS TOO SCARY.
STILL, THERE'S "WYLD" IN HOLLYWOOD. SEE? WE INFILTRATED THEM.

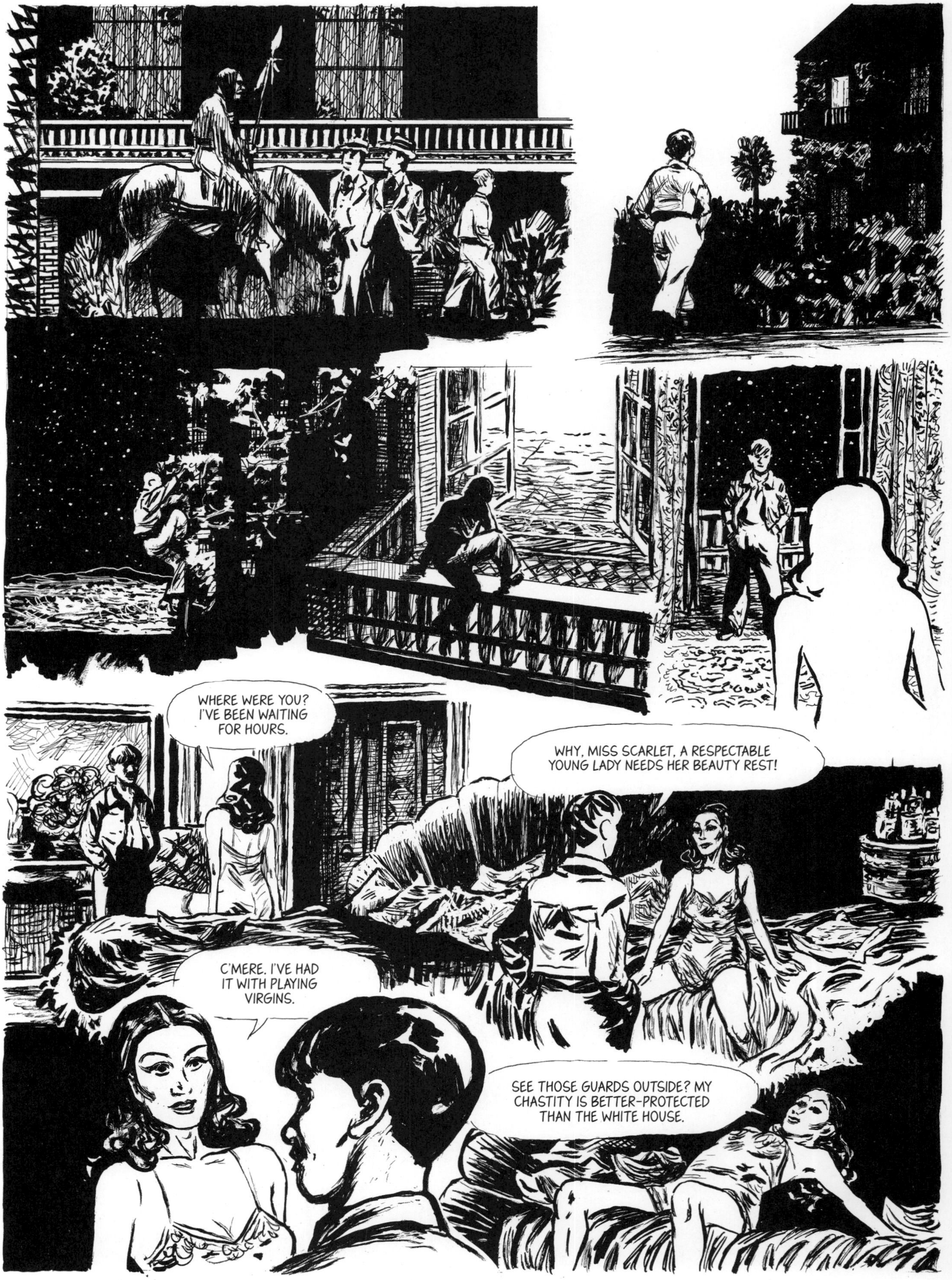
WHERE WERE YOU? I'VE BEEN WAITING FOR HOURS.
WHY, MISS SCARLET, A RESPECTABLE YOUNG LADY NEEDS HER BEAUTY REST!
C'MERE. I'VE HAD IT WITH PLAYING VIRGINS.
SEE THOSE GUARDS OUTSIDE? MY CHASTITY IS BETTER-PROTECTED THAN THE WHITE HOUSE.

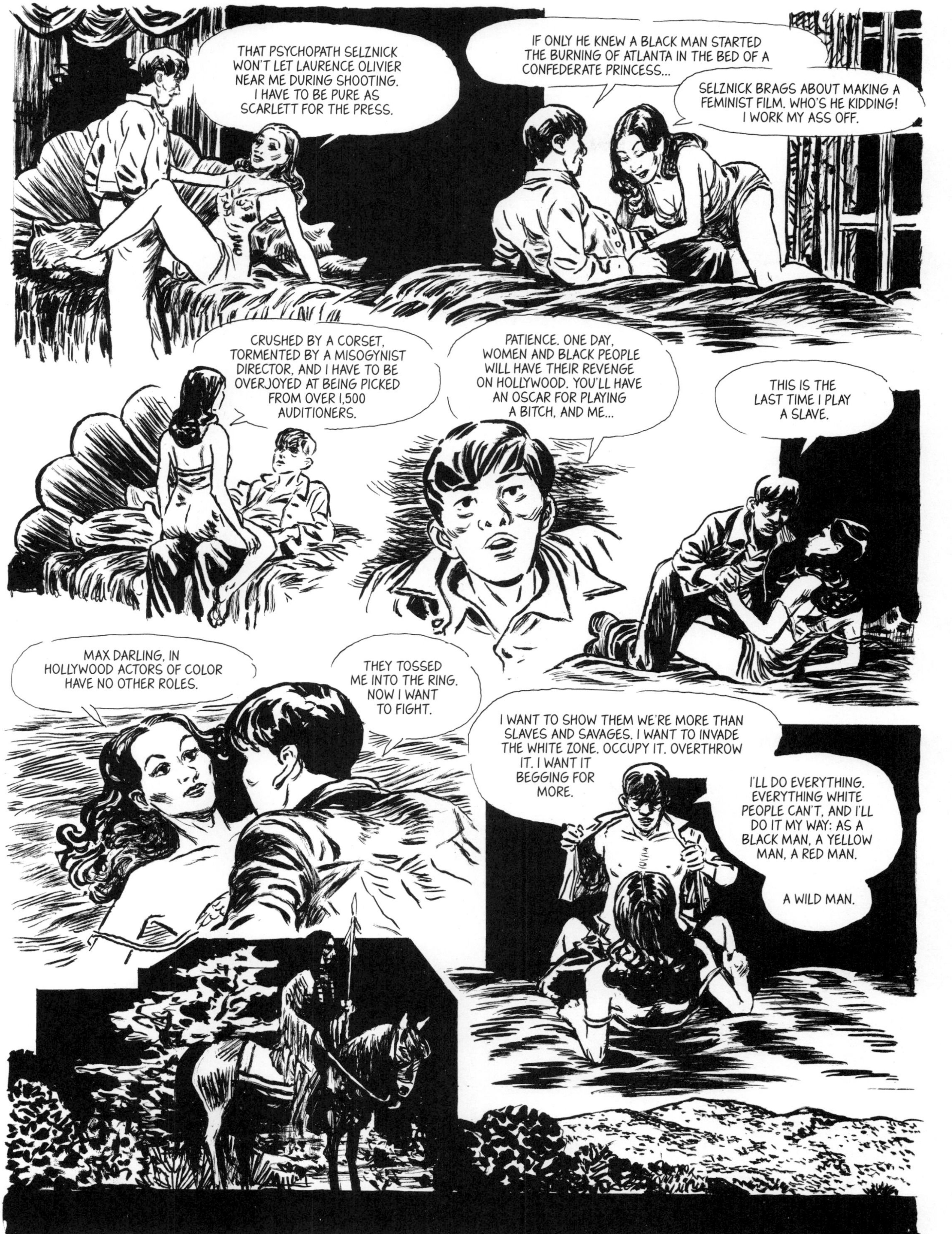
THAT PSYCHOPATH SELZNICK WON'T LET LAURENCE OLIVIER NEAR ME DURING SHOOTING. I HAVE TO BE PURE AS SCARLETT FOR THE PRESS.
IF ONLY HE KNEW A BLACK MAN STARTED THE BURNING OF ATLANTA IN THE BED OF A CONFEDERATE PRINCESS...
SELZNICK BRAGS ABOUT MAKING A FEMINIST FILM. WHO'S HE KIDDING! I WORK MY ASS OFF.
CRUSHED BY A CORSET, TORMENTED BY A MISOGYNIST DIRECTOR, AND I HAVE TO BE OVERJOYED AT BEING PICKED FROM OVER 1,500 AUDITIONERS.
PATIENCE. ONE DAY, WOMEN AND BLACK PEOPLE WILL HAVE THEIR REVENGE ON HOLLYWOOD. YOU'LL HAVE AN OSCAR FOR PLAYING A BITCH, AND ME...
THIS IS THE LAST TIME I PLAY A SLAVE.
MAX DARLING, IN HOLLYWOOD ACTORS OF COLOR HAVE NO OTHER ROLES.
THEY TOSSED ME INTO THE RING. NOW I WANT TO FIGHT.
I WANT TO SHOW THEM WE'RE MORE THAN SLAVES AND SAVAGES. I WANT TO INVADE THE WHITE ZONE. OCCUPY IT. OVERTHROW IT. I WANT IT BEGGING FOR MORE.
I'LL DO EVERYTHING. EVERYTHING WHITE PEOPLE CAN'T, AND I'LL DO IT MY WAY: AS A BLACK MAN, A YELLOW MAN, A RED MAN.
A WILD MAN.

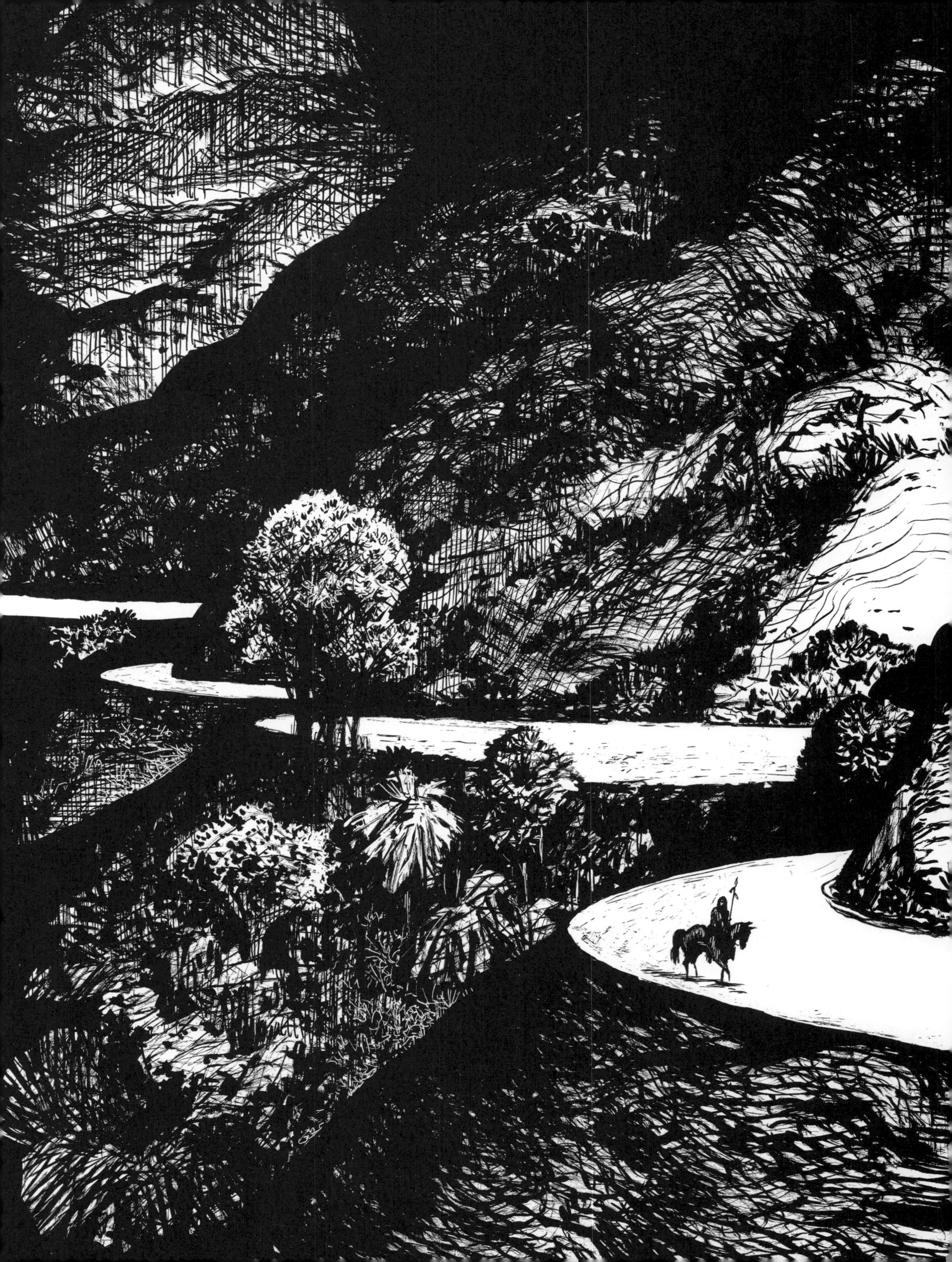

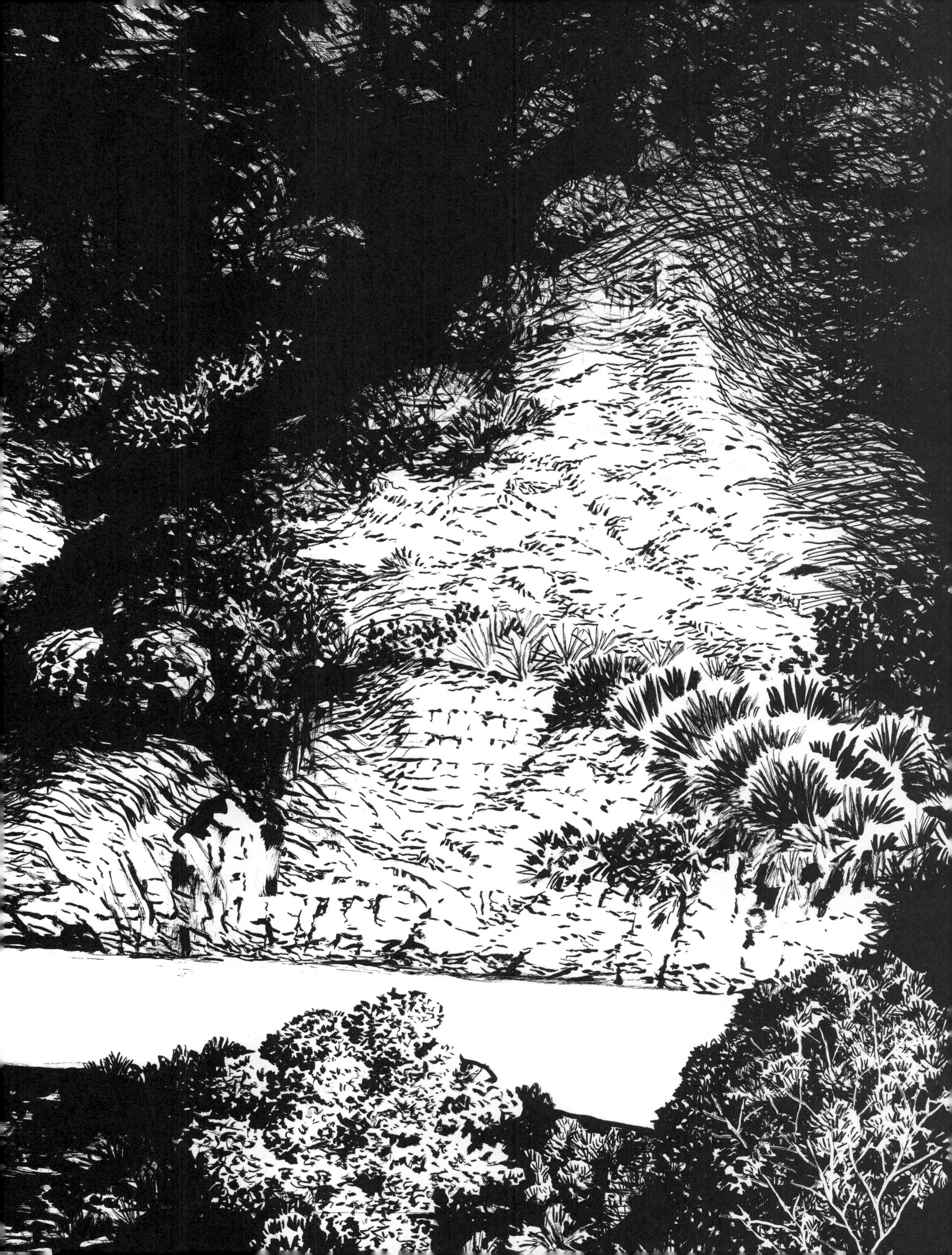

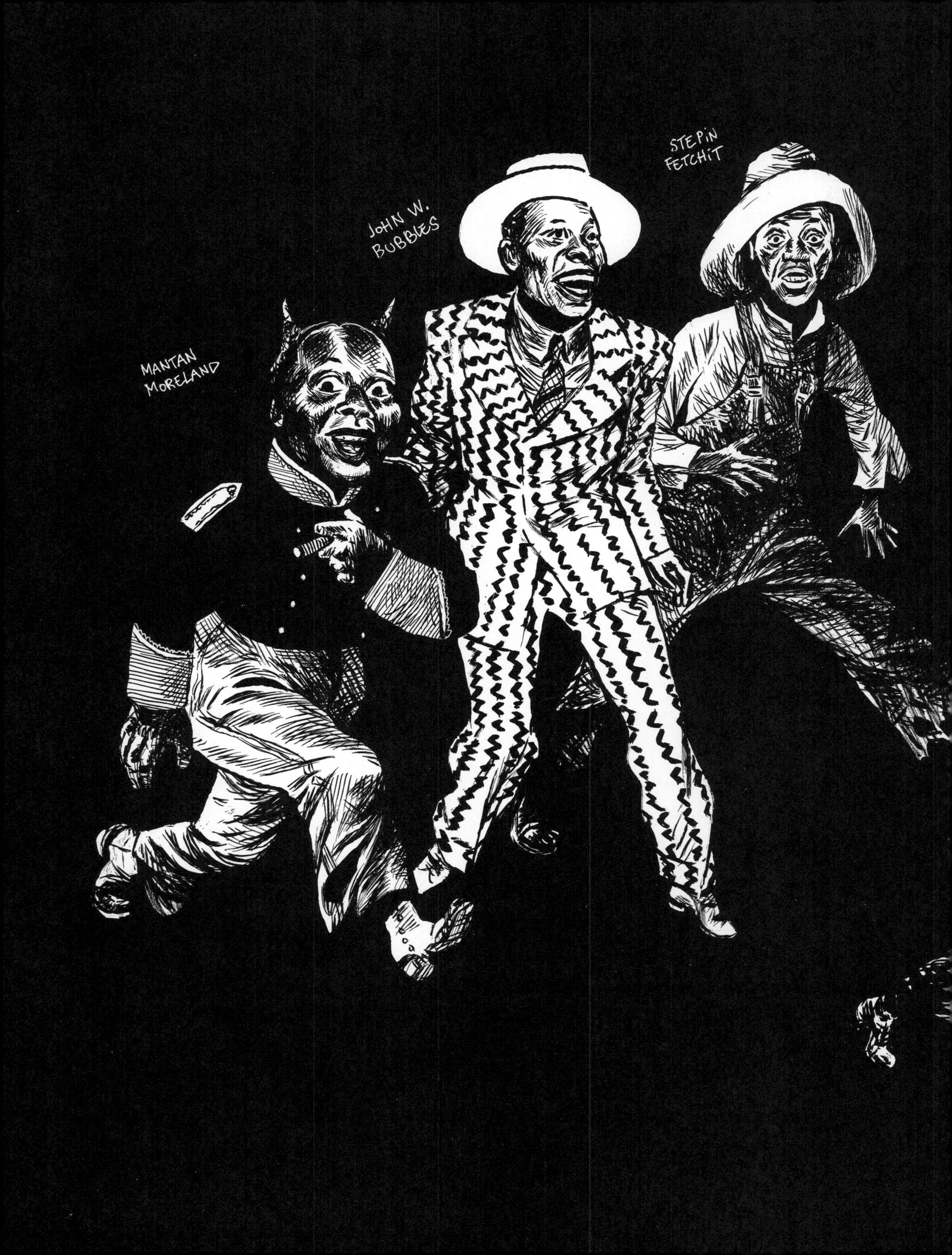
MANTAN MORELAND
JOHN W. BUBBLES
STEPIN FETCHIT

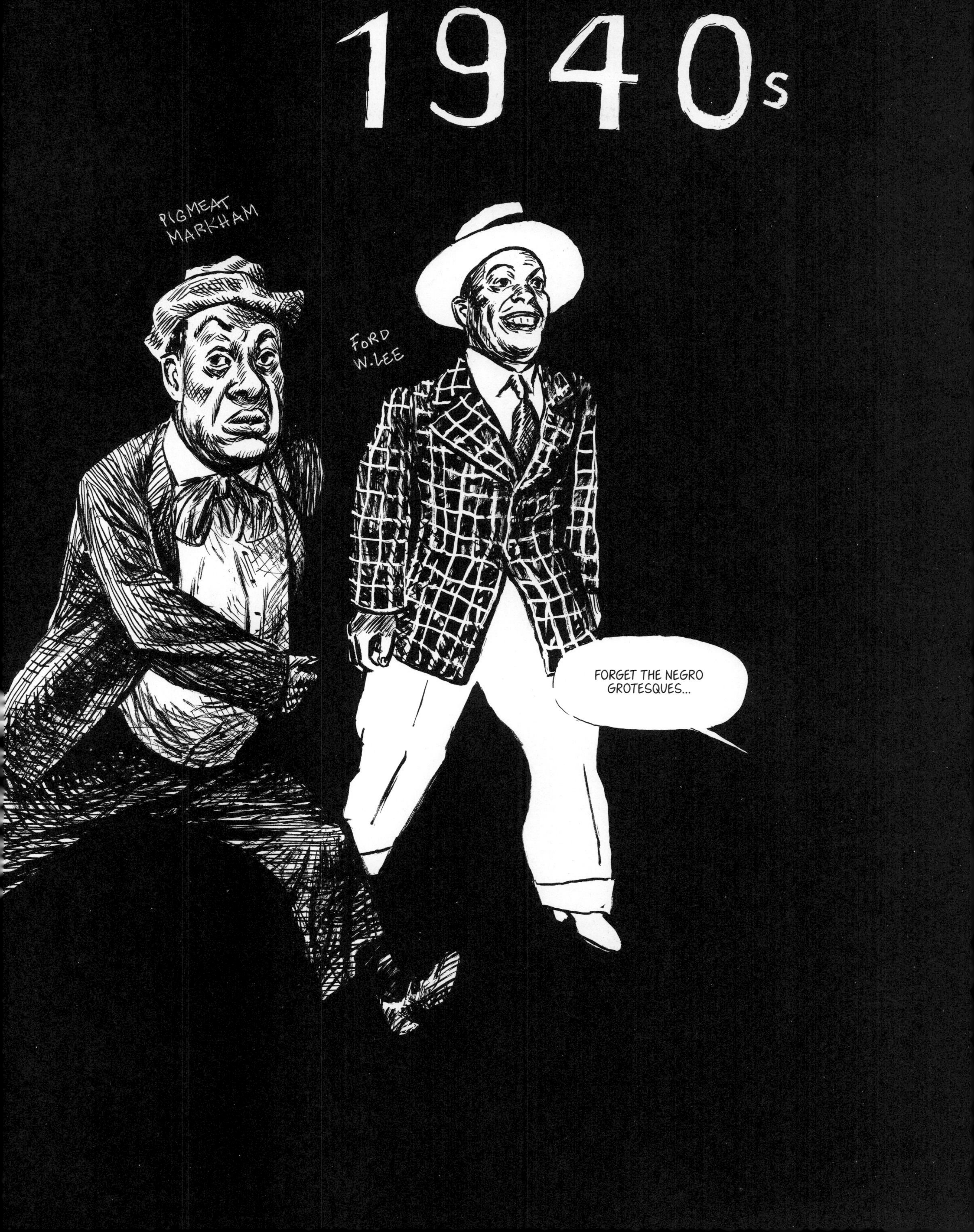
1940s
PIGMEAT MARKHAM
FORD W. LEE
FORGET THE NEGRO GROTESQUES...

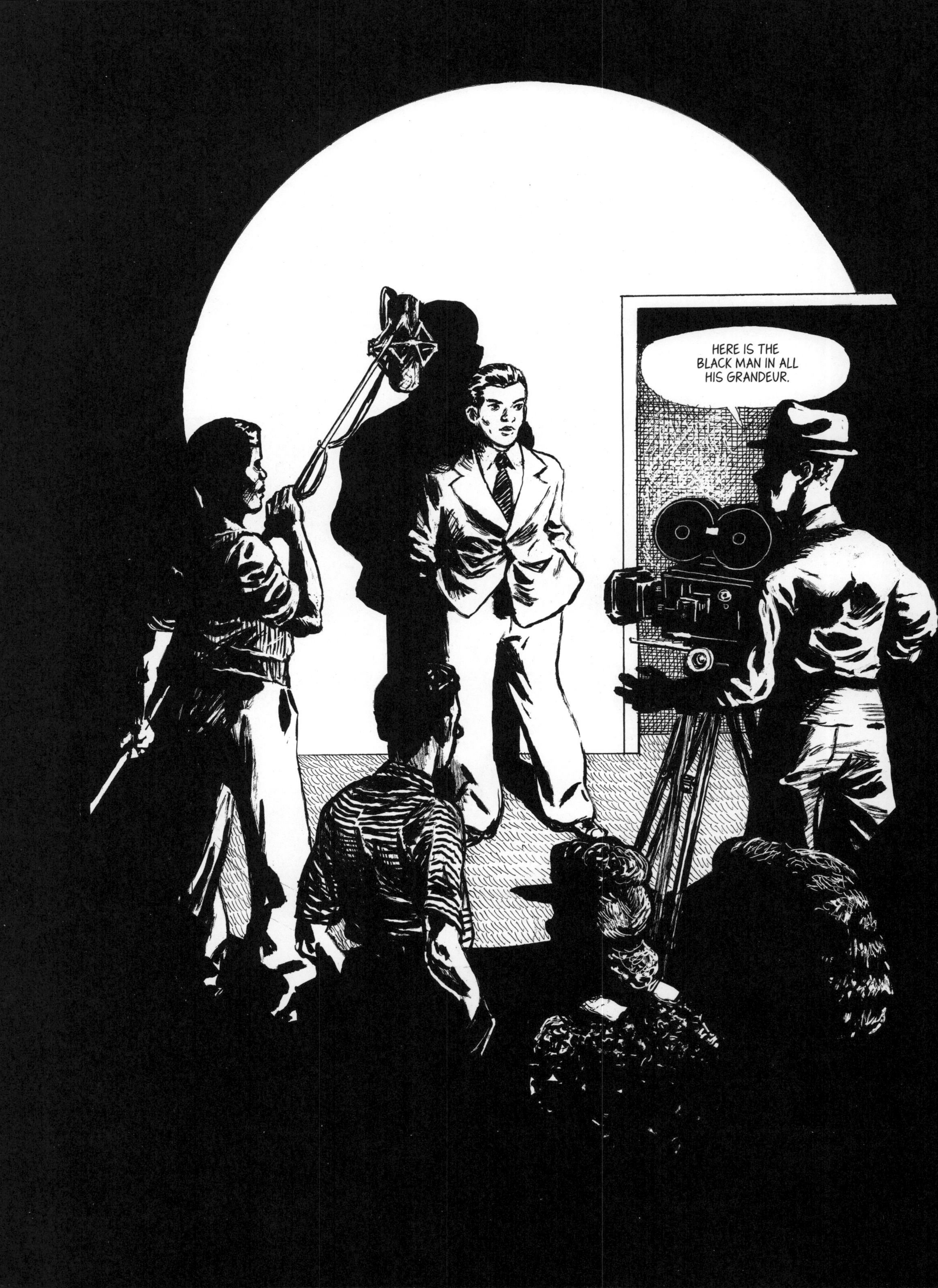
HERE IS THE BLACK MAN IN ALL HIS GRANDEUR.

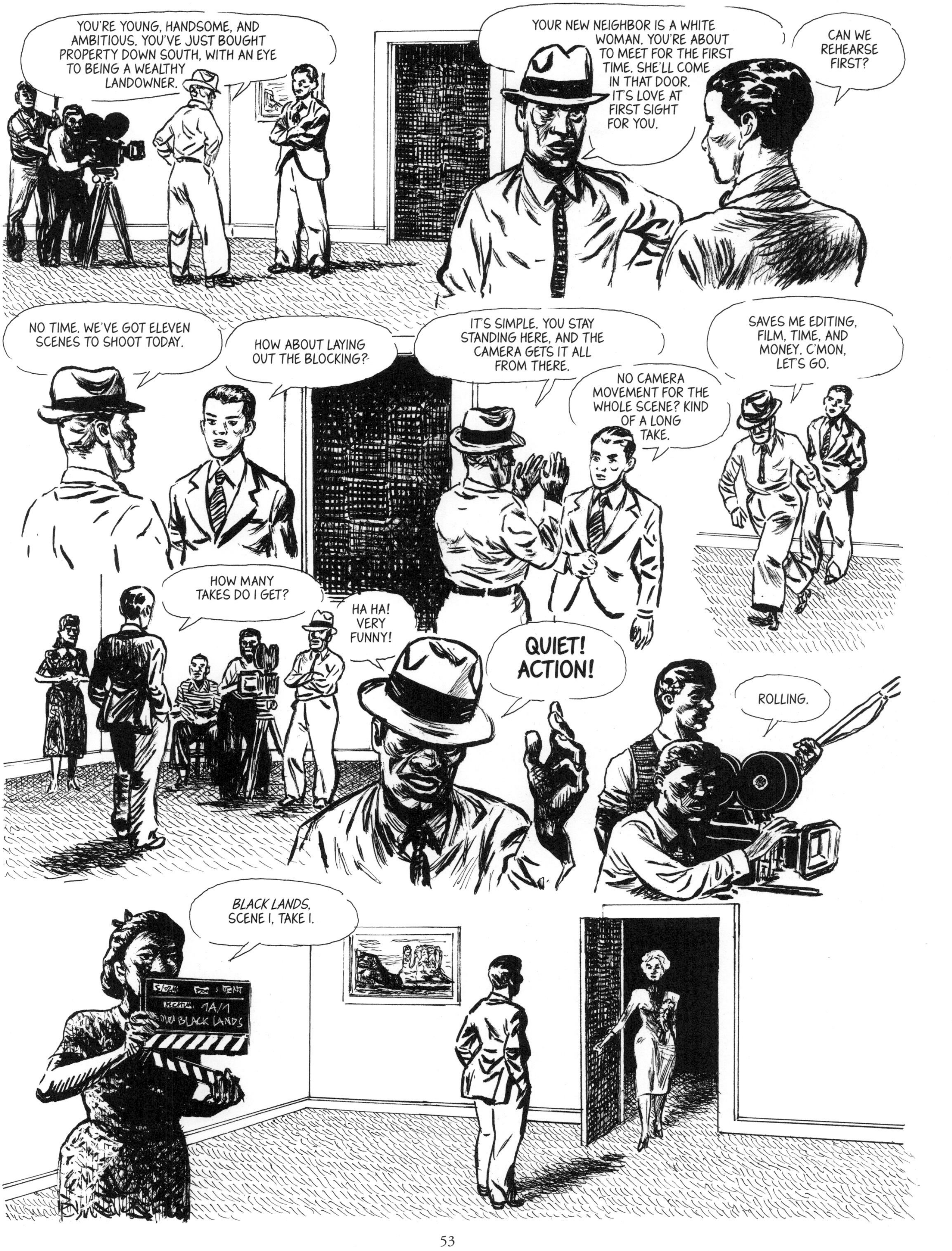
YOU'RE YOUNG, HANDSOME, AND AMBITIOUS. YOU'VE JUST BOUGHT PROPERTY DOWN SOUTH, WITH AN EYE TO BEING A WEALTHY LANDOWNER.
YOUR NEW NEIGHBOR IS A WHITE WOMAN. YOU'RE ABOUT TO MEET FOR THE FIRST TIME. SHE'LL COME IN THAT DOOR. IT'S LOVE AT FIRST SIGHT FOR YOU.
CAN WE REHEARSE FIRST?
NO TIME. WE'VE GOT ELEVEN SCENES TO SHOOT TODAY.
HOW ABOUT LAYING OUT THE BLOCKING?
IT'S SIMPLE. YOU STAY STANDING HERE, AND THE CAMERA GETS IT ALL FROM THERE.
NO CAMERA MOVEMENT FOR THE WHOLE SCENE? KIND OF A LONG TAKE.
SAVES ME EDITING, FILM, TIME, AND MONEY. C'MON, LET'S GO.
HOW MANY TAKES DO I GET?
HA HA! VERY FUNNY!
QUIET! ACTION!
ROLLING.
BLACK LANDS, SCENE 1, TAKE 1.
BLACK LANDS

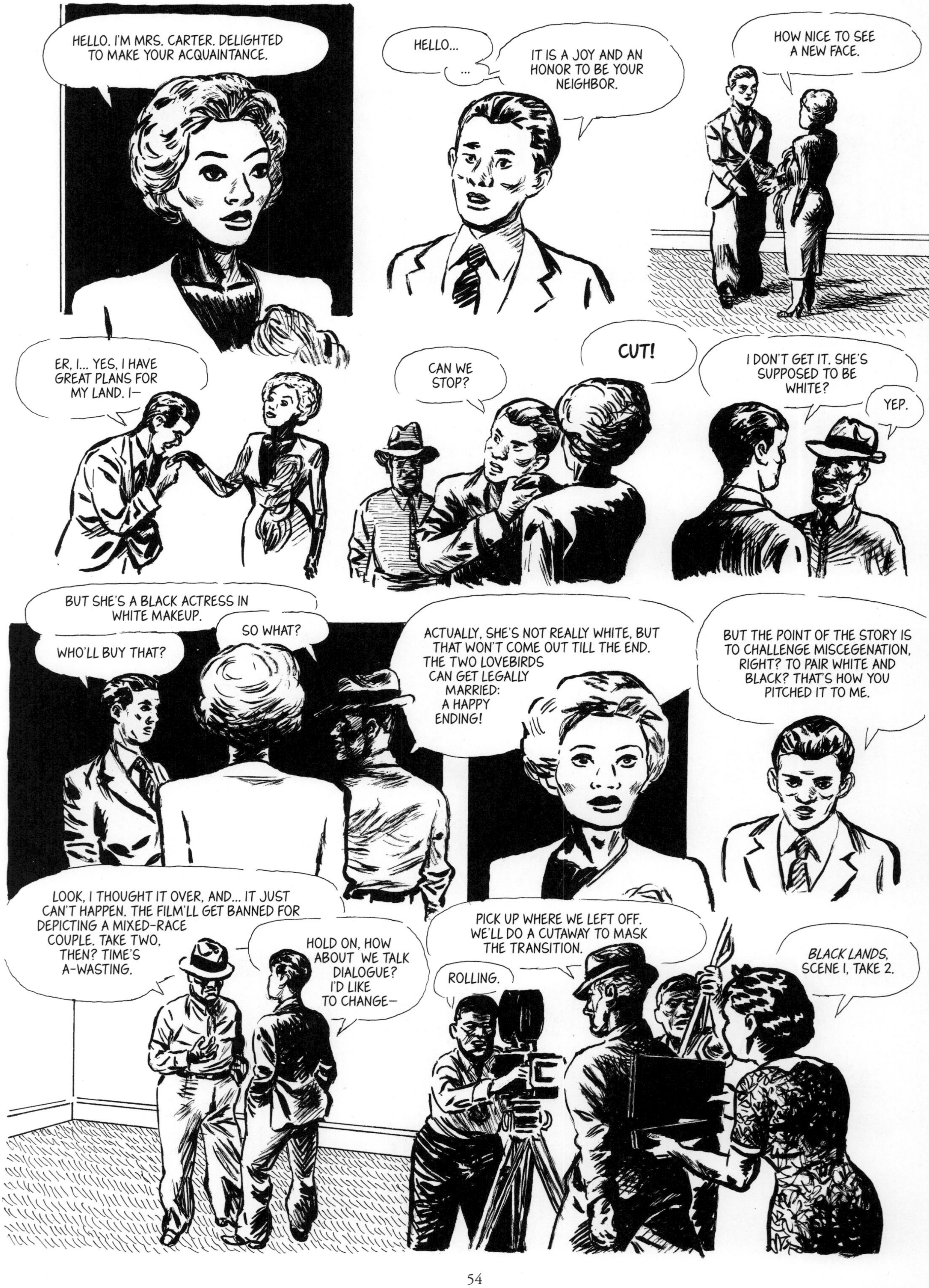
HELLO. I'M MRS. CARTER. DELIGHTED TO MAKE YOUR ACQUAINTANCE.
HELLO...
...
IT IS A JOY AND AN HONOR TO BE YOUR NEIGHBOR.
HOW NICE TO SEE A NEW FACE.
ER, I... YES, I HAVE GREAT PLANS FOR MY LAND. I–
CAN WE STOP?
CUT!
I DON'T GET IT. SHE'S SUPPOSED TO BE WHITE?
YEP.
BUT SHE'S A BLACK ACTRESS IN WHITE MAKEUP.
WHO'LL BUY THAT?
SO WHAT?
ACTUALLY, SHE'S NOT REALLY WHITE, BUT THAT WON'T COME OUT TILL THE END. THE TWO LOVEBIRDS CAN GET LEGALLY MARRIED: A HAPPY ENDING!
BUT THE POINT OF THE STORY IS TO CHALLENGE MISCEGENATION, RIGHT? TO PAIR WHITE AND BLACK? THAT'S HOW YOU PITCHED IT TO ME.
LOOK, I THOUGHT IT OVER, AND... IT JUST CAN'T HAPPEN. THE FILM'LL GET BANNED FOR DEPICTING A MIXED-RACE COUPLE. TAKE TWO, THEN? TIME'S A-WASTING.
HOLD ON, HOW ABOUT WE TALK DIALOGUE? I'D LIKE TO CHANGE–
PICK UP WHERE WE LEFT OFF. WE'LL DO A CUTAWAY TO MASK THE TRANSITION.
ROLLING.
*BLACK LANDS*, SCENE 1, TAKE 2.

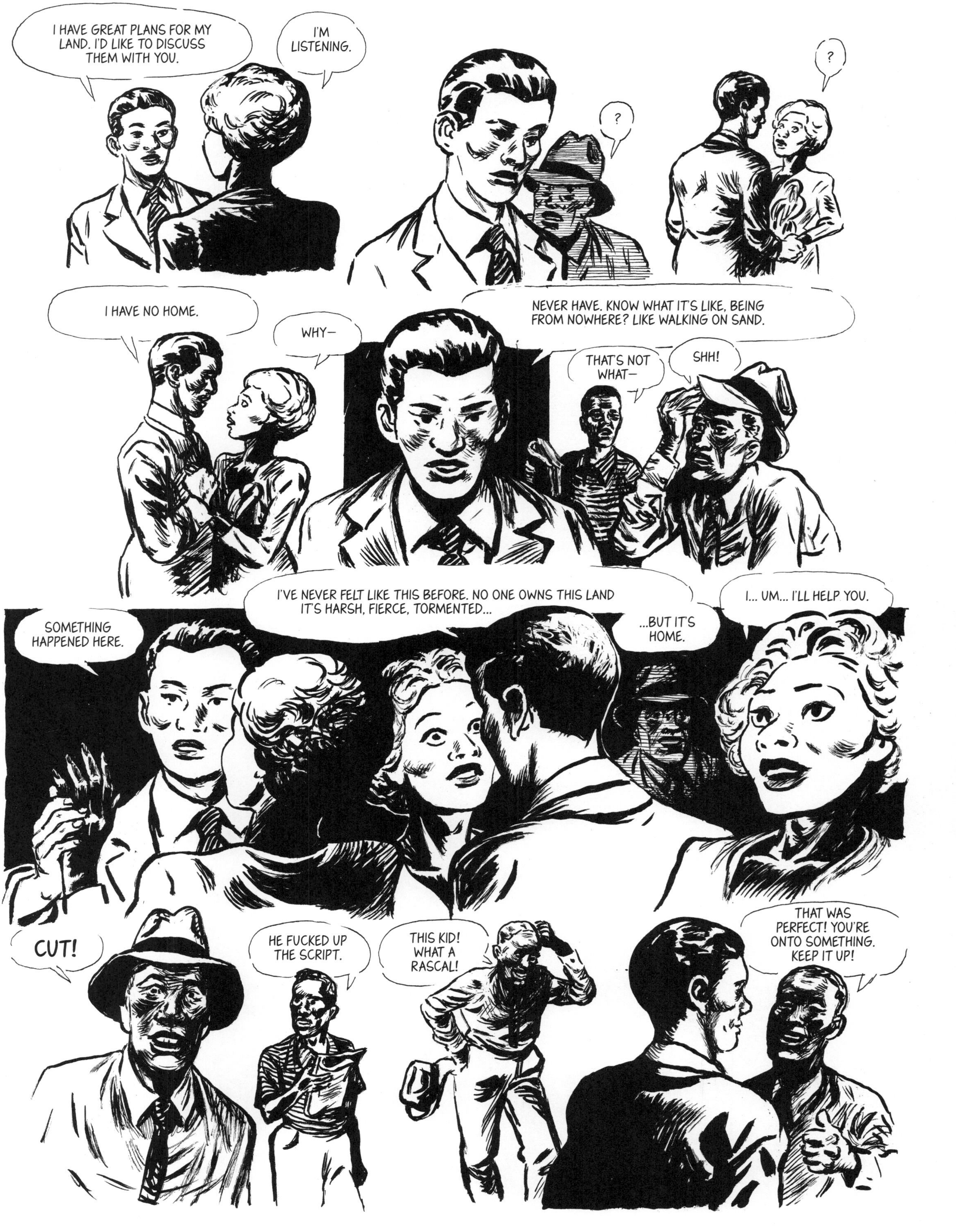
I HAVE GREAT PLANS FOR MY LAND. I'D LIKE TO DISCUSS THEM WITH YOU.
I'M LISTENING.
?
?
I HAVE NO HOME.
WHY–
NEVER HAVE. KNOW WHAT IT'S LIKE, BEING FROM NOWHERE? LIKE WALKING ON SAND.
THAT'S NOT WHAT–
SHH!
SOMETHING HAPPENED HERE.
I'VE NEVER FELT LIKE THIS BEFORE. NO ONE OWNS THIS LAND IT'S HARSH, FIERCE, TORMENTED...
...BUT IT'S HOME.
I... UM... I'LL HELP YOU.
CUT!
HE FUCKED UP THE SCRIPT.
THIS KID! WHAT A RASCAL!
THAT WAS PERFECT! YOU'RE ONTO SOMETHING. KEEP IT UP!

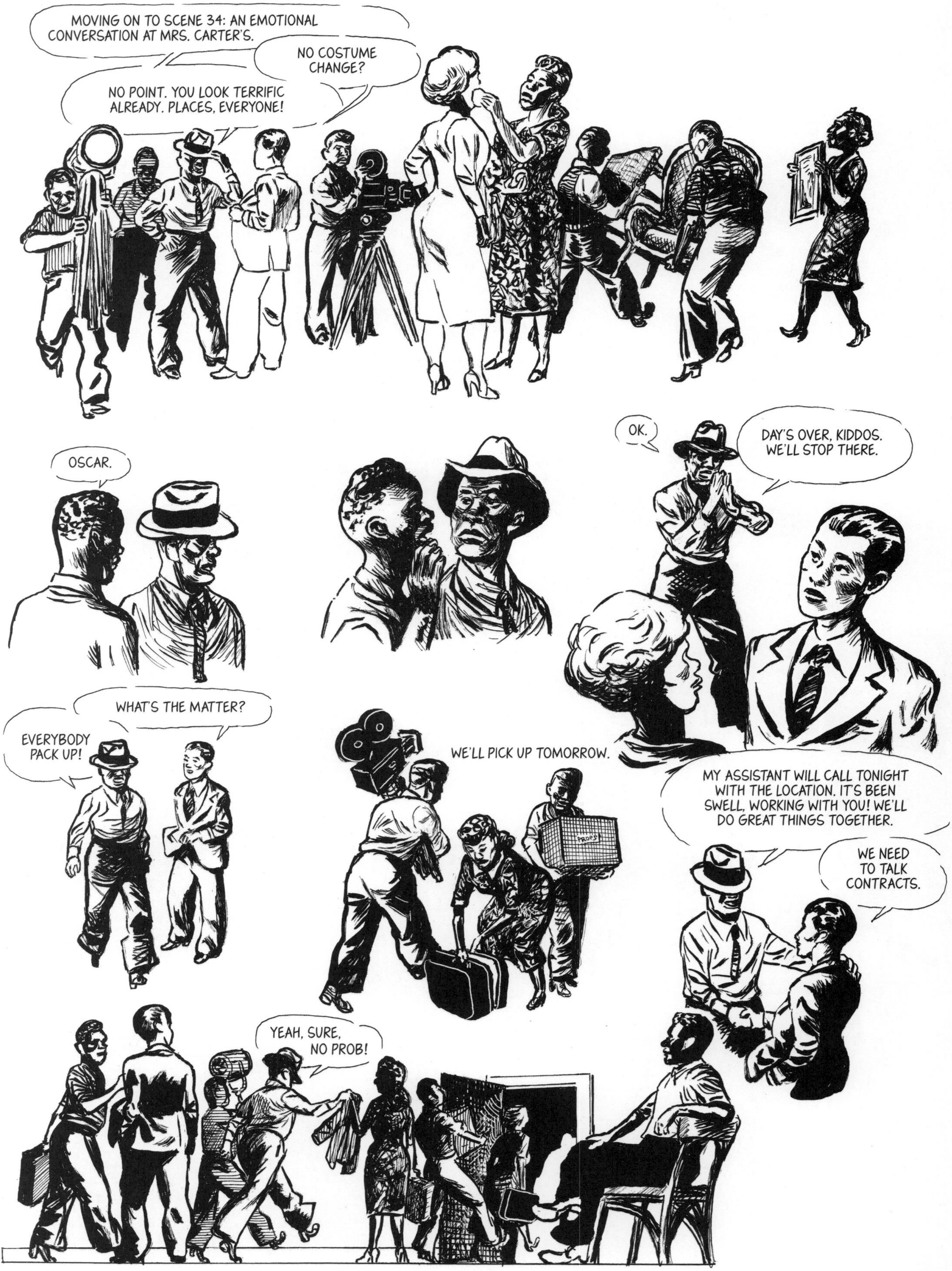
MOVING ON TO SCENE 34: AN EMOTIONAL CONVERSATION AT MRS. CARTER'S.
NO COSTUME CHANGE?
NO POINT. YOU LOOK TERRIFIC ALREADY. PLACES, EVERYONE!
OSCAR.
OK.
DAY'S OVER, KIDDOS. WE'LL STOP THERE.
WHAT'S THE MATTER?
EVERYBODY PACK UP!
WE'LL PICK UP TOMORROW.
PROPS
MY ASSISTANT WILL CALL TONIGHT WITH THE LOCATION. IT'S BEEN SWELL, WORKING WITH YOU! WE'LL DO GREAT THINGS TOGETHER.
WE NEED TO TALK CONTRACTS.
YEAH, SURE, NO PROB!

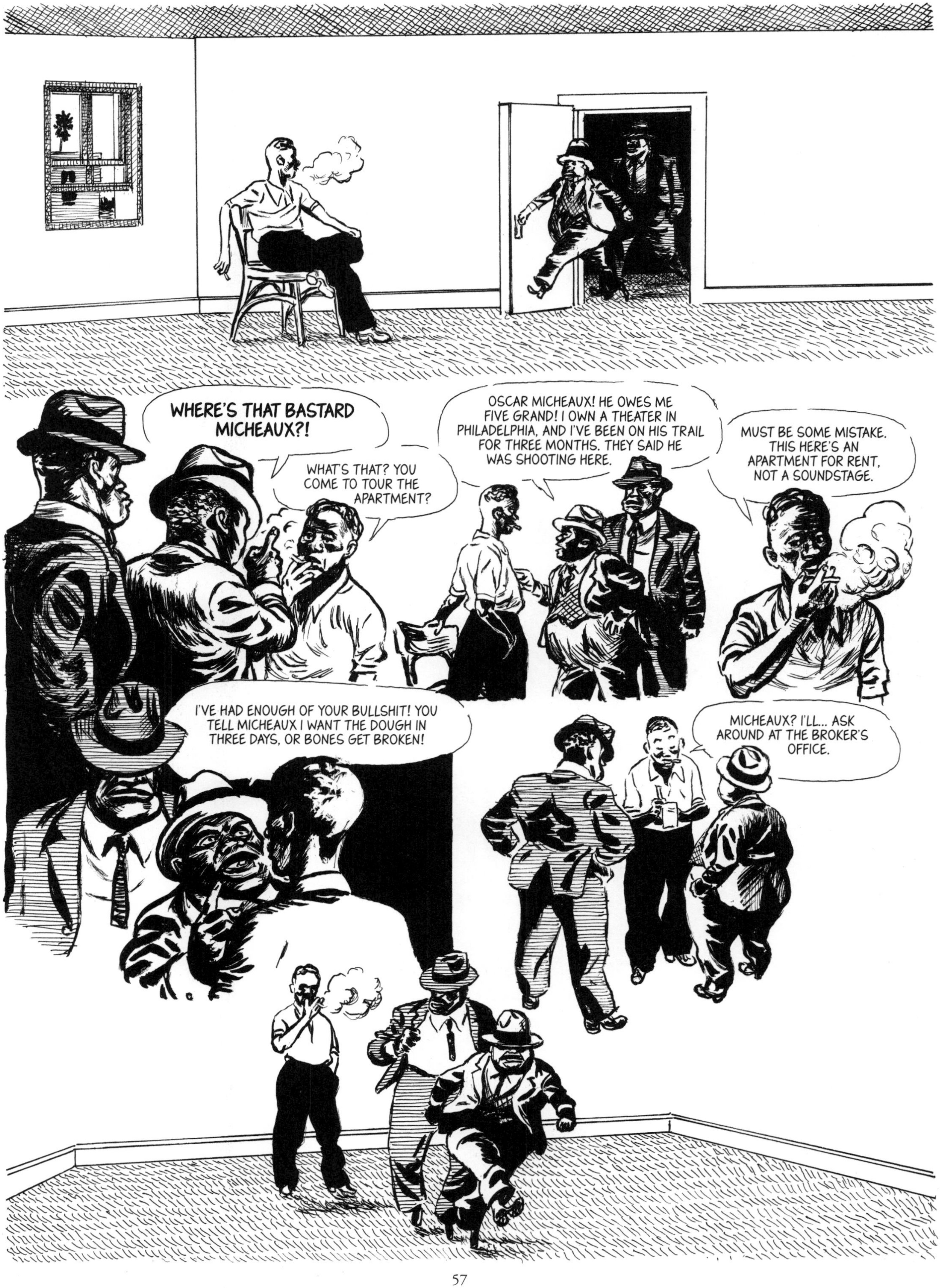
WHERE'S THAT BASTARD MICHEAUX?!
WHAT'S THAT? YOU COME TO TOUR THE APARTMENT?
OSCAR MICHEAUX! HE OWES ME FIVE GRAND! I OWN A THEATER IN PHILADELPHIA, AND I'VE BEEN ON HIS TRAIL FOR THREE MONTHS. THEY SAID HE WAS SHOOTING HERE.
MUST BE SOME MISTAKE. THIS HERE'S AN APARTMENT FOR RENT, NOT A SOUNDSTAGE.
I'VE HAD ENOUGH OF YOUR BULLSHIT! YOU TELL MICHEAUX I WANT THE DOUGH IN THREE DAYS, OR BONES GET BROKEN!
MICHEAUX? I'LL... ASK AROUND AT THE BROKER'S OFFICE.

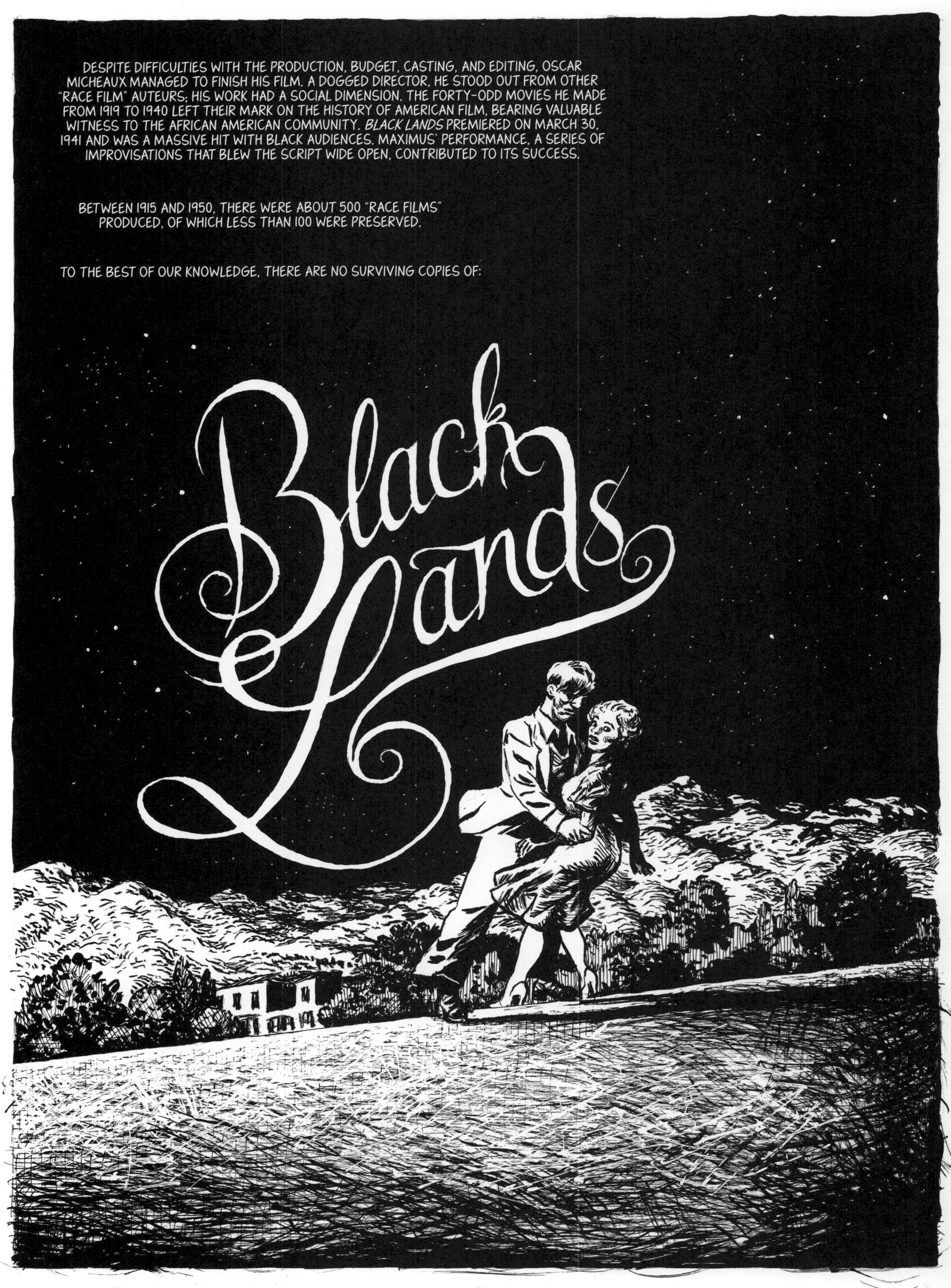
DESPITE DIFFICULTIES WITH THE PRODUCTION, BUDGET, CASTING, AND EDITING, OSCAR MICHEAUX MANAGED TO FINISH HIS FILM. A DOGGED DIRECTOR, HE STOOD OUT FROM OTHER "RACE FILM" AUTEURS; HIS WORK HAD A SOCIAL DIMENSION. THE FORTY-ODD MOVIES HE MADE FROM 1919 TO 1940 LEFT THEIR MARK ON THE HISTORY OF AMERICAN FILM, BEARING VALUABLE WITNESS TO THE AFRICAN AMERICAN COMMUNITY. *BLACK LANDS* PREMIERED ON MARCH 30, 1941 AND WAS A MASSIVE HIT WITH BLACK AUDIENCES. MAXIMUS' PERFORMANCE, A SERIES OF IMPROVISATIONS THAT BLEW THE SCRIPT WIDE OPEN, CONTRIBUTED TO ITS SUCCESS.
BETWEEN 1915 AND 1950, THERE WERE ABOUT 500 "RACE FILMS" PRODUCED, OF WHICH LESS THAN 100 WERE PRESERVED.
TO THE BEST OF OUR KNOWLEDGE, THERE ARE NO SURVIVING COPIES OF:
Black Lands

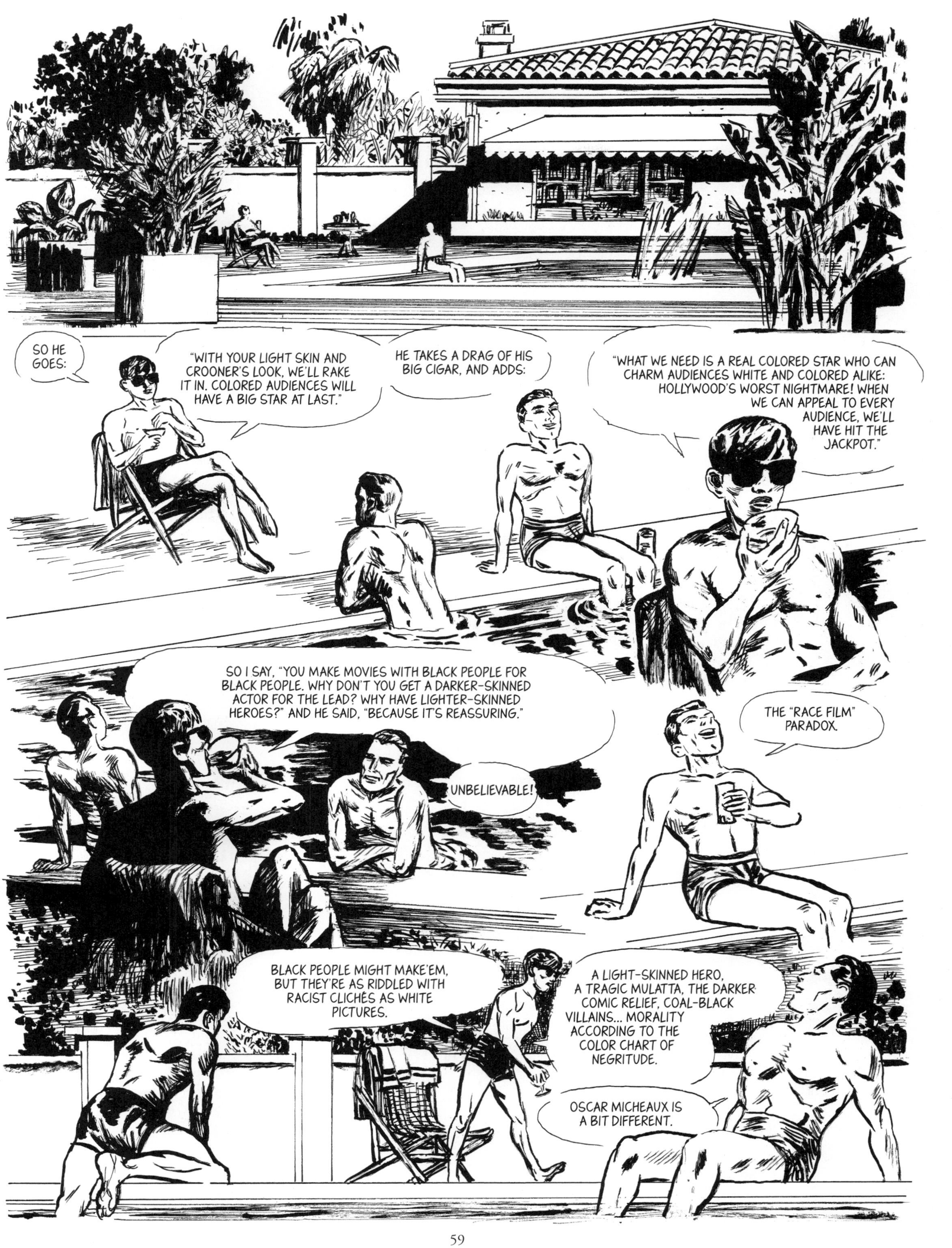
SO HE GOES:
"WITH YOUR LIGHT SKIN AND CROONER'S LOOK, WE'LL RAKE IT IN. COLORED AUDIENCES WILL HAVE A BIG STAR AT LAST."
HE TAKES A DRAG OF HIS BIG CIGAR, AND ADDS:
"WHAT WE NEED IS A REAL COLORED STAR WHO CAN CHARM AUDIENCES WHITE AND COLORED ALIKE: HOLLYWOOD'S WORST NIGHTMARE! WHEN WE CAN APPEAL TO EVERY AUDIENCE, WE'LL HAVE HIT THE JACKPOT."
SO I SAY, "YOU MAKE MOVIES WITH BLACK PEOPLE FOR BLACK PEOPLE. WHY DON'T YOU GET A DARKER-SKINNED ACTOR FOR THE LEAD? WHY HAVE LIGHTER-SKINNED HEROES?" AND HE SAID, "BECAUSE IT'S REASSURING."
UNBELIEVABLE!
THE "RACE FILM" PARADOX.
BLACK PEOPLE MIGHT MAKE'EM, BUT THEY'RE AS RIDDLED WITH RACIST CLICHÉS AS WHITE PICTURES.
A LIGHT-SKINNED HERO, A TRAGIC MULATTA, THE DARKER COMIC RELIEF, COAL-BLACK VILLAINS... MORALITY ACCORDING TO THE COLOR CHART OF NEGRITUDE.
OSCAR MICHEAUX IS A BIT DIFFERENT.

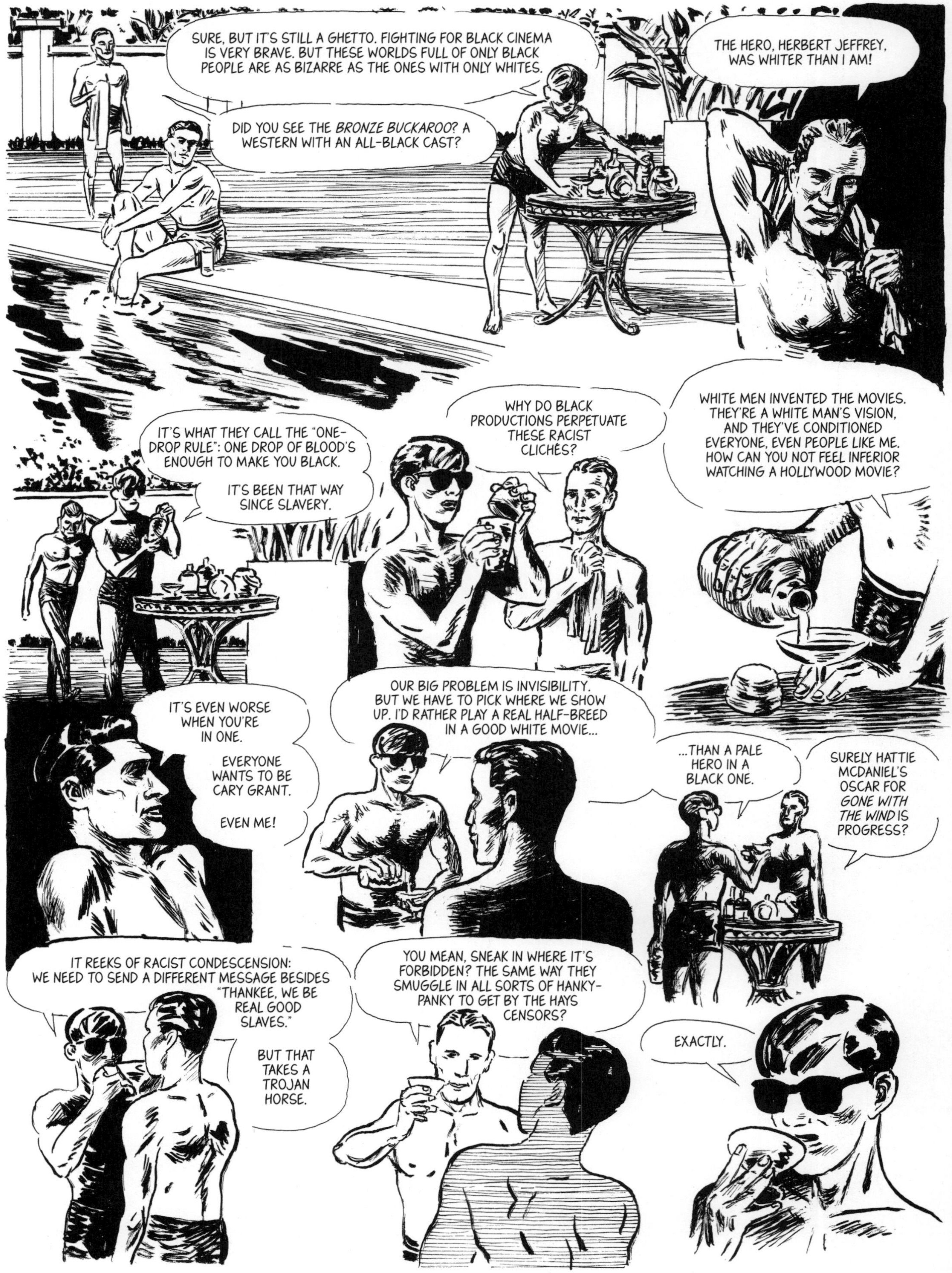
SURE, BUT IT'S STILL A GHETTO. FIGHTING FOR BLACK CINEMA IS VERY BRAVE. BUT THESE WORLDS FULL OF ONLY BLACK PEOPLE ARE AS BIZARRE AS THE ONES WITH ONLY WHITES.
DID YOU SEE THE *BRONZE BUCKAROO*? A WESTERN WITH AN ALL-BLACK CAST?
THE HERO, HERBERT JEFFREY, WAS WHITER THAN I AM!
IT'S WHAT THEY CALL THE "ONE-DROP RULE": ONE DROP OF BLOOD'S ENOUGH TO MAKE YOU BLACK.
IT'S BEEN THAT WAY SINCE SLAVERY.
WHY DO BLACK PRODUCTIONS PERPETUATE THESE RACIST CLICHÉS?
WHITE MEN INVENTED THE MOVIES. THEY'RE A WHITE MAN'S VISION, AND THEY'VE CONDITIONED EVERYONE, EVEN PEOPLE LIKE ME. HOW CAN YOU NOT FEEL INFERIOR WATCHING A HOLLYWOOD MOVIE?
IT'S EVEN WORSE WHEN YOU'RE IN ONE.
EVERYONE WANTS TO BE CARY GRANT.
EVEN ME!
OUR BIG PROBLEM IS INVISIBILITY. BUT WE HAVE TO PICK WHERE WE SHOW UP. I'D RATHER PLAY A REAL HALF-BREED IN A GOOD WHITE MOVIE...
...THAN A PALE HERO IN A BLACK ONE.
SURELY HATTIE MCDANIEL'S OSCAR FOR *GONE WITH THE WIND* IS PROGRESS?
IT REEKS OF RACIST CONDESCENSION: WE NEED TO SEND A DIFFERENT MESSAGE BESIDES "THANKEE, WE BE REAL GOOD SLAVES."
BUT THAT TAKES A TROJAN HORSE.
YOU MEAN, SNEAK IN WHERE IT'S FORBIDDEN? THE SAME WAY THEY SMUGGLE IN ALL SORTS OF HANKY-PANKY TO GET BY THE HAYS CENSORS?
EXACTLY.

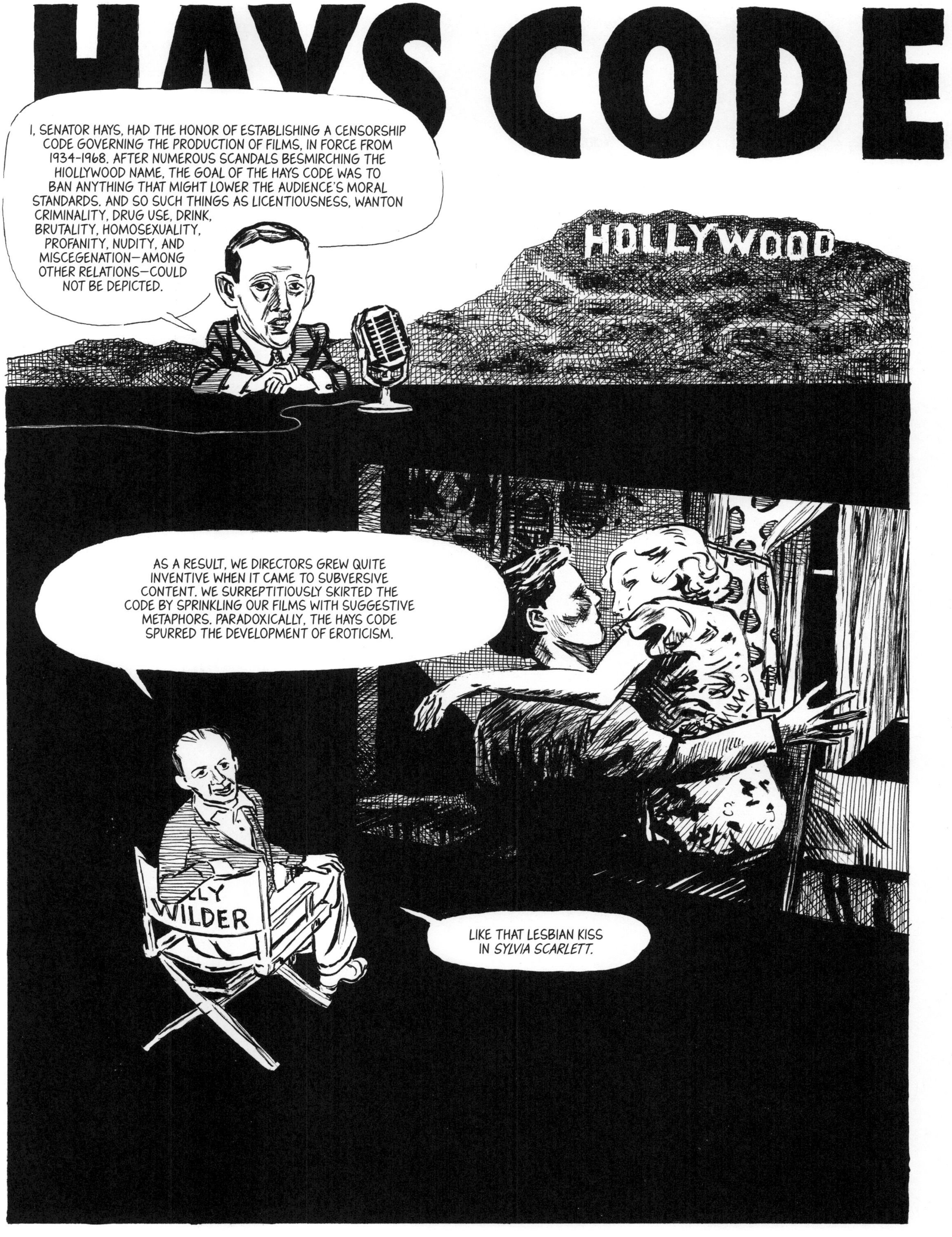
HAYS CODE
I, SENATOR HAYS, HAD THE HONOR OF ESTABLISHING A CENSORSHIP CODE GOVERNING THE PRODUCTION OF FILMS, IN FORCE FROM 1934–1968. AFTER NUMEROUS SCANDALS BESMIRCHING THE HIOLLYWOOD NAME, THE GOAL OF THE HAYS CODE WAS TO BAN ANYTHING THAT MIGHT LOWER THE AUDIENCE'S MORAL STANDARDS. AND SO SUCH THINGS AS LICENTIOUSNESS, WANTON CRIMINALITY, DRUG USE, DRINK, BRUTALITY, HOMOSEXUALITY, PROFANITY, NUDITY, AND MISCEGENATION—AMONG OTHER RELATIONS—COULD NOT BE DEPICTED.
HOLLYWOOD
AS A RESULT, WE DIRECTORS GREW QUITE INVENTIVE WHEN IT CAME TO SUBVERSIVE CONTENT. WE SURREPTITIOUSLY SKIRTED THE CODE BY SPRINKLING OUR FILMS WITH SUGGESTIVE METAPHORS. PARADOXICALLY, THE HAYS CODE SPURRED THE DEVELOPMENT OF EROTICISM.
LLY WILDER
LIKE THAT LESBIAN KISS IN *SYLVIA SCARLETT.*

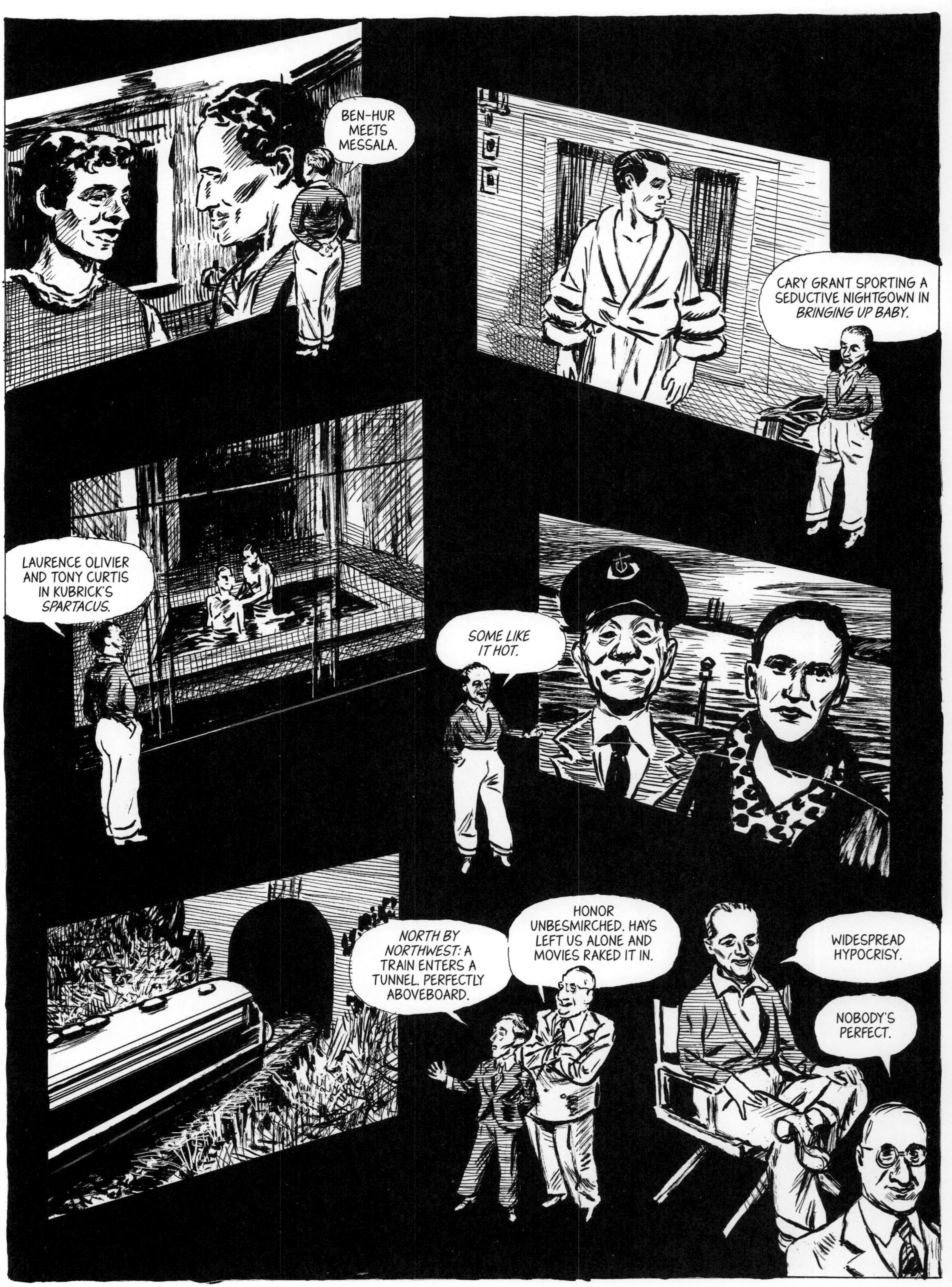
BEN-HUR MEETS MESSALA.
CARY GRANT SPORTING A SEDUCTIVE NIGHTGOWN IN *BRINGING UP BABY*.
LAURENCE OLIVIER AND TONY CURTIS IN KUBRICK'S *SPARTACUS*.
*SOME LIKE IT HOT*.
*NORTH BY NORTHWEST*: A TRAIN ENTERS A TUNNEL. PERFECTLY ABOVEBOARD.
HONOR UNBESMIRCHED. HAYS LEFT US ALONE AND MOVIES RAKED IT IN.
WIDESPREAD HYPOCRISY.
NOBODY'S PERFECT.

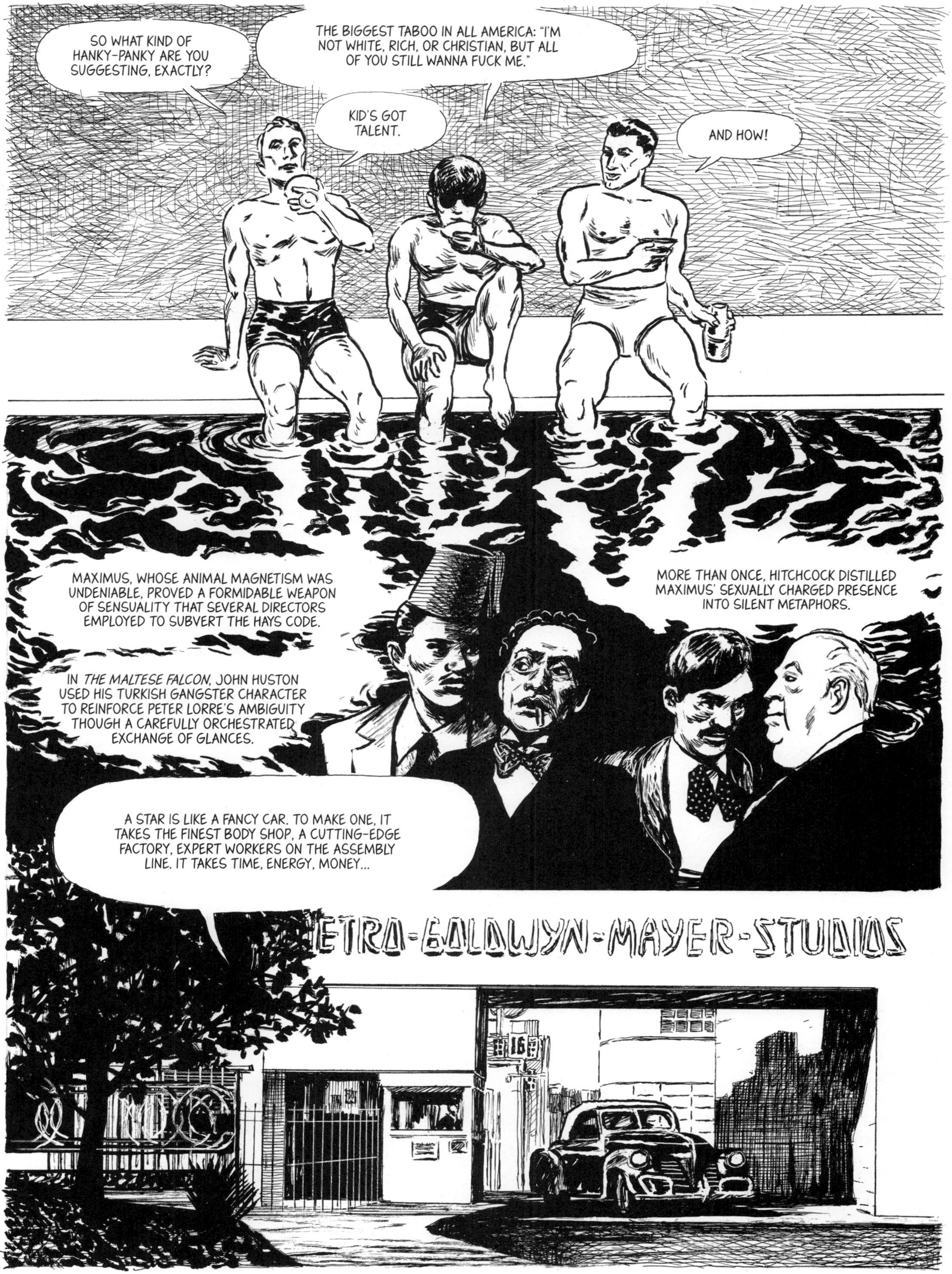
SO WHAT KIND OF HANKY-PANKY ARE YOU SUGGESTING, EXACTLY?
THE BIGGEST TABOO IN ALL AMERICA: "I'M NOT WHITE, RICH, OR CHRISTIAN, BUT ALL OF YOU STILL WANNA FUCK ME."
KID'S GOT TALENT.
AND HOW!
MAXIMUS, WHOSE ANIMAL MAGNETISM WAS UNDENIABLE, PROVED A FORMIDABLE WEAPON OF SENSUALITY THAT SEVERAL DIRECTORS EMPLOYED TO SUBVERT THE HAYS CODE.
MORE THAN ONCE, HITCHCOCK DISTILLED MAXIMUS' SEXUALLY CHARGED PRESENCE INTO SILENT METAPHORS.
IN *THE MALTESE FALCON*, JOHN HUSTON USED HIS TURKISH GANGSTER CHARACTER TO REINFORCE PETER LORRE'S AMBIGUITY THOUGH A CAREFULLY ORCHESTRATED EXCHANGE OF GLANCES.
A STAR IS LIKE A FANCY CAR. TO MAKE ONE, IT TAKES THE FINEST BODY SHOP, A CUTTING-EDGE FACTORY, EXPERT WORKERS ON THE ASSEMBLY LINE. IT TAKES TIME, ENERGY, MONEY...
ETRO-GOLDWYN-MAYER-STUDIOS
16

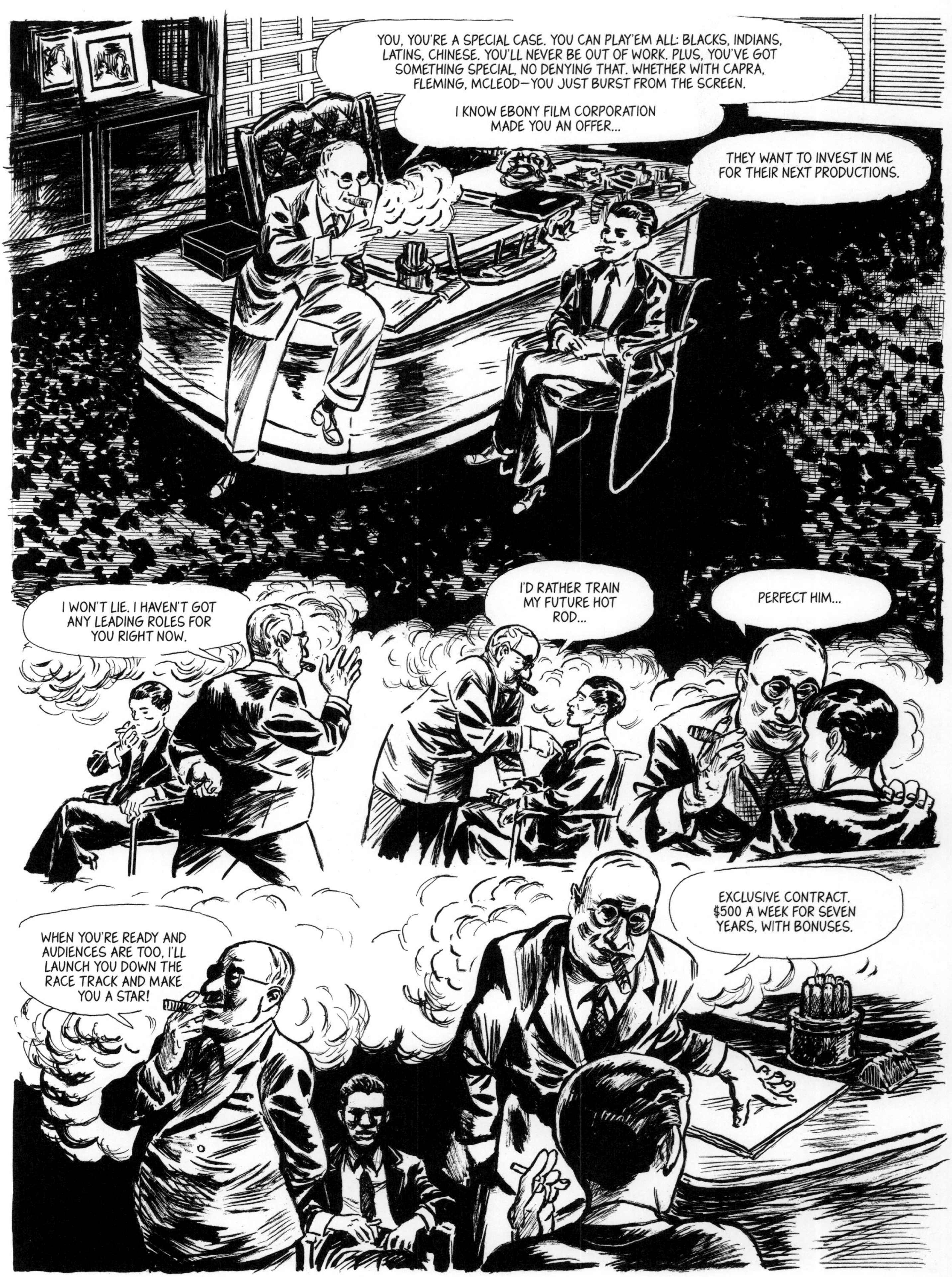
YOU, YOU'RE A SPECIAL CASE. YOU CAN PLAY'EM ALL: BLACKS, INDIANS, LATINS, CHINESE. YOU'LL NEVER BE OUT OF WORK. PLUS, YOU'VE GOT SOMETHING SPECIAL, NO DENYING THAT. WHETHER WITH CAPRA, FLEMING, MCLEOD—YOU JUST BURST FROM THE SCREEN.
I KNOW EBONY FILM CORPORATION MADE YOU AN OFFER...
THEY WANT TO INVEST IN ME FOR THEIR NEXT PRODUCTIONS.
I WON'T LIE. I HAVEN'T GOT ANY LEADING ROLES FOR YOU RIGHT NOW.
I'D RATHER TRAIN MY FUTURE HOT ROD...
PERFECT HIM...
WHEN YOU'RE READY AND AUDIENCES ARE TOO, I'LL LAUNCH YOU DOWN THE RACE TRACK AND MAKE YOU A STAR!
EXCLUSIVE CONTRACT. $500 A WEEK FOR SEVEN YEARS, WITH BONUSES.

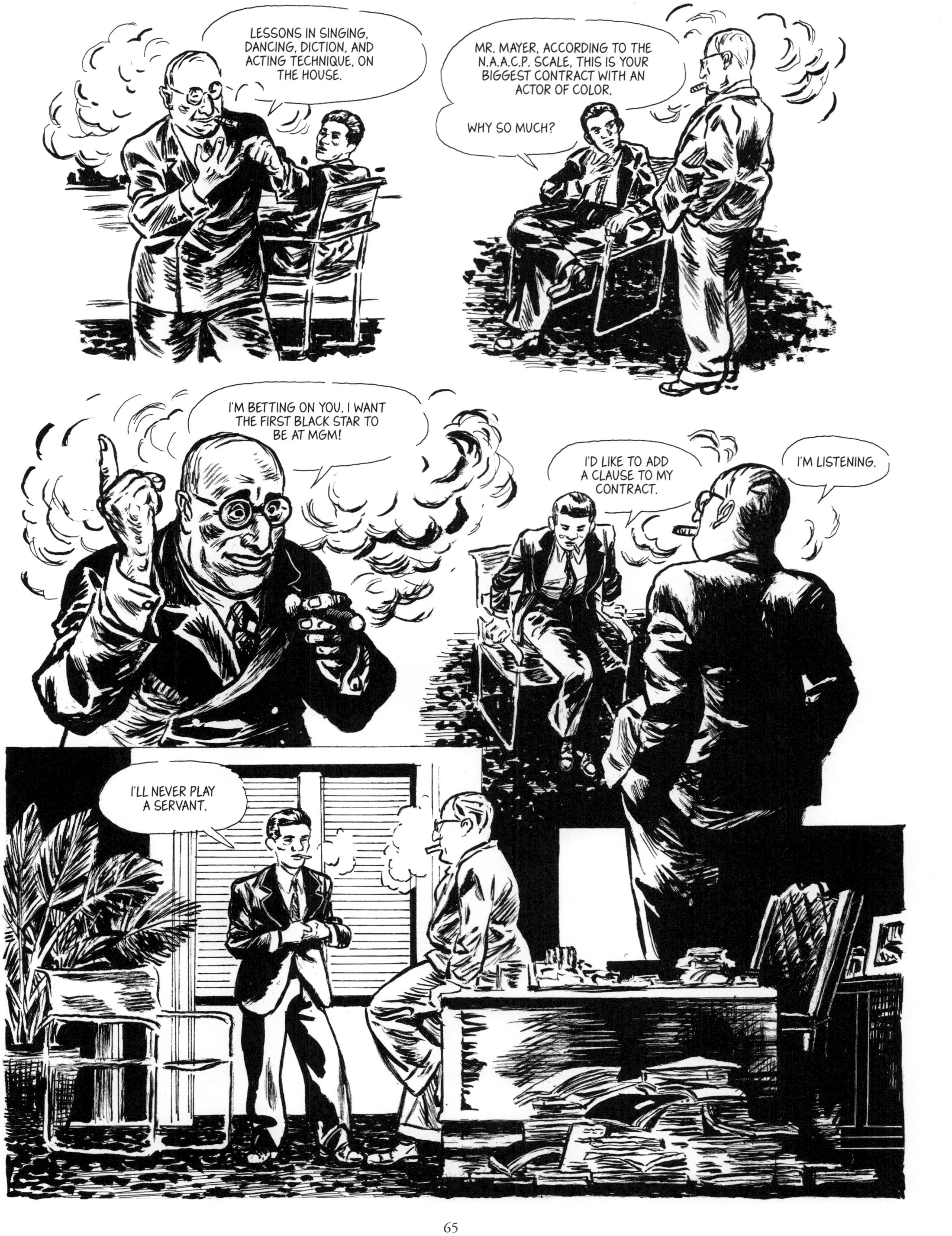
LESSONS IN SINGING, DANCING, DICTION, AND ACTING TECHNIQUE, ON THE HOUSE.
MR. MAYER, ACCORDING TO THE N.A.A.C.P. SCALE, THIS IS YOUR BIGGEST CONTRACT WITH AN ACTOR OF COLOR.
WHY SO MUCH?
I'M BETTING ON YOU. I WANT THE FIRST BLACK STAR TO BE AT MGM!
I'D LIKE TO ADD A CLAUSE TO MY CONTRACT.
I'M LISTENING.
I'LL NEVER PLAY A SERVANT.

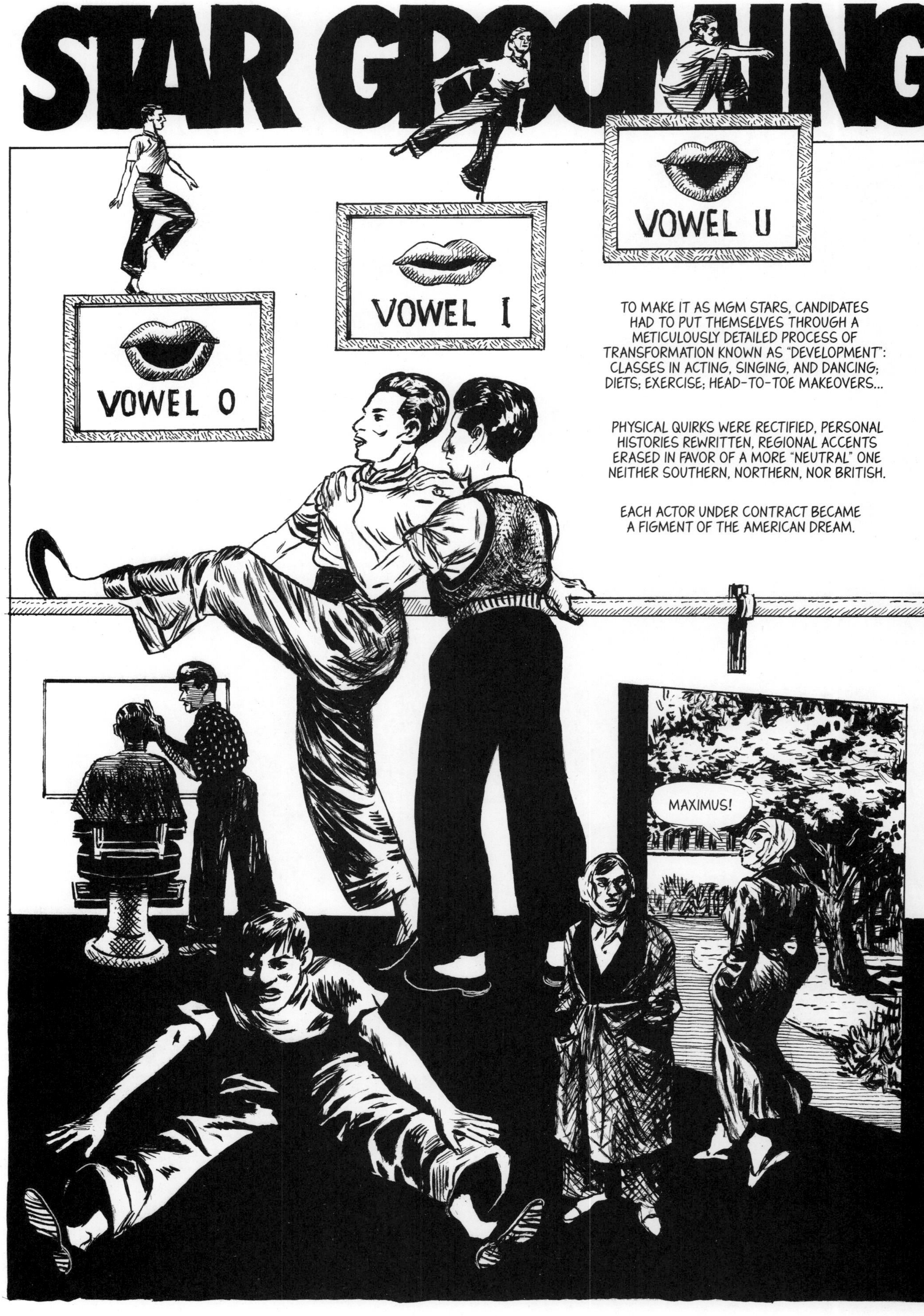
STAR GROOMING
VOWEL O
VOWEL I
VOWEL U
TO MAKE IT AS MGM STARS, CANDIDATES HAD TO PUT THEMSELVES THROUGH A METICULOUSLY DETAILED PROCESS OF TRANSFORMATION KNOWN AS "DEVELOPMENT": CLASSES IN ACTING, SINGING, AND DANCING; DIETS; EXERCISE; HEAD-TO-TOE MAKEOVERS...
PHYSICAL QUIRKS WERE RECTIFIED, PERSONAL HISTORIES REWRITTEN, REGIONAL ACCENTS ERASED IN FAVOR OF A MORE "NEUTRAL" ONE NEITHER SOUTHERN, NORTHERN, NOR BRITISH.
EACH ACTOR UNDER CONTRACT BECAME A FIGMENT OF THE AMERICAN DREAM.
MAXIMUS!

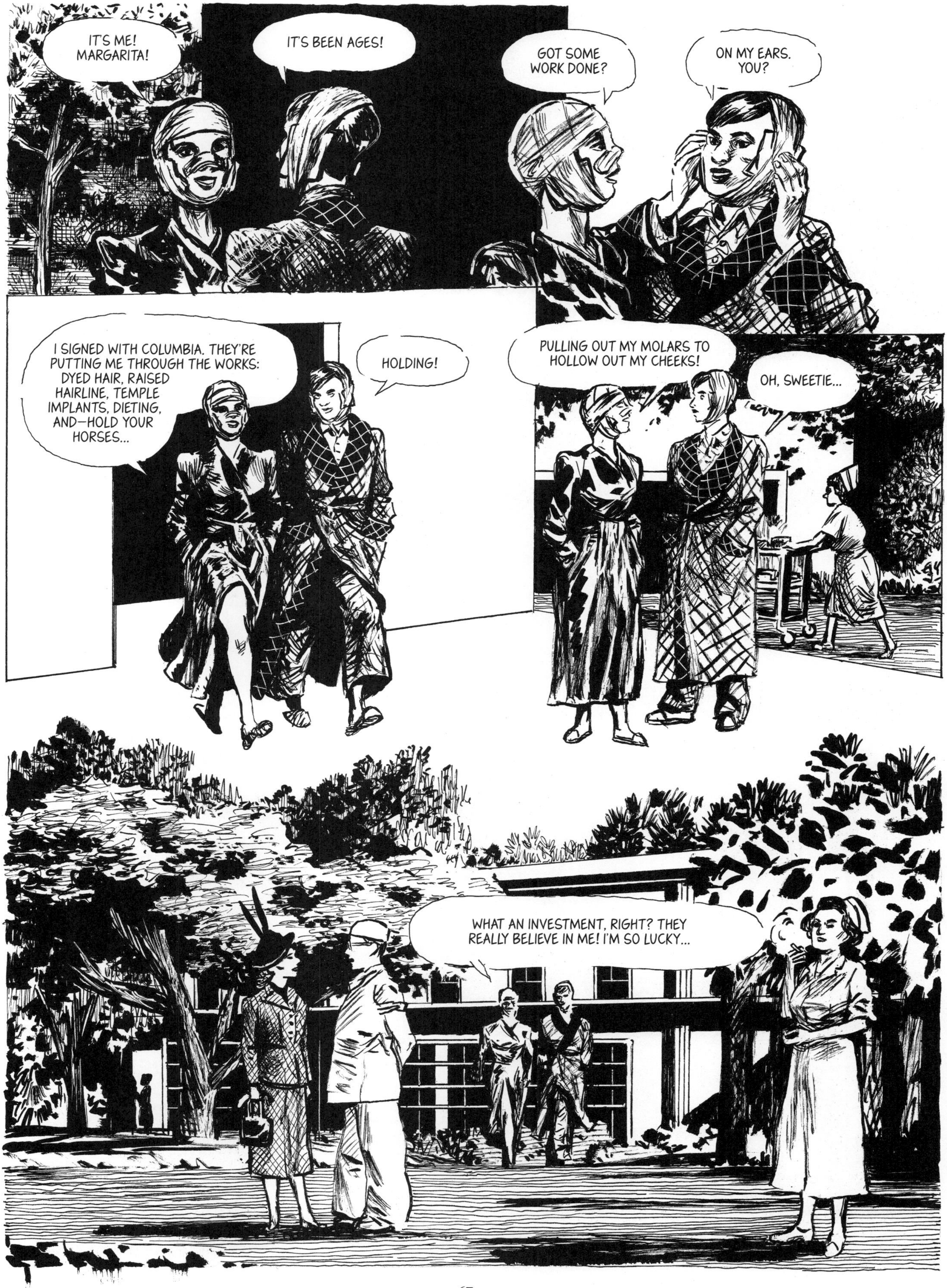
IT'S ME! MARGARITA!
IT'S BEEN AGES!
GOT SOME WORK DONE?
ON MY EARS. YOU?
I SIGNED WITH COLUMBIA. THEY'RE PUTTING ME THROUGH THE WORKS: DYED HAIR, RAISED HAIRLINE, TEMPLE IMPLANTS, DIETING, AND—HOLD YOUR HORSES...
HOLDING!
PULLING OUT MY MOLARS TO HOLLOW OUT MY CHEEKS!
OH, SWEETIE...
WHAT AN INVESTMENT, RIGHT? THEY REALLY BELIEVE IN ME! I'M SO LUCKY...

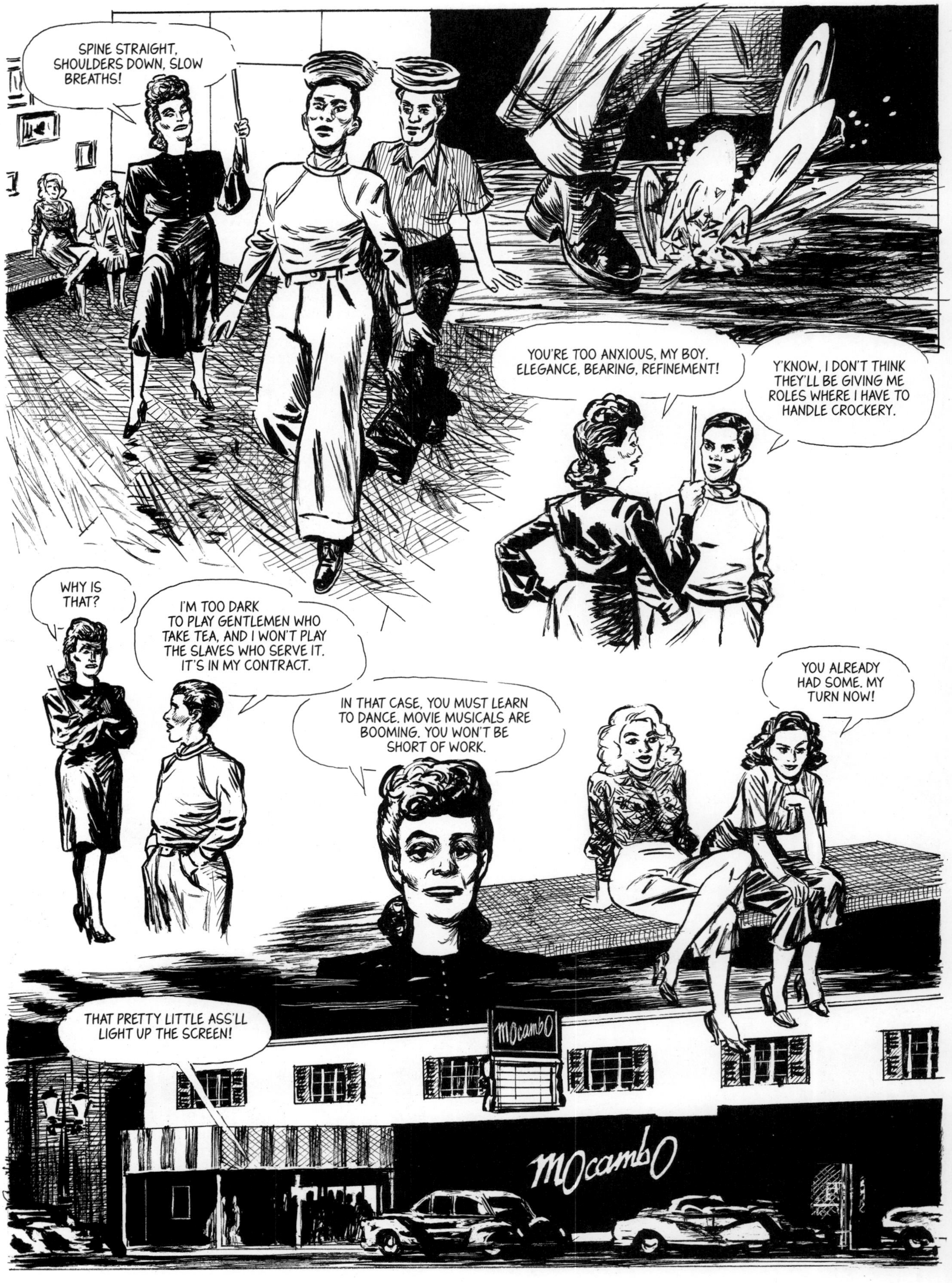
SPINE STRAIGHT, SHOULDERS DOWN, SLOW BREATHS!
YOU'RE TOO ANXIOUS, MY BOY. ELEGANCE, BEARING, REFINEMENT!
Y'KNOW, I DON'T THINK THEY'LL BE GIVING ME ROLES WHERE I HAVE TO HANDLE CROCKERY.
WHY IS THAT?
I'M TOO DARK TO PLAY GENTLEMEN WHO TAKE TEA, AND I WON'T PLAY THE SLAVES WHO SERVE IT. IT'S IN MY CONTRACT.
IN THAT CASE, YOU MUST LEARN TO DANCE. MOVIE MUSICALS ARE BOOMING. YOU WON'T BE SHORT OF WORK.
YOU ALREADY HAD SOME. MY TURN NOW!
THAT PRETTY LITTLE ASS'LL LIGHT UP THE SCREEN!
MOcambO
MOcambO

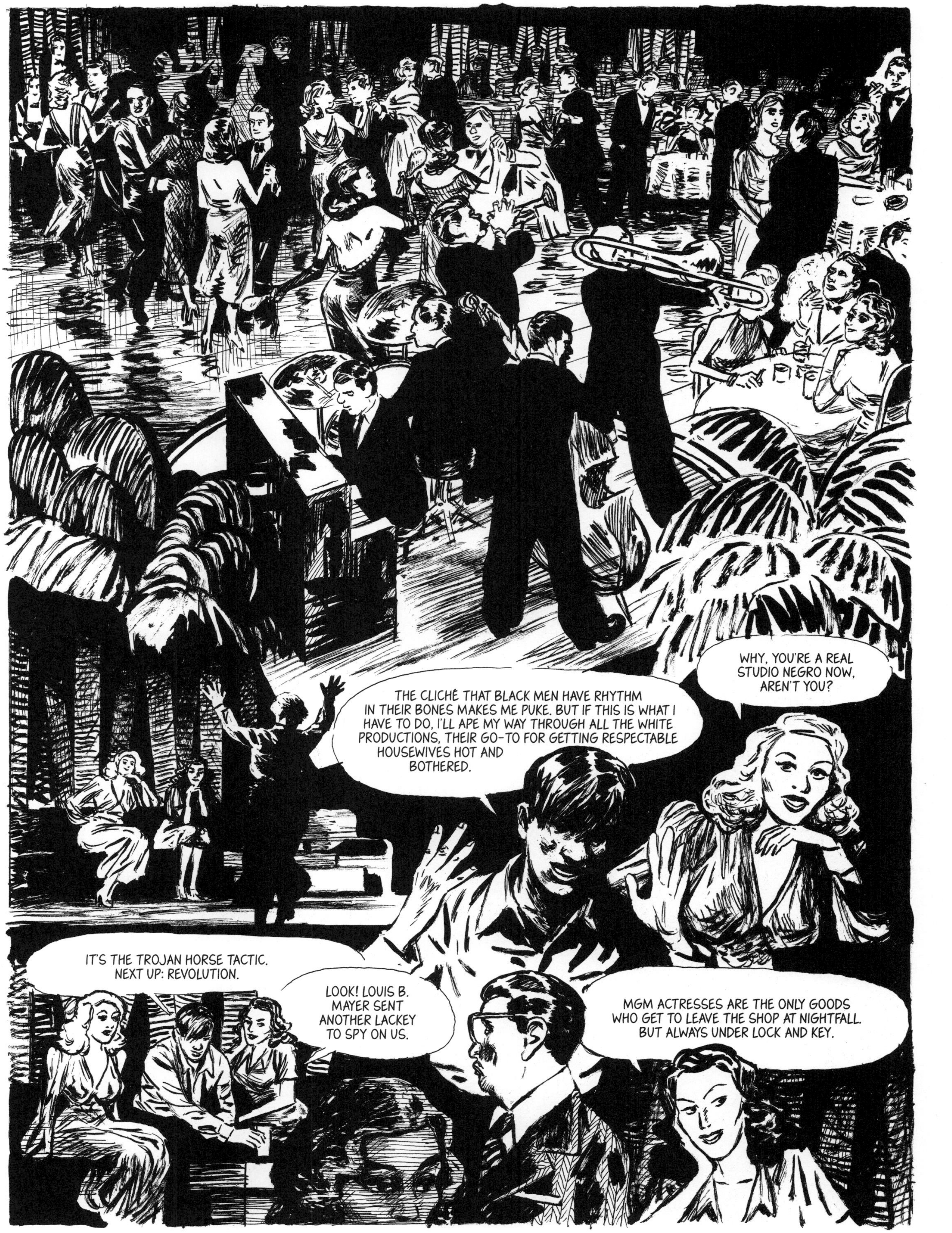
THE CLICHÉ THAT BLACK MEN HAVE RHYTHM IN THEIR BONES MAKES ME PUKE. BUT IF THIS IS WHAT I HAVE TO DO, I'LL APE MY WAY THROUGH ALL THE WHITE PRODUCTIONS, THEIR GO-TO FOR GETTING RESPECTABLE HOUSEWIVES HOT AND BOTHERED.
WHY, YOU'RE A REAL STUDIO NEGRO NOW, AREN'T YOU?
IT'S THE TROJAN HORSE TACTIC. NEXT UP: REVOLUTION.
LOOK! LOUIS B. MAYER SENT ANOTHER LACKEY TO SPY ON US.
MGM ACTRESSES ARE THE ONLY GOODS WHO GET TO LEAVE THE SHOP AT NIGHTFALL. BUT ALWAYS UNDER LOCK AND KEY.

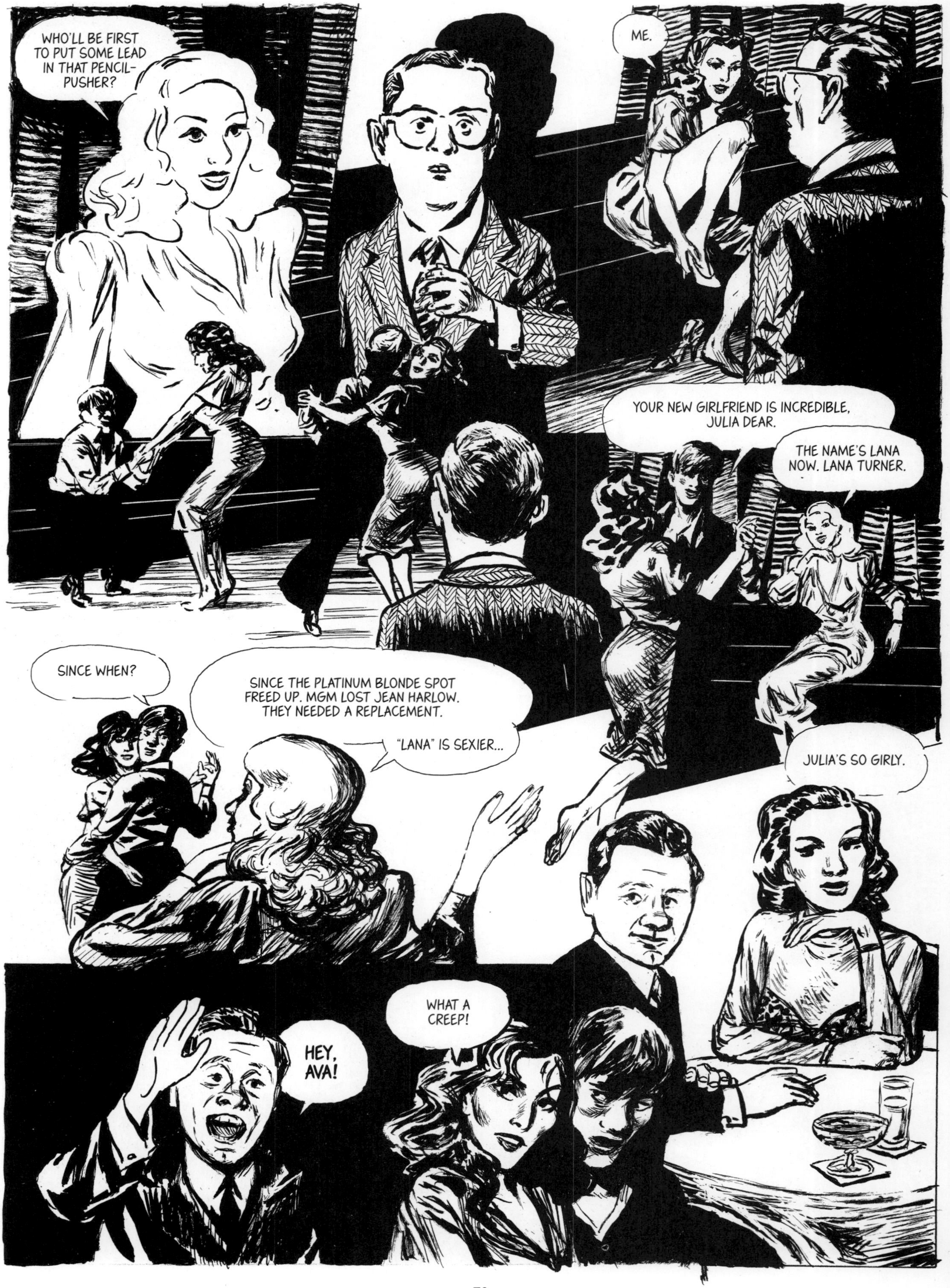
WHO'LL BE FIRST TO PUT SOME LEAD IN THAT PENCIL-PUSHER?
ME.
YOUR NEW GIRLFRIEND IS INCREDIBLE, JULIA DEAR.
THE NAME'S LANA NOW. LANA TURNER.
SINCE WHEN?
SINCE THE PLATINUM BLONDE SPOT FREED UP. MGM LOST JEAN HARLOW. THEY NEEDED A REPLACEMENT.
"LANA" IS SEXIER...
JULIA'S SO GIRLY.
HEY, AVA!
WHAT A CREEP!

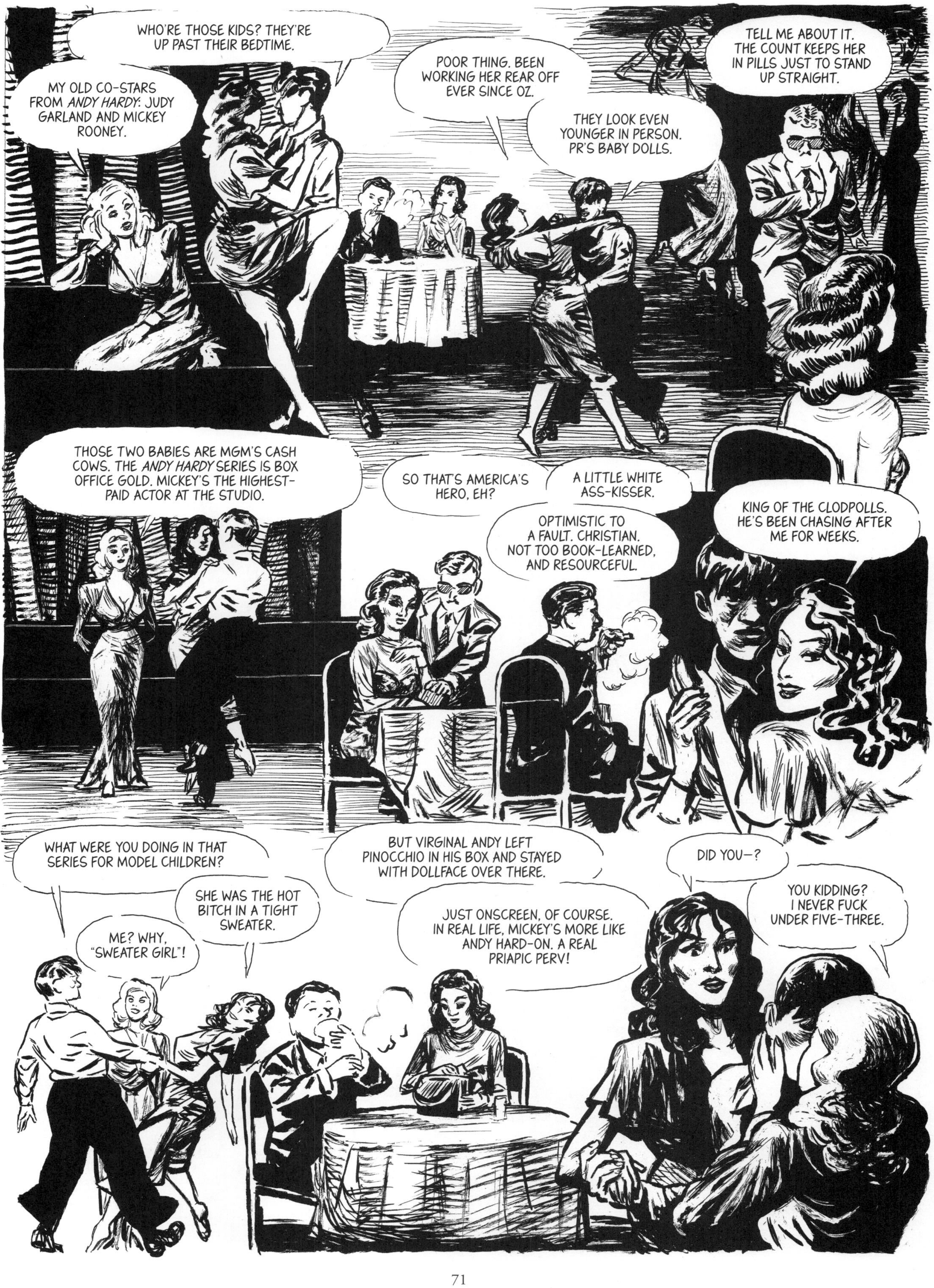
WHO'RE THOSE KIDS? THEY'RE UP PAST THEIR BEDTIME.
MY OLD CO-STARS FROM *ANDY HARDY*: JUDY GARLAND AND MICKEY ROONEY.
POOR THING. BEEN WORKING HER REAR OFF EVER SINCE OZ.
THEY LOOK EVEN YOUNGER IN PERSON. PR'S BABY DOLLS.
TELL ME ABOUT IT. THE COUNT KEEPS HER IN PILLS JUST TO STAND UP STRAIGHT.
THOSE TWO BABIES ARE MGM'S CASH COWS. THE *ANDY HARDY* SERIES IS BOX OFFICE GOLD. MICKEY'S THE HIGHEST-PAID ACTOR AT THE STUDIO.
SO THAT'S AMERICA'S HERO, EH?
A LITTLE WHITE ASS-KISSER.
OPTIMISTIC TO A FAULT. CHRISTIAN. NOT TOO BOOK-LEARNED, AND RESOURCEFUL.
KING OF THE CLODPOLLS. HE'S BEEN CHASING AFTER ME FOR WEEKS.
WHAT WERE YOU DOING IN THAT SERIES FOR MODEL CHILDREN?
ME? WHY, "SWEATER GIRL"!
SHE WAS THE HOT BITCH IN A TIGHT SWEATER.
BUT VIRGINAL ANDY LEFT PINOCCHIO IN HIS BOX AND STAYED WITH DOLLFACE OVER THERE.
JUST ONSCREEN, OF COURSE. IN REAL LIFE, MICKEY'S MORE LIKE ANDY HARD-ON. A REAL PRIAPIC PERV!
DID YOU—?
YOU KIDDING? I NEVER FUCK UNDER FIVE-THREE.

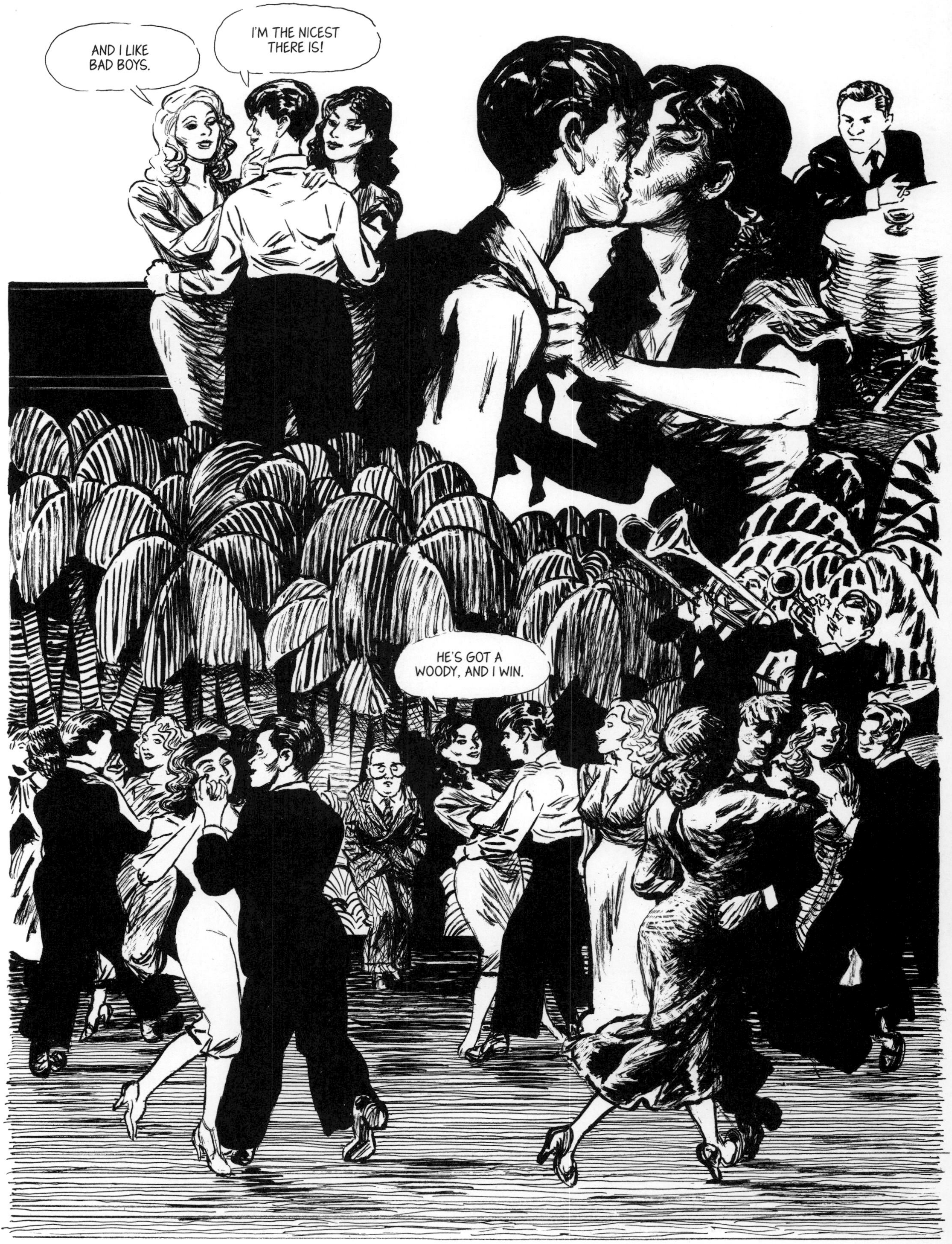
AND I LIKE BAD BOYS.
I'M THE NICEST THERE IS!
HE'S GOT A WOODY, AND I WIN.

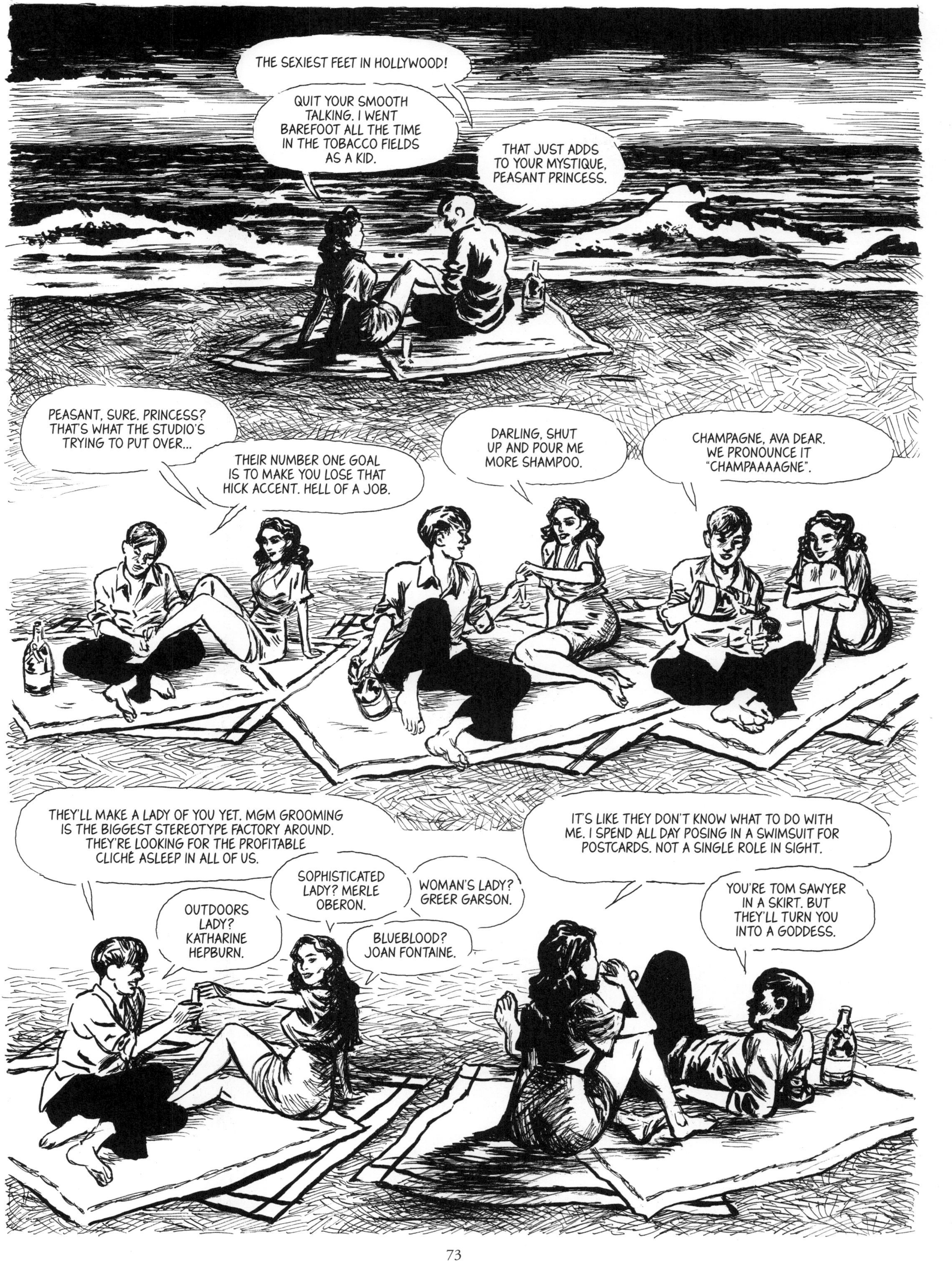
THE SEXIEST FEET IN HOLLYWOOD!
QUIT YOUR SMOOTH TALKING. I WENT BAREFOOT ALL THE TIME IN THE TOBACCO FIELDS AS A KID.
THAT JUST ADDS TO YOUR MYSTIQUE, PEASANT PRINCESS.
PEASANT, SURE. PRINCESS? THAT'S WHAT THE STUDIO'S TRYING TO PUT OVER...
THEIR NUMBER ONE GOAL IS TO MAKE YOU LOSE THAT HICK ACCENT. HELL OF A JOB.
DARLING, SHUT UP AND POUR ME MORE SHAMPOO.
CHAMPAGNE, AVA DEAR. WE PRONOUNCE IT "CHAMPAAAAGNE".
THEY'LL MAKE A LADY OF YOU YET. MGM GROOMING IS THE BIGGEST STEREOTYPE FACTORY AROUND. THEY'RE LOOKING FOR THE PROFITABLE CLICHÉ ASLEEP IN ALL OF US.
OUTDOORS LADY? KATHARINE HEPBURN.
SOPHISTICATED LADY? MERLE OBERON.
WOMAN'S LADY? GREER GARSON.
BLUEBLOOD? JOAN FONTAINE.
IT'S LIKE THEY DON'T KNOW WHAT TO DO WITH ME. I SPEND ALL DAY POSING IN A SWIMSUIT FOR POSTCARDS. NOT A SINGLE ROLE IN SIGHT.
YOU'RE TOM SAWYER IN A SKIRT. BUT THEY'LL TURN YOU INTO A GODDESS.

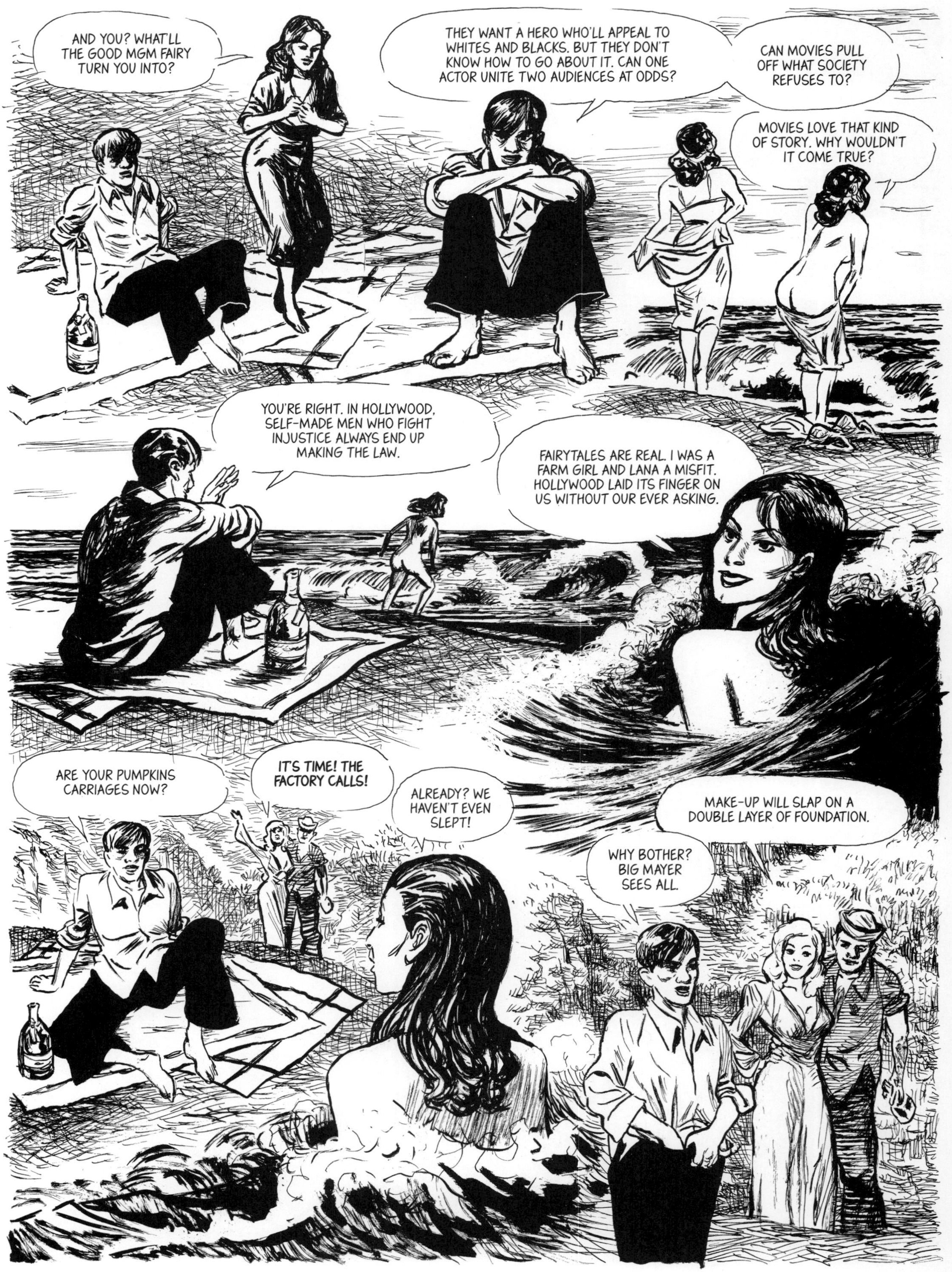
AND YOU? WHAT'LL THE GOOD MGM FAIRY TURN YOU INTO?
THEY WANT A HERO WHO'LL APPEAL TO WHITES AND BLACKS. BUT THEY DON'T KNOW HOW TO GO ABOUT IT. CAN ONE ACTOR UNITE TWO AUDIENCES AT ODDS?
CAN MOVIES PULL OFF WHAT SOCIETY REFUSES TO?
MOVIES LOVE THAT KIND OF STORY. WHY WOULDN'T IT COME TRUE?
YOU'RE RIGHT. IN HOLLYWOOD, SELF-MADE MEN WHO FIGHT INJUSTICE ALWAYS END UP MAKING THE LAW.
FAIRYTALES ARE REAL. I WAS A FARM GIRL AND LANA A MISFIT. HOLLYWOOD LAID ITS FINGER ON US WITHOUT OUR EVER ASKING.
ARE YOUR PUMPKINS CARRIAGES NOW?
IT'S TIME! THE FACTORY CALLS!
ALREADY? WE HAVEN'T EVEN SLEPT!
MAKE-UP WILL SLAP ON A DOUBLE LAYER OF FOUNDATION.
WHY BOTHER? BIG MAYER SEES ALL.

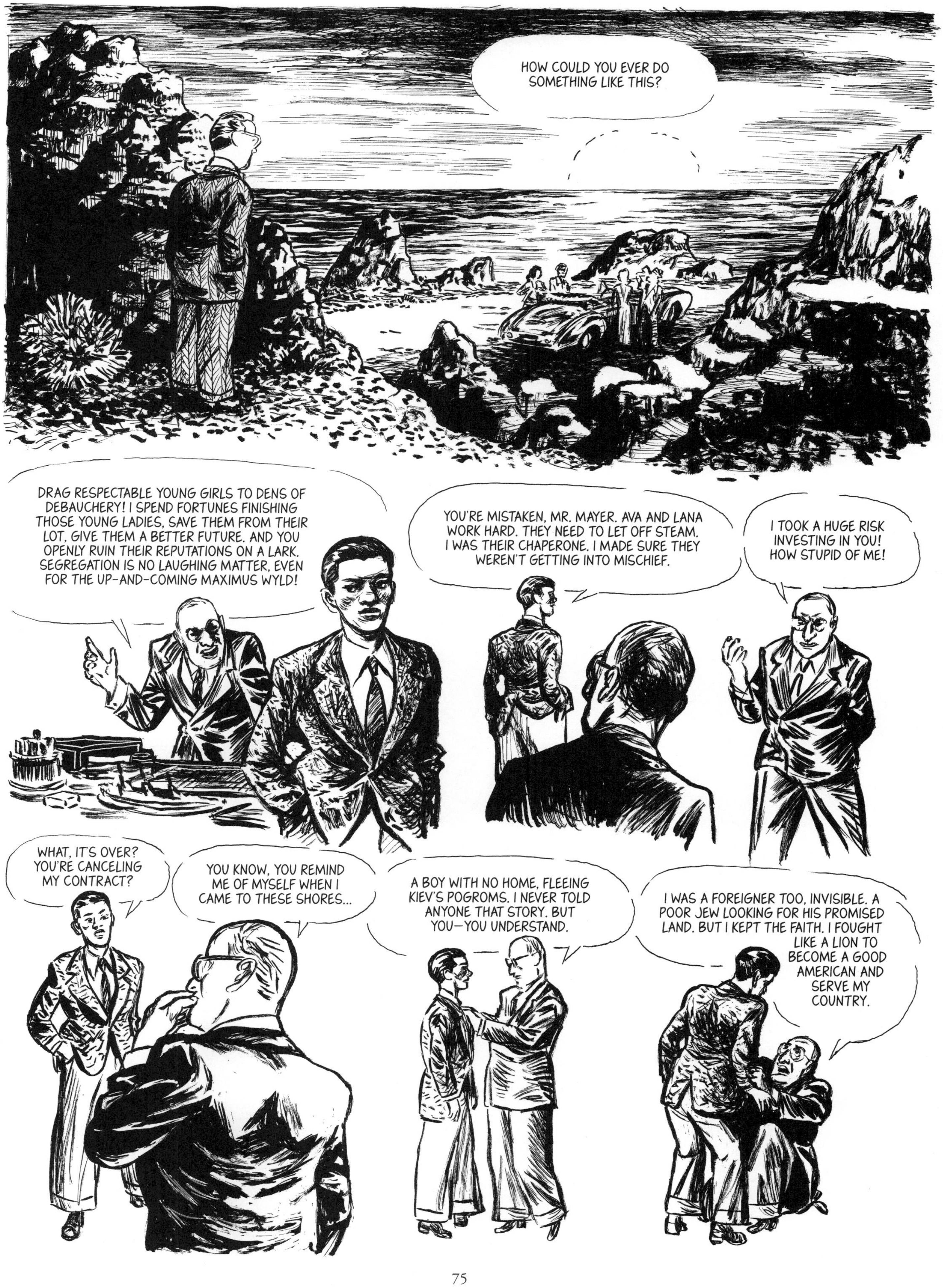
HOW COULD YOU EVER DO SOMETHING LIKE THIS?
DRAG RESPECTABLE YOUNG GIRLS TO DENS OF DEBAUCHERY! I SPEND FORTUNES FINISHING THOSE YOUNG LADIES, SAVE THEM FROM THEIR LOT, GIVE THEM A BETTER FUTURE. AND YOU OPENLY RUIN THEIR REPUTATIONS ON A LARK. SEGREGATION IS NO LAUGHING MATTER, EVEN FOR THE UP-AND-COMING MAXIMUS WYLD!
YOU'RE MISTAKEN, MR. MAYER. AVA AND LANA WORK HARD. THEY NEED TO LET OFF STEAM. I WAS THEIR CHAPERONE. I MADE SURE THEY WEREN'T GETTING INTO MISCHIEF.
I TOOK A HUGE RISK INVESTING IN YOU! HOW STUPID OF ME!
WHAT, IT'S OVER? YOU'RE CANCELING MY CONTRACT?
YOU KNOW, YOU REMIND ME OF MYSELF WHEN I CAME TO THESE SHORES...
A BOY WITH NO HOME, FLEEING KIEV'S POGROMS. I NEVER TOLD ANYONE THAT STORY. BUT YOU—YOU UNDERSTAND.
I WAS A FOREIGNER TOO, INVISIBLE. A POOR JEW LOOKING FOR HIS PROMISED LAND. BUT I KEPT THE FAITH. I FOUGHT LIKE A LION TO BECOME A GOOD AMERICAN AND SERVE MY COUNTRY.

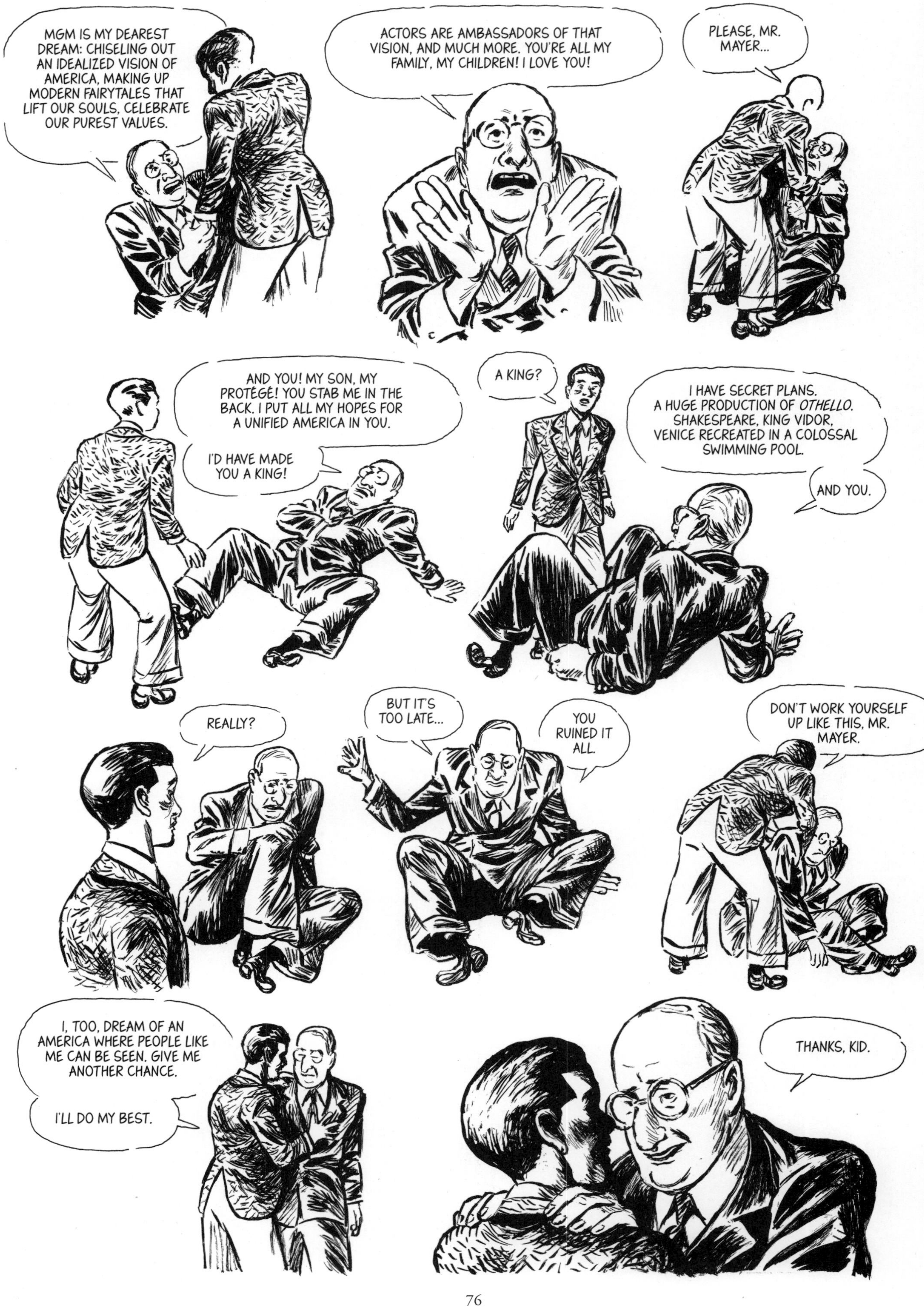

MGM IS MY DEAREST DREAM: CHISELING OUT AN IDEALIZED VISION OF AMERICA, MAKING UP MODERN FAIRYTALES THAT LIFT OUR SOULS, CELEBRATE OUR PUREST VALUES.
ACTORS ARE AMBASSADORS OF THAT VISION, AND MUCH MORE. YOU'RE ALL MY FAMILY, MY CHILDREN! I LOVE YOU!
PLEASE, MR. MAYER...
AND YOU! MY SON, MY PROTÉGÉ! YOU STAB ME IN THE BACK. I PUT ALL MY HOPES FOR A UNIFIED AMERICA IN YOU.
I'D HAVE MADE YOU A KING!
A KING?
I HAVE SECRET PLANS. A HUGE PRODUCTION OF *OTHELLO*. SHAKESPEARE, KING VIDOR, VENICE RECREATED IN A COLOSSAL SWIMMING POOL.
AND YOU.
REALLY?
BUT IT'S TOO LATE...
YOU RUINED IT ALL.
DON'T WORK YOURSELF UP LIKE THIS, MR. MAYER.
I, TOO, DREAM OF AN AMERICA WHERE PEOPLE LIKE ME CAN BE SEEN. GIVE ME ANOTHER CHANCE.
I'LL DO MY BEST.
THANKS, KID.

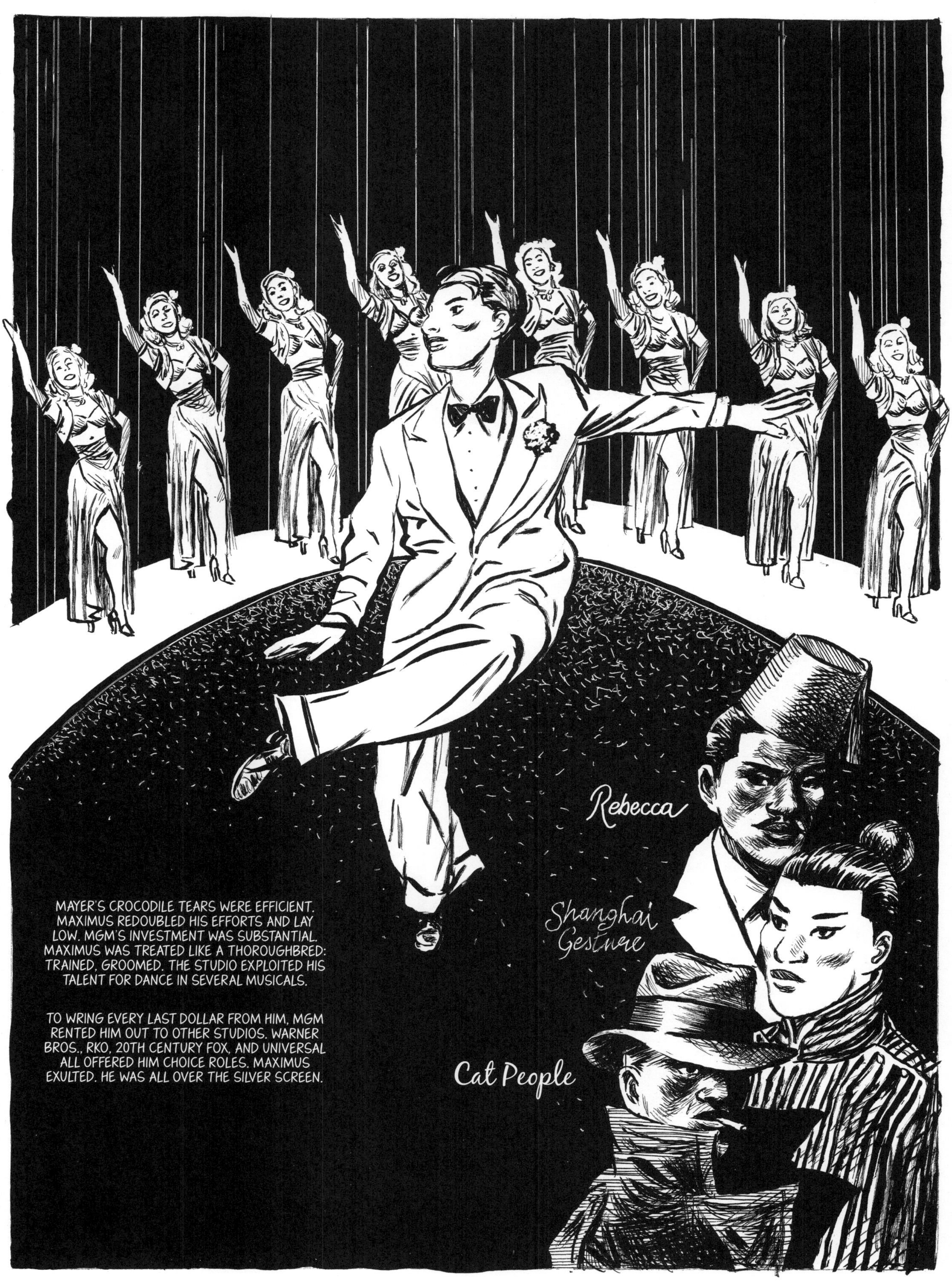
Rebecca
Shanghai Gesture
MAYER'S CROCODILE TEARS WERE EFFICIENT. MAXIMUS REDOUBLED HIS EFFORTS AND LAY LOW. MGM'S INVESTMENT WAS SUBSTANTIAL. MAXIMUS WAS TREATED LIKE A THOROUGHBRED: TRAINED, GROOMED. THE STUDIO EXPLOITED HIS TALENT FOR DANCE IN SEVERAL MUSICALS.
TO WRING EVERY LAST DOLLAR FROM HIM, MGM RENTED HIM OUT TO OTHER STUDIOS. WARNER BROS., RKO, 20TH CENTURY FOX, AND UNIVERSAL ALL OFFERED HIM CHOICE ROLES. MAXIMUS EXULTED. HE WAS ALL OVER THE SILVER SCREEN.
Cat People

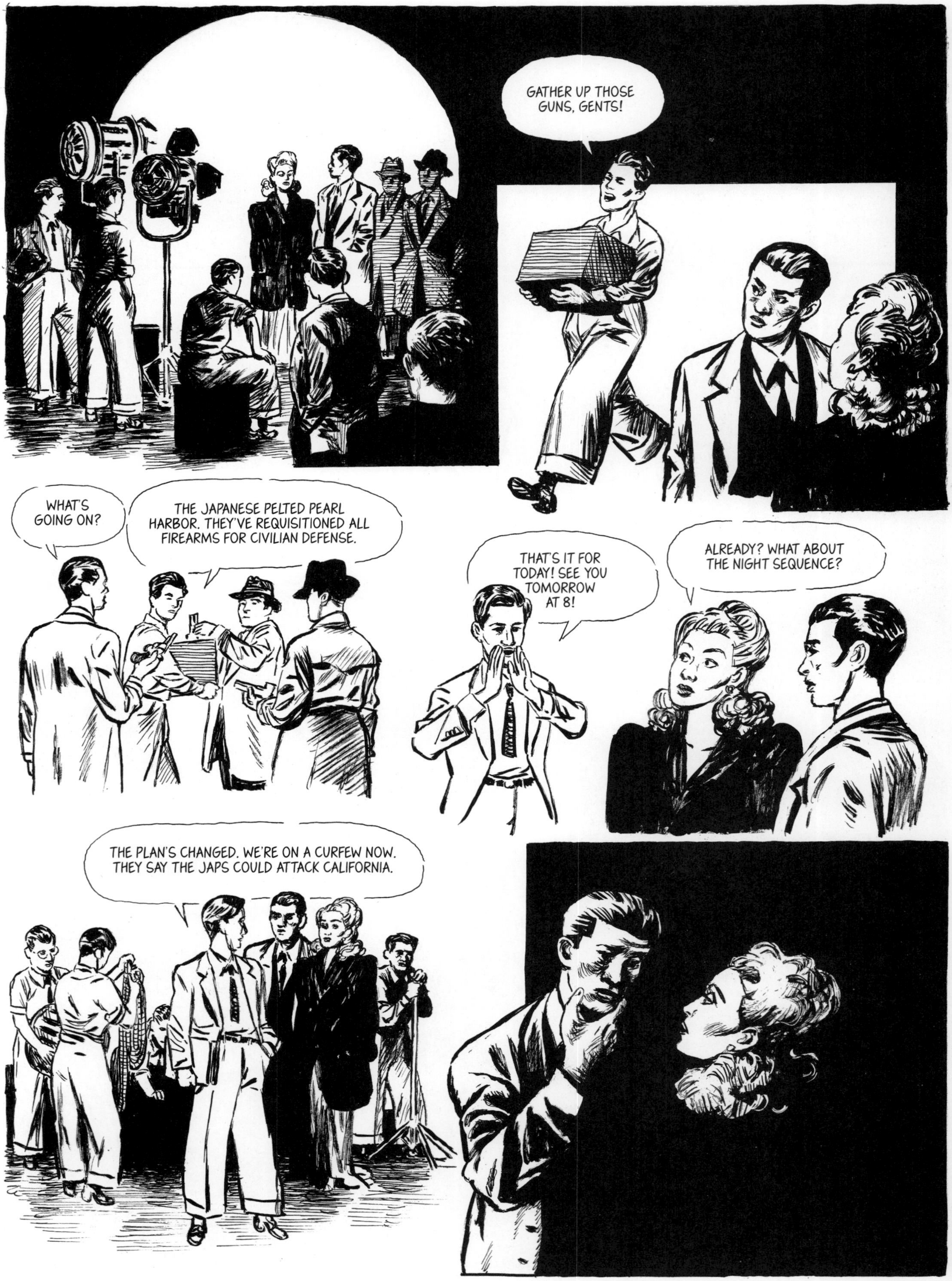
GATHER UP THOSE GUNS, GENTS!
WHAT'S GOING ON?
THE JAPANESE PELTED PEARL HARBOR. THEY'VE REQUISITIONED ALL FIREARMS FOR CIVILIAN DEFENSE.
THAT'S IT FOR TODAY! SEE YOU TOMORROW AT 8!
ALREADY? WHAT ABOUT THE NIGHT SEQUENCE?
THE PLAN'S CHANGED. WE'RE ON A CURFEW NOW. THEY SAY THE JAPS COULD ATTACK CALIFORNIA.

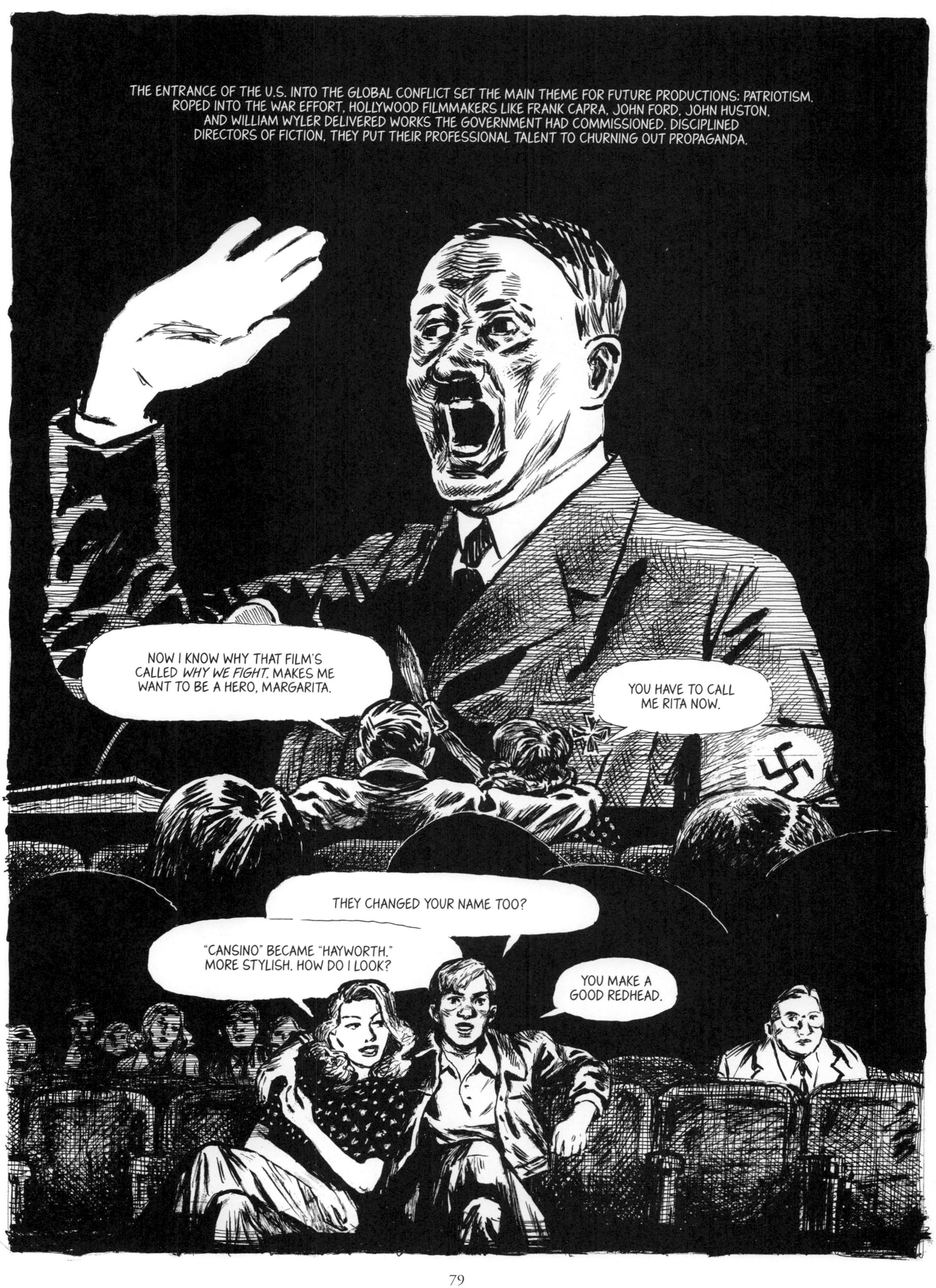
THE ENTRANCE OF THE U.S. INTO THE GLOBAL CONFLICT SET THE MAIN THEME FOR FUTURE PRODUCTIONS: PATRIOTISM. ROPED INTO THE WAR EFFORT, HOLLYWOOD FILMMAKERS LIKE FRANK CAPRA, JOHN FORD, JOHN HUSTON, AND WILLIAM WYLER DELIVERED WORKS THE GOVERNMENT HAD COMMISSIONED. DISCIPLINED DIRECTORS OF FICTION, THEY PUT THEIR PROFESSIONAL TALENT TO CHURNING OUT PROPAGANDA.
NOW I KNOW WHY THAT FILM'S CALLED *WHY WE FIGHT*. MAKES ME WANT TO BE A HERO, MARGARITA.
YOU HAVE TO CALL ME RITA NOW.
THEY CHANGED YOUR NAME TOO?
"CANSINO" BECAME "HAYWORTH." MORE STYLISH. HOW DO I LOOK?
YOU MAKE A GOOD REDHEAD.

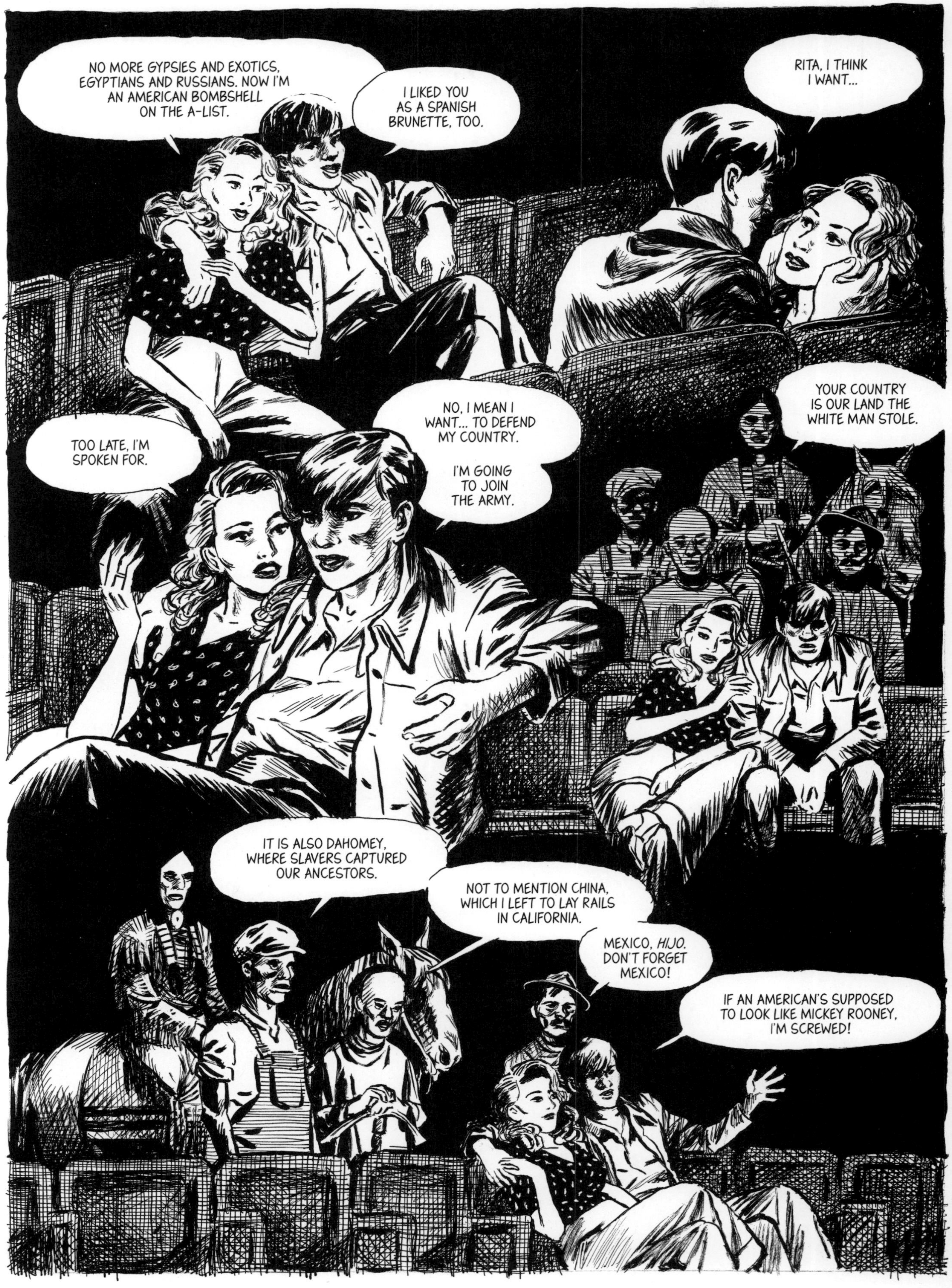
NO MORE GYPSIES AND EXOTICS, EGYPTIANS AND RUSSIANS. NOW I'M AN AMERICAN BOMBSHELL ON THE A-LIST.
I LIKED YOU AS A SPANISH BRUNETTE, TOO.
RITA, I THINK I WANT...
TOO LATE, I'M SPOKEN FOR.
NO, I MEAN I WANT... TO DEFEND MY COUNTRY.
I'M GOING TO JOIN THE ARMY.
YOUR COUNTRY IS OUR LAND THE WHITE MAN STOLE.
IT IS ALSO DAHOMEY, WHERE SLAVERS CAPTURED OUR ANCESTORS.
NOT TO MENTION CHINA, WHICH I LEFT TO LAY RAILS IN CALIFORNIA.
MEXICO, *HIJO*. DON'T FORGET MEXICO!
IF AN AMERICAN'S SUPPOSED TO LOOK LIKE MICKEY ROONEY, I'M SCREWED!

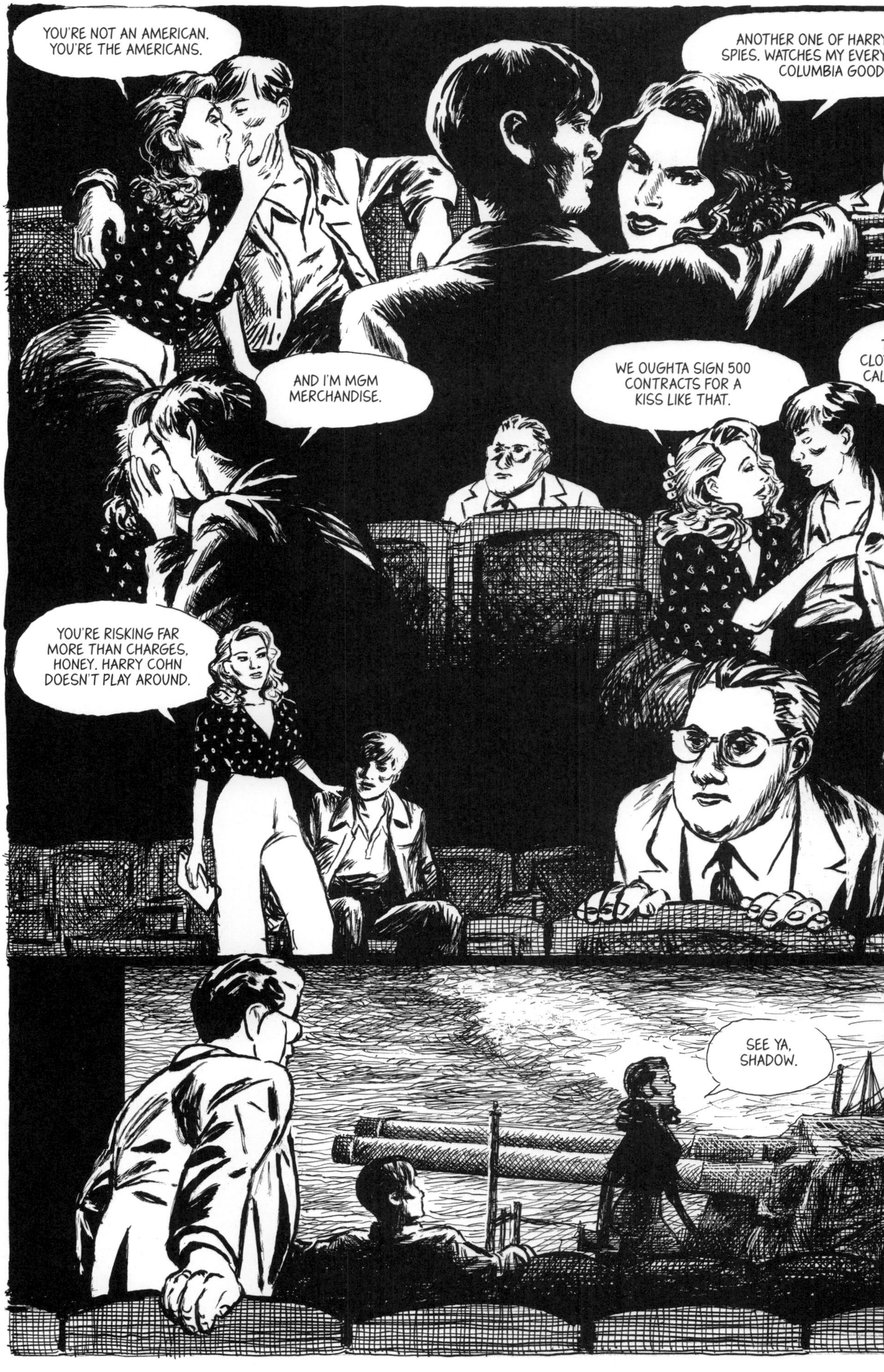
YOU'RE NOT AN AMERICAN. YOU'RE THE AMERICANS.
ANOTHER ONE OF HARRY COHN'S SPIES. WATCHES MY EVERY MOVE. I'M COLUMBIA GOODS.
AND I'M MGM MERCHANDISE.
WE OUGHTA SIGN 500 CONTRACTS FOR A KISS LIKE THAT.
TAKE YOUR CLOTHES OFF. I'LL CALL MY AGENT.
YOU'RE RISKING FAR MORE THAN CHARGES, HONEY. HARRY COHN DOESN'T PLAY AROUND.
SEE YA, SHADOW.

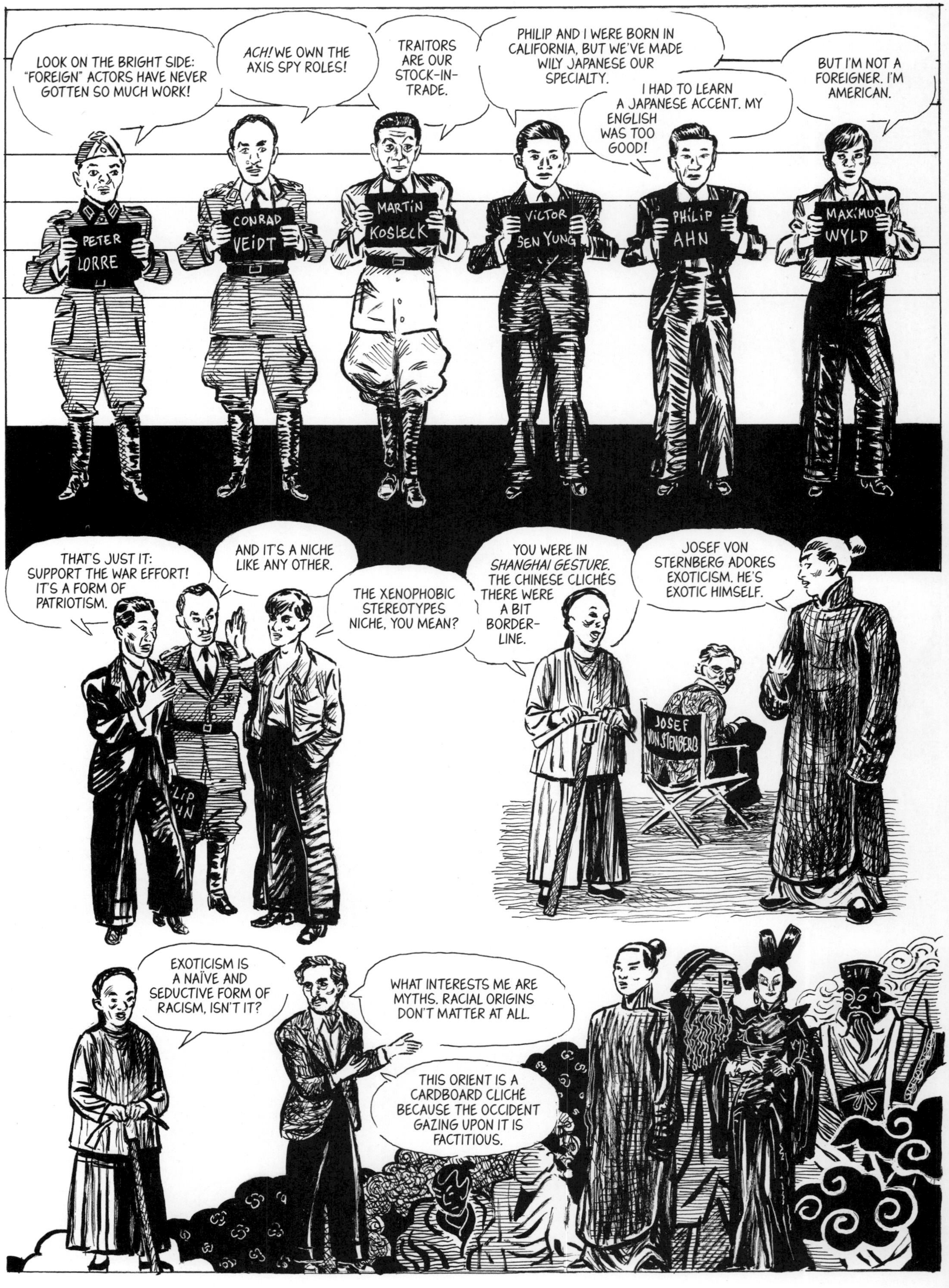

LOOK ON THE BRIGHT SIDE: "FOREIGN" ACTORS HAVE NEVER GOTTEN SO MUCH WORK!
ACH! WE OWN THE AXIS SPY ROLES!
TRAITORS ARE OUR STOCK-IN-TRADE.
PHILIP AND I WERE BORN IN CALIFORNIA, BUT WE'VE MADE WILY JAPANESE OUR SPECIALTY.
I HAD TO LEARN A JAPANESE ACCENT. MY ENGLISH WAS TOO GOOD!
BUT I'M NOT A FOREIGNER. I'M AMERICAN.
PETER LORRE
CONRAD VEIDT
MARTIN KOSLECK
VICTOR SEN YUNG
PHILIP AHN
MAXIMUS WYLD
THAT'S JUST IT: SUPPORT THE WAR EFFORT! IT'S A FORM OF PATRIOTISM.
AND IT'S A NICHE LIKE ANY OTHER.
THE XENOPHOBIC STEREOTYPES NICHE, YOU MEAN?
YOU WERE IN SHANGHAI GESTURE. THE CHINESE CLICHÉS THERE WERE A BIT BORDER-LINE.
JOSEF VON STERNBERG ADORES EXOTICISM. HE'S EXOTIC HIMSELF.
JOSEF VON STENBERG
EXOTICISM IS A NAÏVE AND SEDUCTIVE FORM OF RACISM, ISN'T IT?
WHAT INTERESTS ME ARE MYTHS. RACIAL ORIGINS DON'T MATTER AT ALL.
THIS ORIENT IS A CARDBOARD CLICHÉ BECAUSE THE OCCIDENT GAZING UPON IT IS FACTITIOUS.

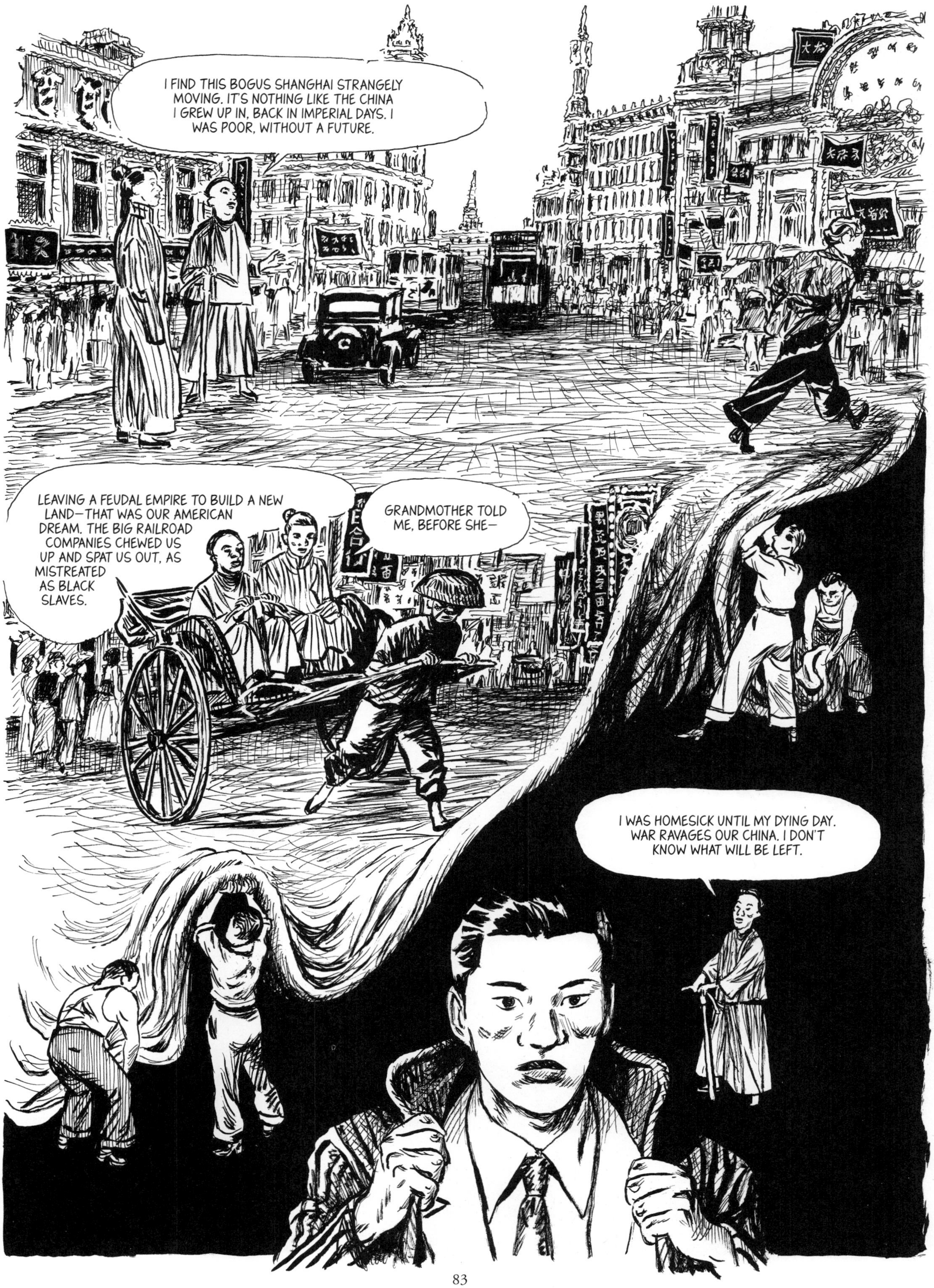
I FIND THIS BOGUS SHANGHAI STRANGELY MOVING. IT'S NOTHING LIKE THE CHINA I GREW UP IN, BACK IN IMPERIAL DAYS. I WAS POOR, WITHOUT A FUTURE.
LEAVING A FEUDAL EMPIRE TO BUILD A NEW LAND—THAT WAS OUR AMERICAN DREAM. THE BIG RAILROAD COMPANIES CHEWED US UP AND SPAT US OUT, AS MISTREATED AS BLACK SLAVES.
GRANDMOTHER TOLD ME, BEFORE SHE—
I WAS HOMESICK UNTIL MY DYING DAY. WAR RAVAGES OUR CHINA. I DON'T KNOW WHAT WILL BE LEFT.

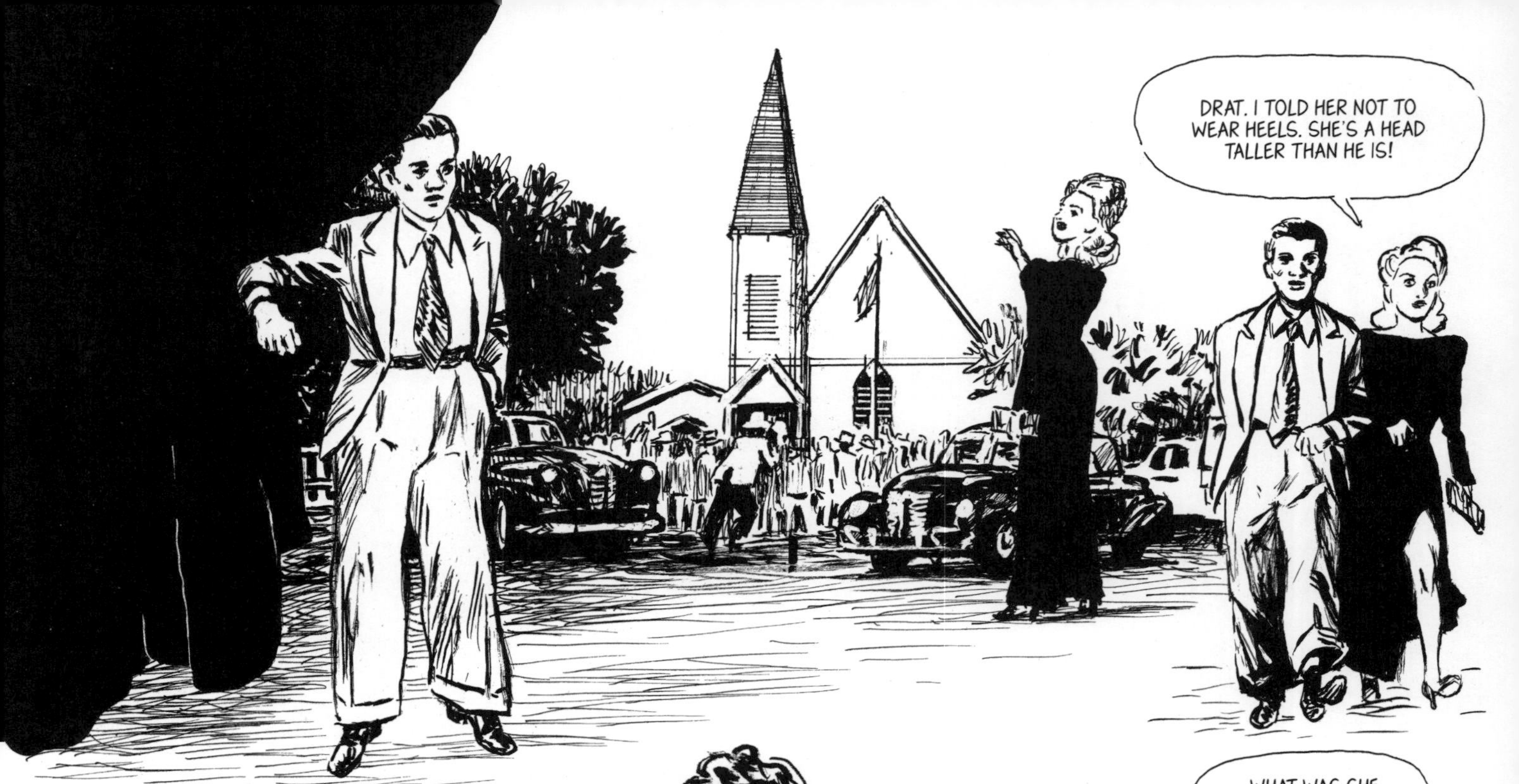
DRAT. I TOLD HER NOT TO WEAR HEELS. SHE'S A HEAD TALLER THAN HE IS!

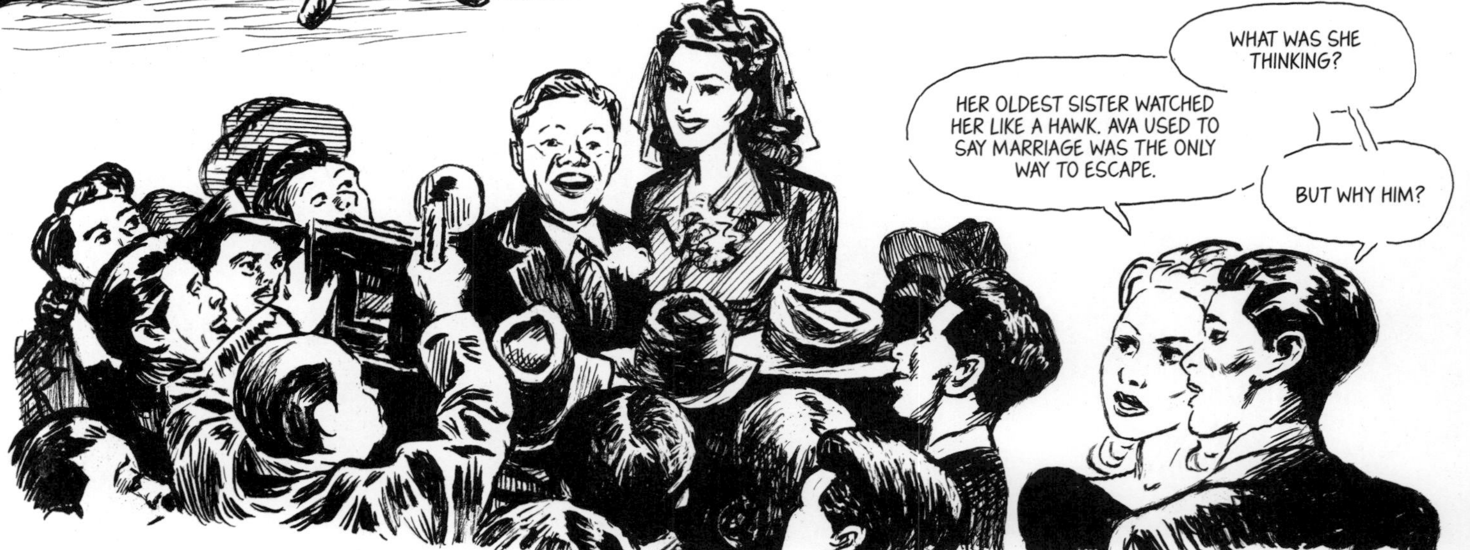
WHAT WAS SHE THINKING?
HER OLDEST SISTER WATCHED HER LIKE A HAWK. AVA USED TO SAY MARRIAGE WAS THE ONLY WAY TO ESCAPE.
BUT WHY HIM?

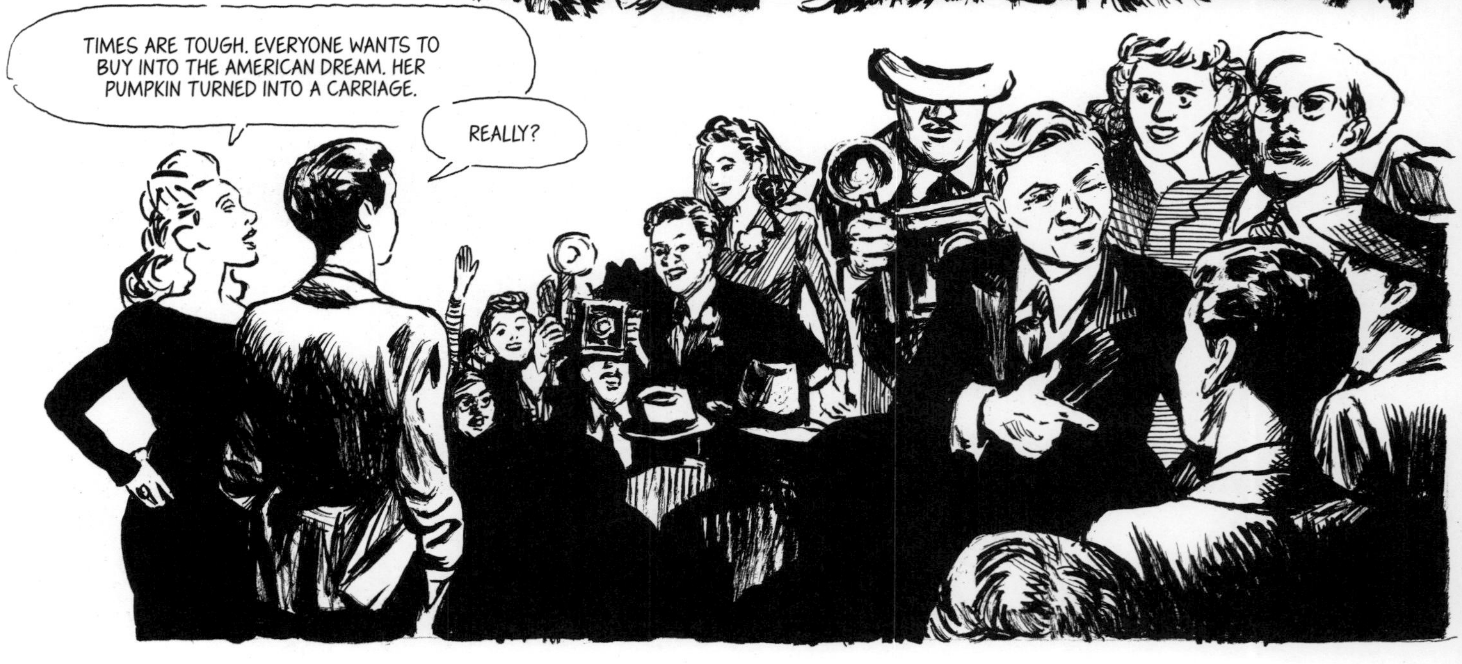
TIMES ARE TOUGH. EVERYONE WANTS TO BUY INTO THE AMERICAN DREAM. HER PUMPKIN TURNED INTO A CARRIAGE.
REALLY?

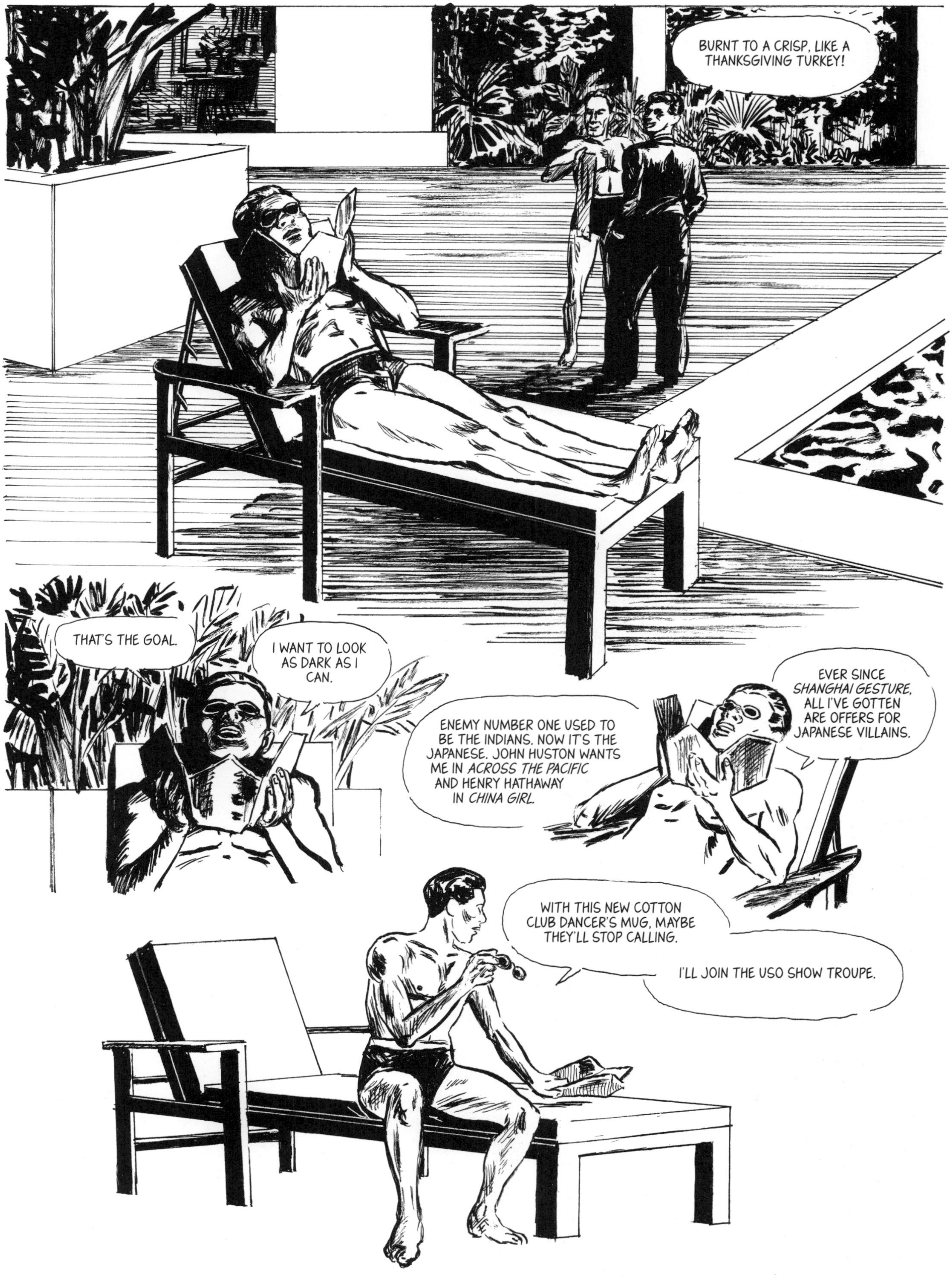

BURNT TO A CRISP, LIKE A THANKSGIVING TURKEY!
THAT'S THE GOAL.
I WANT TO LOOK AS DARK AS I CAN.
ENEMY NUMBER ONE USED TO BE THE INDIANS. NOW IT'S THE JAPANESE. JOHN HUSTON WANTS ME IN *ACROSS THE PACIFIC* AND HENRY HATHAWAY IN *CHINA GIRL.*
EVER SINCE *SHANGHAI GESTURE,* ALL I'VE GOTTEN ARE OFFERS FOR JAPANESE VILLAINS.
WITH THIS NEW COTTON CLUB DANCER'S MUG, MAYBE THEY'LL STOP CALLING.
I'LL JOIN THE USO SHOW TROUPE.

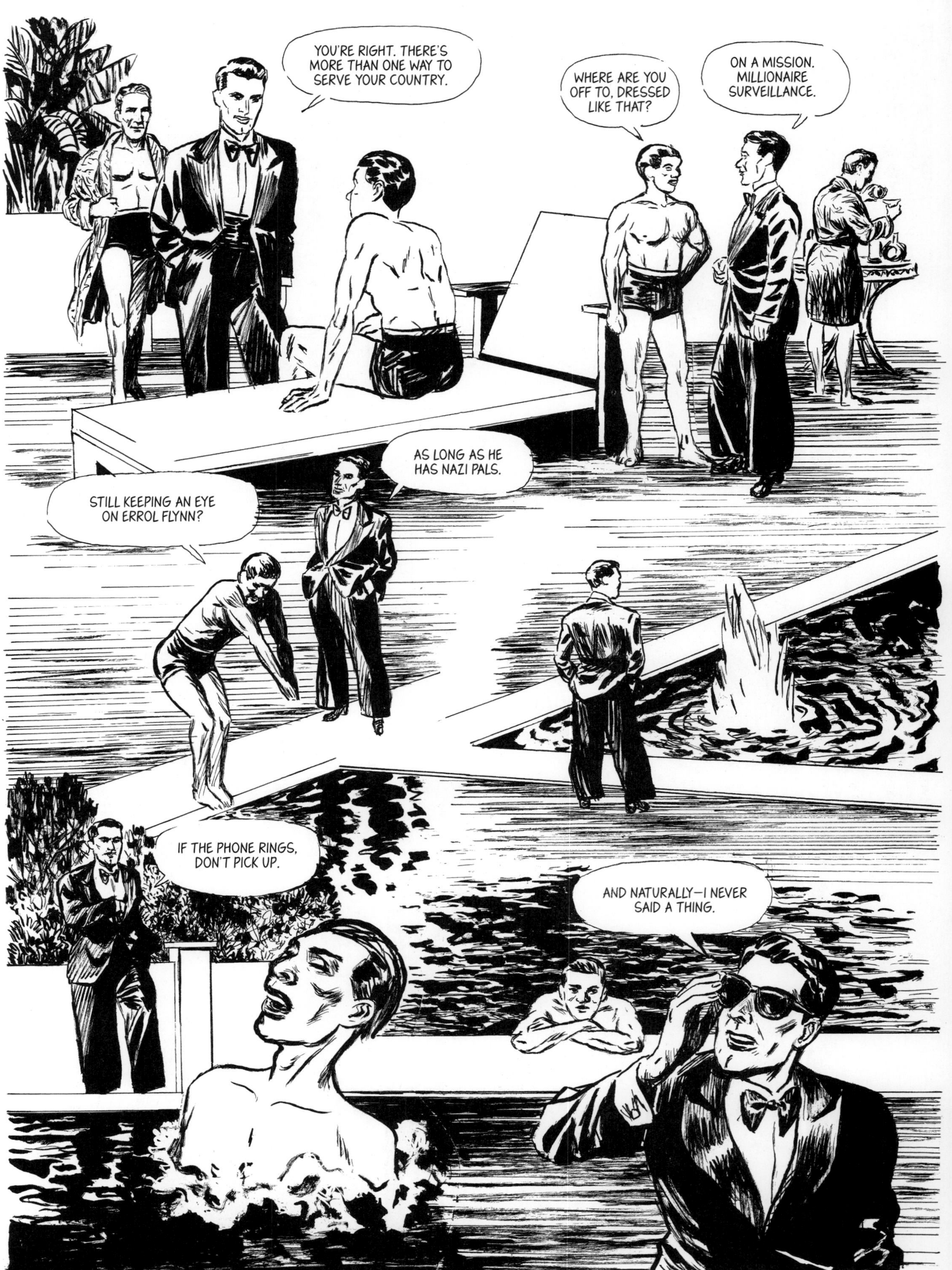
YOU'RE RIGHT. THERE'S MORE THAN ONE WAY TO SERVE YOUR COUNTRY.
WHERE ARE YOU OFF TO, DRESSED LIKE THAT?
ON A MISSION. MILLIONAIRE SURVEILLANCE.
STILL KEEPING AN EYE ON ERROL FLYNN?
AS LONG AS HE HAS NAZI PALS.
IF THE PHONE RINGS, DON'T PICK UP.
AND NATURALLY—I NEVER SAID A THING.

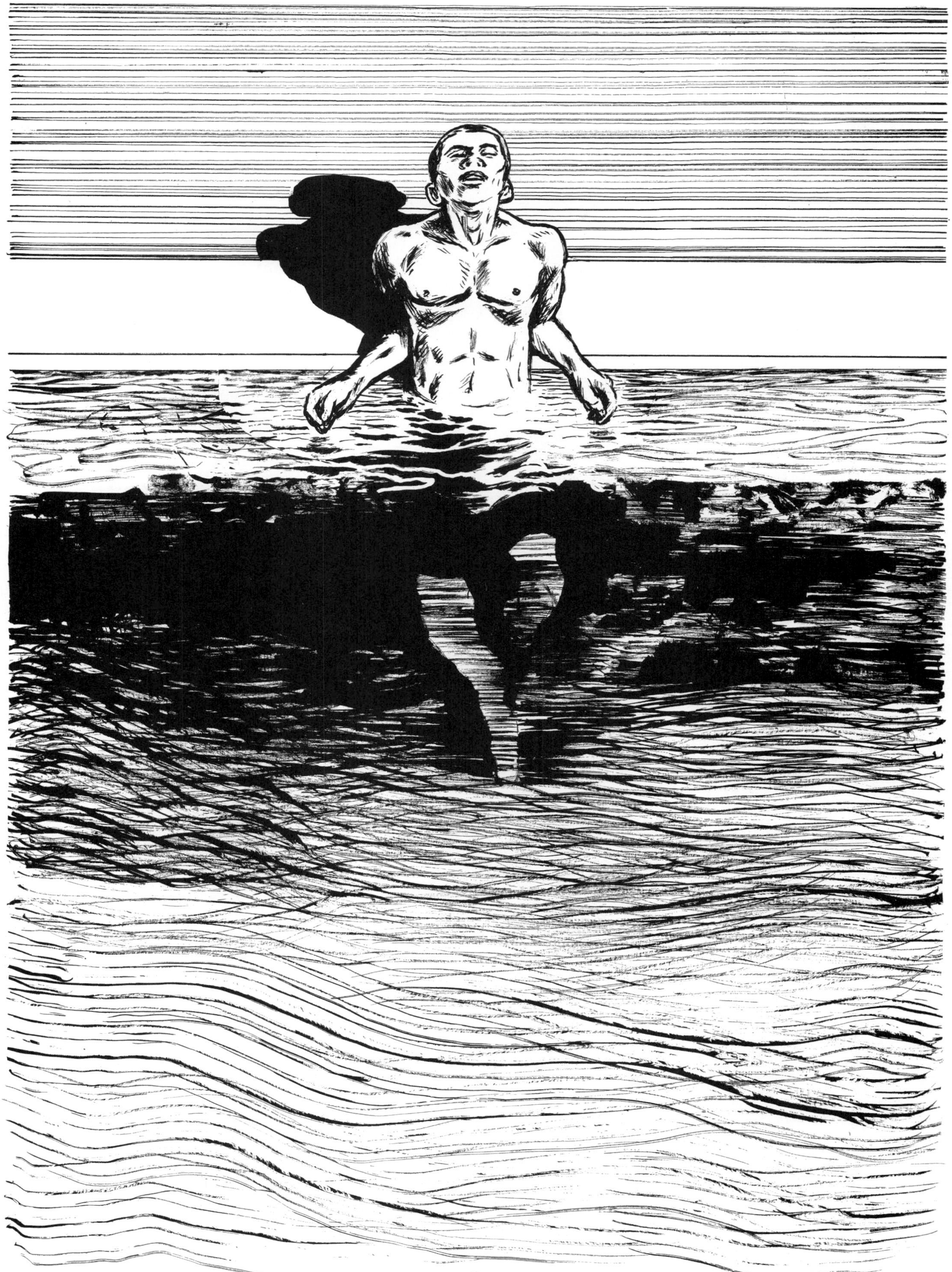

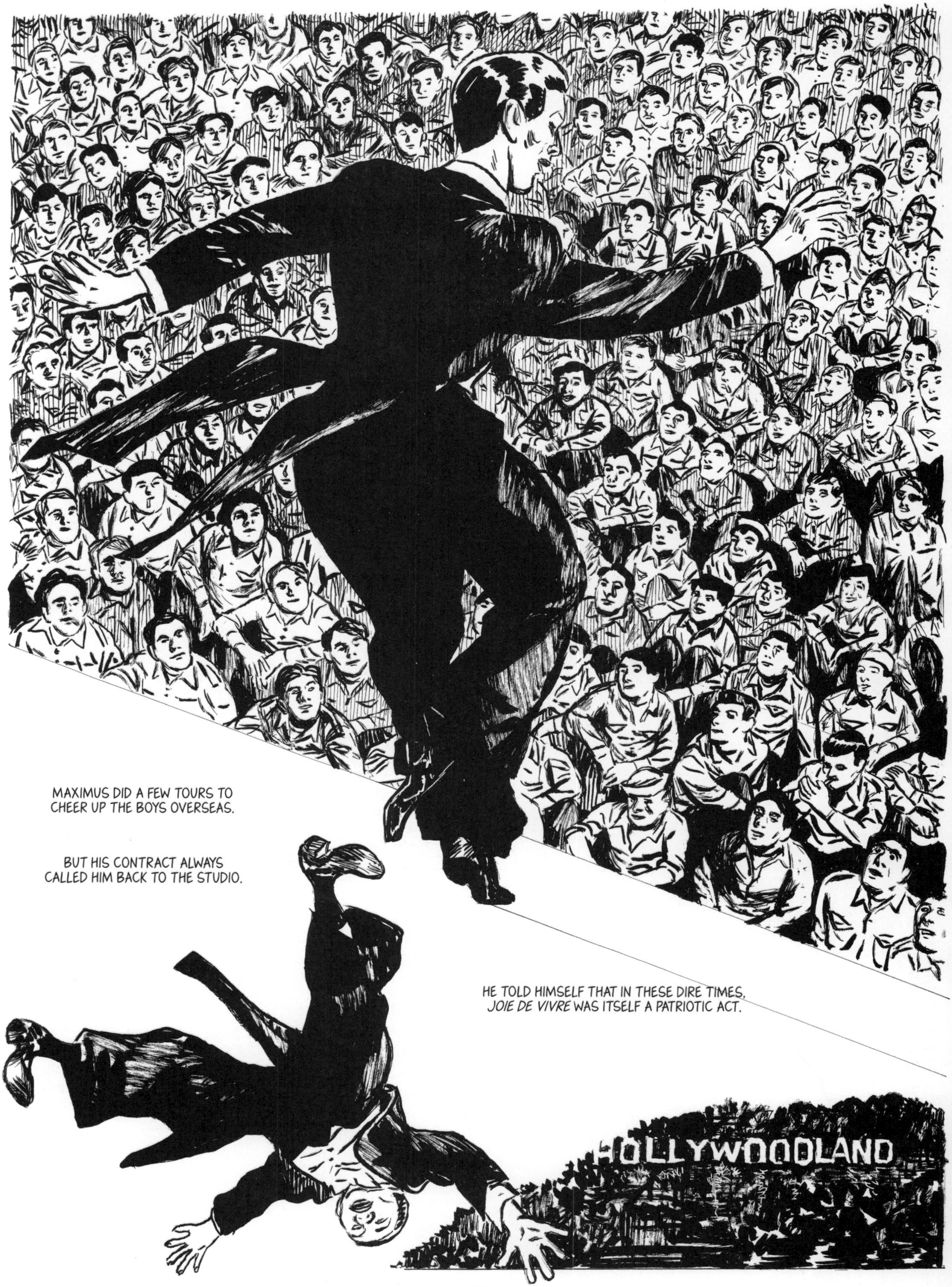
MAXIMUS DID A FEW TOURS TO CHEER UP THE BOYS OVERSEAS.
BUT HIS CONTRACT ALWAYS CALLED HIM BACK TO THE STUDIO.
HE TOLD HIMSELF THAT IN THESE DIRE TIMES, *JOIE DE VIVRE* WAS ITSELF A PATRIOTIC ACT.
HOLLYWOODLAND

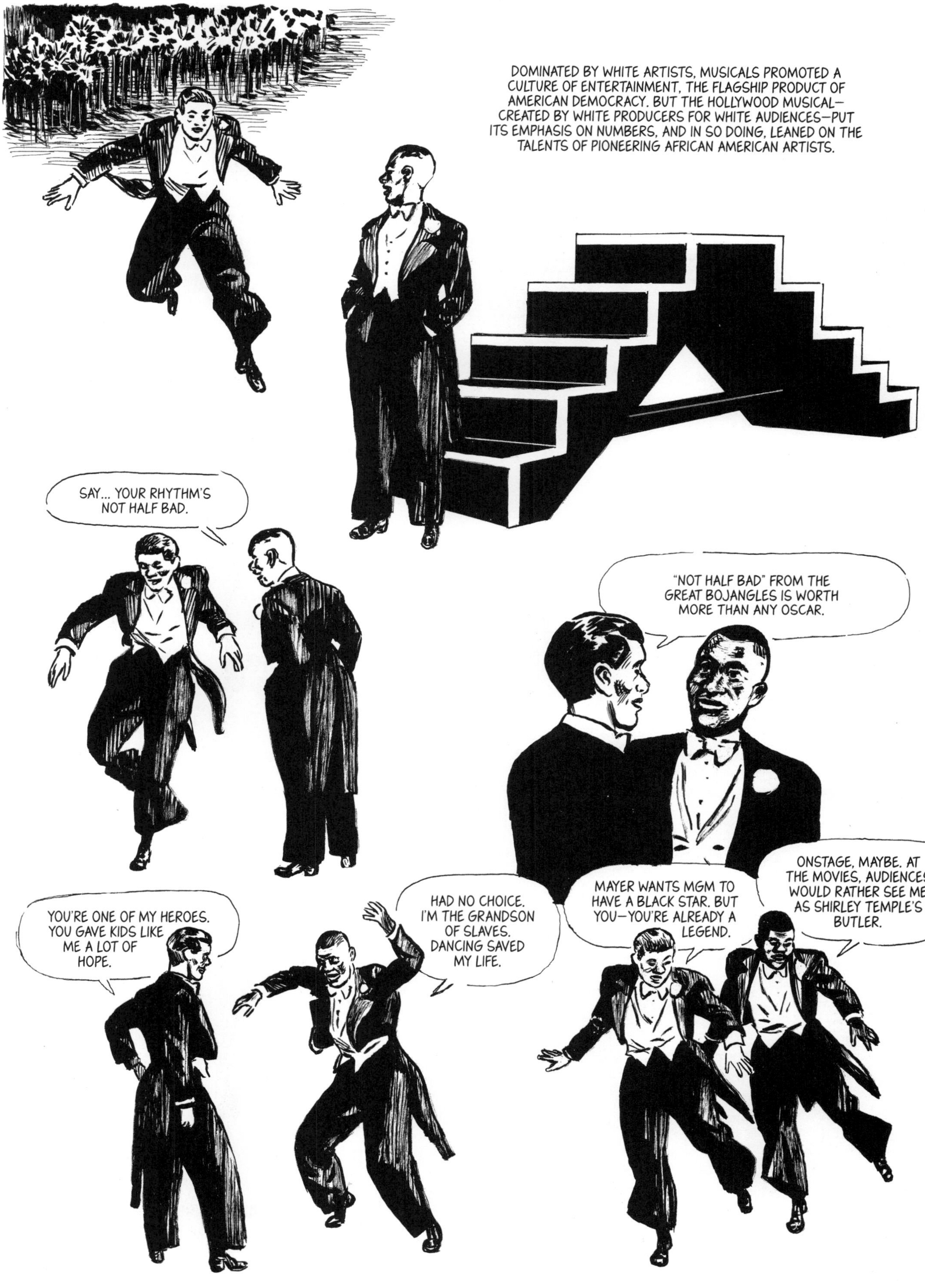
DOMINATED BY WHITE ARTISTS, MUSICALS PROMOTED A CULTURE OF ENTERTAINMENT, THE FLAGSHIP PRODUCT OF AMERICAN DEMOCRACY. BUT THE HOLLYWOOD MUSICAL—CREATED BY WHITE PRODUCERS FOR WHITE AUDIENCES—PUT ITS EMPHASIS ON NUMBERS, AND IN SO DOING, LEANED ON THE TALENTS OF PIONEERING AFRICAN AMERICAN ARTISTS.
SAY... YOUR RHYTHM'S NOT HALF BAD.
"NOT HALF BAD" FROM THE GREAT BOJANGLES IS WORTH MORE THAN ANY OSCAR.
YOU'RE ONE OF MY HEROES. YOU GAVE KIDS LIKE ME A LOT OF HOPE.
HAD NO CHOICE. I'M THE GRANDSON OF SLAVES. DANCING SAVED MY LIFE.
MAYER WANTS MGM TO HAVE A BLACK STAR. BUT YOU—YOU'RE ALREADY A LEGEND.
ONSTAGE, MAYBE. AT THE MOVIES, AUDIENCES WOULD RATHER SEE ME AS SHIRLEY TEMPLE'S BUTLER.

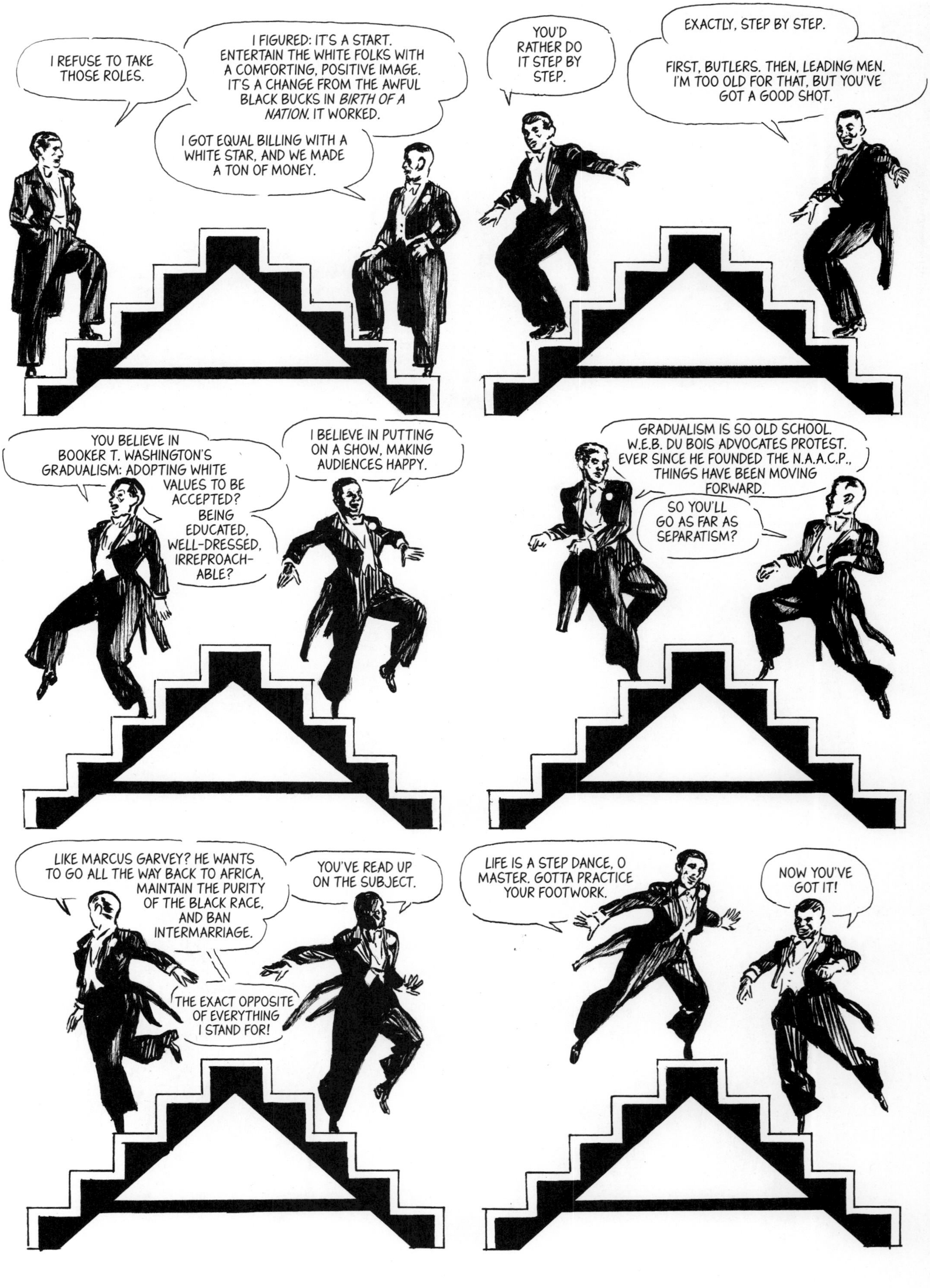
I REFUSE TO TAKE THOSE ROLES.
I FIGURED: IT'S A START. ENTERTAIN THE WHITE FOLKS WITH A COMFORTING, POSITIVE IMAGE. IT'S A CHANGE FROM THE AWFUL BLACK BUCKS IN *BIRTH OF A NATION*. IT WORKED.
I GOT EQUAL BILLING WITH A WHITE STAR, AND WE MADE A TON OF MONEY.
YOU'D RATHER DO IT STEP BY STEP.
EXACTLY, STEP BY STEP.
FIRST, BUTLERS. THEN, LEADING MEN. I'M TOO OLD FOR THAT, BUT YOU'VE GOT A GOOD SHOT.
YOU BELIEVE IN BOOKER T. WASHINGTON'S GRADUALISM: ADOPTING WHITE VALUES TO BE ACCEPTED? BEING EDUCATED, WELL-DRESSED, IRREPROACH-ABLE?
I BELIEVE IN PUTTING ON A SHOW, MAKING AUDIENCES HAPPY.
GRADUALISM IS SO OLD SCHOOL. W.E.B. DU BOIS ADVOCATES PROTEST. EVER SINCE HE FOUNDED THE N.A.A.C.P., THINGS HAVE BEEN MOVING FORWARD.
SO YOU'LL GO AS FAR AS SEPARATISM?
LIKE MARCUS GARVEY? HE WANTS TO GO ALL THE WAY BACK TO AFRICA, MAINTAIN THE PURITY OF THE BLACK RACE, AND BAN INTERMARRIAGE.
THE EXACT OPPOSITE OF EVERYTHING I STAND FOR!
YOU'VE READ UP ON THE SUBJECT.
LIFE IS A STEP DANCE, O MASTER. GOTTA PRACTICE YOUR FOOTWORK.
NOW YOU'VE GOT IT!

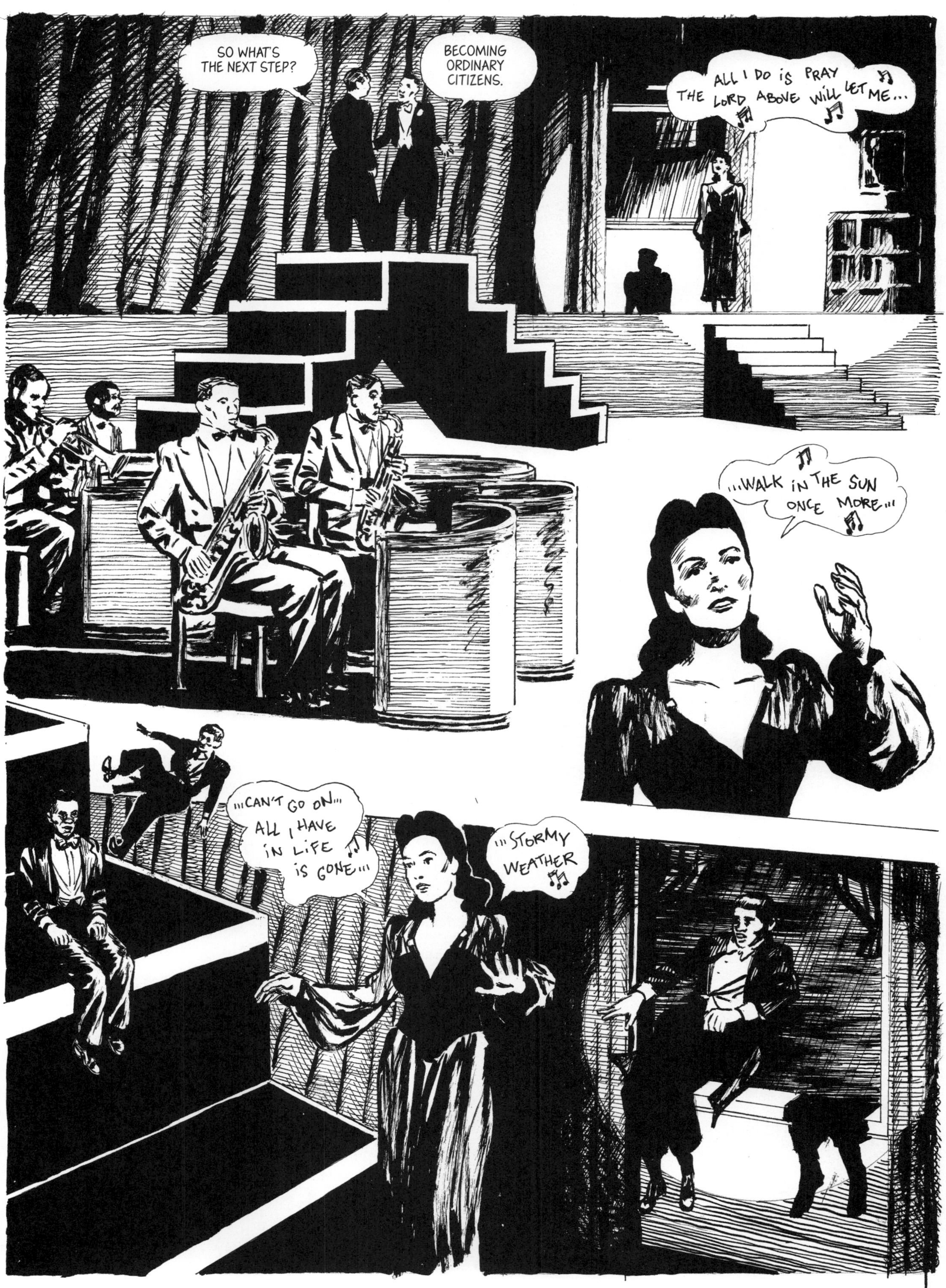
SO WHAT'S THE NEXT STEP?
BECOMING ORDINARY CITIZENS.
ALL I DO IS PRAY THE LORD ABOVE WILL LET ME...
...WALK IN THE SUN ONCE MORE...
...CAN'T GO ON... ALL I HAVE IN LIFE IS GONE...
...STORMY WEATHER

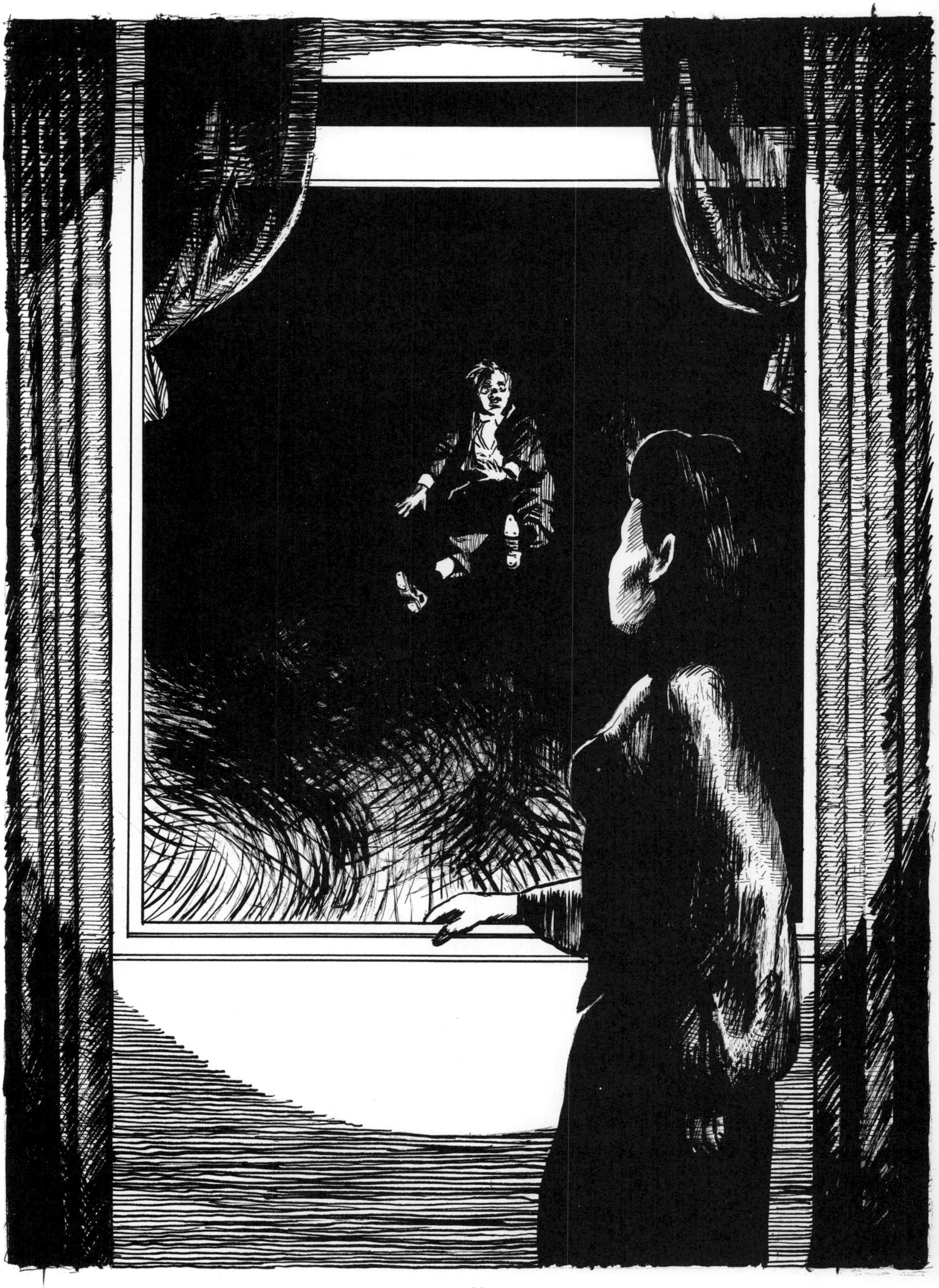

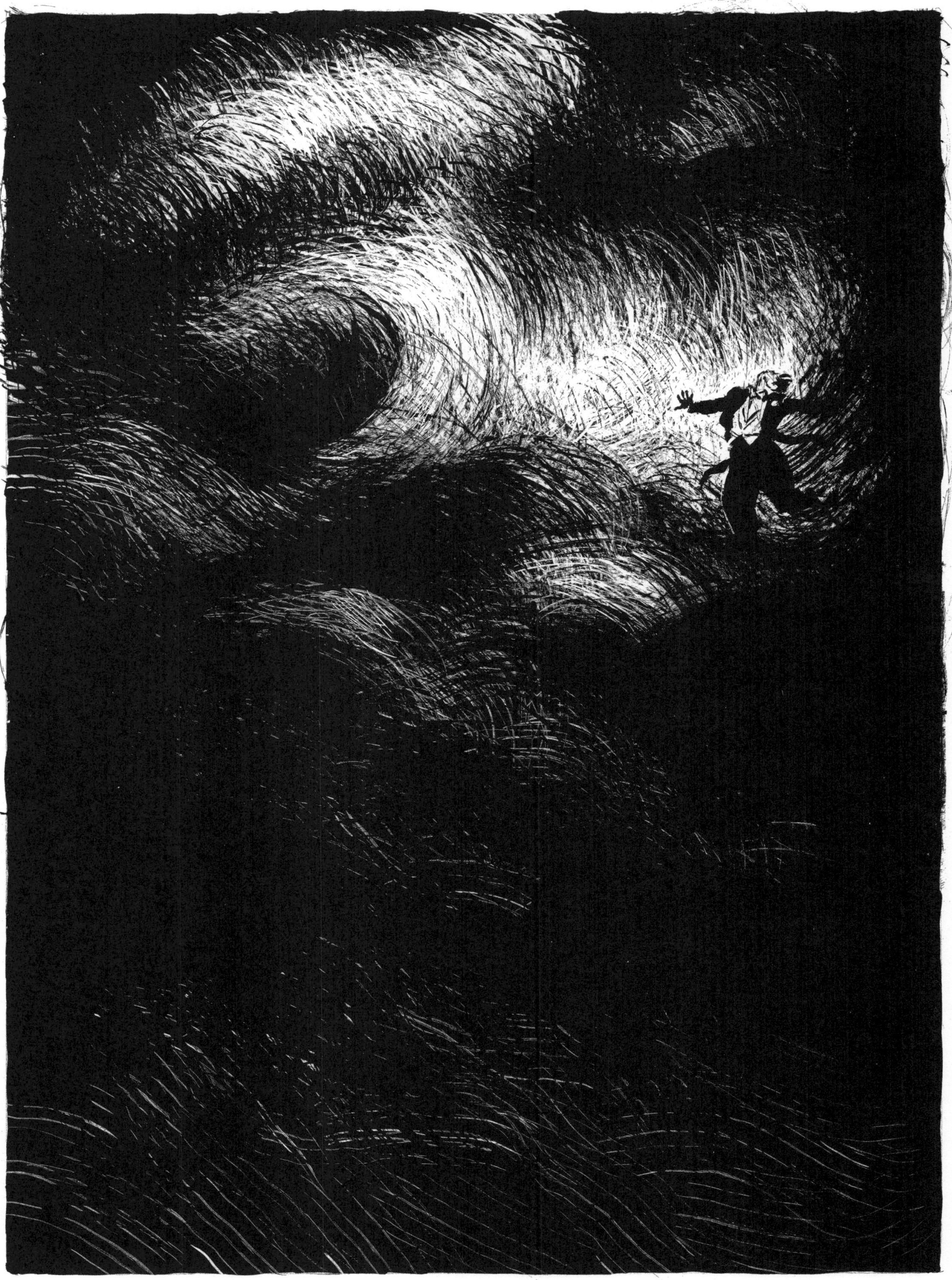

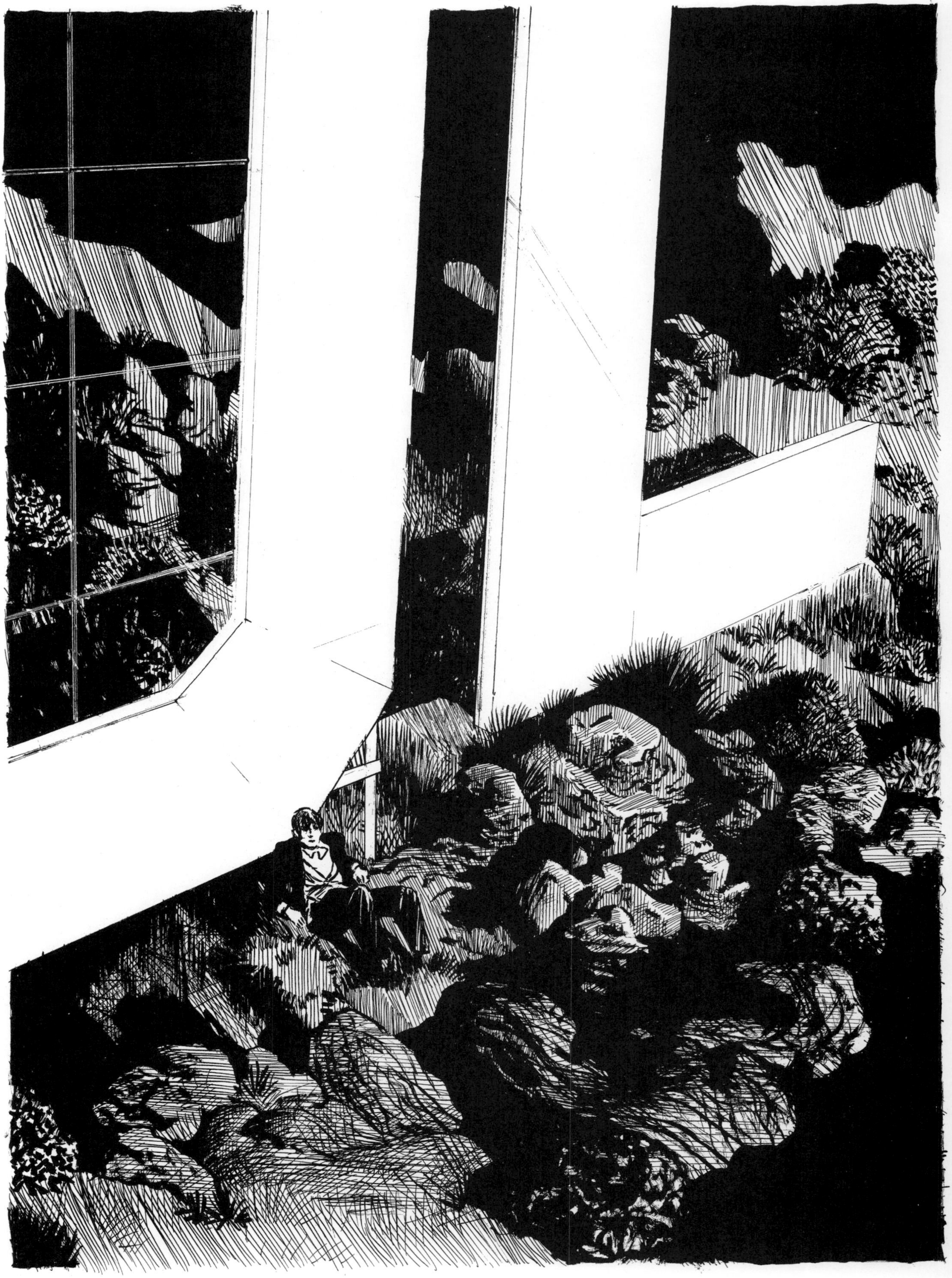

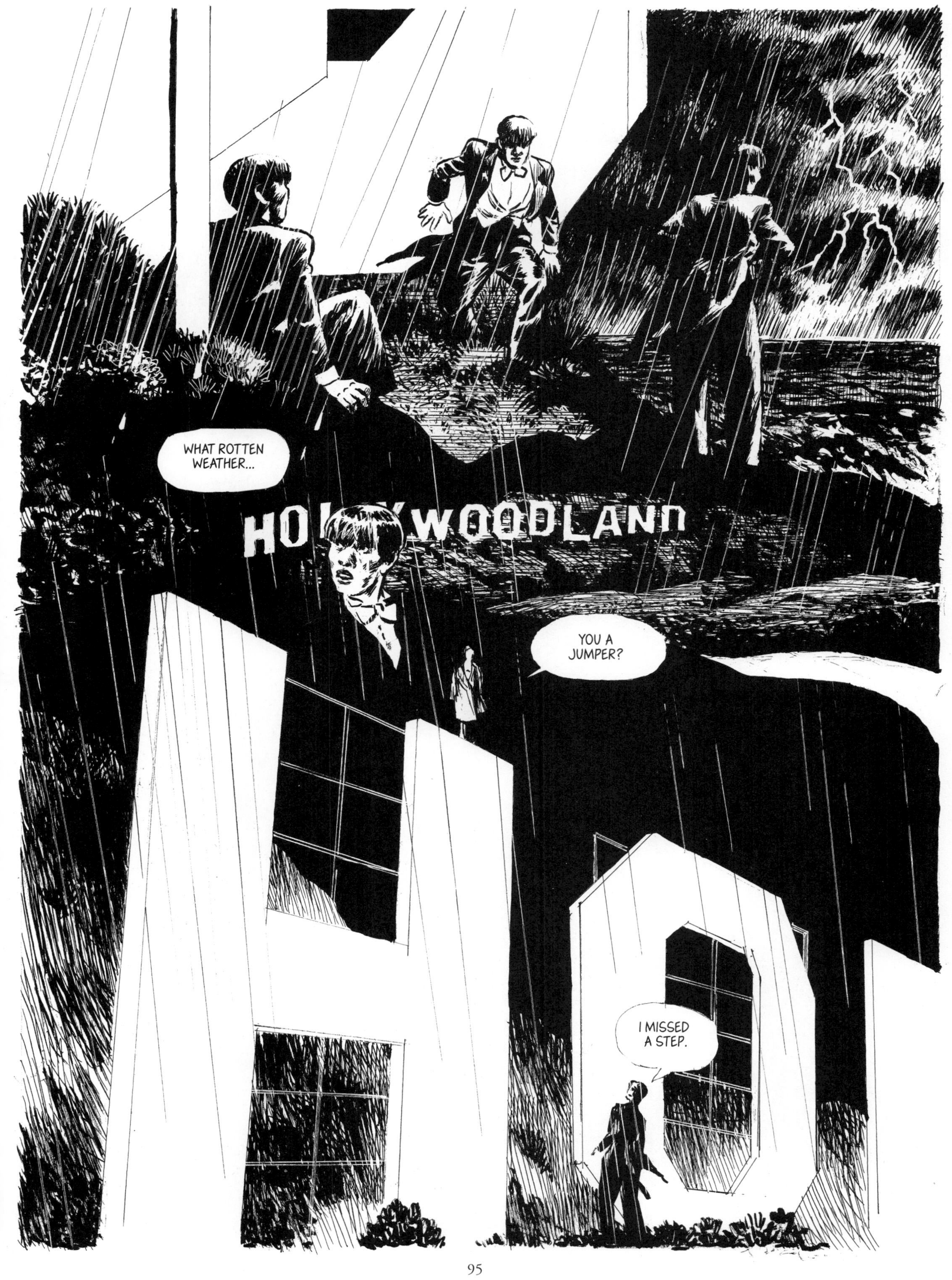
WHAT ROTTEN WEATHER...
HOLLYWOODLAND
YOU A JUMPER?
I MISSED A STEP.

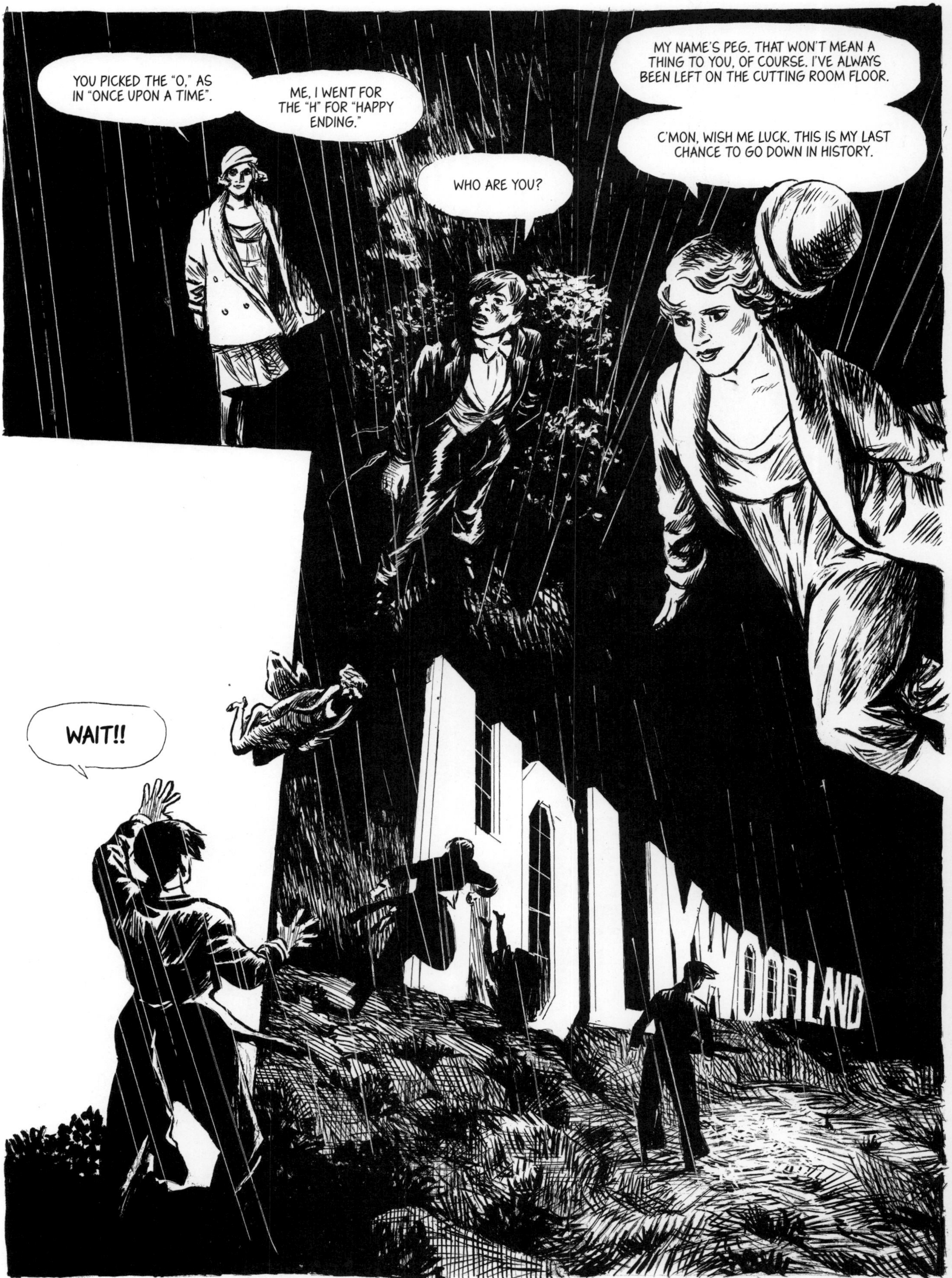
YOU PICKED THE "O," AS IN "ONCE UPON A TIME".
ME, I WENT FOR THE "H" FOR "HAPPY ENDING."
WHO ARE YOU?
MY NAME'S PEG. THAT WON'T MEAN A THING TO YOU, OF COURSE. I'VE ALWAYS BEEN LEFT ON THE CUTTING ROOM FLOOR.
C'MON, WISH ME LUCK. THIS IS MY LAST CHANCE TO GO DOWN IN HISTORY.
WAIT!!
WOODLAND

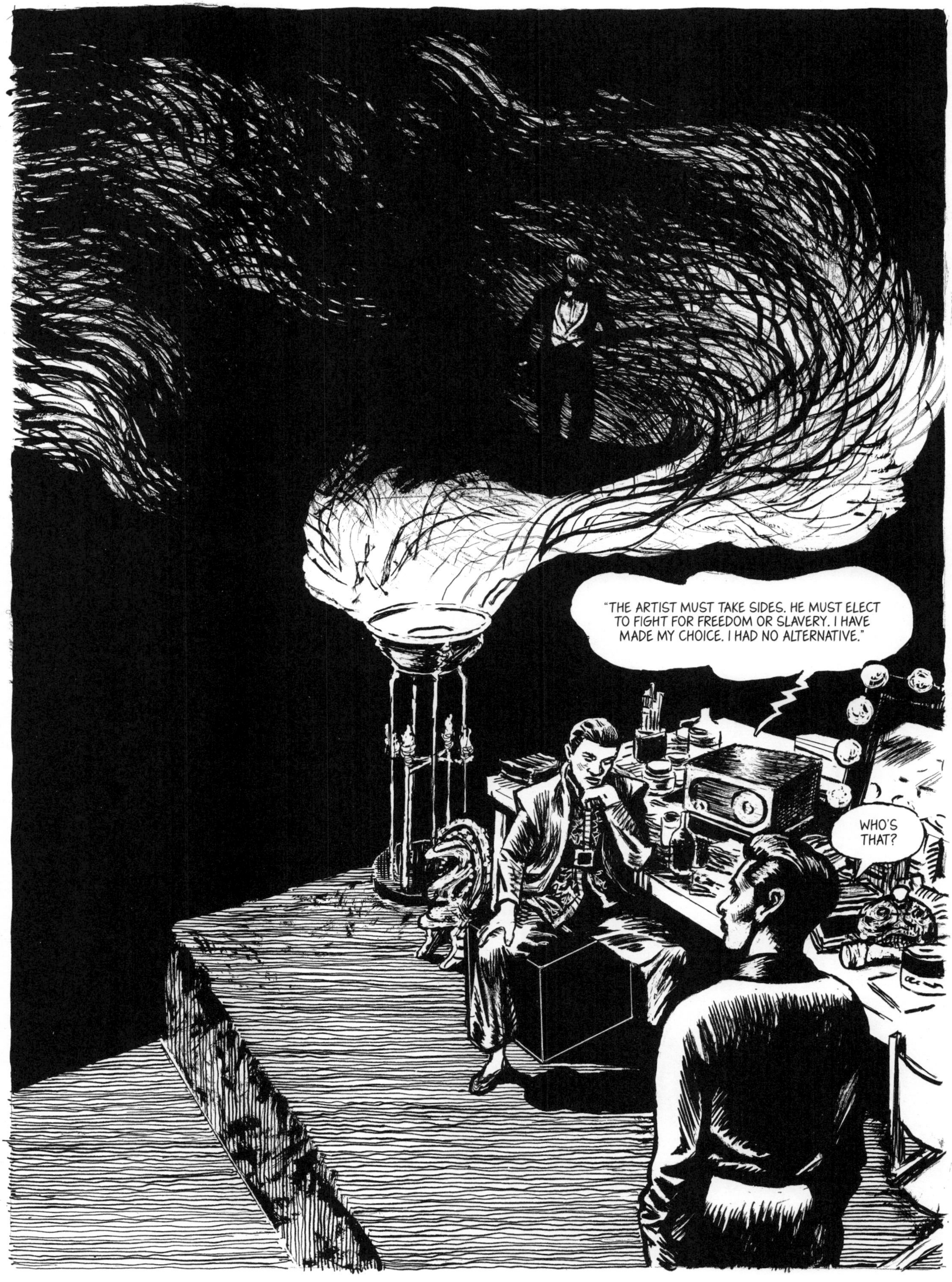
"THE ARTIST MUST TAKE SIDES. HE MUST ELECT TO FIGHT FOR FREEDOM OR SLAVERY. I HAVE MADE MY CHOICE. I HAD NO ALTERNATIVE."
WHO'S THAT?

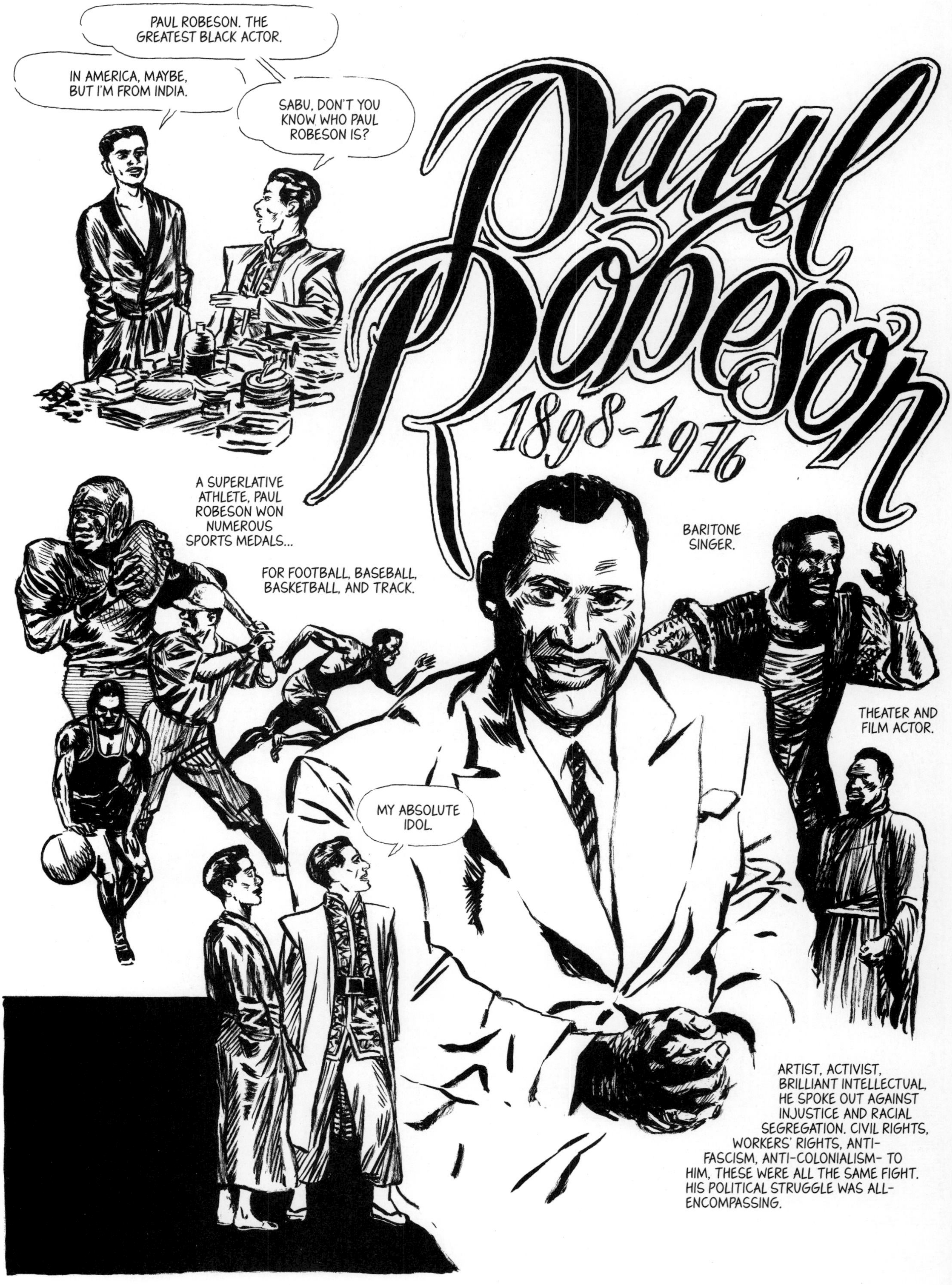
PAUL ROBESON. THE GREATEST BLACK ACTOR.
IN AMERICA, MAYBE, BUT I'M FROM INDIA.
SABU, DON'T YOU KNOW WHO PAUL ROBESON IS?
Paul Robeson
1898-1976
A SUPERLATIVE ATHLETE, PAUL ROBESON WON NUMEROUS SPORTS MEDALS...
FOR FOOTBALL, BASEBALL, BASKETBALL, AND TRACK.
BARITONE SINGER.
THEATER AND FILM ACTOR.
MY ABSOLUTE IDOL.
ARTIST, ACTIVIST, BRILLIANT INTELLECTUAL, HE SPOKE OUT AGAINST INJUSTICE AND RACIAL SEGREGATION. CIVIL RIGHTS, WORKERS' RIGHTS, ANTI-FASCISM, ANTI-COLONIALISM– TO HIM, THESE WERE ALL THE SAME FIGHT. HIS POLITICAL STRUGGLE WAS ALL-ENCOMPASSING.

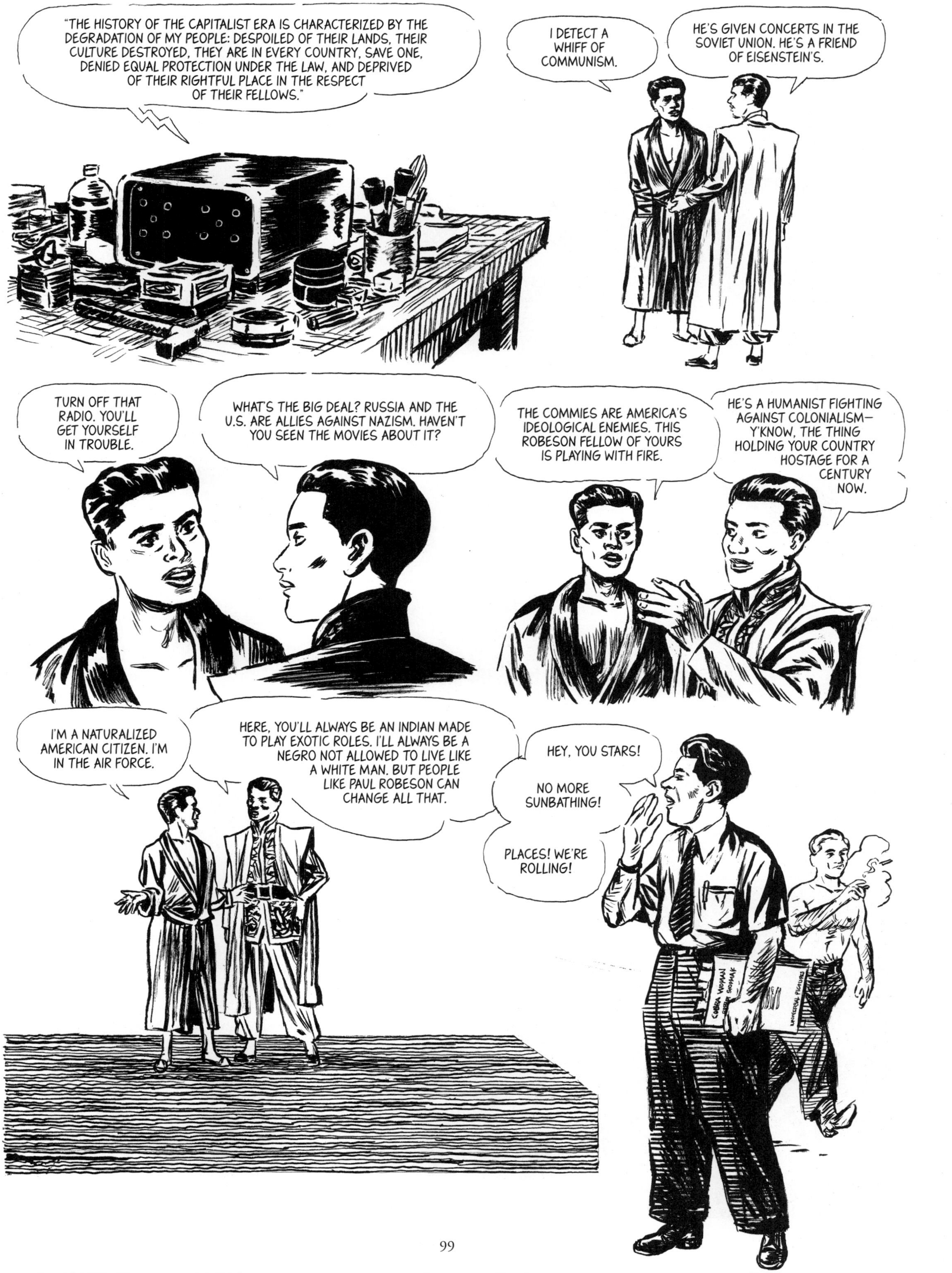
"THE HISTORY OF THE CAPITALIST ERA IS CHARACTERIZED BY THE DEGRADATION OF MY PEOPLE: DESPOILED OF THEIR LANDS, THEIR CULTURE DESTROYED, THEY ARE IN EVERY COUNTRY, SAVE ONE, DENIED EQUAL PROTECTION UNDER THE LAW, AND DEPRIVED OF THEIR RIGHTFUL PLACE IN THE RESPECT OF THEIR FELLOWS."
I DETECT A WHIFF OF COMMUNISM.
HE'S GIVEN CONCERTS IN THE SOVIET UNION. HE'S A FRIEND OF EISENSTEIN'S.
TURN OFF THAT RADIO. YOU'LL GET YOURSELF IN TROUBLE.
WHAT'S THE BIG DEAL? RUSSIA AND THE U.S. ARE ALLIES AGAINST NAZISM. HAVEN'T YOU SEEN THE MOVIES ABOUT IT?
THE COMMIES ARE AMERICA'S IDEOLOGICAL ENEMIES. THIS ROBESON FELLOW OF YOURS IS PLAYING WITH FIRE.
HE'S A HUMANIST FIGHTING AGAINST COLONIALISM— Y'KNOW, THE THING HOLDING YOUR COUNTRY HOSTAGE FOR A CENTURY NOW.
I'M A NATURALIZED AMERICAN CITIZEN. I'M IN THE AIR FORCE.
HERE, YOU'LL ALWAYS BE AN INDIAN MADE TO PLAY EXOTIC ROLES. I'LL ALWAYS BE A NEGRO NOT ALLOWED TO LIVE LIKE A WHITE MAN. BUT PEOPLE LIKE PAUL ROBESON CAN CHANGE ALL THAT.
HEY, YOU STARS!
NO MORE SUNBATHING!
PLACES! WE'RE ROLLING!
COBRA WOMAN
SIODMAK
UNIVERSAL PICTURES

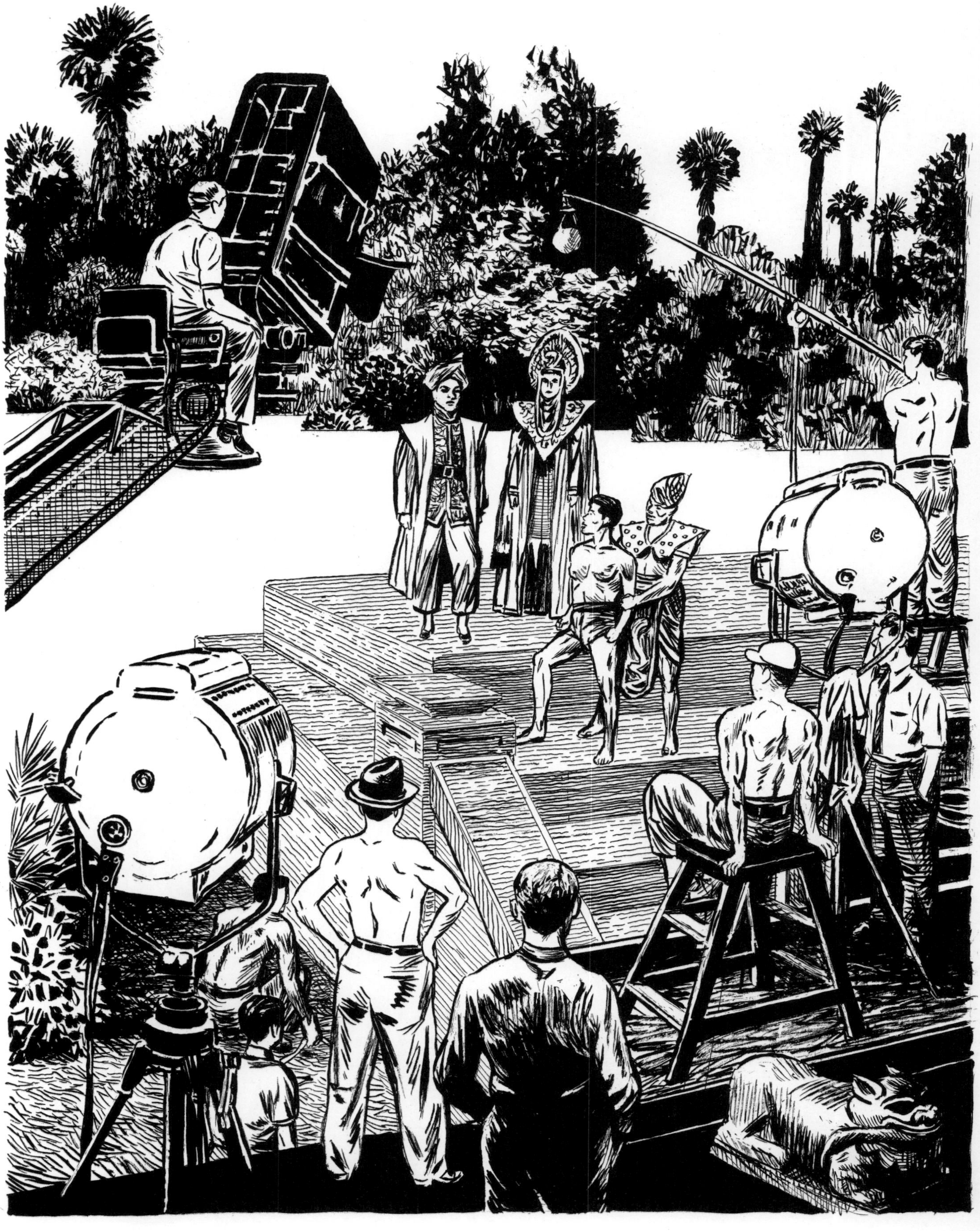

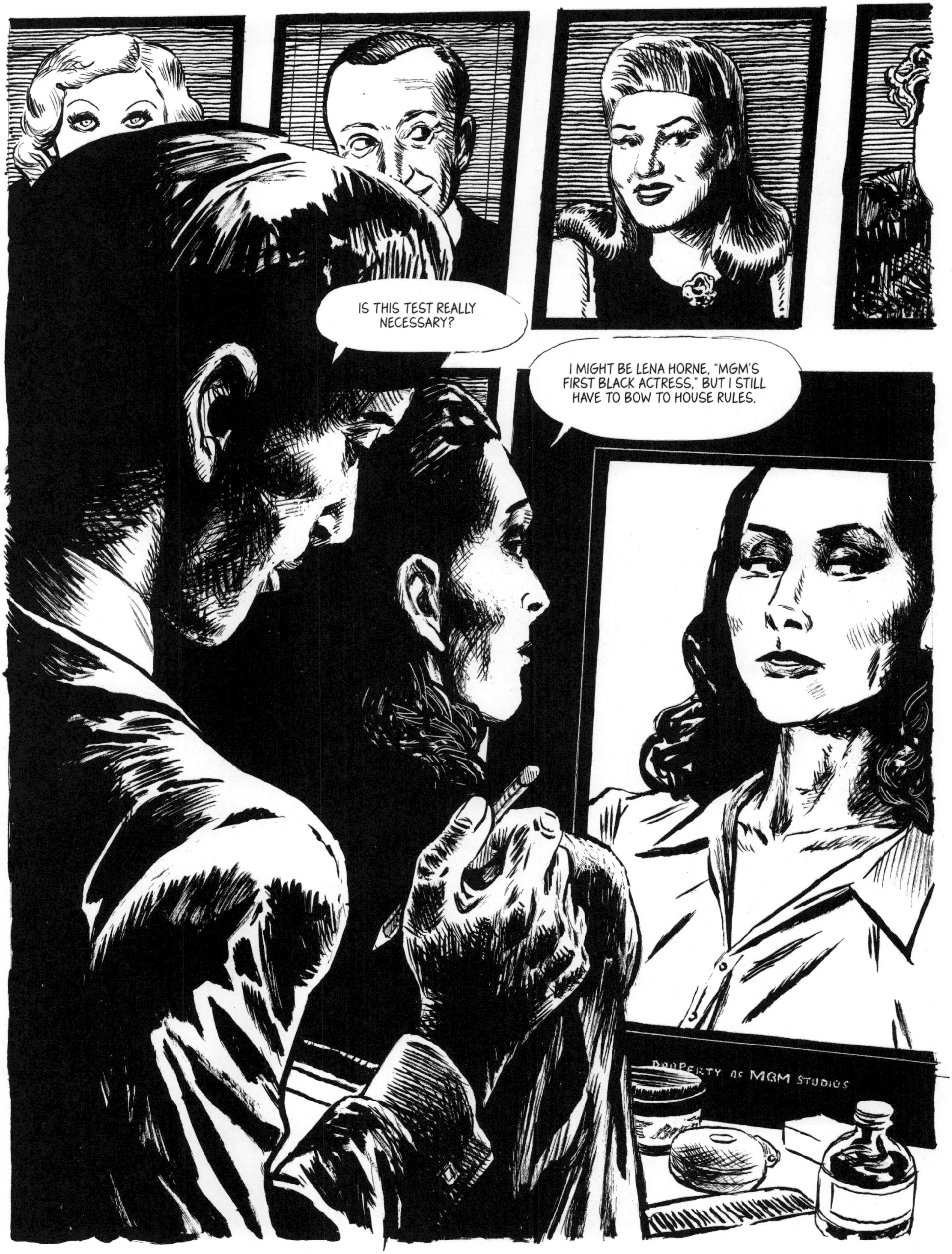
IS THIS TEST REALLY NECESSARY?
I MIGHT BE LENA HORNE, "MGM'S FIRST BLACK ACTRESS," BUT I STILL HAVE TO BOW TO HOUSE RULES.
PROPERTY OF MGM STUDIOS

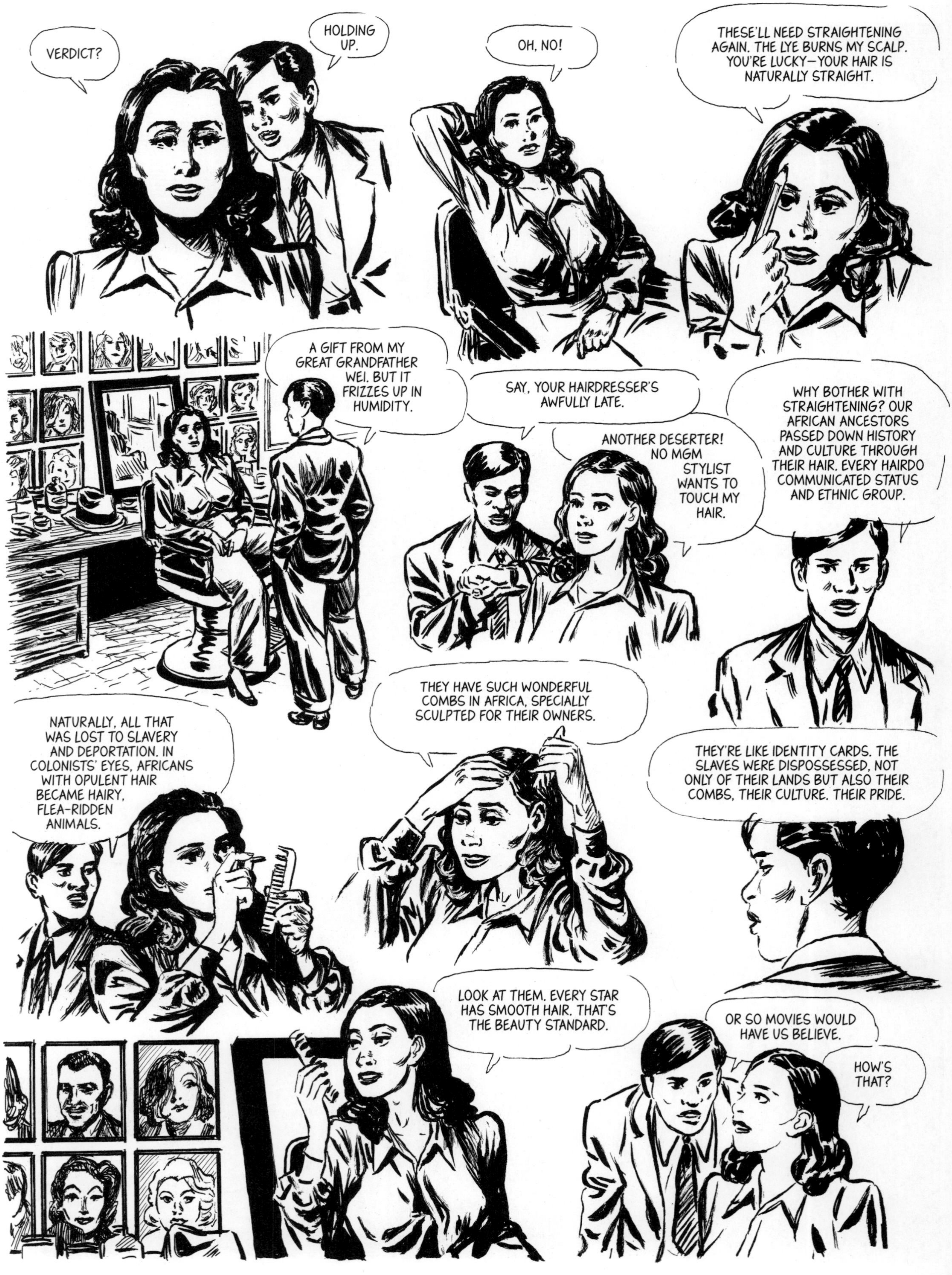
VERDICT?
HOLDING UP.
OH, NO!
THESE'LL NEED STRAIGHTENING AGAIN. THE LYE BURNS MY SCALP. YOU'RE LUCKY—YOUR HAIR IS NATURALLY STRAIGHT.
A GIFT FROM MY GREAT GRANDFATHER WEI. BUT IT FRIZZES UP IN HUMIDITY.
SAY, YOUR HAIRDRESSER'S AWFULLY LATE.
ANOTHER DESERTER! NO MGM STYLIST WANTS TO TOUCH MY HAIR.
WHY BOTHER WITH STRAIGHTENING? OUR AFRICAN ANCESTORS PASSED DOWN HISTORY AND CULTURE THROUGH THEIR HAIR. EVERY HAIRDO COMMUNICATED STATUS AND ETHNIC GROUP.
NATURALLY, ALL THAT WAS LOST TO SLAVERY AND DEPORTATION. IN COLONISTS' EYES, AFRICANS WITH OPULENT HAIR BECAME HAIRY, FLEA-RIDDEN ANIMALS.
THEY HAVE SUCH WONDERFUL COMBS IN AFRICA, SPECIALLY SCULPTED FOR THEIR OWNERS.
THEY'RE LIKE IDENTITY CARDS. THE SLAVES WERE DISPOSSESSED, NOT ONLY OF THEIR LANDS BUT ALSO THEIR COMBS, THEIR CULTURE. THEIR PRIDE.
LOOK AT THEM. EVERY STAR HAS SMOOTH HAIR. THAT'S THE BEAUTY STANDARD.
OR SO MOVIES WOULD HAVE US BELIEVE.
HOW'S THAT?

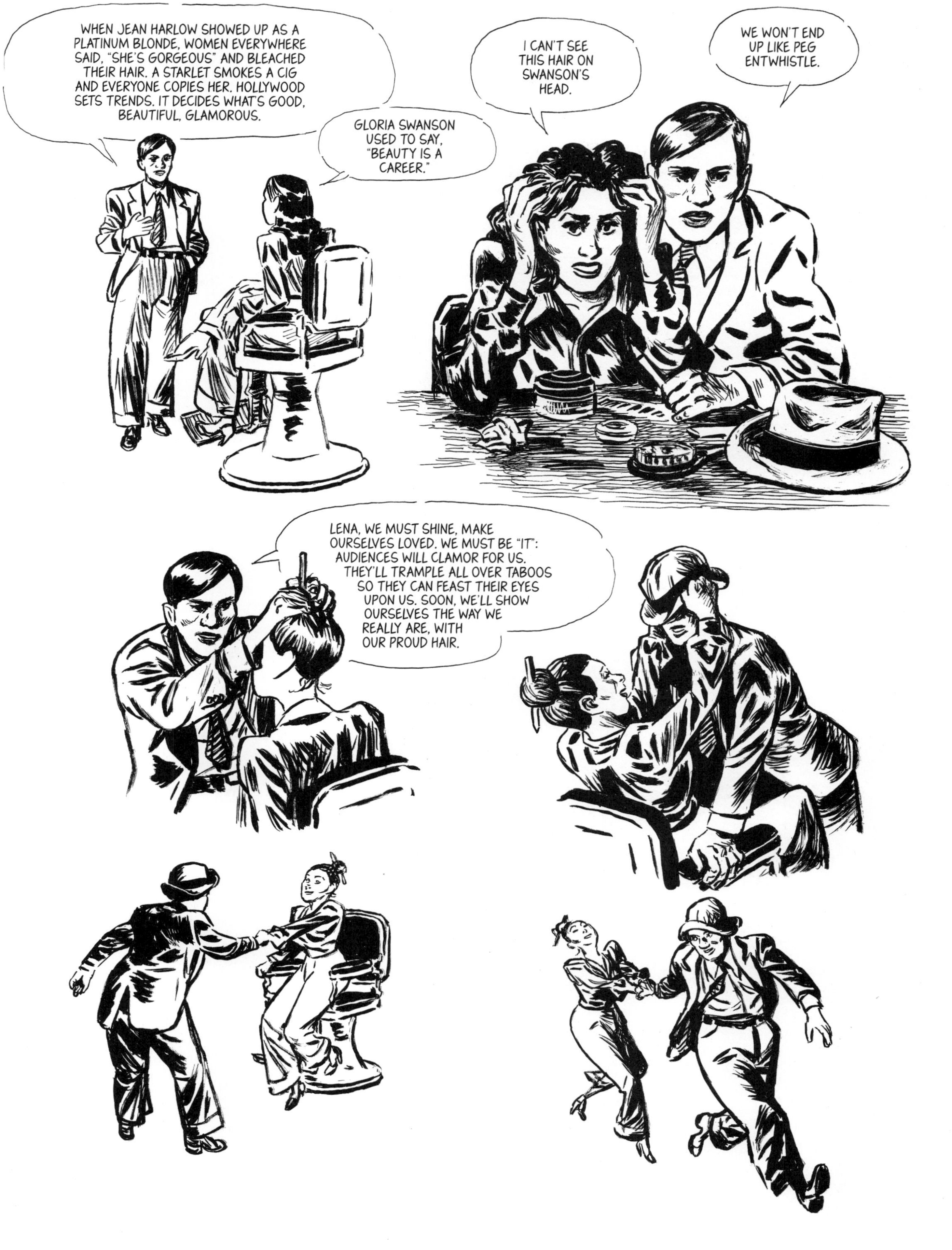
WHEN JEAN HARLOW SHOWED UP AS A PLATINUM BLONDE, WOMEN EVERYWHERE SAID, "SHE'S GORGEOUS" AND BLEACHED THEIR HAIR. A STARLET SMOKES A CIG AND EVERYONE COPIES HER. HOLLYWOOD SETS TRENDS. IT DECIDES WHAT'S GOOD, BEAUTIFUL, GLAMOROUS.
GLORIA SWANSON USED TO SAY, "BEAUTY IS A CAREER."
I CAN'T SEE THIS HAIR ON SWANSON'S HEAD.
WE WON'T END UP LIKE PEG ENTWHISTLE.
LENA, WE MUST SHINE, MAKE OURSELVES LOVED. WE MUST BE "IT": AUDIENCES WILL CLAMOR FOR US. THEY'LL TRAMPLE ALL OVER TABOOS SO THEY CAN FEAST THEIR EYES UPON US. SOON, WE'LL SHOW OURSELVES THE WAY WE REALLY ARE, WITH OUR PROUD HAIR.

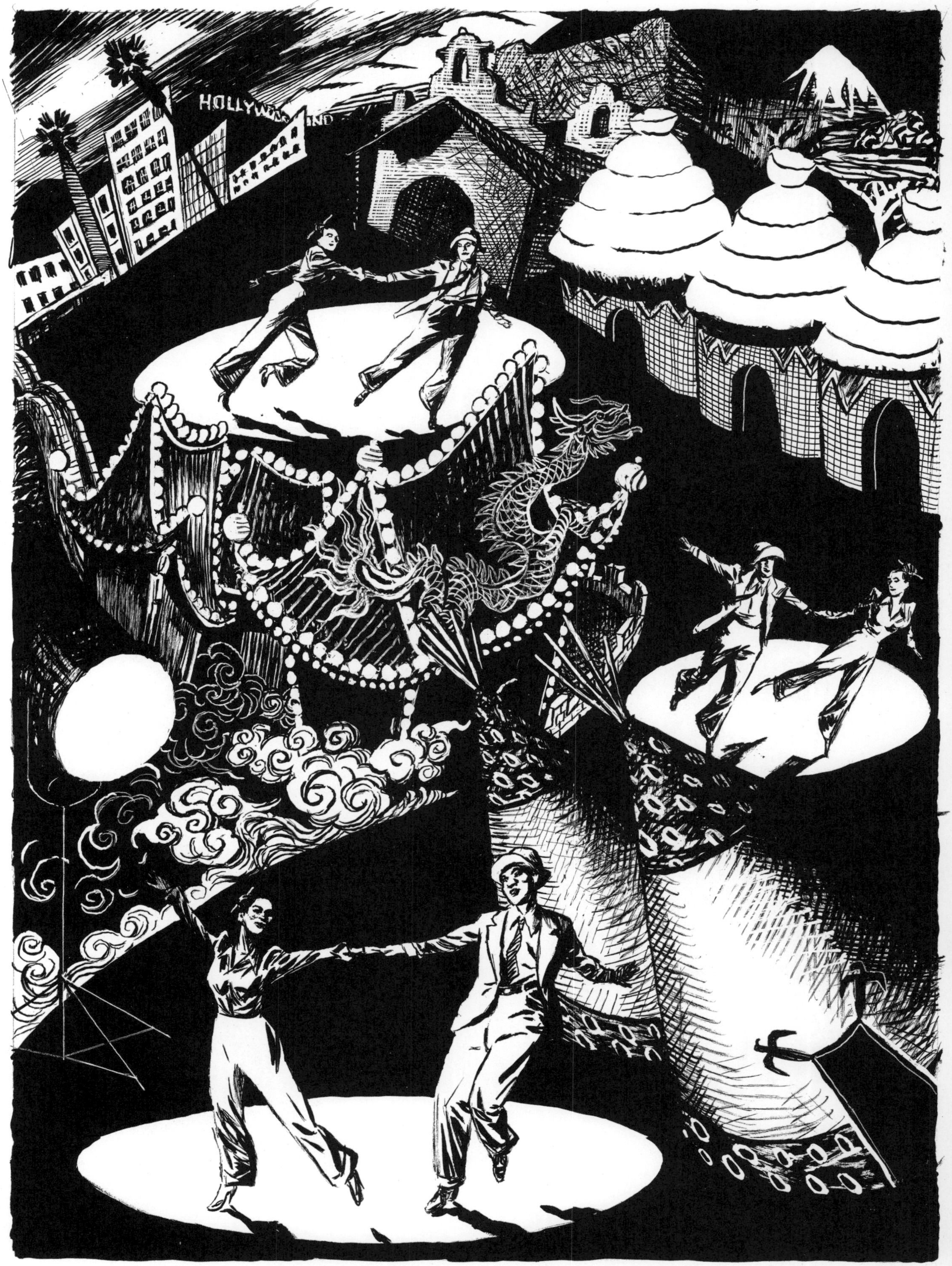
HOLLYW
ND

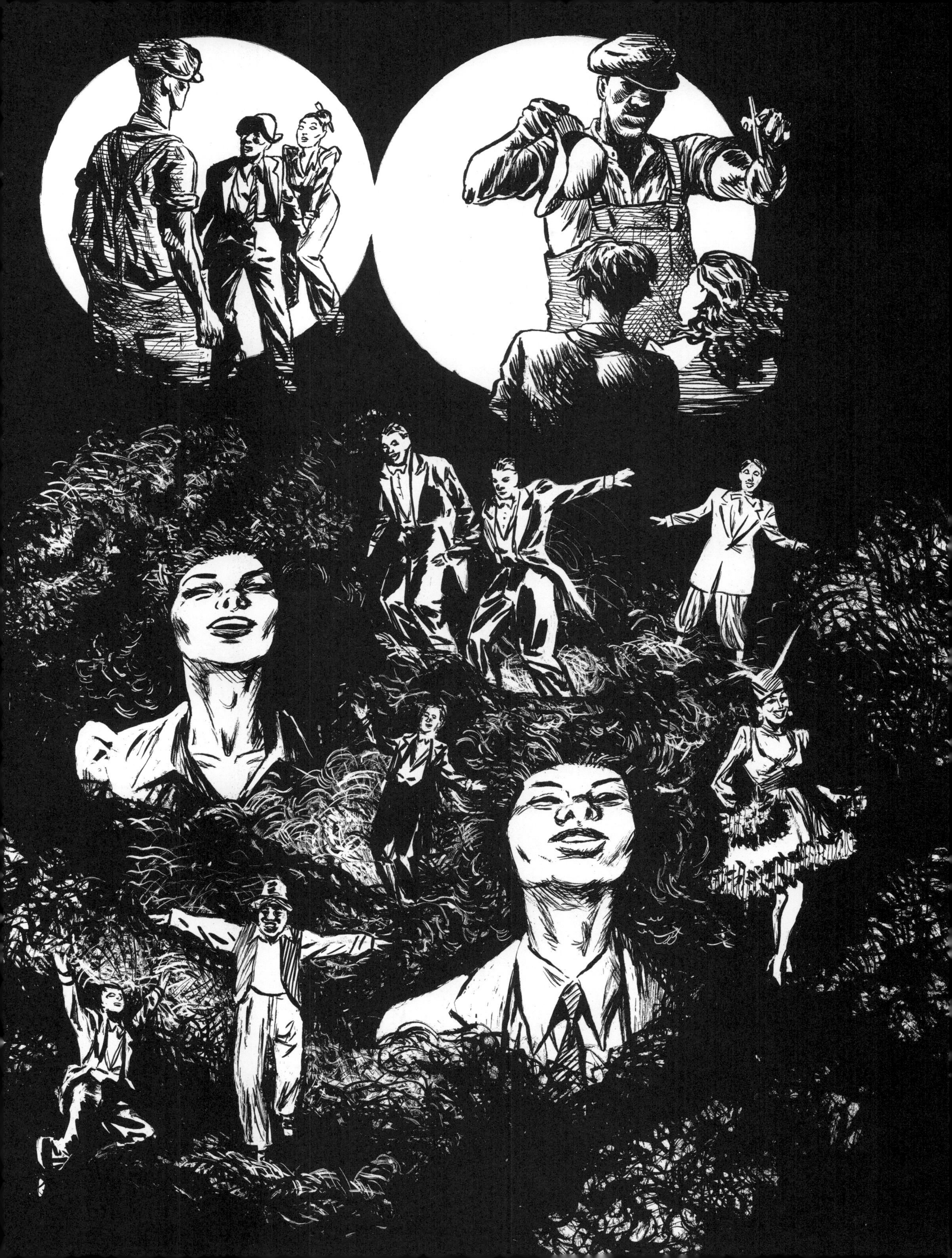

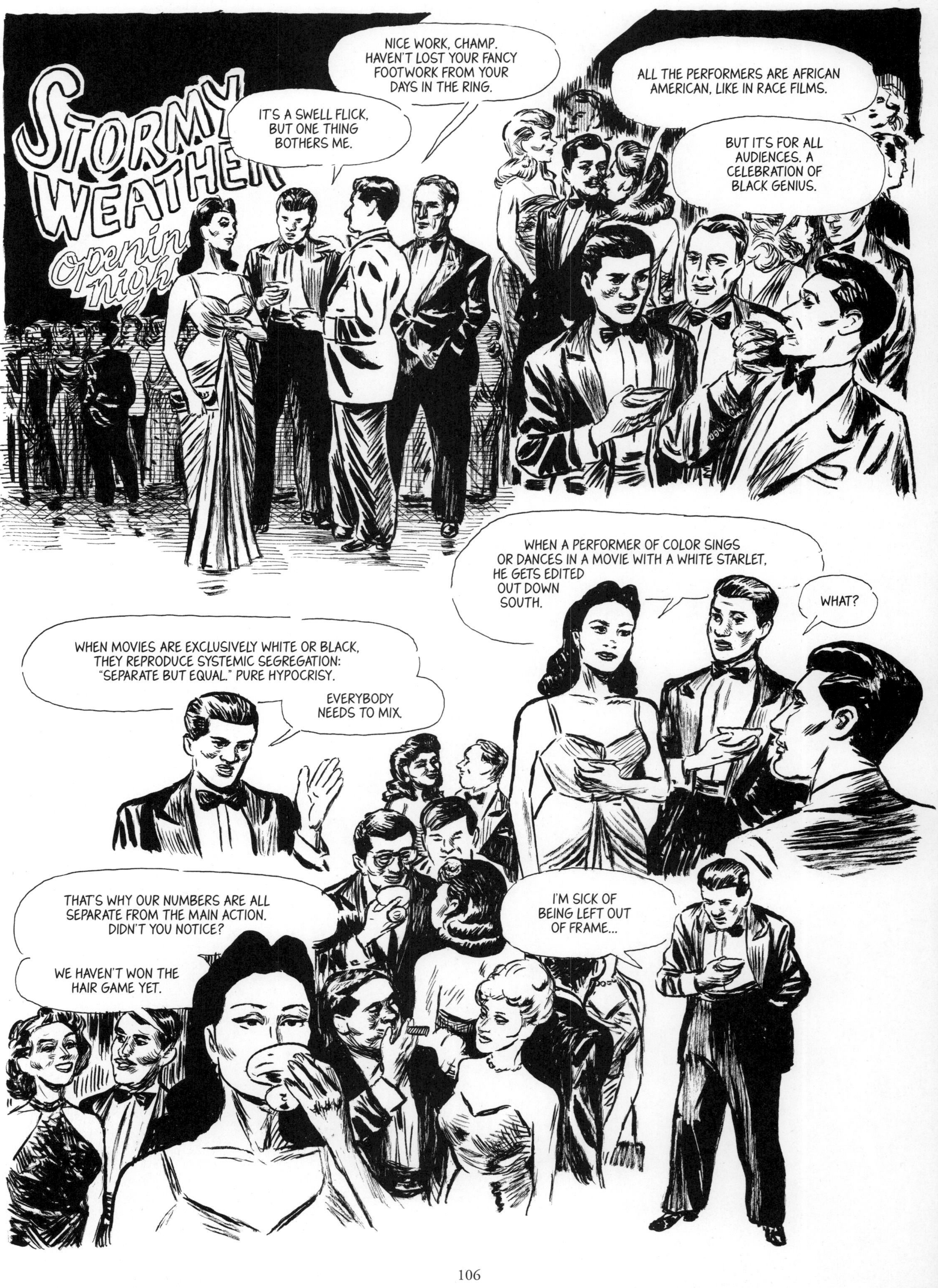
STORMY WEATHER
Opening night
IT'S A SWELL FLICK, BUT ONE THING BOTHERS ME.
NICE WORK, CHAMP. HAVEN'T LOST YOUR FANCY FOOTWORK FROM YOUR DAYS IN THE RING.
ALL THE PERFORMERS ARE AFRICAN AMERICAN, LIKE IN RACE FILMS.
BUT IT'S FOR ALL AUDIENCES. A CELEBRATION OF BLACK GENIUS.
WHEN A PERFORMER OF COLOR SINGS OR DANCES IN A MOVIE WITH A WHITE STARLET, HE GETS EDITED OUT DOWN SOUTH.
WHAT?
WHEN MOVIES ARE EXCLUSIVELY WHITE OR BLACK, THEY REPRODUCE SYSTEMIC SEGREGATION: "SEPARATE BUT EQUAL." PURE HYPOCRISY.
EVERYBODY NEEDS TO MIX.
THAT'S WHY OUR NUMBERS ARE ALL SEPARATE FROM THE MAIN ACTION. DIDN'T YOU NOTICE?
WE HAVEN'T WON THE HAIR GAME YET.
I'M SICK OF BEING LEFT OUT OF FRAME...

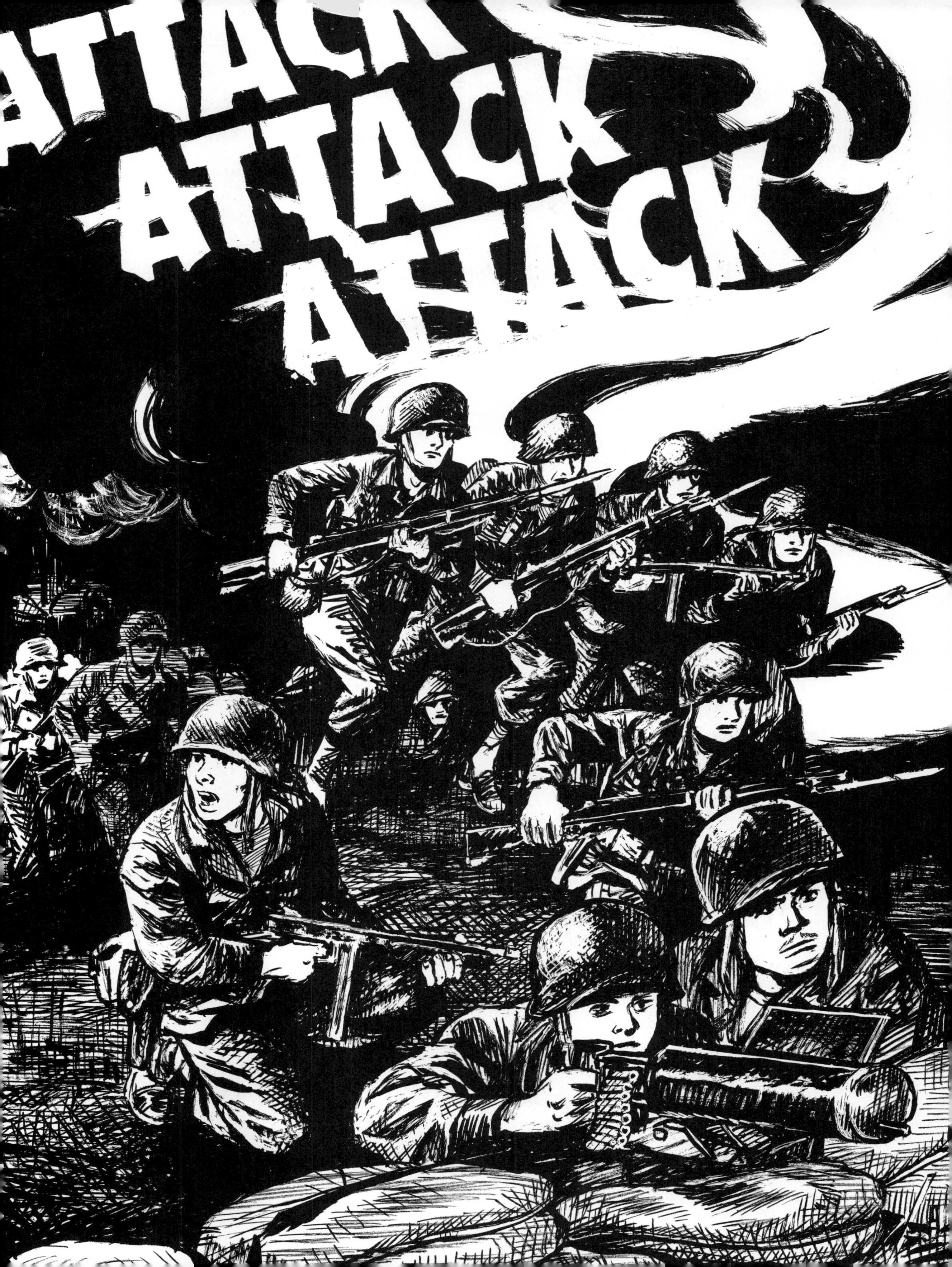
ATTACK
ATTACK
ATTACK
ATTACK

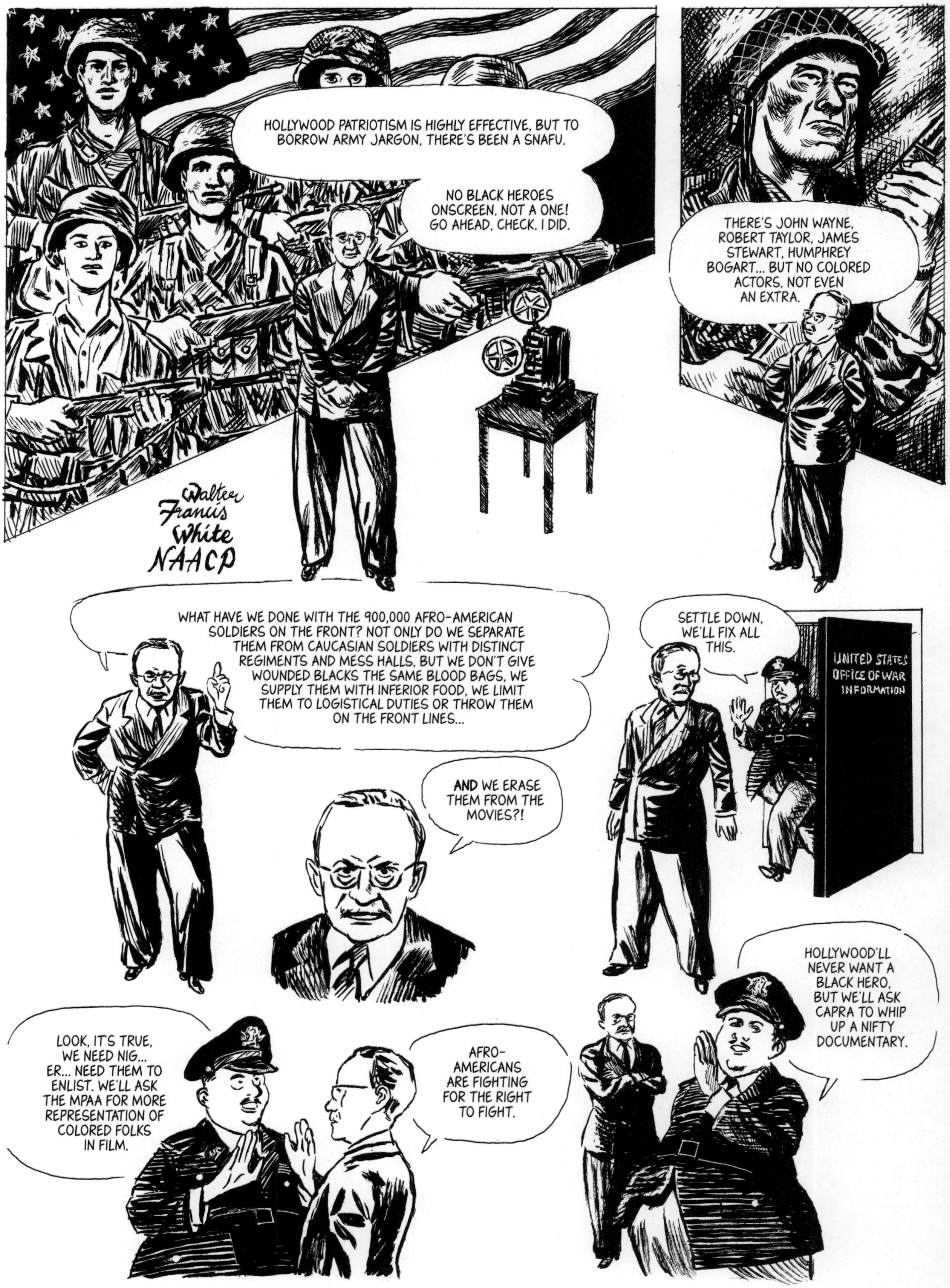
HOLLYWOOD PATRIOTISM IS HIGHLY EFFECTIVE, BUT TO BORROW ARMY JARGON, THERE'S BEEN A SNAFU.
NO BLACK HEROES ONSCREEN. NOT A ONE! GO AHEAD, CHECK. I DID.
Walter Francis White NAACP
THERE'S JOHN WAYNE, ROBERT TAYLOR, JAMES STEWART, HUMPHREY BOGART... BUT NO COLORED ACTORS. NOT EVEN AN EXTRA.
WHAT HAVE WE DONE WITH THE 900,000 AFRO-AMERICAN SOLDIERS ON THE FRONT? NOT ONLY DO WE SEPARATE THEM FROM CAUCASIAN SOLDIERS WITH DISTINCT REGIMENTS AND MESS HALLS, BUT WE DON'T GIVE WOUNDED BLACKS THE SAME BLOOD BAGS, WE SUPPLY THEM WITH INFERIOR FOOD, WE LIMIT THEM TO LOGISTICAL DUTIES OR THROW THEM ON THE FRONT LINES...
AND WE ERASE THEM FROM THE MOVIES?!
SETTLE DOWN, WE'LL FIX ALL THIS.
UNITED STATES OFFICE OF WAR INFORMATION
LOOK, IT'S TRUE, WE NEED NIG... ER... NEED THEM TO ENLIST. WE'LL ASK THE MPAA FOR MORE REPRESENTATION OF COLORED FOLKS IN FILM.
AFRO-AMERICANS ARE FIGHTING FOR THE RIGHT TO FIGHT.
HOLLYWOOD'LL NEVER WANT A BLACK HERO, BUT WE'LL ASK CAPRA TO WHIP UP A NIFTY DOCUMENTARY.

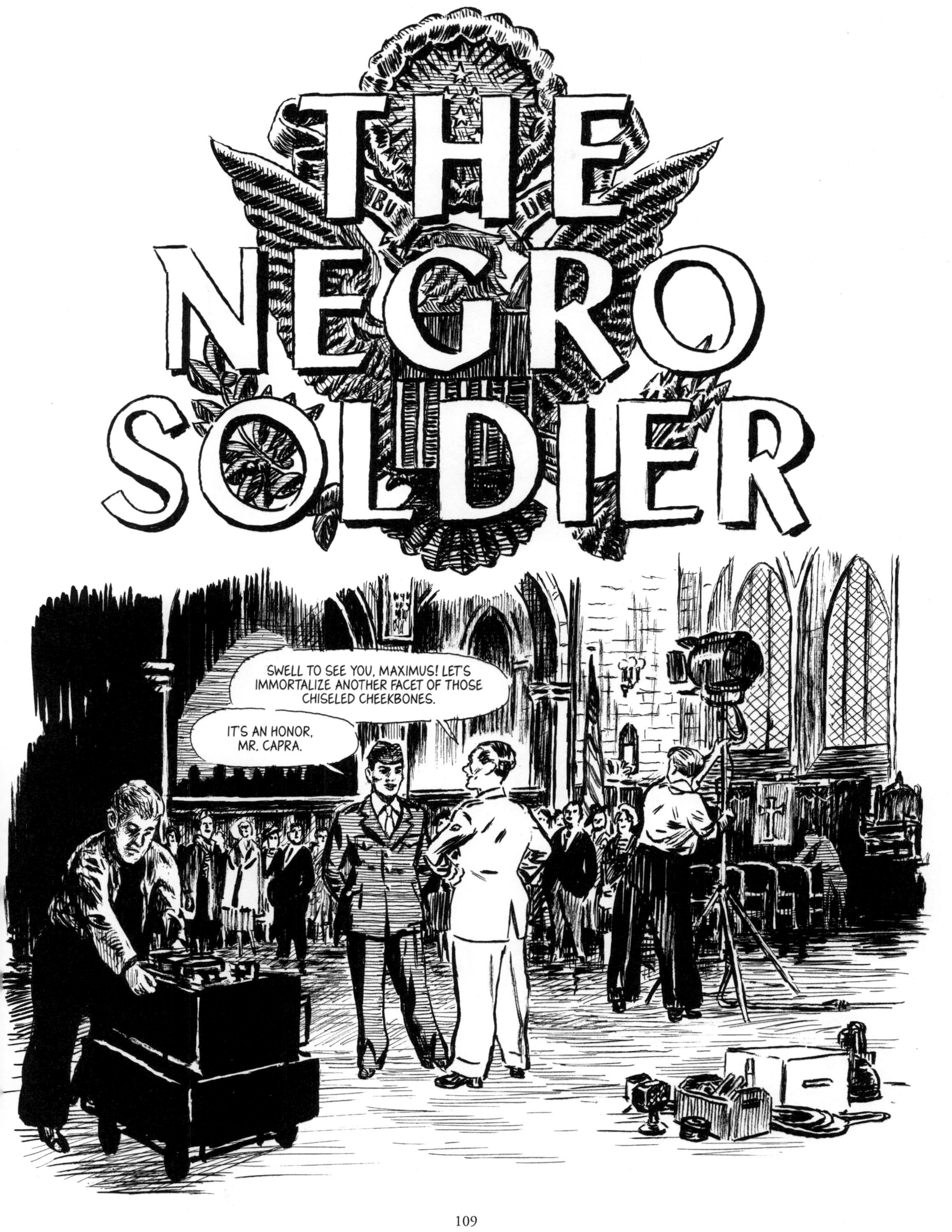
THE NEGRO SOLDIER
SWELL TO SEE YOU, MAXIMUS! LET'S IMMORTALIZE ANOTHER FACET OF THOSE CHISELED CHEEKBONES.
IT'S AN HONOR, MR. CAPRA.

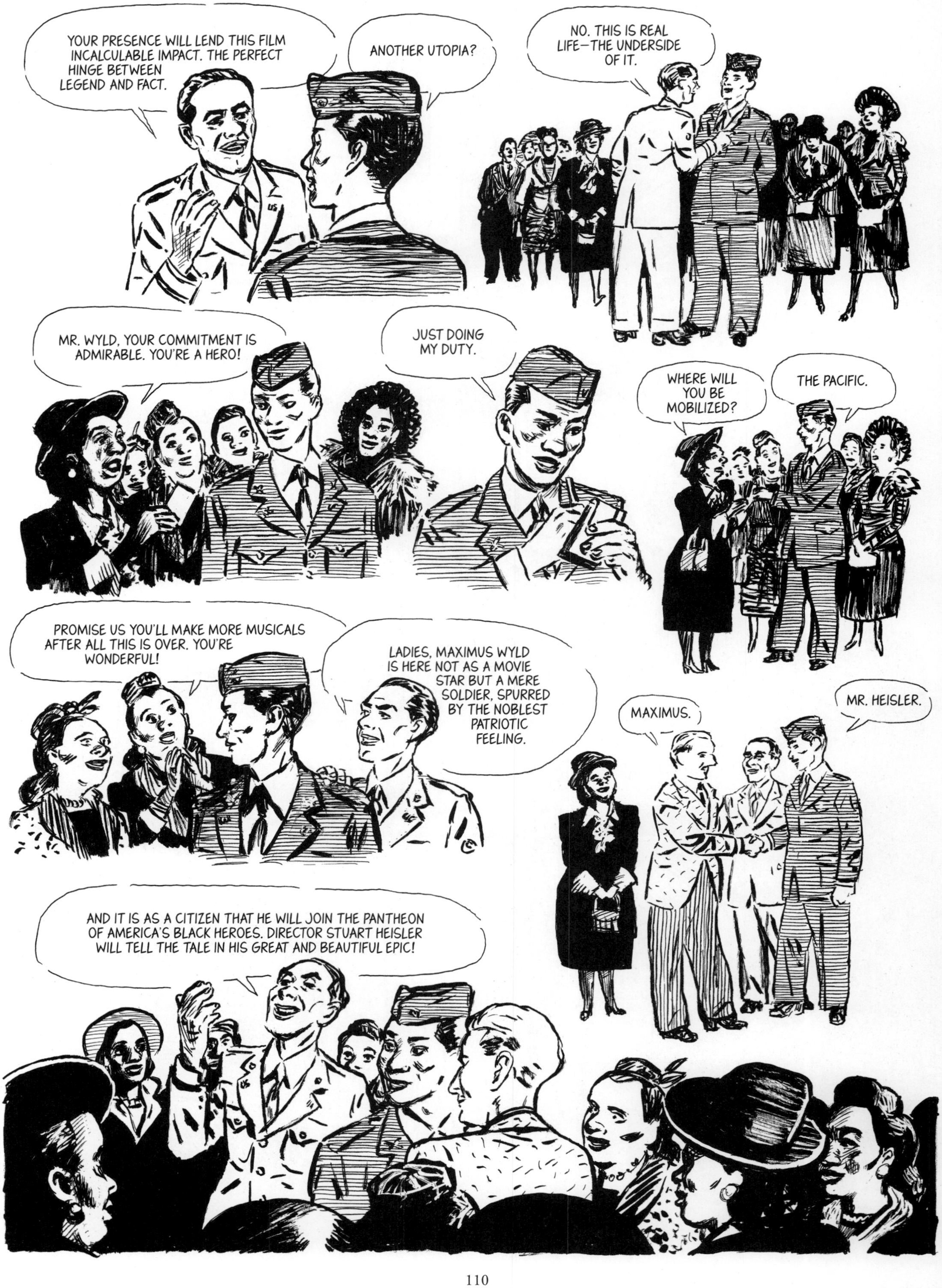
YOUR PRESENCE WILL LEND THIS FILM INCALCULABLE IMPACT. THE PERFECT HINGE BETWEEN LEGEND AND FACT.
ANOTHER UTOPIA?
NO. THIS IS REAL LIFE—THE UNDERSIDE OF IT.
MR. WYLD, YOUR COMMITMENT IS ADMIRABLE. YOU'RE A HERO!
JUST DOING MY DUTY.
WHERE WILL YOU BE MOBILIZED?
THE PACIFIC.
PROMISE US YOU'LL MAKE MORE MUSICALS AFTER ALL THIS IS OVER. YOU'RE WONDERFUL!
LADIES, MAXIMUS WYLD IS HERE NOT AS A MOVIE STAR BUT A MERE SOLDIER, SPURRED BY THE NOBLEST PATRIOTIC FEELING.
MAXIMUS.
MR. HEISLER.
AND IT IS AS A CITIZEN THAT HE WILL JOIN THE PANTHEON OF AMERICA'S BLACK HEROES. DIRECTOR STUART HEISLER WILL TELL THE TALE IN HIS GREAT AND BEAUTIFUL EPIC!

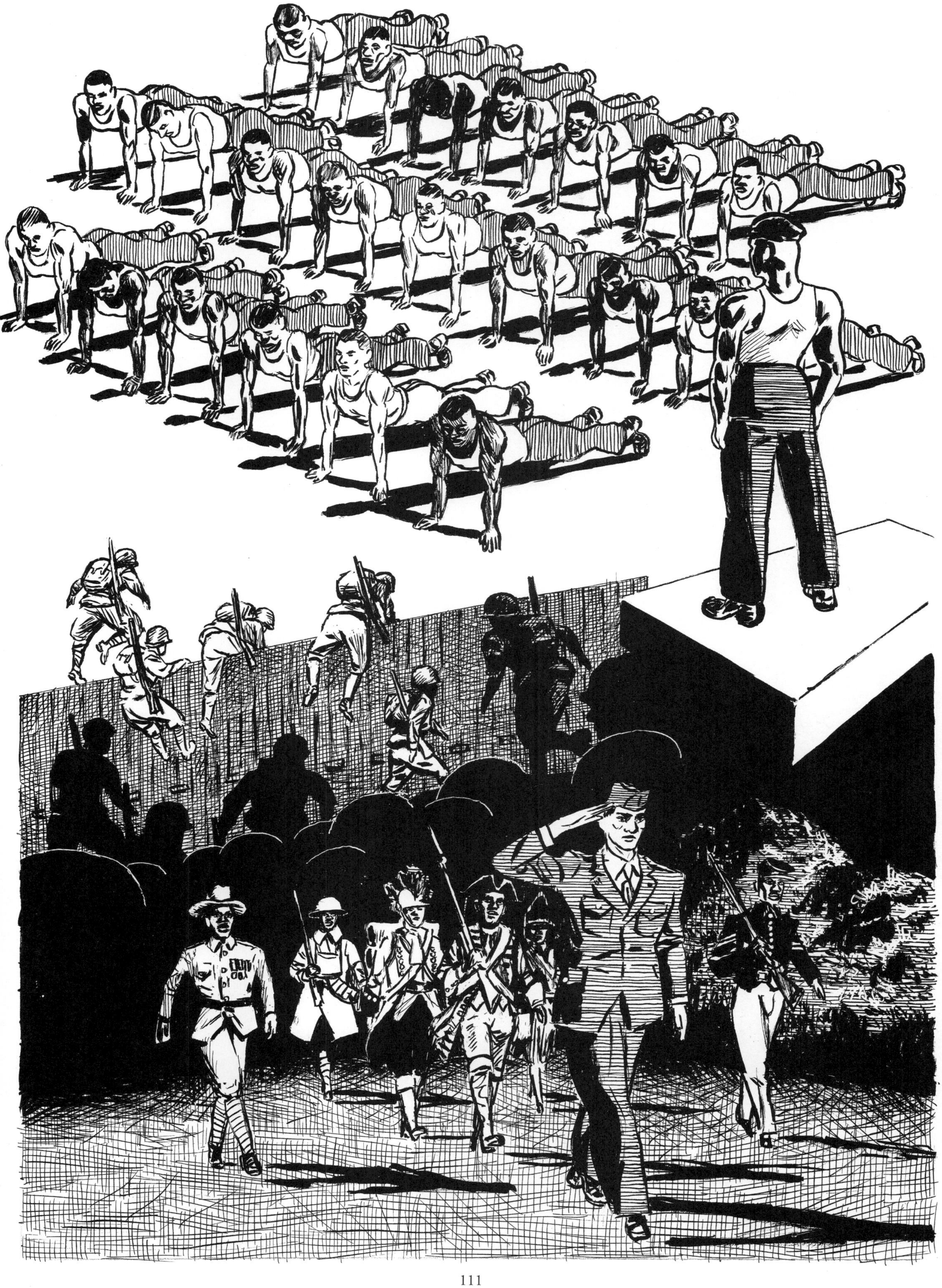

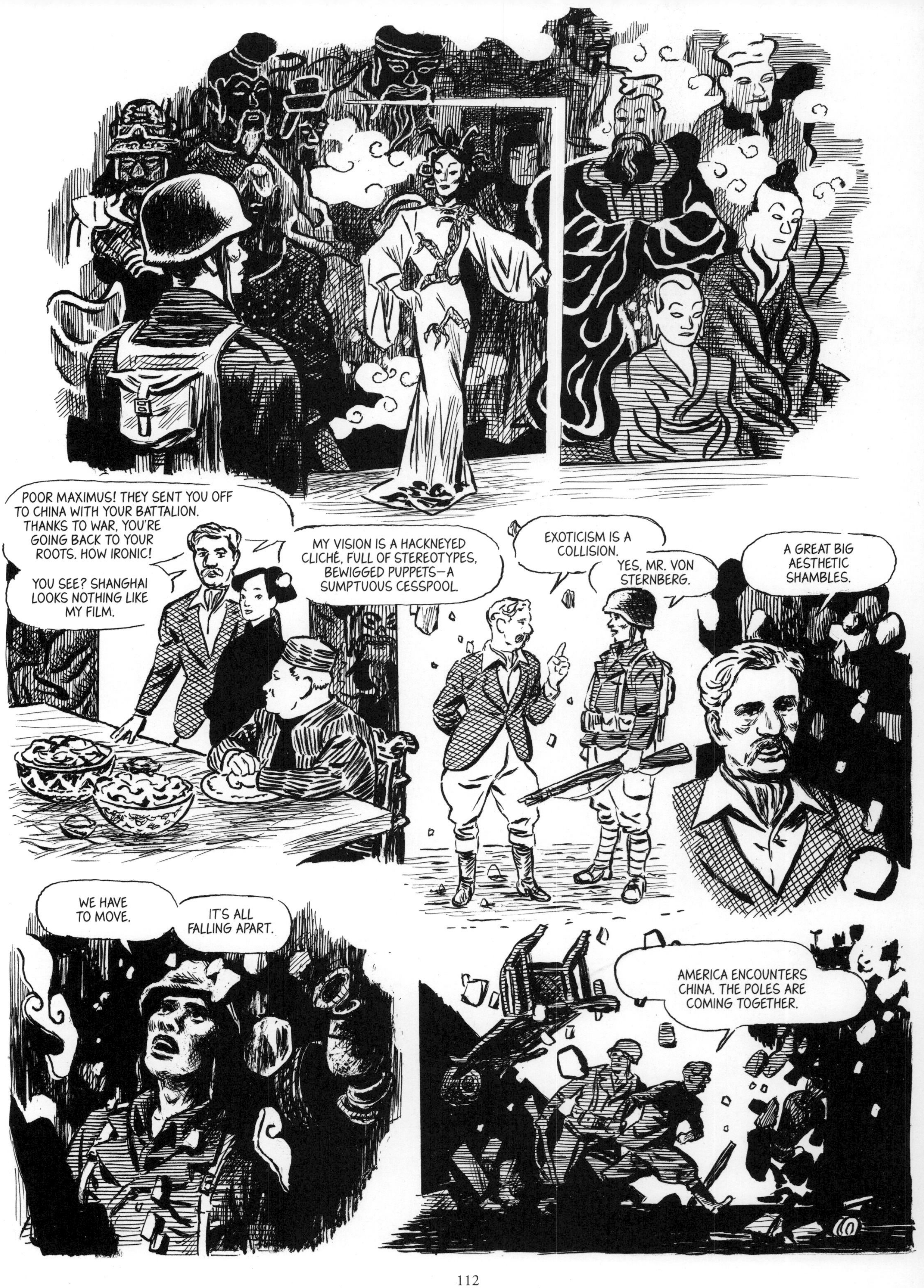

POOR MAXIMUS! THEY SENT YOU OFF TO CHINA WITH YOUR BATTALION. THANKS TO WAR, YOU'RE GOING BACK TO YOUR ROOTS. HOW IRONIC!
YOU SEE? SHANGHAI LOOKS NOTHING LIKE MY FILM.
MY VISION IS A HACKNEYED CLICHÉ, FULL OF STEREOTYPES, BEWIGGED PUPPETS—A SUMPTUOUS CESSPOOL.
EXOTICISM IS A COLLISION.
YES, MR. VON STERNBERG.
A GREAT BIG AESTHETIC SHAMBLES.
WE HAVE TO MOVE.
IT'S ALL FALLING APART.
AMERICA ENCOUNTERS CHINA. THE POLES ARE COMING TOGETHER.

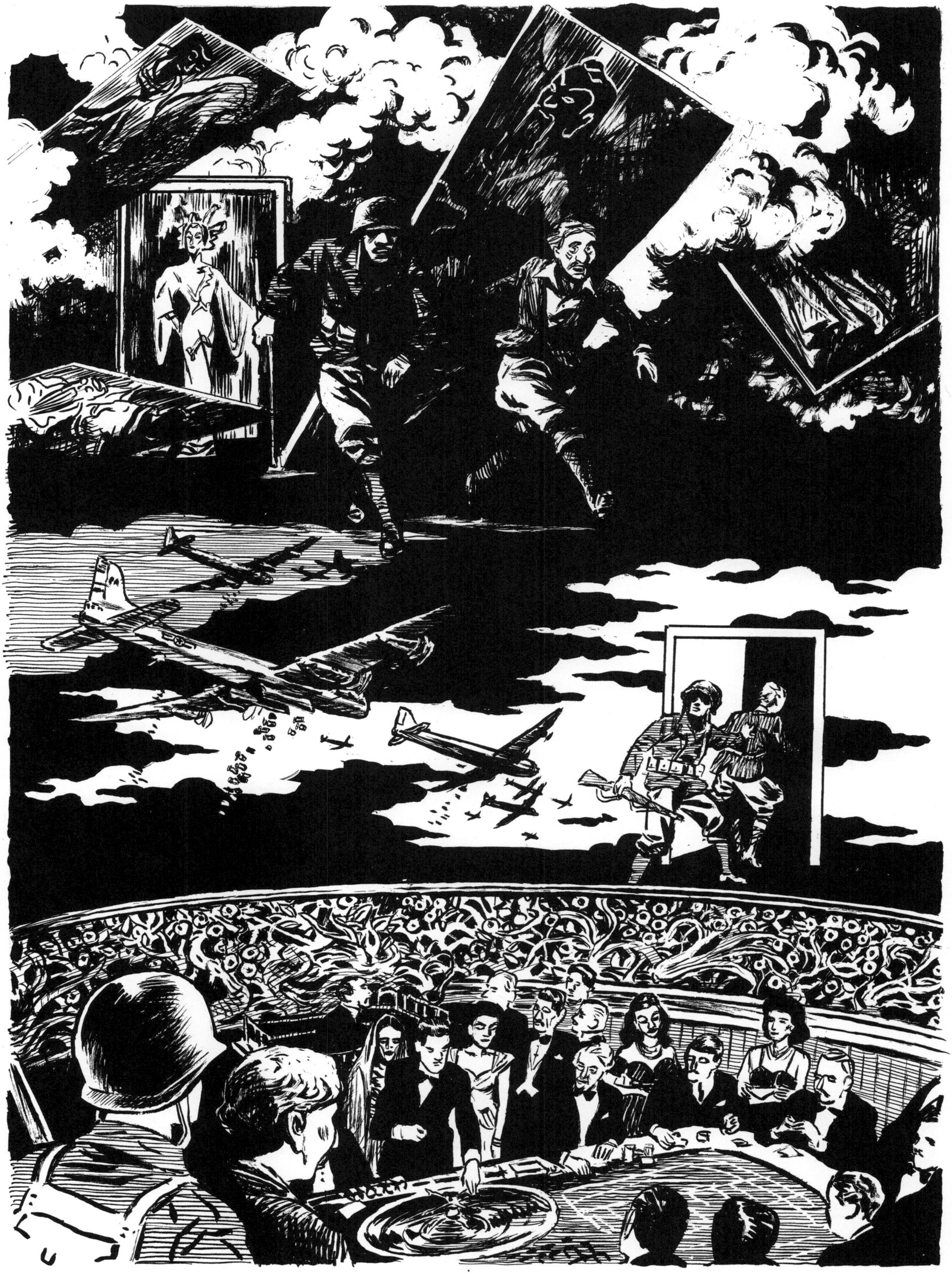

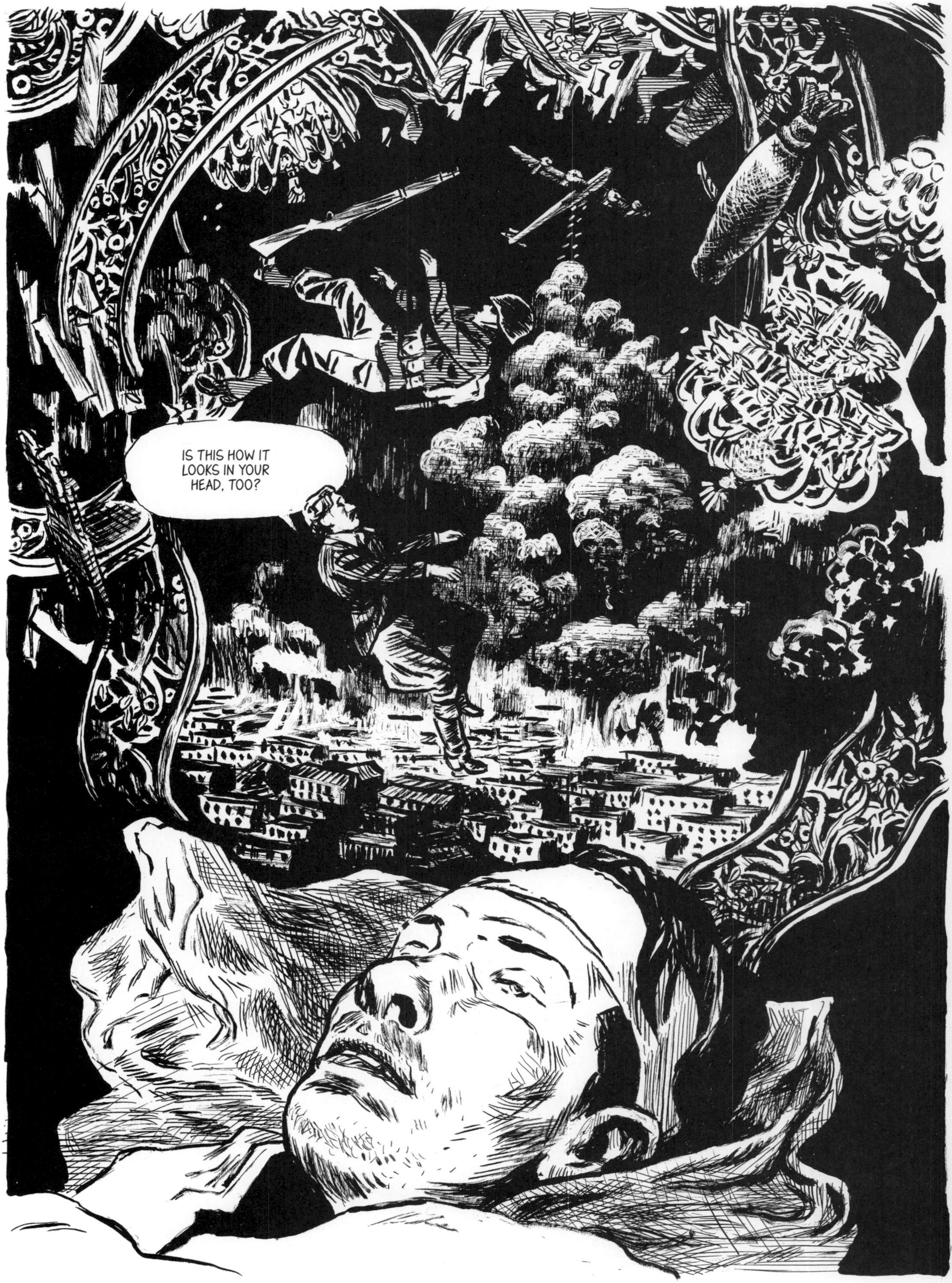
IS THIS HOW IT LOOKS IN YOUR HEAD, TOO?

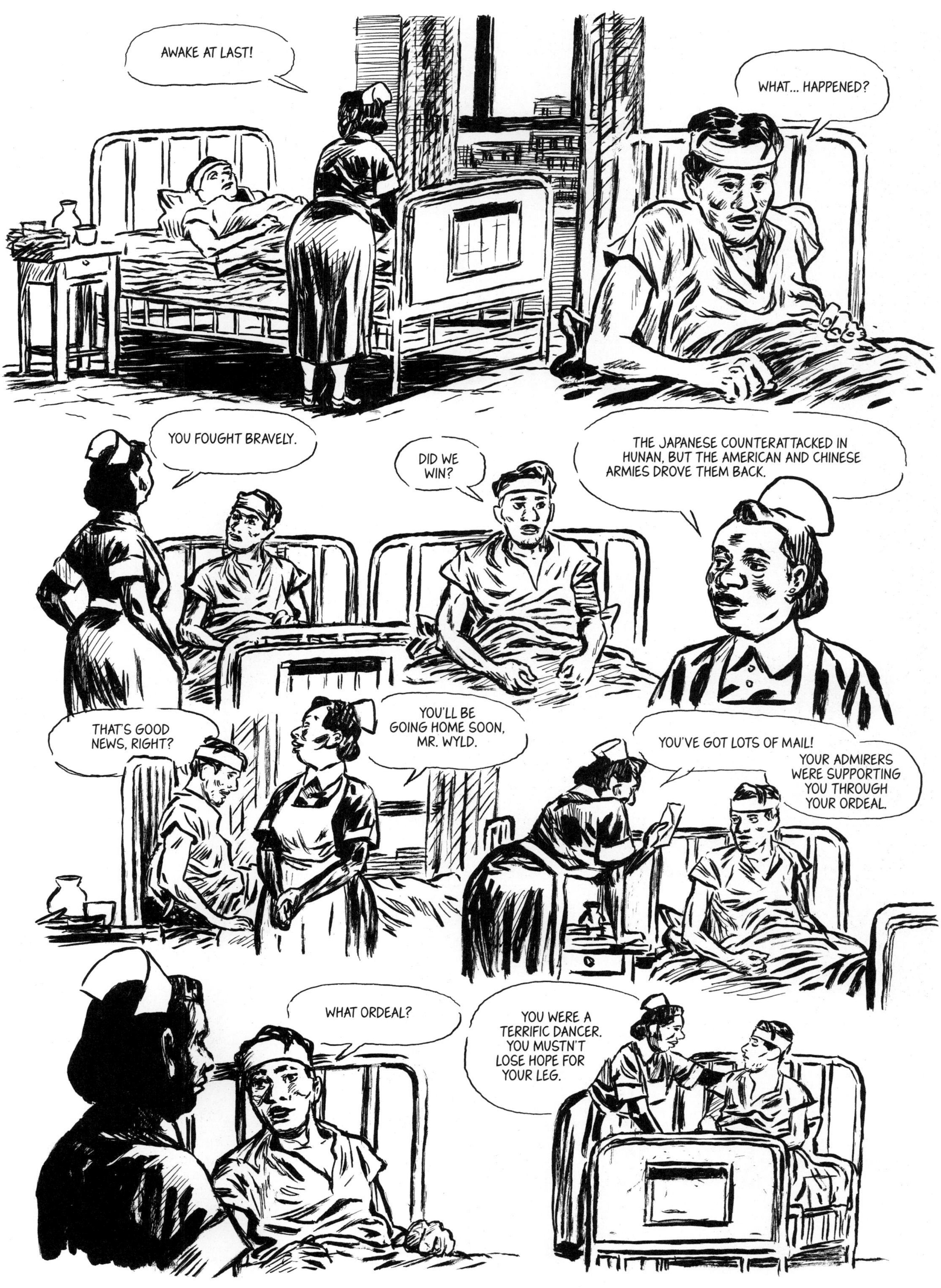
AWAKE AT LAST!
WHAT... HAPPENED?
YOU FOUGHT BRAVELY.
DID WE WIN?
THE JAPANESE COUNTERATTACKED IN HUNAN, BUT THE AMERICAN AND CHINESE ARMIES DROVE THEM BACK.
THAT'S GOOD NEWS, RIGHT?
YOU'LL BE GOING HOME SOON, MR. WYLD.
YOU'VE GOT LOTS OF MAIL!
YOUR ADMIRERS WERE SUPPORTING YOU THROUGH YOUR ORDEAL.
WHAT ORDEAL?
YOU WERE A TERRIFIC DANCER. YOU MUSTN'T LOSE HOPE FOR YOUR LEG.

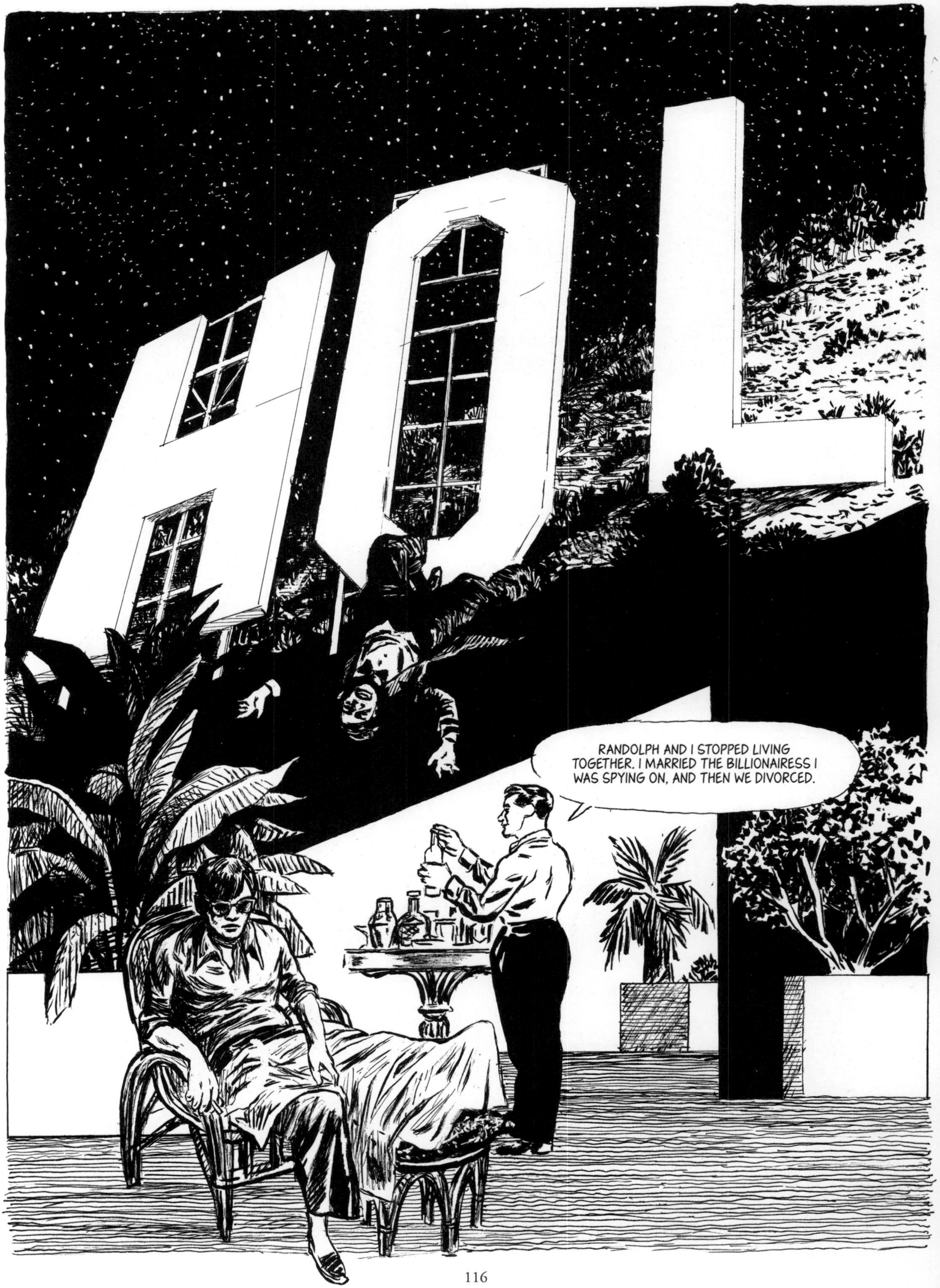
RANDOLPH AND I STOPPED LIVING TOGETHER. I MARRIED THE BILLIONAIRESS I WAS SPYING ON, AND THEN WE DIVORCED.

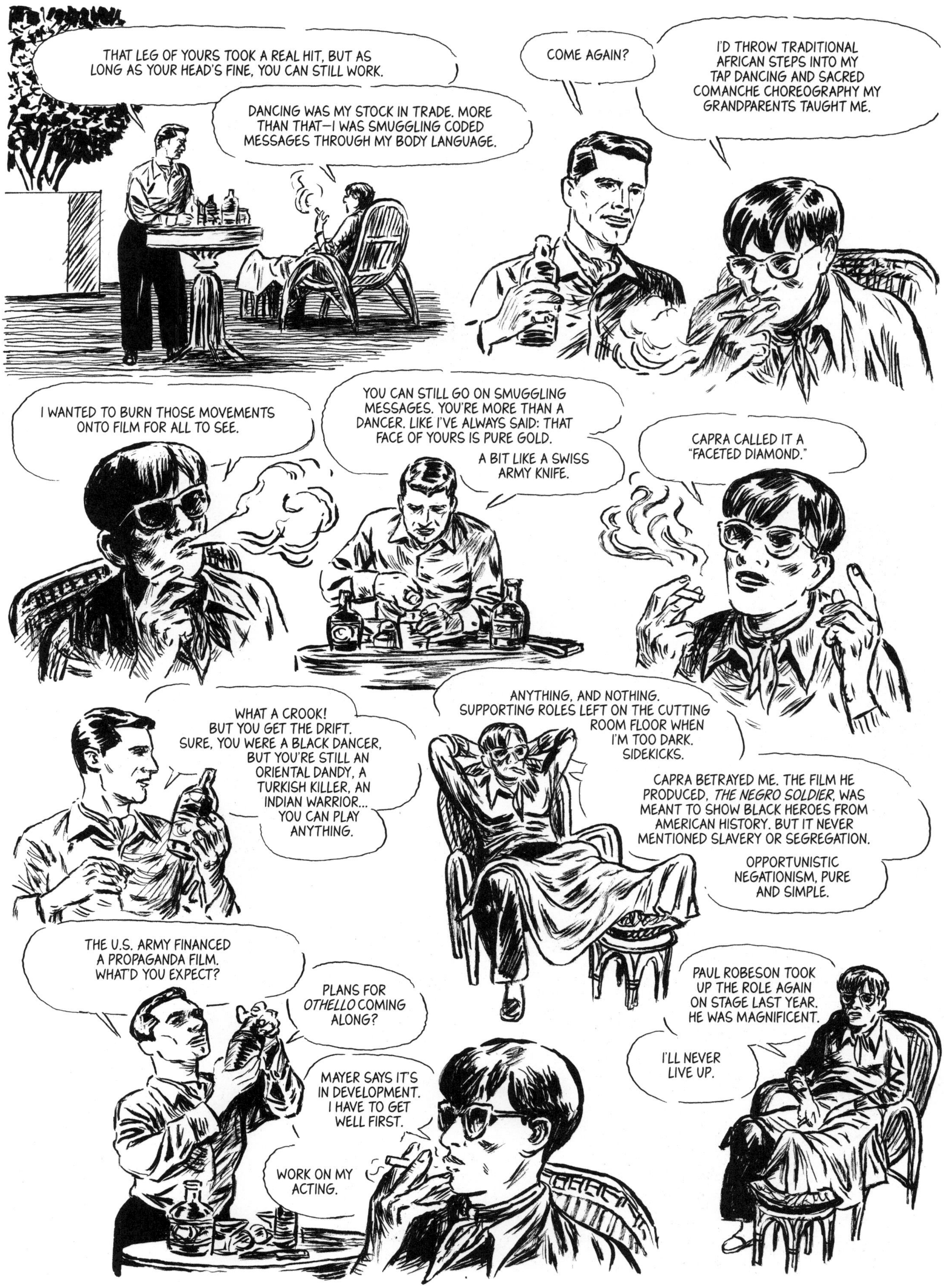
THAT LEG OF YOURS TOOK A REAL HIT, BUT AS LONG AS YOUR HEAD'S FINE, YOU CAN STILL WORK.
DANCING WAS MY STOCK IN TRADE. MORE THAN THAT—I WAS SMUGGLING CODED MESSAGES THROUGH MY BODY LANGUAGE.
COME AGAIN?
I'D THROW TRADITIONAL AFRICAN STEPS INTO MY TAP DANCING AND SACRED COMANCHE CHOREOGRAPHY MY GRANDPARENTS TAUGHT ME.
I WANTED TO BURN THOSE MOVEMENTS ONTO FILM FOR ALL TO SEE.
YOU CAN STILL GO ON SMUGGLING MESSAGES. YOU'RE MORE THAN A DANCER. LIKE I'VE ALWAYS SAID: THAT FACE OF YOURS IS PURE GOLD.
A BIT LIKE A SWISS ARMY KNIFE.
CAPRA CALLED IT A "FACETED DIAMOND."
WHAT A CROOK! BUT YOU GET THE DRIFT. SURE, YOU WERE A BLACK DANCER, BUT YOU'RE STILL AN ORIENTAL DANDY, A TURKISH KILLER, AN INDIAN WARRIOR... YOU CAN PLAY ANYTHING.
ANYTHING, AND NOTHING. SUPPORTING ROLES LEFT ON THE CUTTING ROOM FLOOR WHEN I'M TOO DARK. SIDEKICKS.
CAPRA BETRAYED ME. THE FILM HE PRODUCED, *THE NEGRO SOLDIER*, WAS MEANT TO SHOW BLACK HEROES FROM AMERICAN HISTORY. BUT IT NEVER MENTIONED SLAVERY OR SEGREGATION.
OPPORTUNISTIC NEGATIONISM, PURE AND SIMPLE.
THE U.S. ARMY FINANCED A PROPAGANDA FILM. WHAT'D YOU EXPECT?
PLANS FOR *OTHELLO* COMING ALONG?
MAYER SAYS IT'S IN DEVELOPMENT. I HAVE TO GET WELL FIRST.
WORK ON MY ACTING.
PAUL ROBESON TOOK UP THE ROLE AGAIN ON STAGE LAST YEAR. HE WAS MAGNIFICENT.
I'LL NEVER LIVE UP.

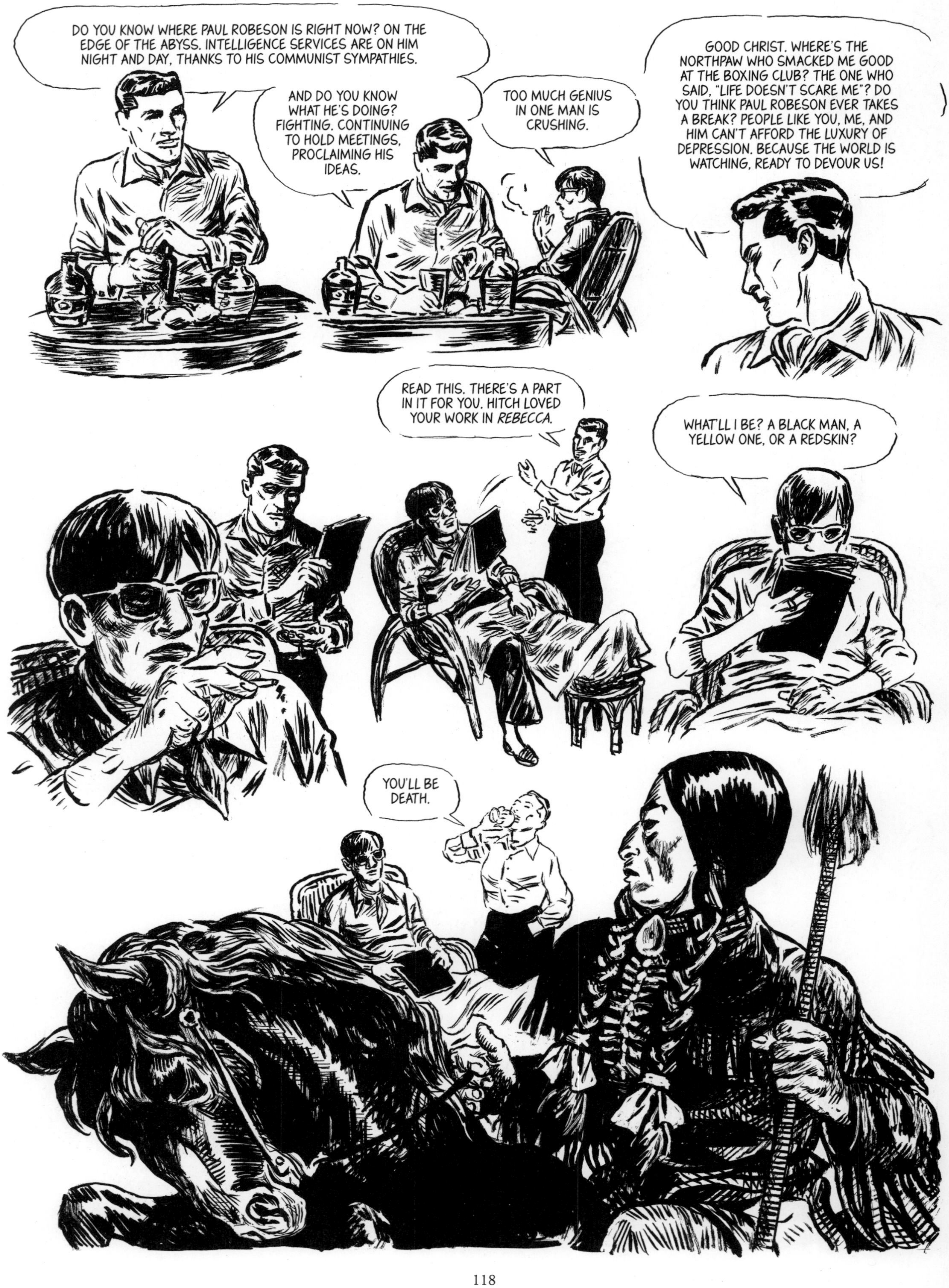
DO YOU KNOW WHERE PAUL ROBESON IS RIGHT NOW? ON THE EDGE OF THE ABYSS. INTELLIGENCE SERVICES ARE ON HIM NIGHT AND DAY, THANKS TO HIS COMMUNIST SYMPATHIES.
AND DO YOU KNOW WHAT HE'S DOING? FIGHTING. CONTINUING TO HOLD MEETINGS, PROCLAIMING HIS IDEAS.
TOO MUCH GENIUS IN ONE MAN IS CRUSHING.
GOOD CHRIST. WHERE'S THE NORTHPAW WHO SMACKED ME GOOD AT THE BOXING CLUB? THE ONE WHO SAID, "LIFE DOESN'T SCARE ME"? DO YOU THINK PAUL ROBESON EVER TAKES A BREAK? PEOPLE LIKE YOU, ME, AND HIM CAN'T AFFORD THE LUXURY OF DEPRESSION. BECAUSE THE WORLD IS WATCHING, READY TO DEVOUR US!
READ THIS. THERE'S A PART IN IT FOR YOU. HITCH LOVED YOUR WORK IN *REBECCA*.
WHAT'LL I BE? A BLACK MAN, A YELLOW ONE, OR A REDSKIN?
YOU'LL BE DEATH.

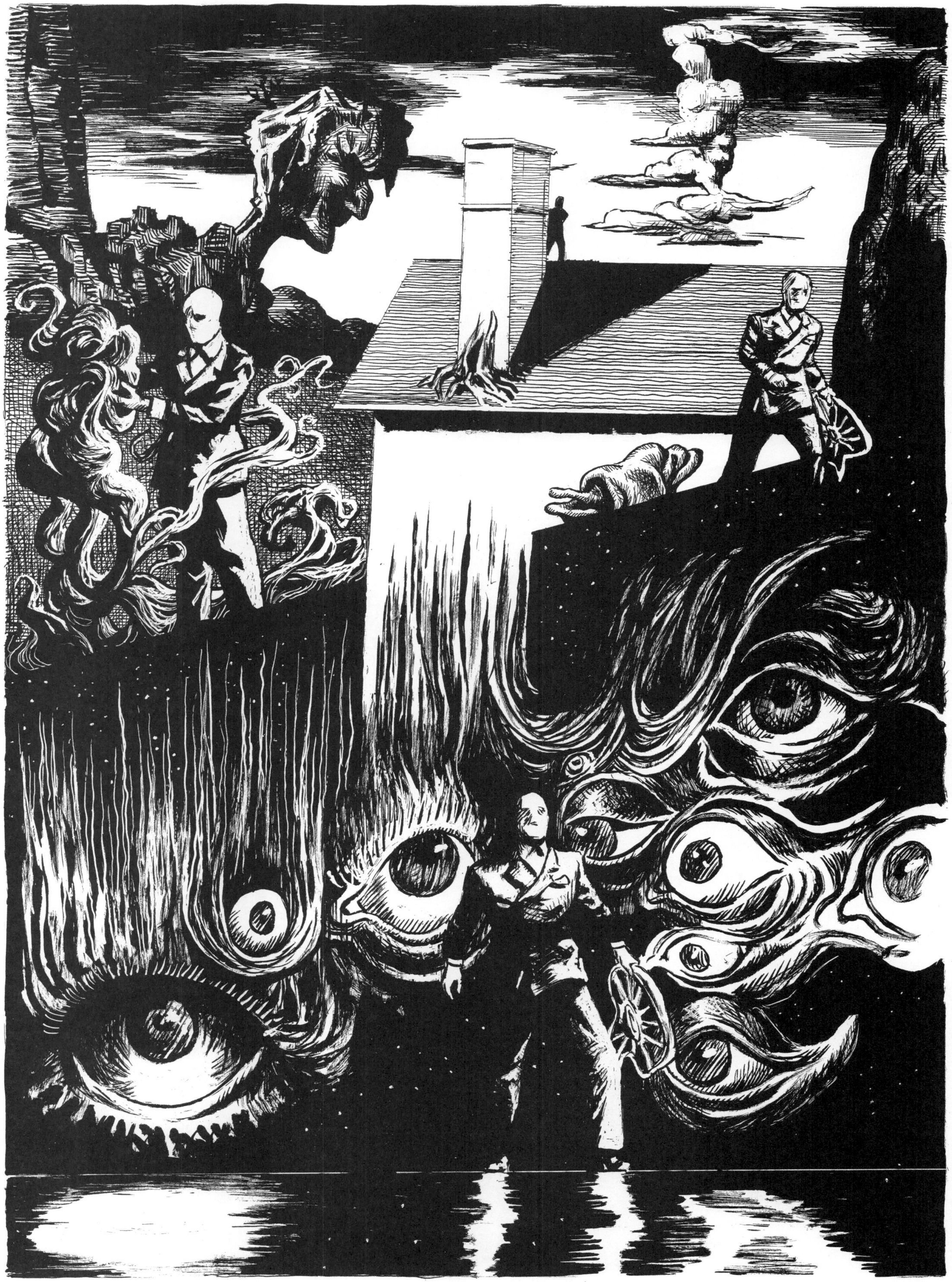

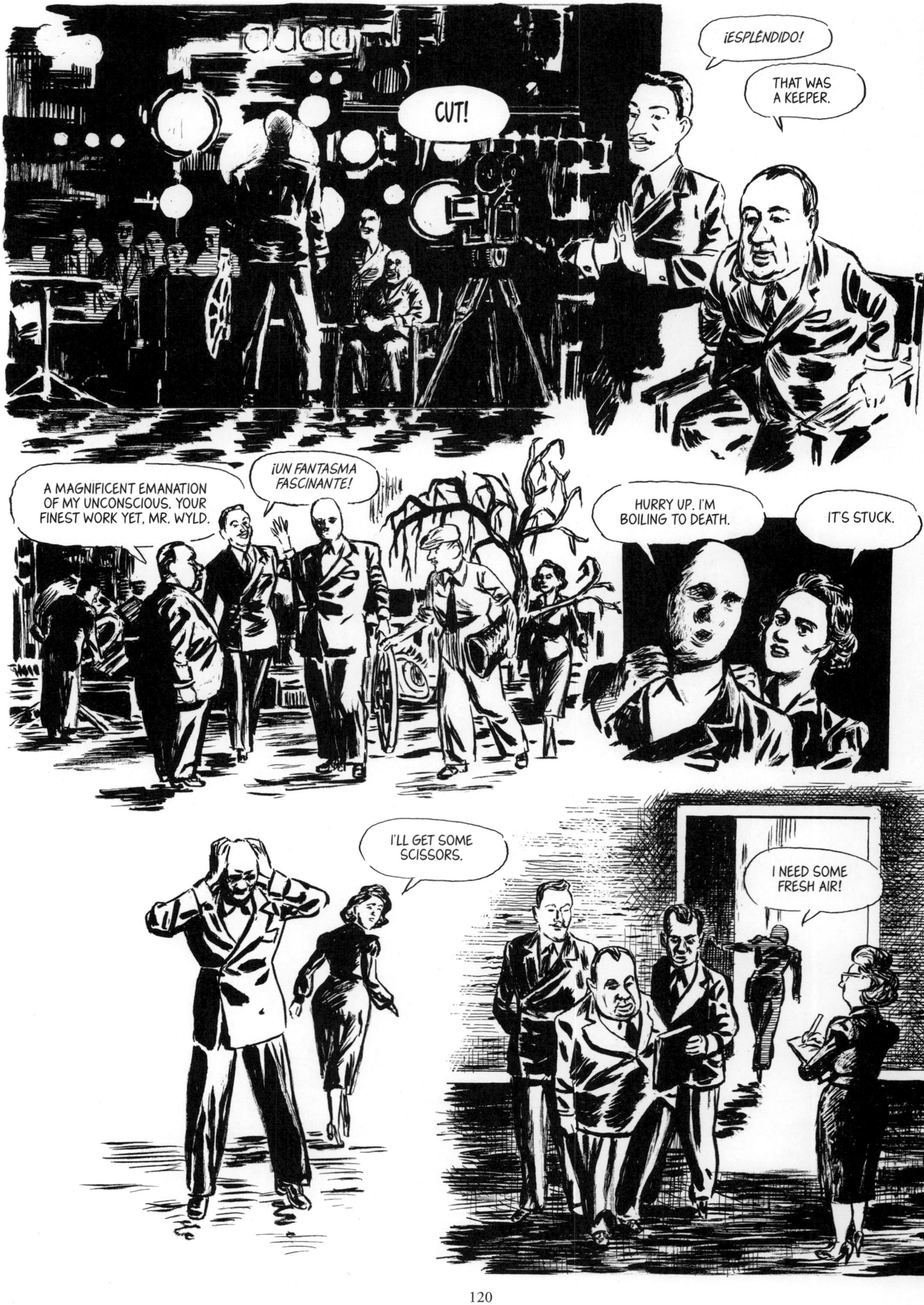
CUT!
¡ESPLÉNDIDO!
THAT WAS A KEEPER.
A MAGNIFICENT EMANATION OF MY UNCONSCIOUS. YOUR FINEST WORK YET, MR. WYLD.
¡UN FANTASMA FASCINANTE!
HURRY UP. I'M BOILING TO DEATH.
IT'S STUCK.
I'LL GET SOME SCISSORS.
I NEED SOME FRESH AIR!

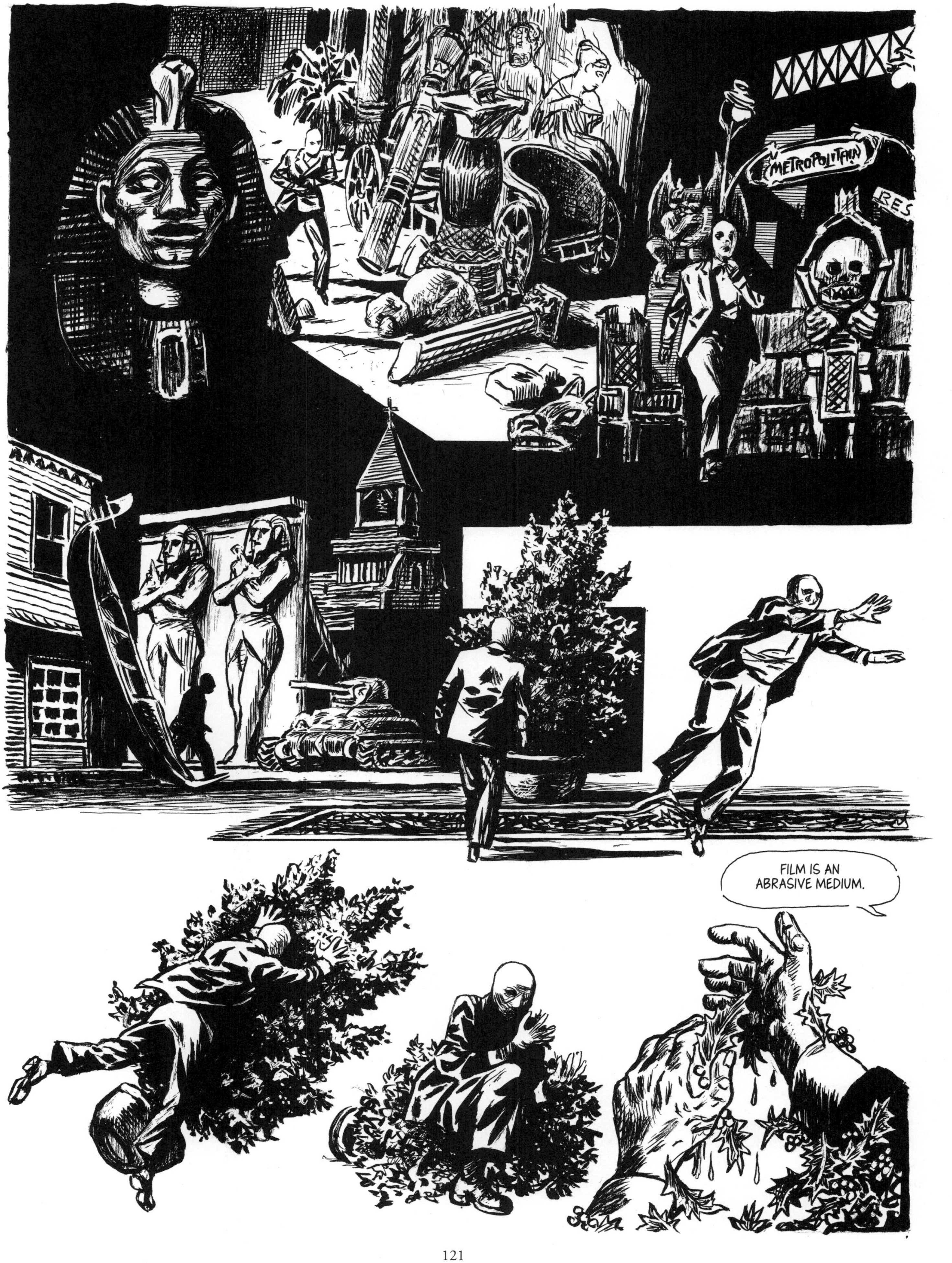
METROPOLITAIN
RES
FILM IS AN ABRASIVE MEDIUM.

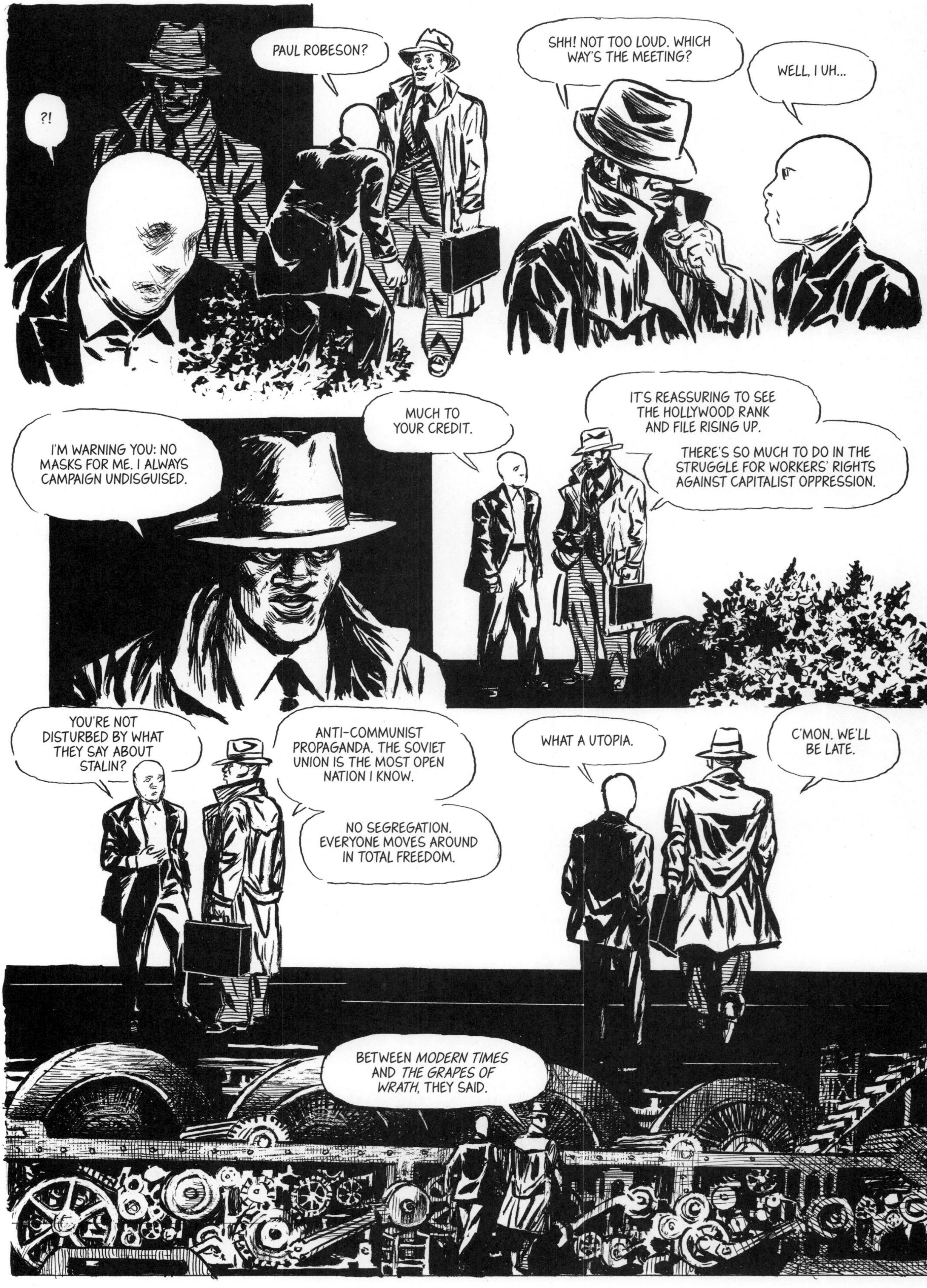
?!
PAUL ROBESON?
SHH! NOT TOO LOUD. WHICH WAY'S THE MEETING?
WELL, I UH...
I'M WARNING YOU: NO MASKS FOR ME. I ALWAYS CAMPAIGN UNDISGUISED.
MUCH TO YOUR CREDIT.
IT'S REASSURING TO SEE THE HOLLYWOOD RANK AND FILE RISING UP.
THERE'S SO MUCH TO DO IN THE STRUGGLE FOR WORKERS' RIGHTS AGAINST CAPITALIST OPPRESSION.
YOU'RE NOT DISTURBED BY WHAT THEY SAY ABOUT STALIN?
ANTI-COMMUNIST PROPAGANDA. THE SOVIET UNION IS THE MOST OPEN NATION I KNOW.
NO SEGREGATION. EVERYONE MOVES AROUND IN TOTAL FREEDOM.
WHAT A UTOPIA.
C'MON. WE'LL BE LATE.
BETWEEN *MODERN TIMES* AND *THE GRAPES OF WRATH*, THEY SAID.

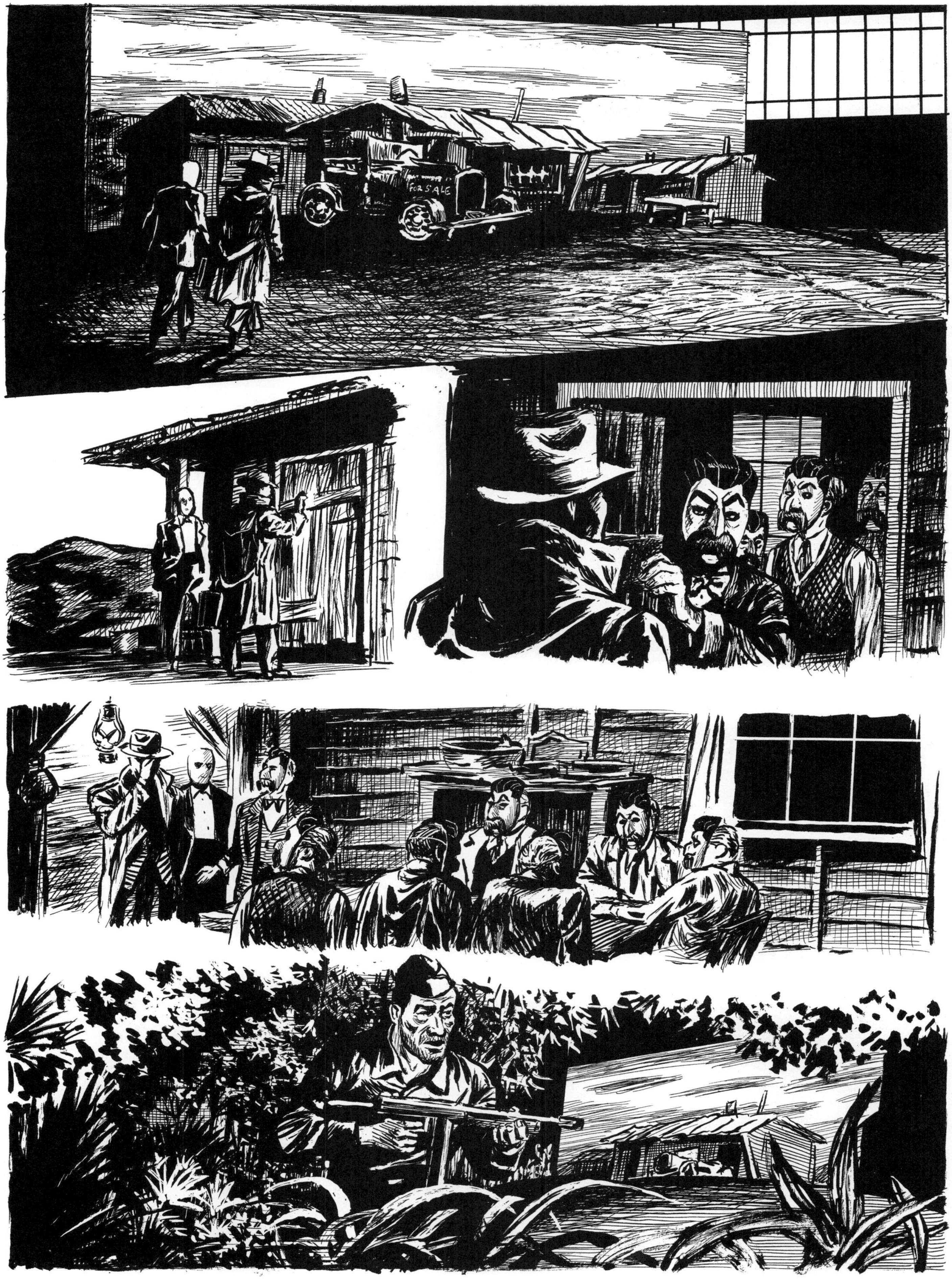
FOR SALE

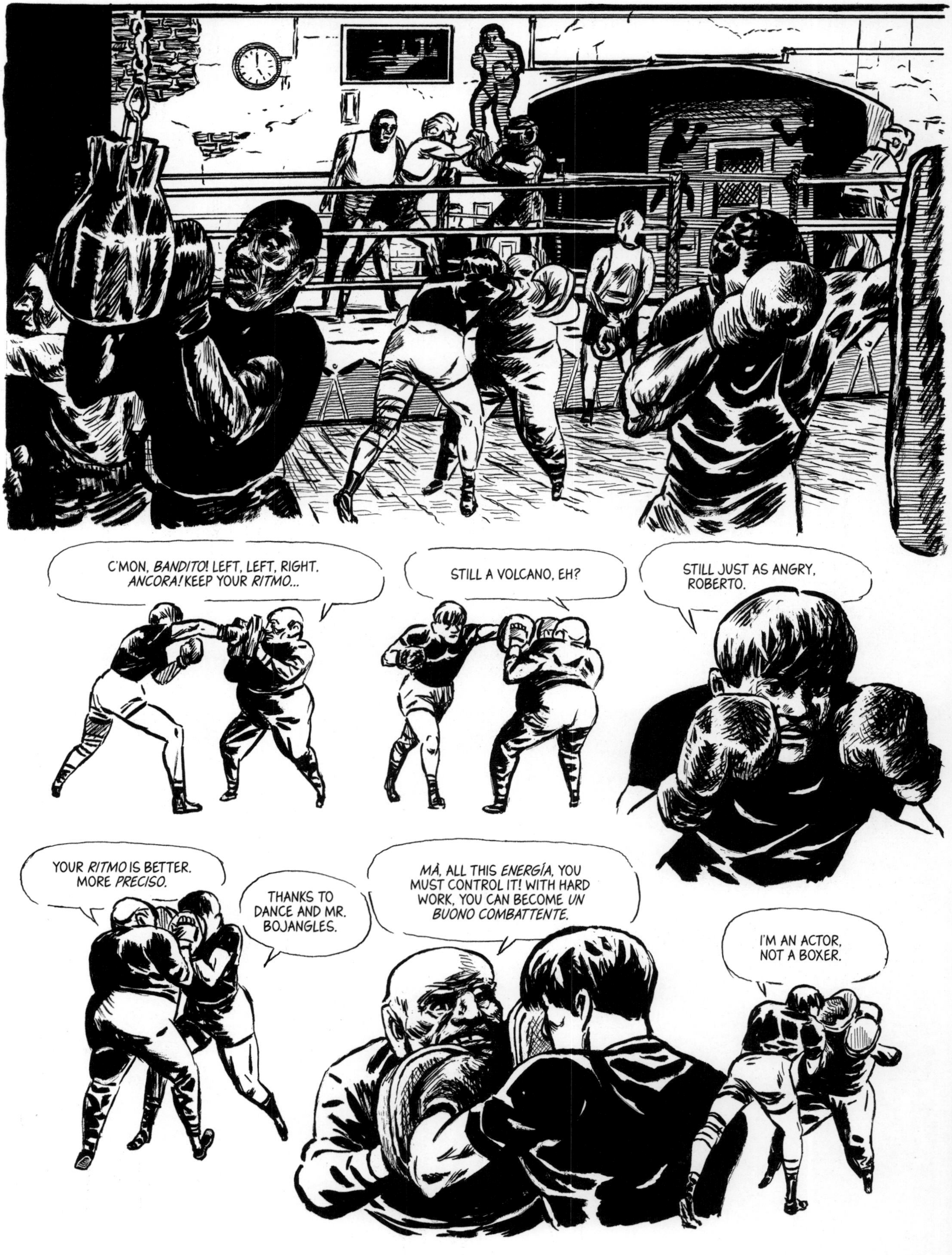
C'MON, *BANDITO!* LEFT, LEFT, RIGHT. *ANCORA!* KEEP YOUR *RITMO*...
STILL A VOLCANO, EH?
STILL JUST AS ANGRY, ROBERTO.
YOUR *RITMO* IS BETTER. MORE *PRECISO.*
THANKS TO DANCE AND MR. BOJANGLES.
*MÀ*, ALL THIS *ENERGÍA*, YOU MUST CONTROL IT! WITH HARD WORK, YOU CAN BECOME *UN BUONO COMBATTENTE.*
I'M AN ACTOR, NOT A BOXER.

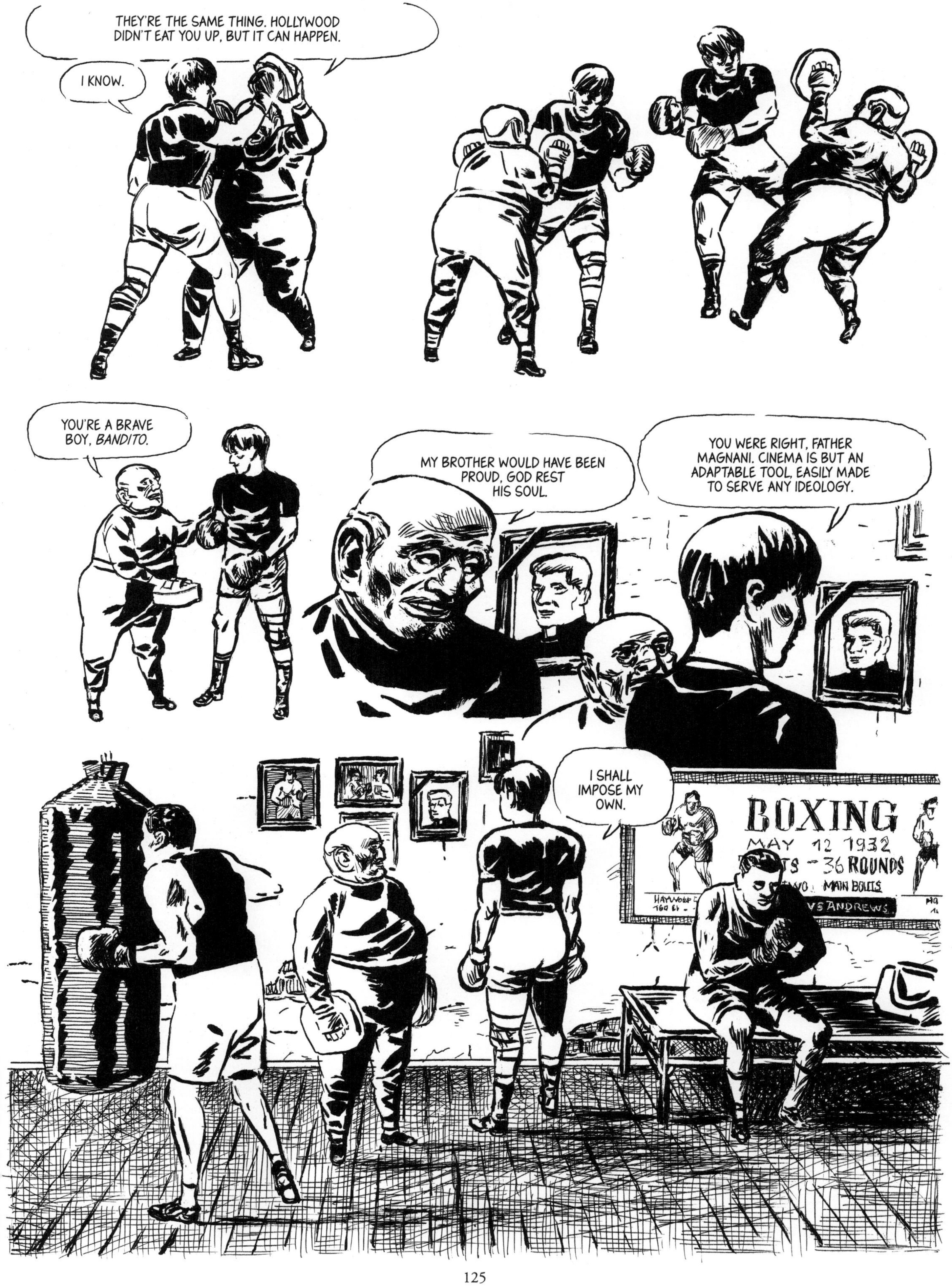
THEY'RE THE SAME THING. HOLLYWOOD DIDN'T EAT YOU UP, BUT IT CAN HAPPEN.
I KNOW.
YOU'RE A BRAVE BOY, *BANDITO.*
MY BROTHER WOULD HAVE BEEN PROUD, GOD REST HIS SOUL.
YOU WERE RIGHT, FATHER MAGNANI. CINEMA IS BUT AN ADAPTABLE TOOL, EASILY MADE TO SERVE ANY IDEOLOGY.
I SHALL IMPOSE MY OWN.
BOXING
MAY 12 1932
36 ROUNDS
MAIN BOUTS
VS ANDREWS

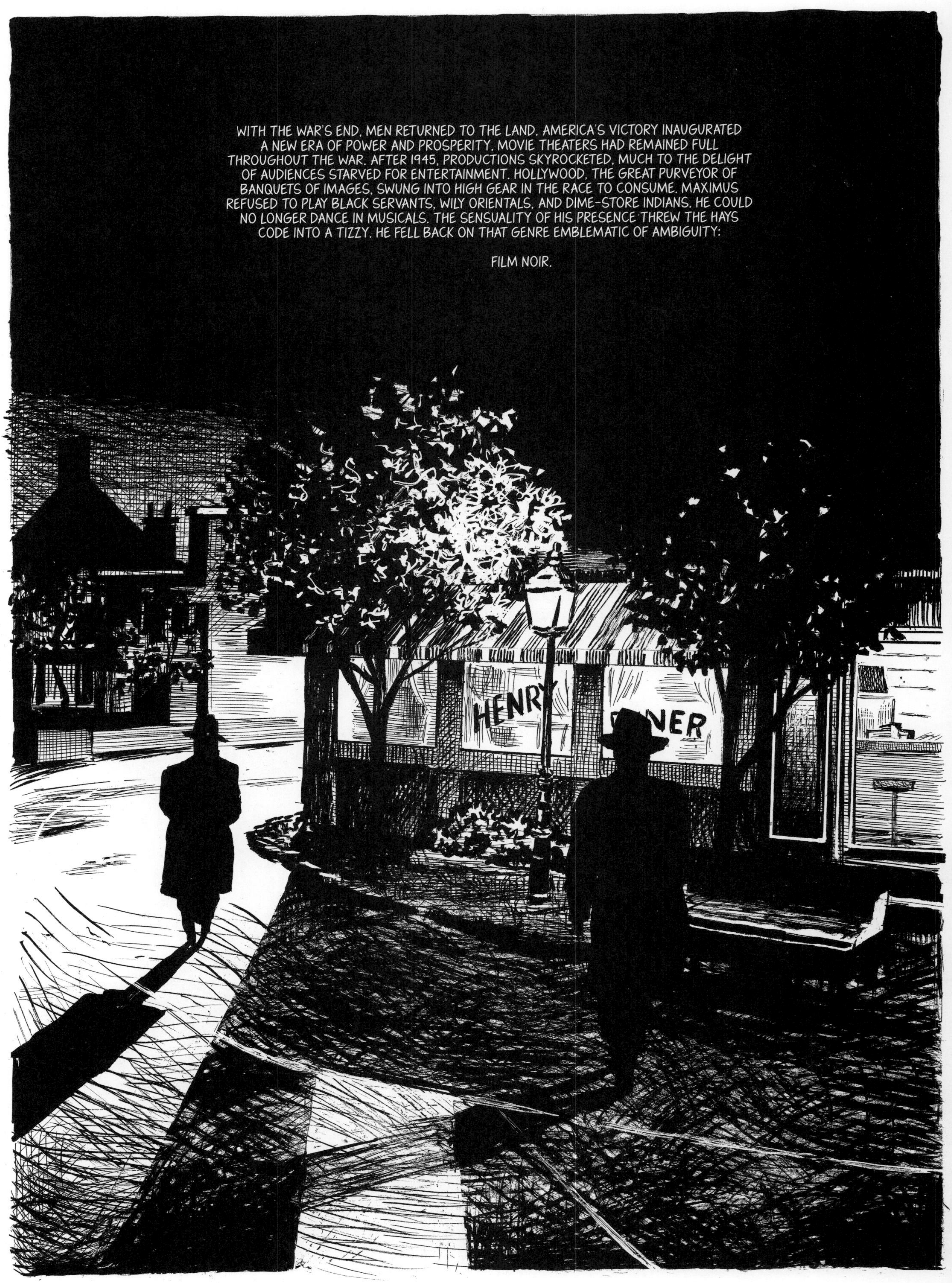
WITH THE WAR'S END, MEN RETURNED TO THE LAND. AMERICA'S VICTORY INAUGURATED A NEW ERA OF POWER AND PROSPERITY. MOVIE THEATERS HAD REMAINED FULL THROUGHOUT THE WAR. AFTER 1945, PRODUCTIONS SKYROCKETED, MUCH TO THE DELIGHT OF AUDIENCES STARVED FOR ENTERTAINMENT. HOLLYWOOD, THE GREAT PURVEYOR OF BANQUETS OF IMAGES, SWUNG INTO HIGH GEAR IN THE RACE TO CONSUME. MAXIMUS REFUSED TO PLAY BLACK SERVANTS, WILY ORIENTALS, AND DIME-STORE INDIANS. HE COULD NO LONGER DANCE IN MUSICALS. THE SENSUALITY OF HIS PRESENCE THREW THE HAYS CODE INTO A TIZZY. HE FELL BACK ON THAT GENRE EMBLEMATIC OF AMBIGUITY:
FILM NOIR.
HENRY

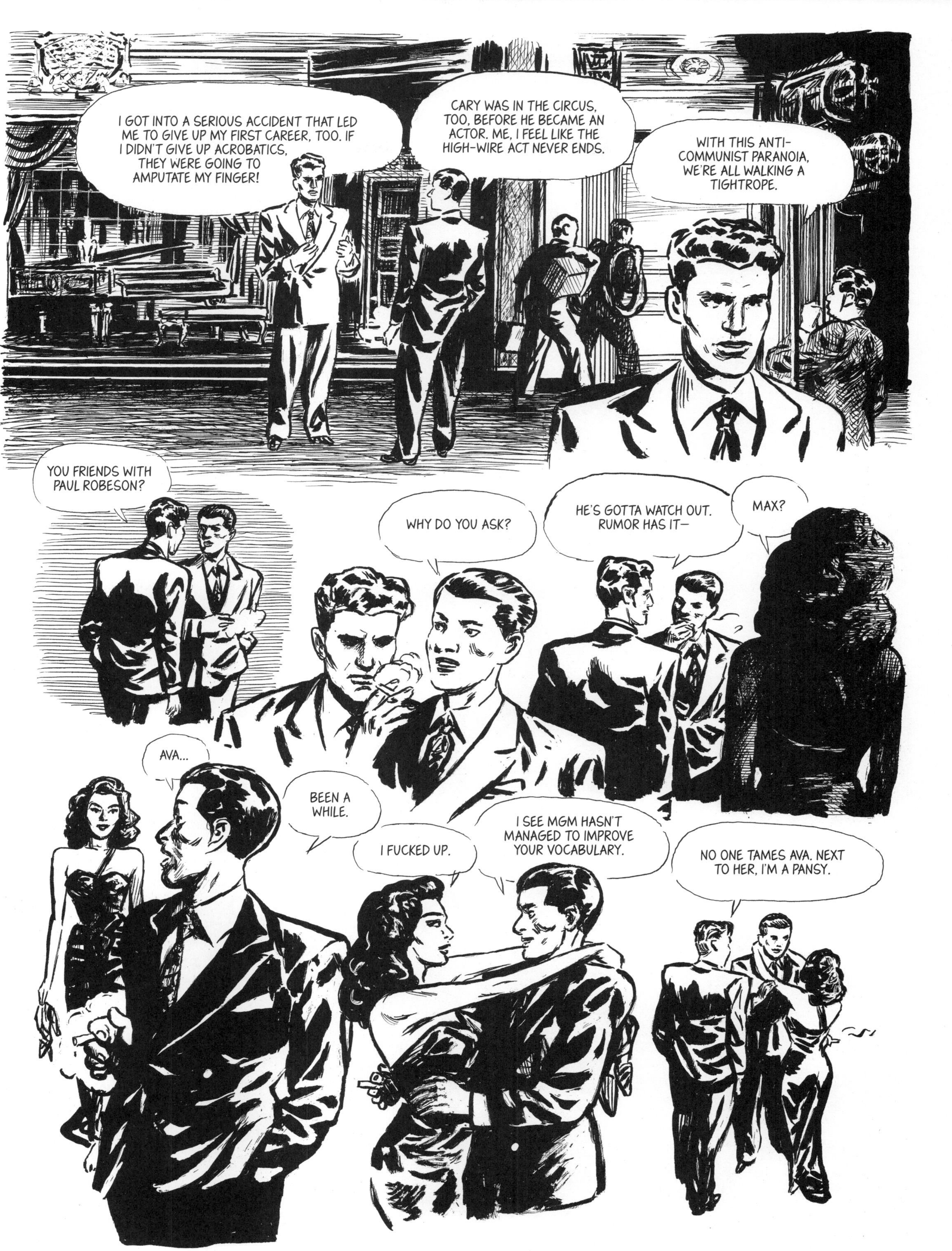
I GOT INTO A SERIOUS ACCIDENT THAT LED ME TO GIVE UP MY FIRST CAREER, TOO. IF I DIDN'T GIVE UP ACROBATICS, THEY WERE GOING TO AMPUTATE MY FINGER!
CARY WAS IN THE CIRCUS, TOO, BEFORE HE BECAME AN ACTOR. ME, I FEEL LIKE THE HIGH-WIRE ACT NEVER ENDS.
WITH THIS ANTI-COMMUNIST PARANOIA, WE'RE ALL WALKING A TIGHTROPE.
YOU FRIENDS WITH PAUL ROBESON?
WHY DO YOU ASK?
HE'S GOTTA WATCH OUT. RUMOR HAS IT—
MAX?
AVA...
BEEN A WHILE.
I FUCKED UP.
I SEE MGM HASN'T MANAGED TO IMPROVE YOUR VOCABULARY.
NO ONE TAMES AVA. NEXT TO HER, I'M A PANSY.

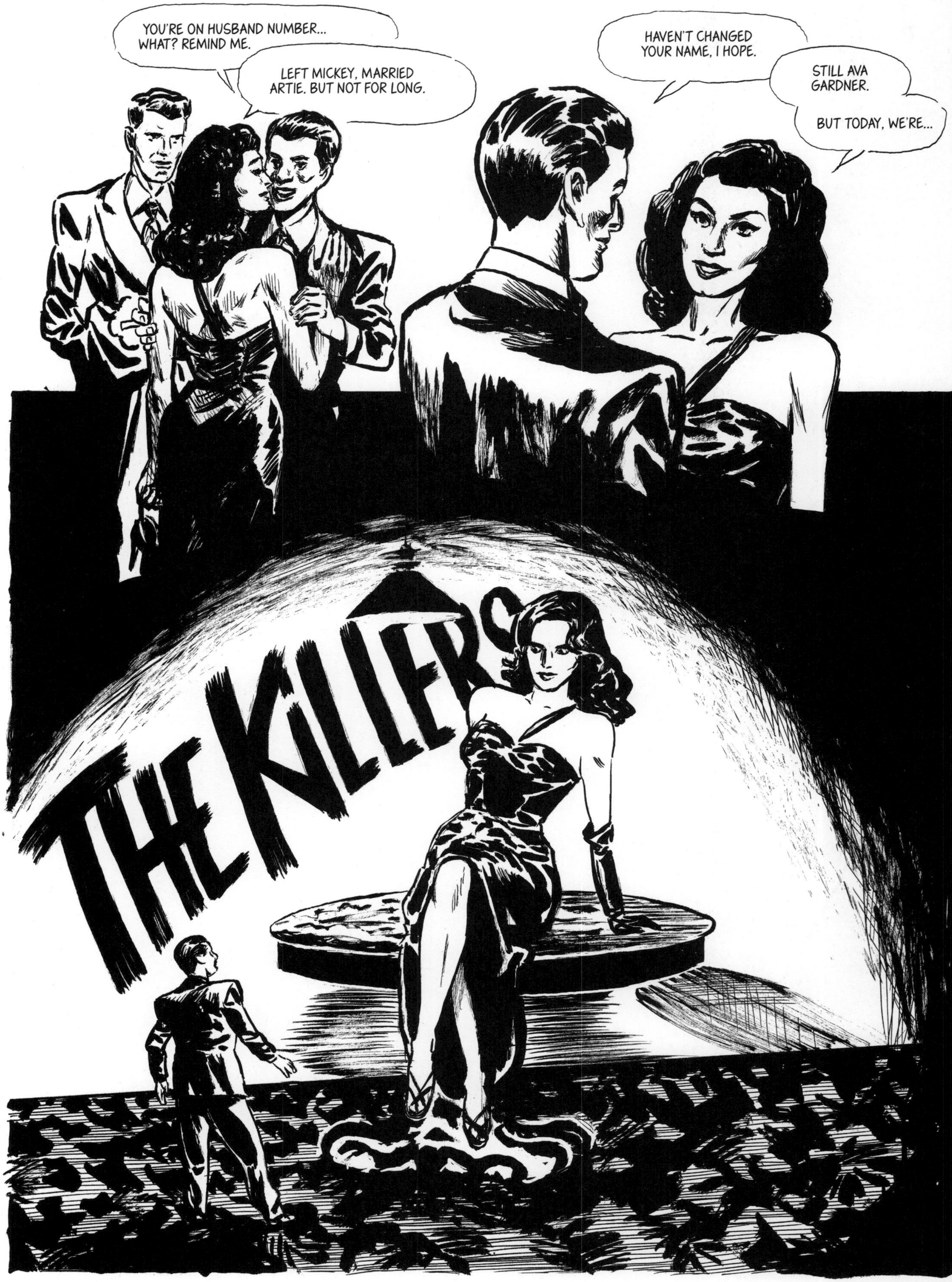
YOU'RE ON HUSBAND NUMBER... WHAT? REMIND ME.
LEFT MICKEY, MARRIED ARTIE. BUT NOT FOR LONG.
HAVEN'T CHANGED YOUR NAME, I HOPE.
STILL AVA GARDNER.
BUT TODAY, WE'RE...
THE KILLERS

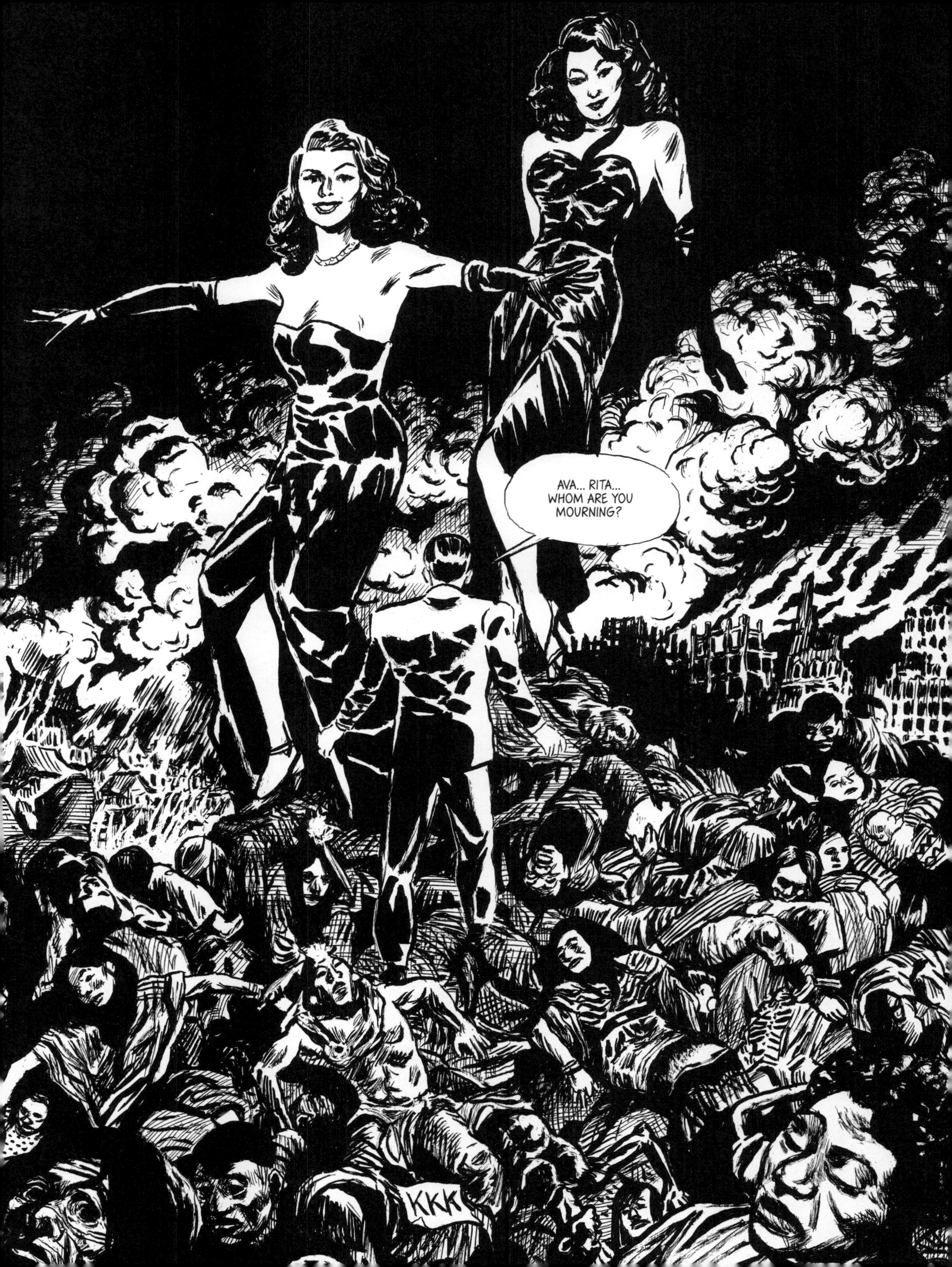
AVA... RITA... WHOM ARE YOU MOURNING?
KKK

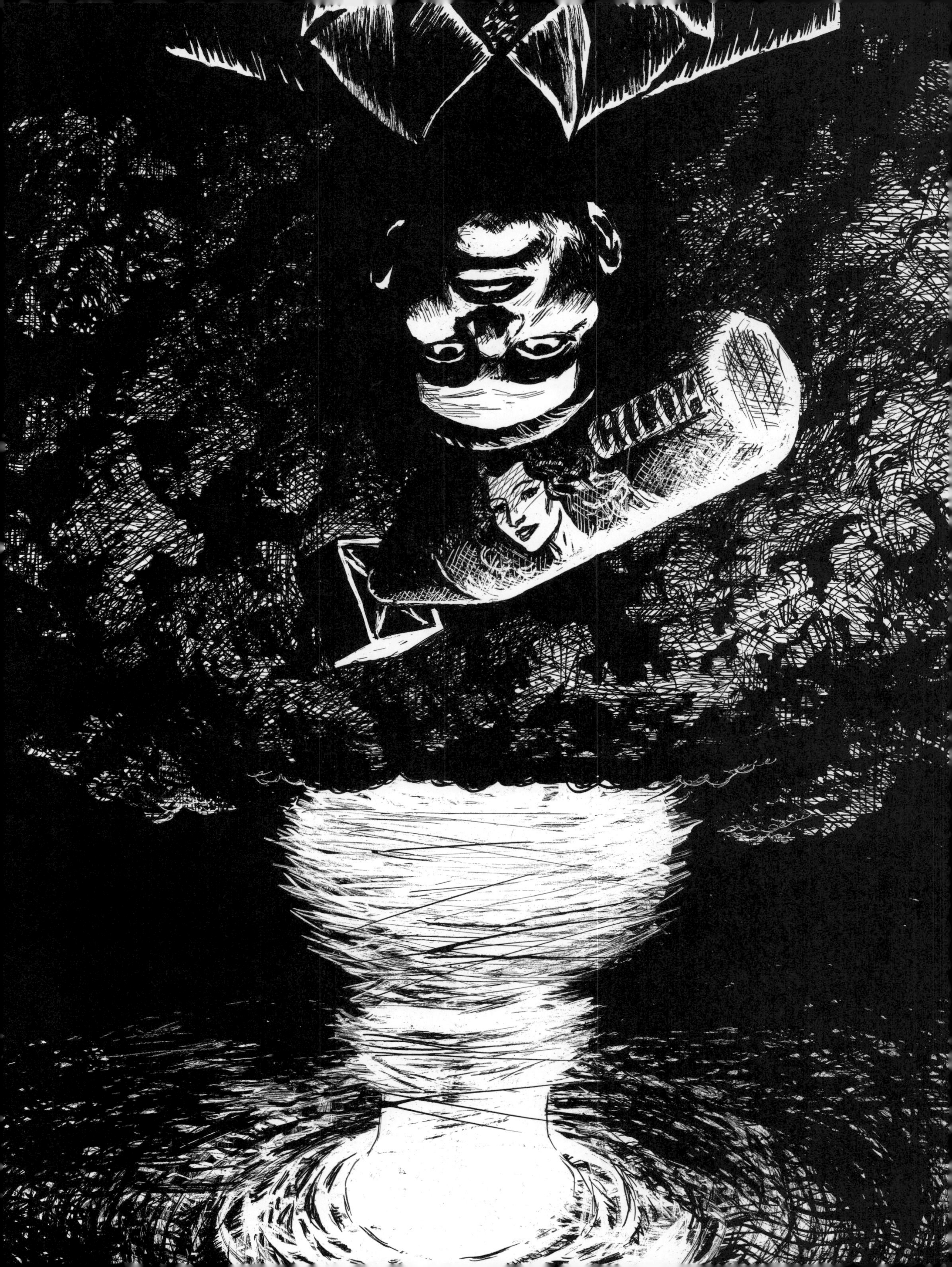

# 1948

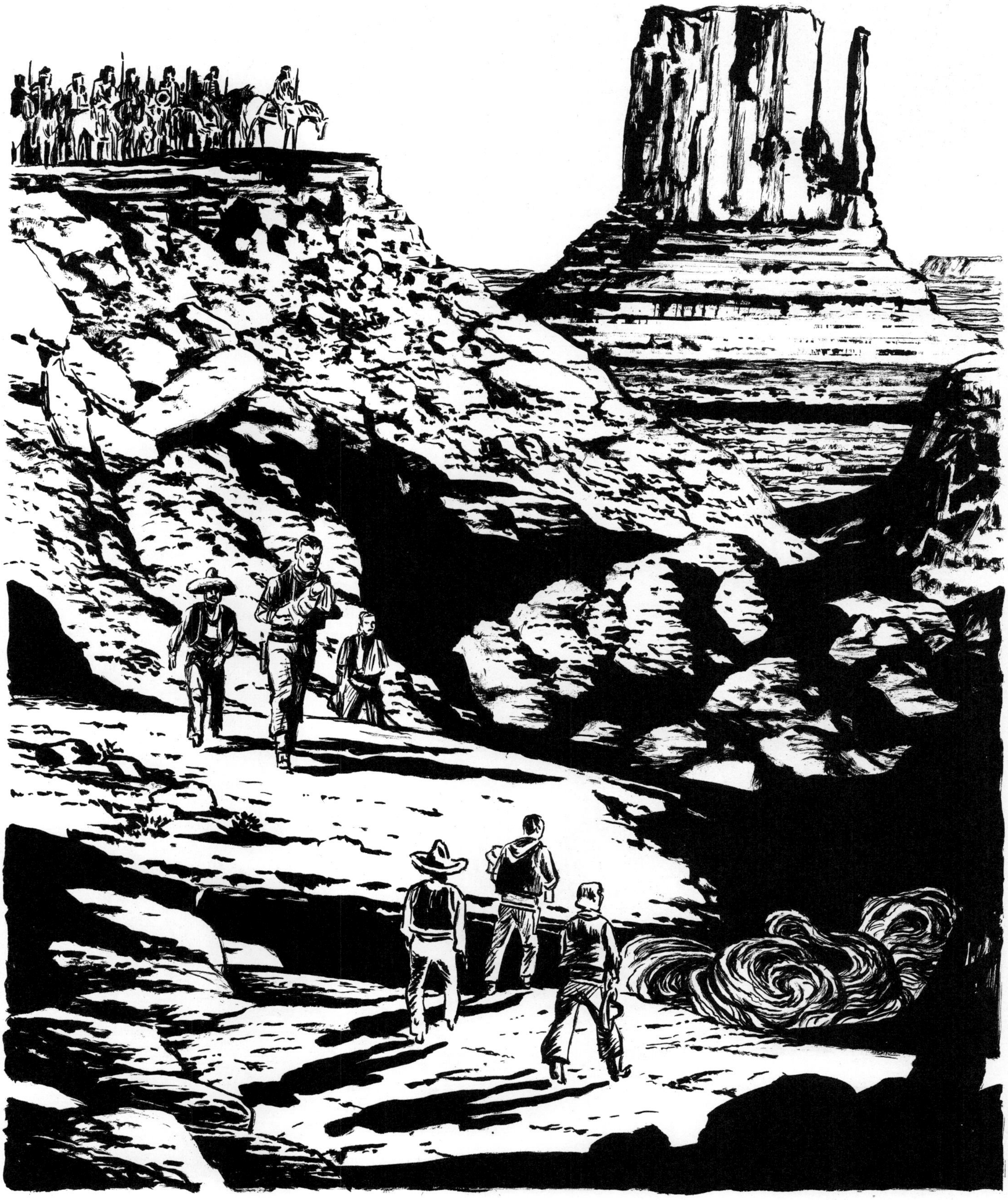

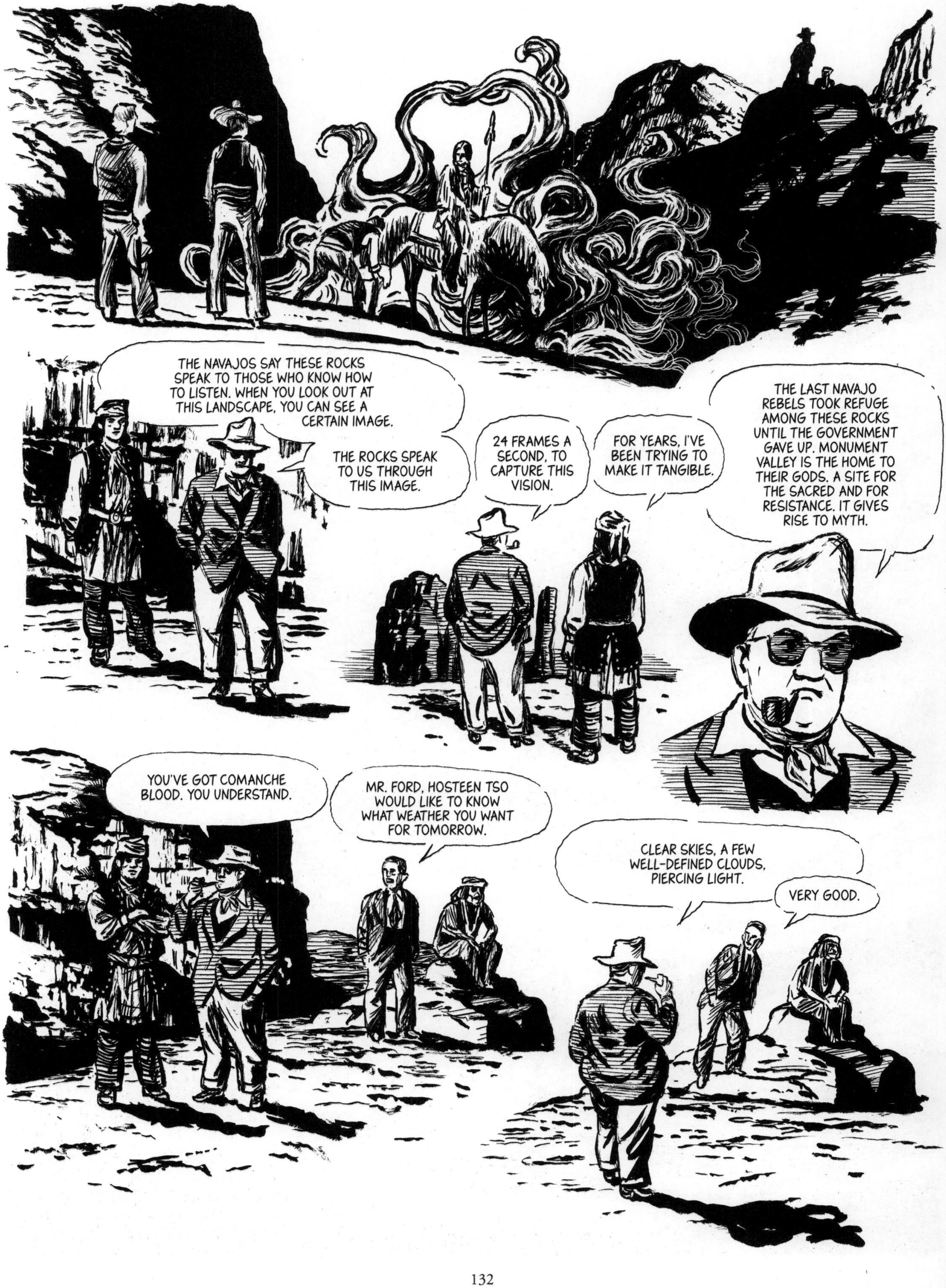

THE NAVAJOS SAY THESE ROCKS SPEAK TO THOSE WHO KNOW HOW TO LISTEN. WHEN YOU LOOK OUT AT THIS LANDSCAPE, YOU CAN SEE A CERTAIN IMAGE.
THE ROCKS SPEAK TO US THROUGH THIS IMAGE.
24 FRAMES A SECOND, TO CAPTURE THIS VISION.
FOR YEARS, I'VE BEEN TRYING TO MAKE IT TANGIBLE.
THE LAST NAVAJO REBELS TOOK REFUGE AMONG THESE ROCKS UNTIL THE GOVERNMENT GAVE UP. MONUMENT VALLEY IS THE HOME TO THEIR GODS. A SITE FOR THE SACRED AND FOR RESISTANCE. IT GIVES RISE TO MYTH.
YOU'VE GOT COMANCHE BLOOD. YOU UNDERSTAND.
MR. FORD, HOSTEEN TSO WOULD LIKE TO KNOW WHAT WEATHER YOU WANT FOR TOMORROW.
CLEAR SKIES, A FEW WELL-DEFINED CLOUDS, PIERCING LIGHT.
VERY GOOD.

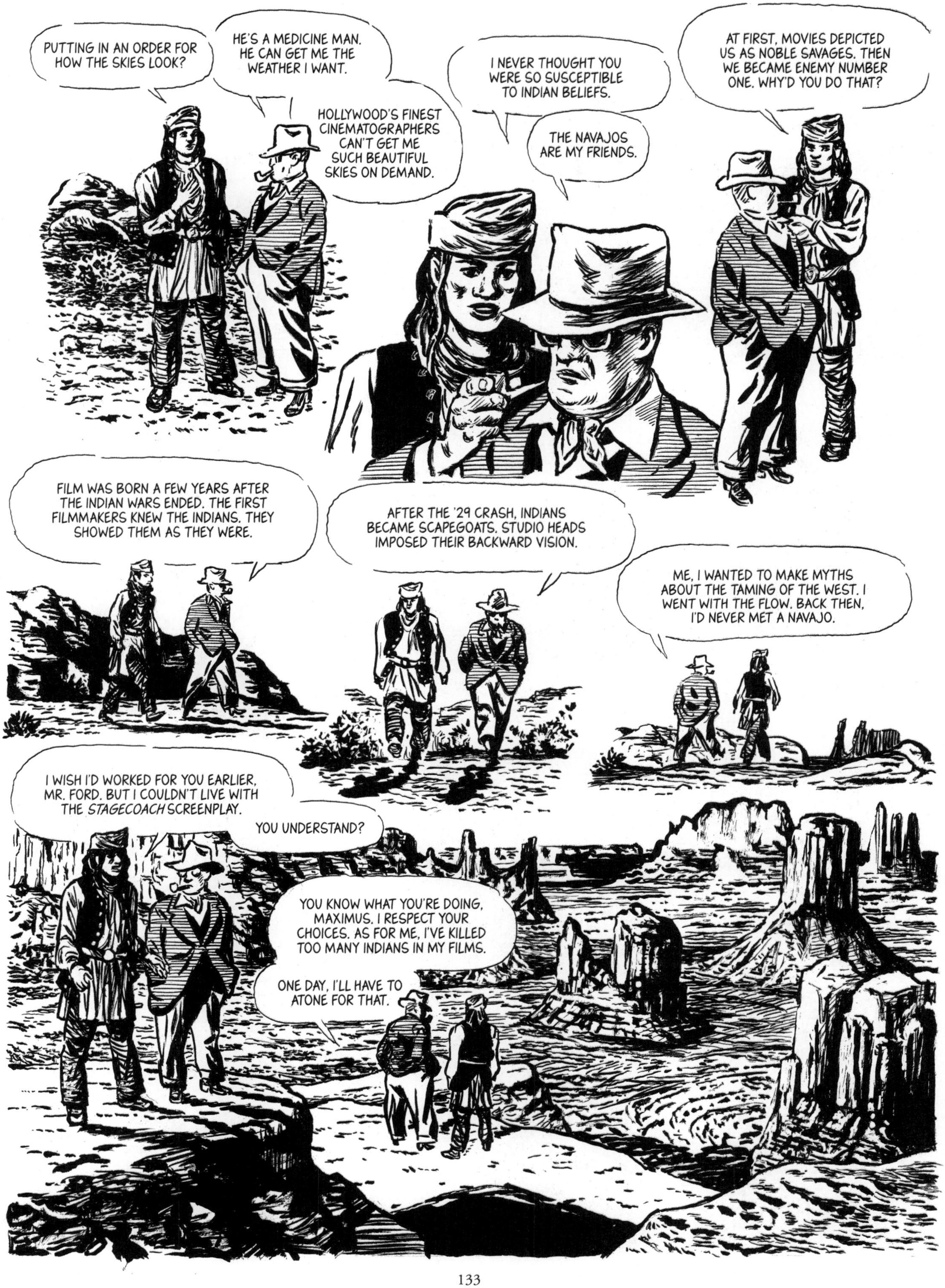
PUTTING IN AN ORDER FOR HOW THE SKIES LOOK?
HE'S A MEDICINE MAN. HE CAN GET ME THE WEATHER I WANT.
HOLLYWOOD'S FINEST CINEMATOGRAPHERS CAN'T GET ME SUCH BEAUTIFUL SKIES ON DEMAND.
I NEVER THOUGHT YOU WERE SO SUSCEPTIBLE TO INDIAN BELIEFS.
THE NAVAJOS ARE MY FRIENDS.
AT FIRST, MOVIES DEPICTED US AS NOBLE SAVAGES. THEN WE BECAME ENEMY NUMBER ONE. WHY'D YOU DO THAT?
FILM WAS BORN A FEW YEARS AFTER THE INDIAN WARS ENDED. THE FIRST FILMMAKERS KNEW THE INDIANS. THEY SHOWED THEM AS THEY WERE.
AFTER THE '29 CRASH, INDIANS BECAME SCAPEGOATS. STUDIO HEADS IMPOSED THEIR BACKWARD VISION.
ME, I WANTED TO MAKE MYTHS ABOUT THE TAMING OF THE WEST. I WENT WITH THE FLOW. BACK THEN, I'D NEVER MET A NAVAJO.
I WISH I'D WORKED FOR YOU EARLIER, MR. FORD. BUT I COULDN'T LIVE WITH THE *STAGECOACH* SCREENPLAY.
YOU UNDERSTAND?
YOU KNOW WHAT YOU'RE DOING, MAXIMUS. I RESPECT YOUR CHOICES. AS FOR ME, I'VE KILLED TOO MANY INDIANS IN MY FILMS.
ONE DAY, I'LL HAVE TO ATONE FOR THAT.

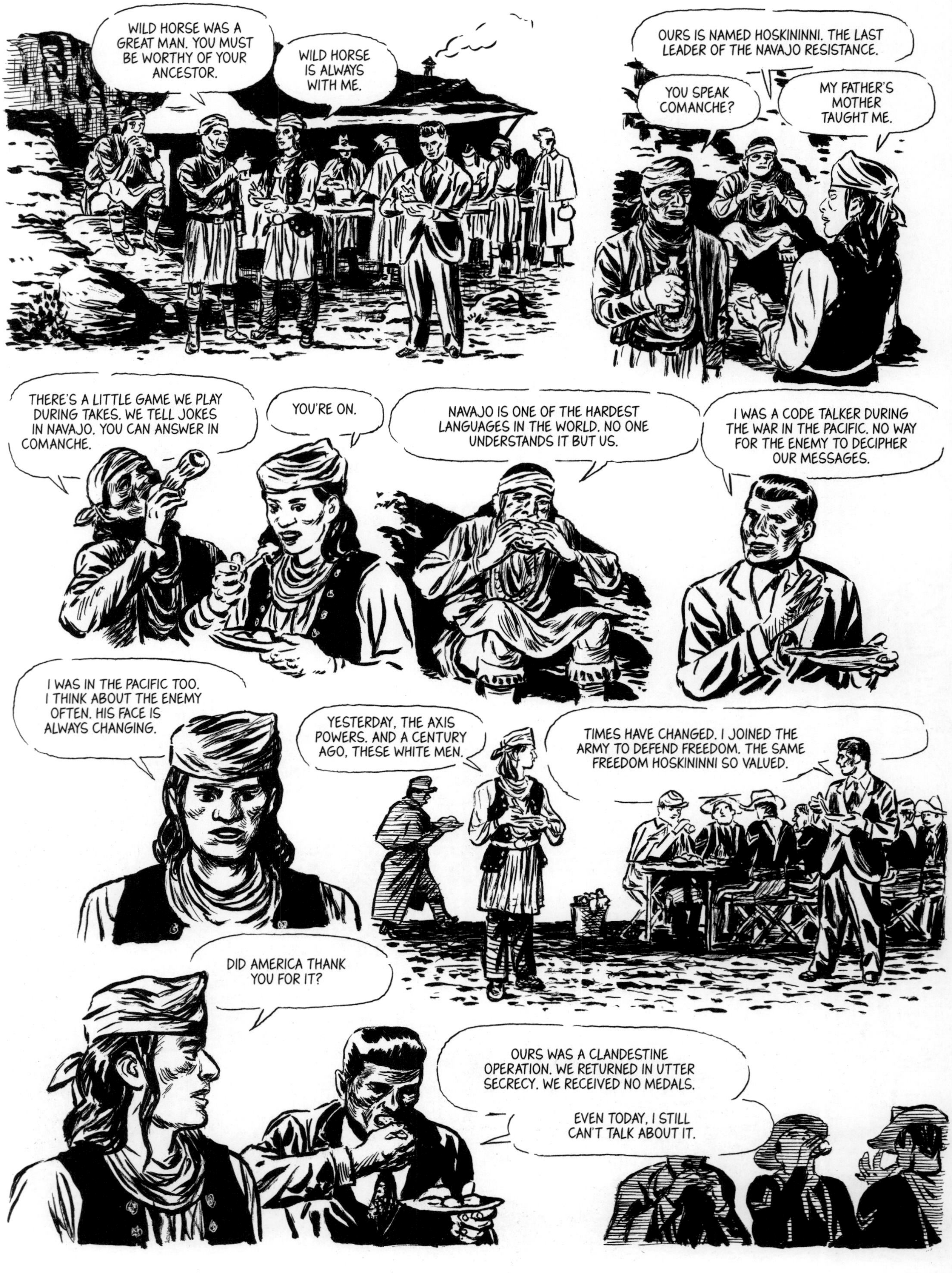
WILD HORSE WAS A GREAT MAN. YOU MUST BE WORTHY OF YOUR ANCESTOR.
WILD HORSE IS ALWAYS WITH ME.
OURS IS NAMED HOSKININNI. THE LAST LEADER OF THE NAVAJO RESISTANCE.
YOU SPEAK COMANCHE?
MY FATHER'S MOTHER TAUGHT ME.
THERE'S A LITTLE GAME WE PLAY DURING TAKES. WE TELL JOKES IN NAVAJO. YOU CAN ANSWER IN COMANCHE.
YOU'RE ON.
NAVAJO IS ONE OF THE HARDEST LANGUAGES IN THE WORLD. NO ONE UNDERSTANDS IT BUT US.
I WAS A CODE TALKER DURING THE WAR IN THE PACIFIC. NO WAY FOR THE ENEMY TO DECIPHER OUR MESSAGES.
I WAS IN THE PACIFIC TOO. I THINK ABOUT THE ENEMY OFTEN. HIS FACE IS ALWAYS CHANGING.
YESTERDAY, THE AXIS POWERS. AND A CENTURY AGO, THESE WHITE MEN.
TIMES HAVE CHANGED. I JOINED THE ARMY TO DEFEND FREEDOM. THE SAME FREEDOM HOSKININNI SO VALUED.
DID AMERICA THANK YOU FOR IT?
OURS WAS A CLANDESTINE OPERATION. WE RETURNED IN UTTER SECRECY. WE RECEIVED NO MEDALS.
EVEN TODAY, I STILL CAN'T TALK ABOUT IT.

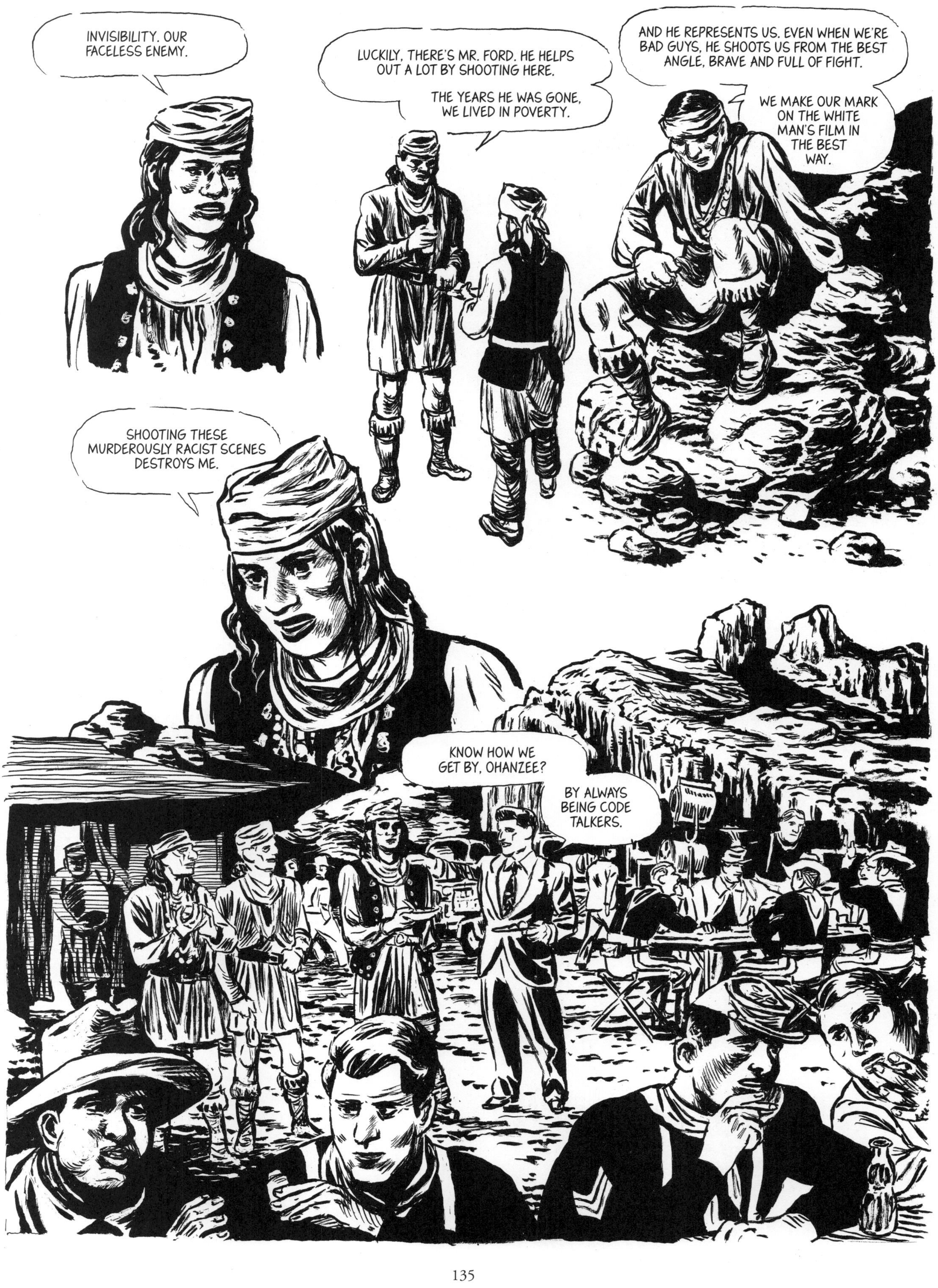
INVISIBILITY. OUR FACELESS ENEMY.
LUCKILY, THERE'S MR. FORD. HE HELPS OUT A LOT BY SHOOTING HERE.
THE YEARS HE WAS GONE, WE LIVED IN POVERTY.
AND HE REPRESENTS US. EVEN WHEN WE'RE BAD GUYS, HE SHOOTS US FROM THE BEST ANGLE, BRAVE AND FULL OF FIGHT.
WE MAKE OUR MARK ON THE WHITE MAN'S FILM IN THE BEST WAY.
SHOOTING THESE MURDEROUSLY RACIST SCENES DESTROYS ME.
KNOW HOW WE GET BY, OHANZEE?
BY ALWAYS BEING CODE TALKERS.

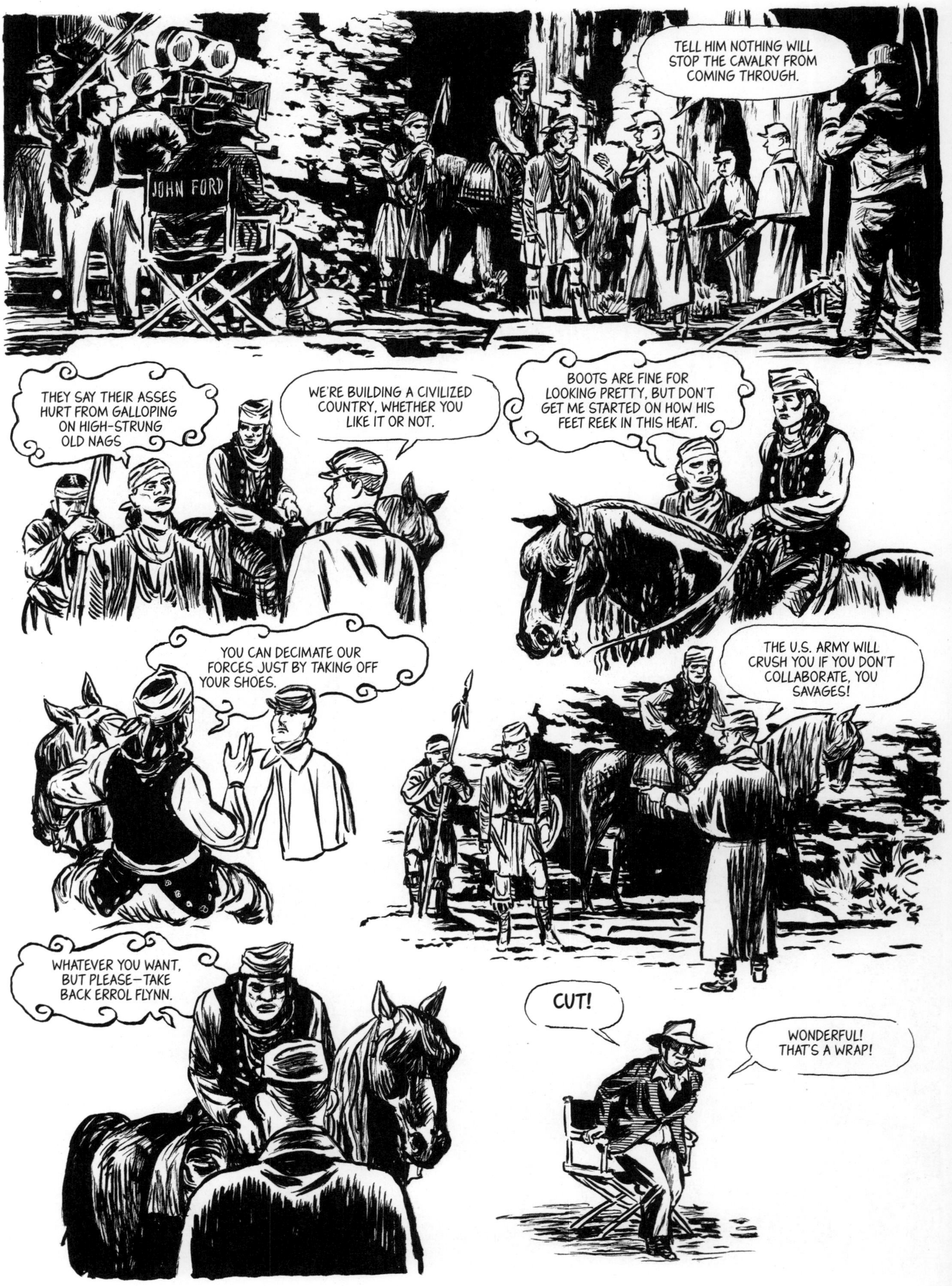
JOHN FORD
TELL HIM NOTHING WILL STOP THE CAVALRY FROM COMING THROUGH.
THEY SAY THEIR ASSES HURT FROM GALLOPING ON HIGH-STRUNG OLD NAGS
WE'RE BUILDING A CIVILIZED COUNTRY, WHETHER YOU LIKE IT OR NOT.
BOOTS ARE FINE FOR LOOKING PRETTY, BUT DON'T GET ME STARTED ON HOW HIS FEET REEK IN THIS HEAT.
YOU CAN DECIMATE OUR FORCES JUST BY TAKING OFF YOUR SHOES.
THE U.S. ARMY WILL CRUSH YOU IF YOU DON'T COLLABORATE, YOU SAVAGES!
WHATEVER YOU WANT, BUT PLEASE—TAKE BACK ERROL FLYNN.
CUT!
WONDERFUL! THAT'S A WRAP!

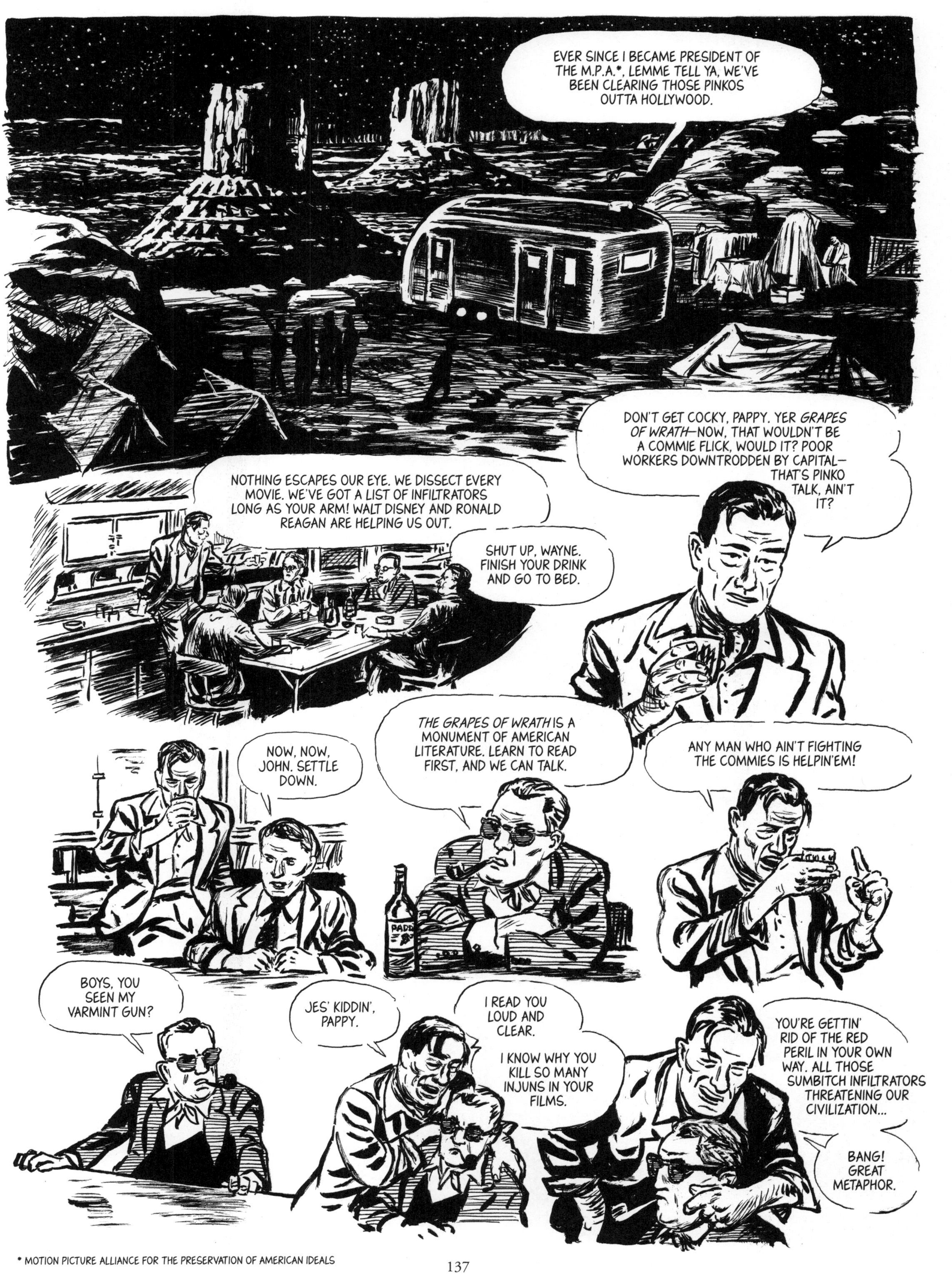
EVER SINCE I BECAME PRESIDENT OF THE M.P.A.*, LEMME TELL YA, WE'VE BEEN CLEARING THOSE PINKOS OUTTA HOLLYWOOD.
NOTHING ESCAPES OUR EYE. WE DISSECT EVERY MOVIE. WE'VE GOT A LIST OF INFILTRATORS LONG AS YOUR ARM! WALT DISNEY AND RONALD REAGAN ARE HELPING US OUT.
SHUT UP, WAYNE. FINISH YOUR DRINK AND GO TO BED.
DON'T GET COCKY, PAPPY. YER *GRAPES OF WRATH*—NOW, THAT WOULDN'T BE A COMMIE FLICK, WOULD IT? POOR WORKERS DOWNTRODDEN BY CAPITAL—THAT'S PINKO TALK, AIN'T IT?
NOW, NOW, JOHN. SETTLE DOWN.
*THE GRAPES OF WRATH* IS A MONUMENT OF AMERICAN LITERATURE. LEARN TO READ FIRST, AND WE CAN TALK.
ANY MAN WHO AIN'T FIGHTING THE COMMIES IS HELPIN'EM!
BOYS, YOU SEEN MY VARMINT GUN?
JES' KIDDIN', PAPPY.
I READ YOU LOUD AND CLEAR.
I KNOW WHY YOU KILL SO MANY INJUNS IN YOUR FILMS.
YOU'RE GETTIN' RID OF THE RED PERIL IN YOUR OWN WAY. ALL THOSE SUMBITCH INFILTRATORS THREATENING OUR CIVILIZATION...
BANG! GREAT METAPHOR.

* MOTION PICTURE ALLIANCE FOR THE PRESERVATION OF AMERICAN IDEALS

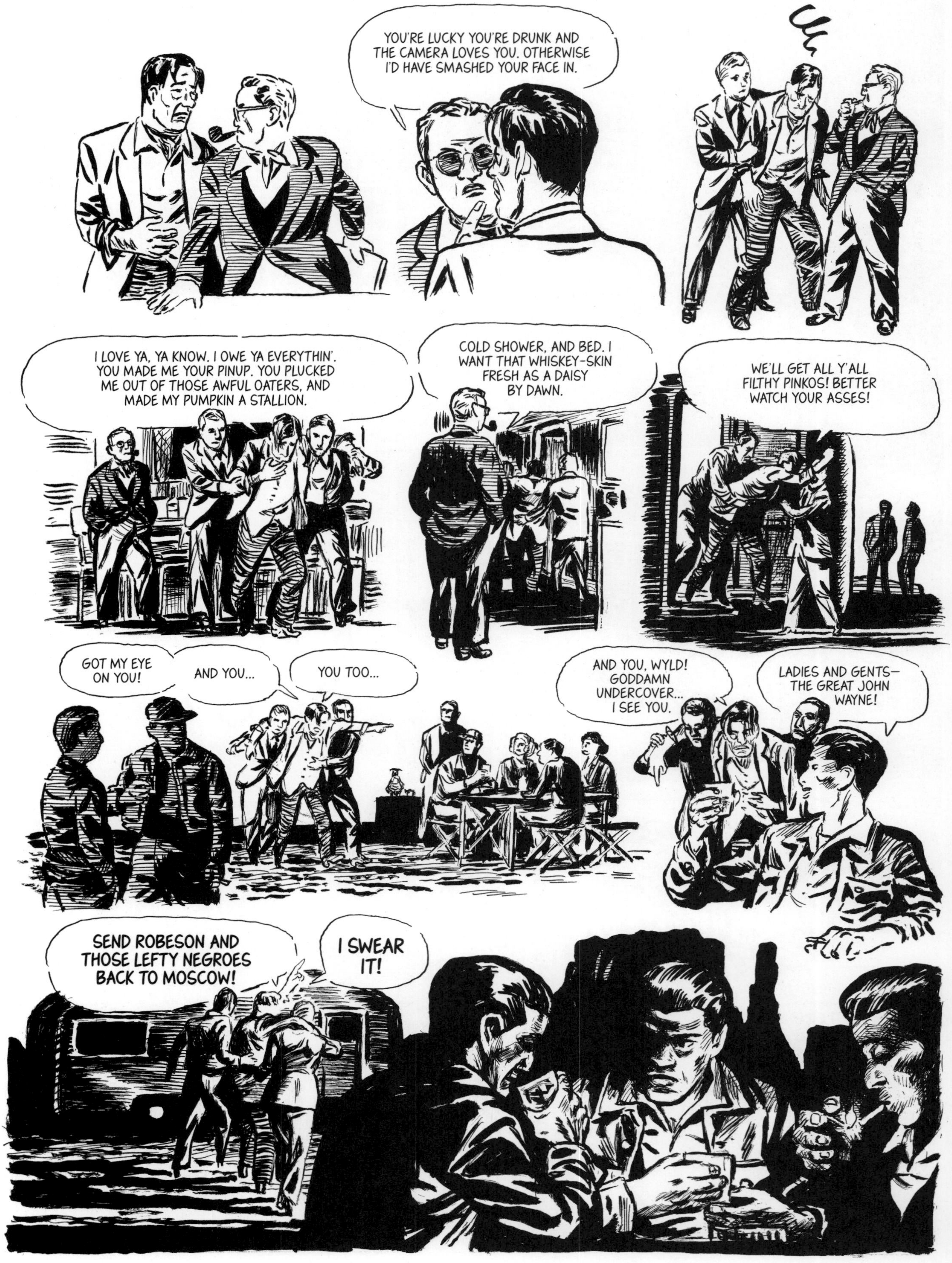
YOU'RE LUCKY YOU'RE DRUNK AND THE CAMERA LOVES YOU. OTHERWISE I'D HAVE SMASHED YOUR FACE IN.
I LOVE YA, YA KNOW. I OWE YA EVERYTHIN'. YOU MADE ME YOUR PINUP. YOU PLUCKED ME OUT OF THOSE AWFUL OATERS, AND MADE MY PUMPKIN A STALLION.
COLD SHOWER, AND BED. I WANT THAT WHISKEY-SKIN FRESH AS A DAISY BY DAWN.
WE'LL GET ALL Y'ALL FILTHY PINKOS! BETTER WATCH YOUR ASSES!
GOT MY EYE ON YOU!
AND YOU...
YOU TOO...
AND YOU, WYLD! GODDAMN UNDERCOVER... I SEE YOU.
LADIES AND GENTS— THE GREAT JOHN WAYNE!
SEND ROBESON AND THOSE LEFTY NEGROES BACK TO MOSCOW!
I SWEAR IT!

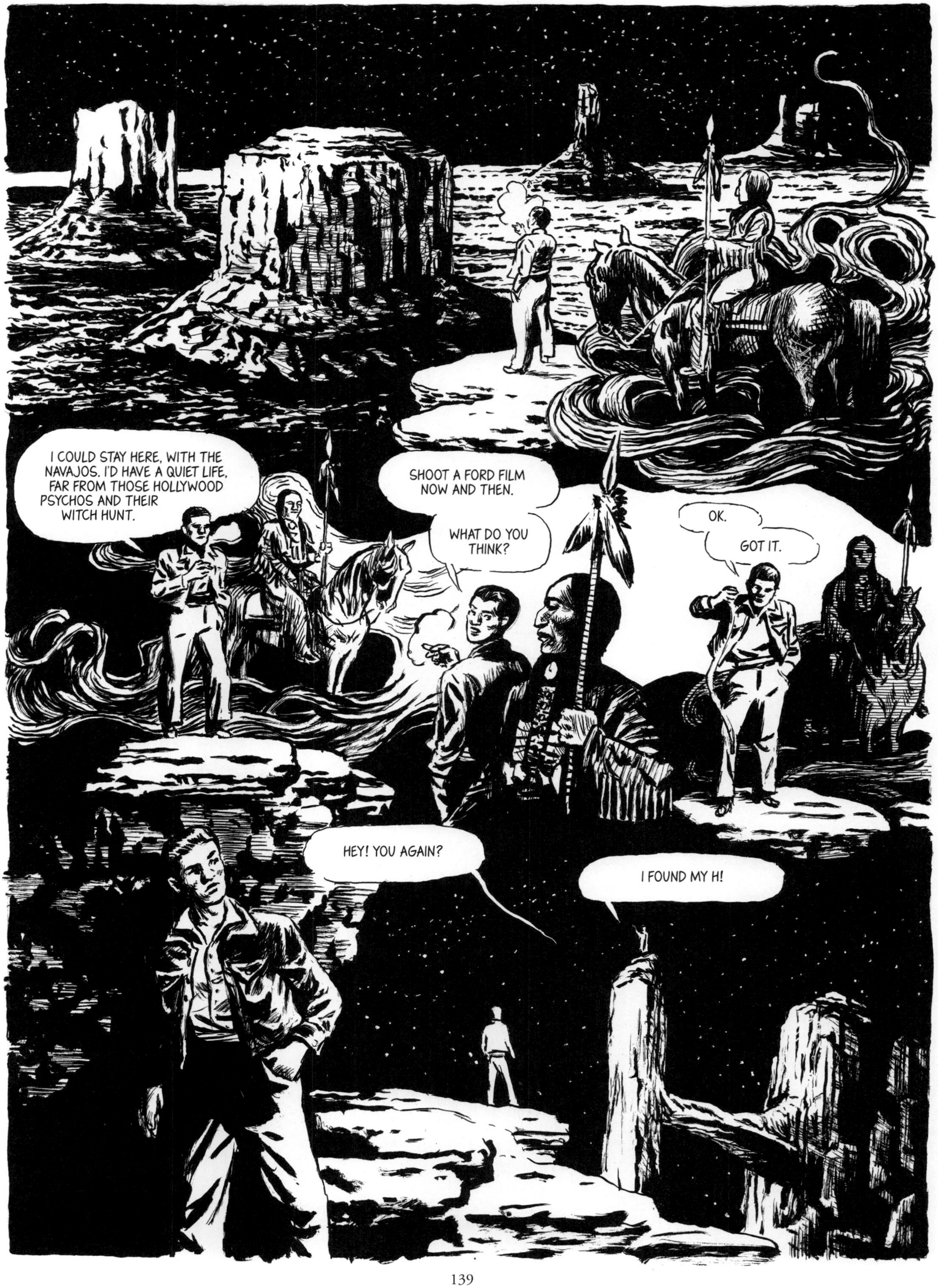
I COULD STAY HERE, WITH THE NAVAJOS. I'D HAVE A QUIET LIFE, FAR FROM THOSE HOLLYWOOD PSYCHOS AND THEIR WITCH HUNT.
SHOOT A FORD FILM NOW AND THEN.
WHAT DO YOU THINK?
OK.
GOT IT.
HEY! YOU AGAIN?
I FOUND MY H!

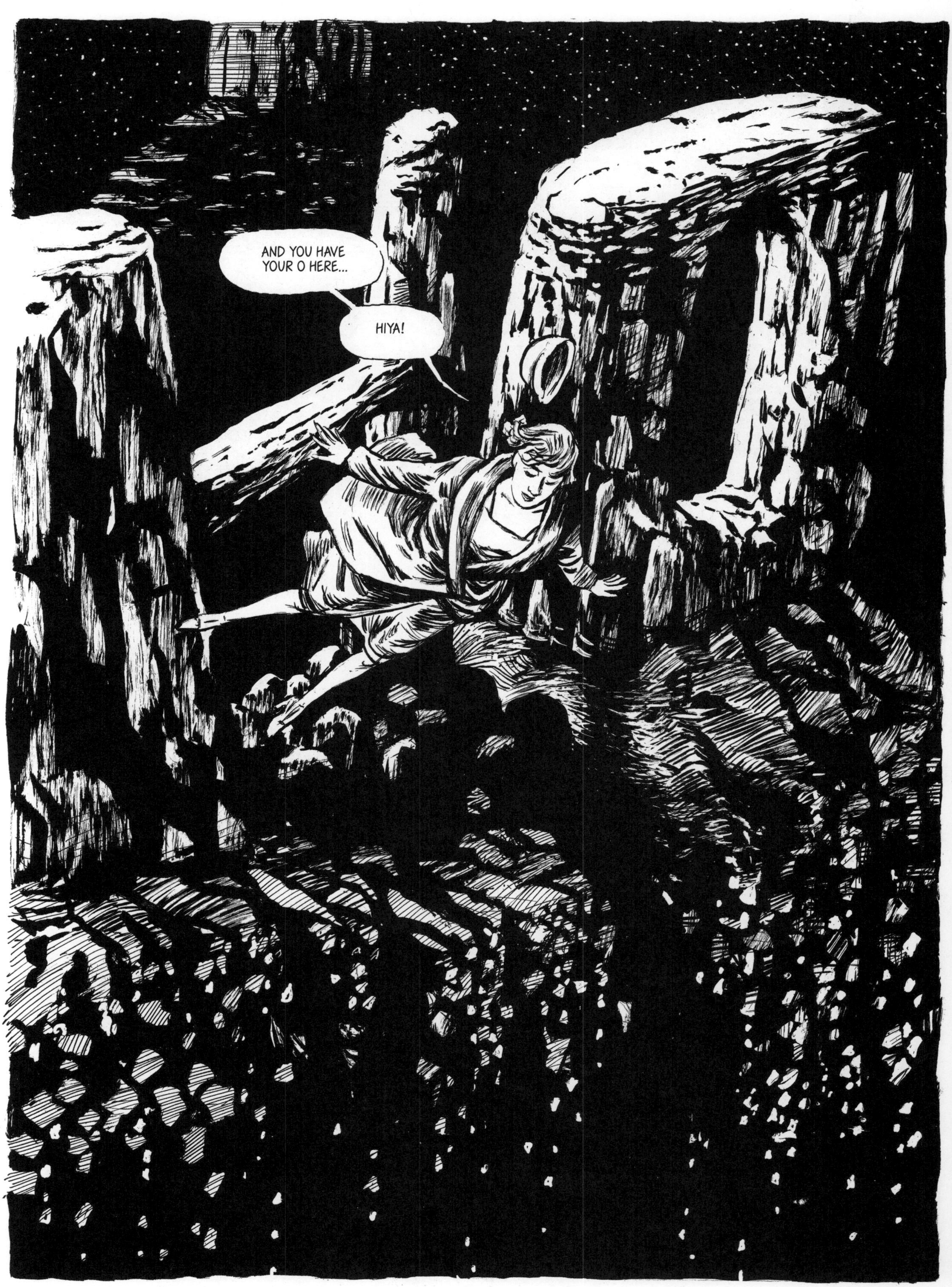
AND YOU HAVE YOUR O HERE...
HIYA!

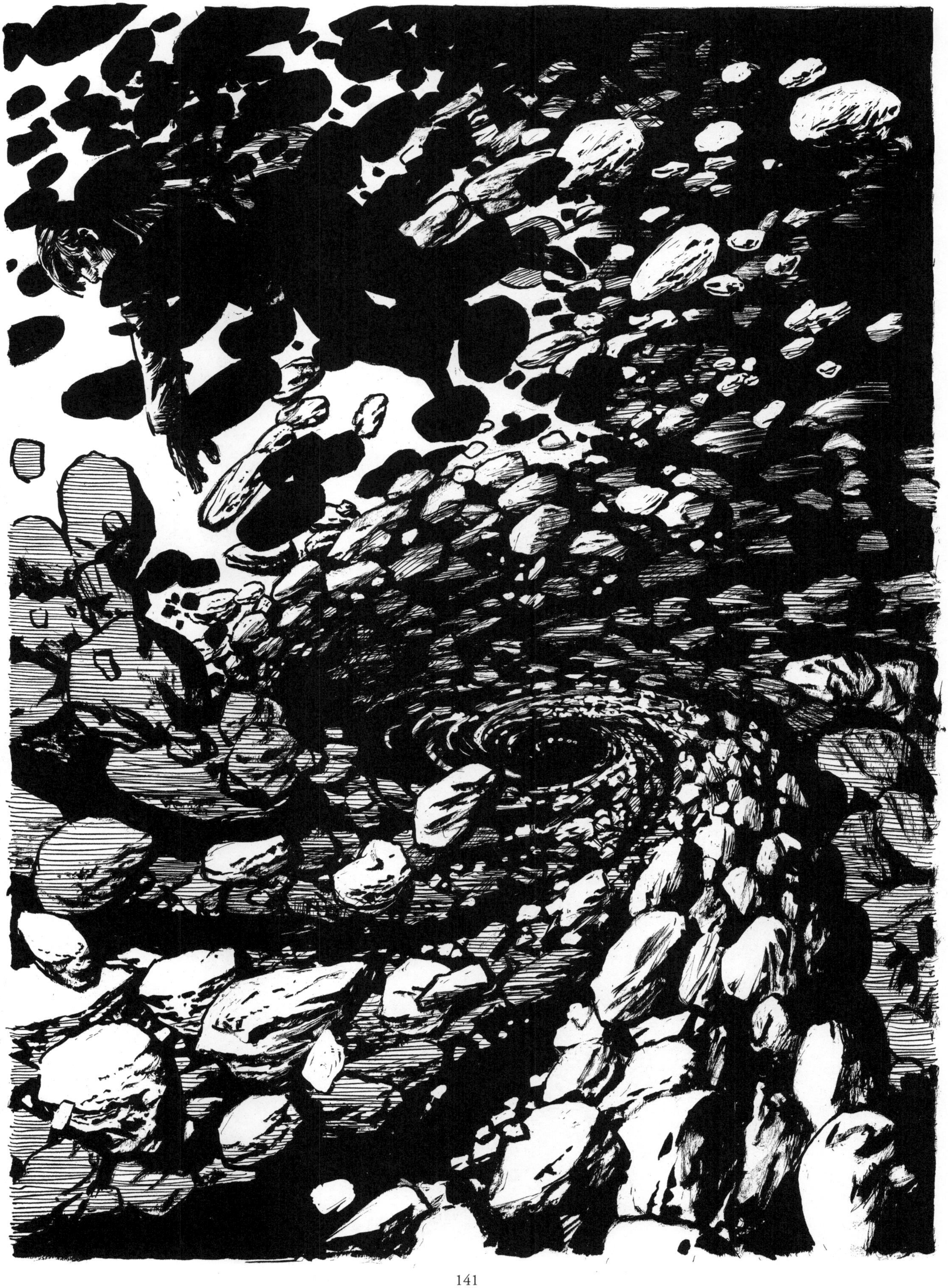

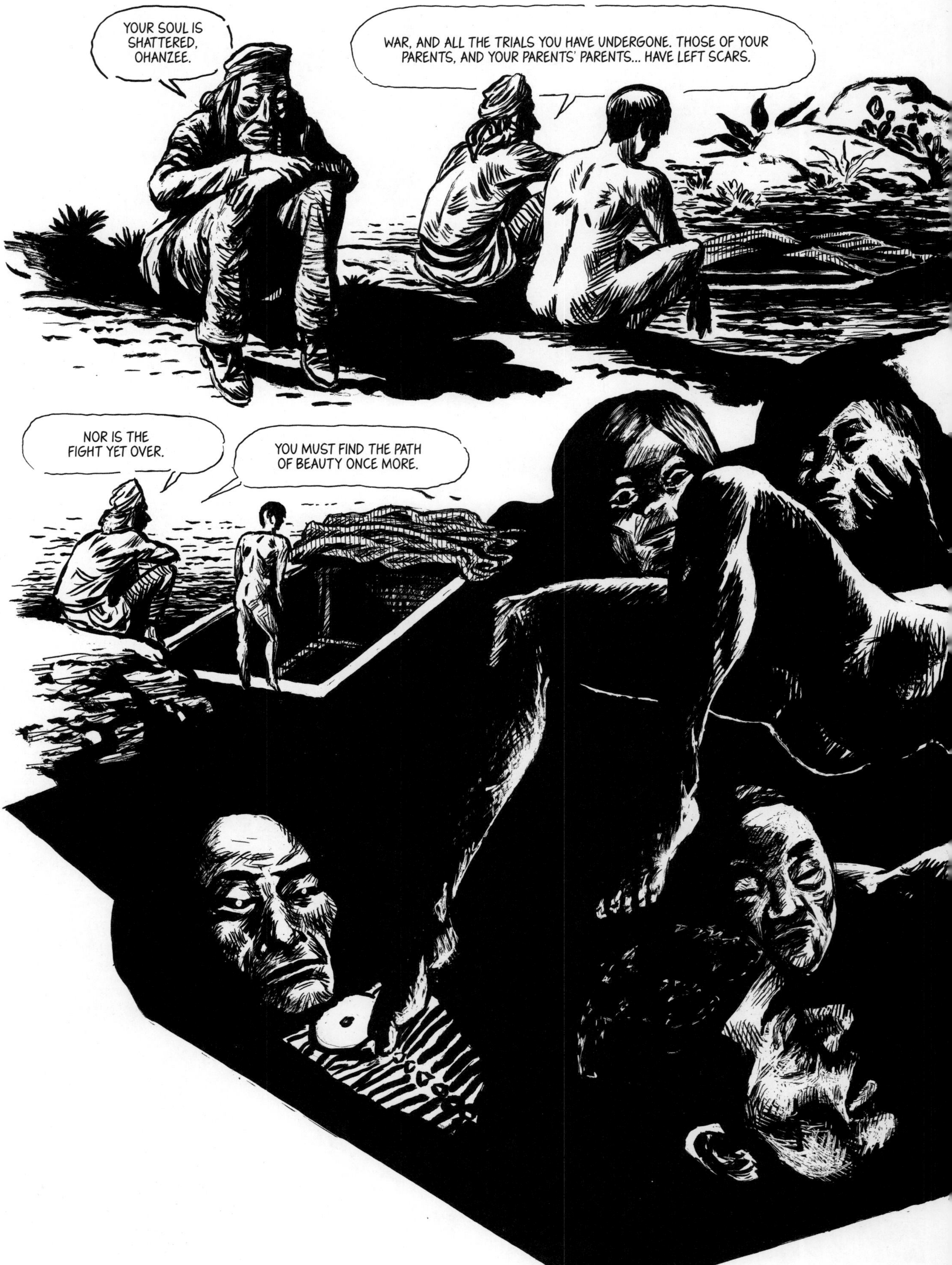
YOUR SOUL IS SHATTERED, OHANZEE.
WAR, AND ALL THE TRIALS YOU HAVE UNDERGONE. THOSE OF YOUR PARENTS, AND YOUR PARENTS' PARENTS... HAVE LEFT SCARS.
NOR IS THE FIGHT YET OVER.
YOU MUST FIND THE PATH OF BEAUTY ONCE MORE.

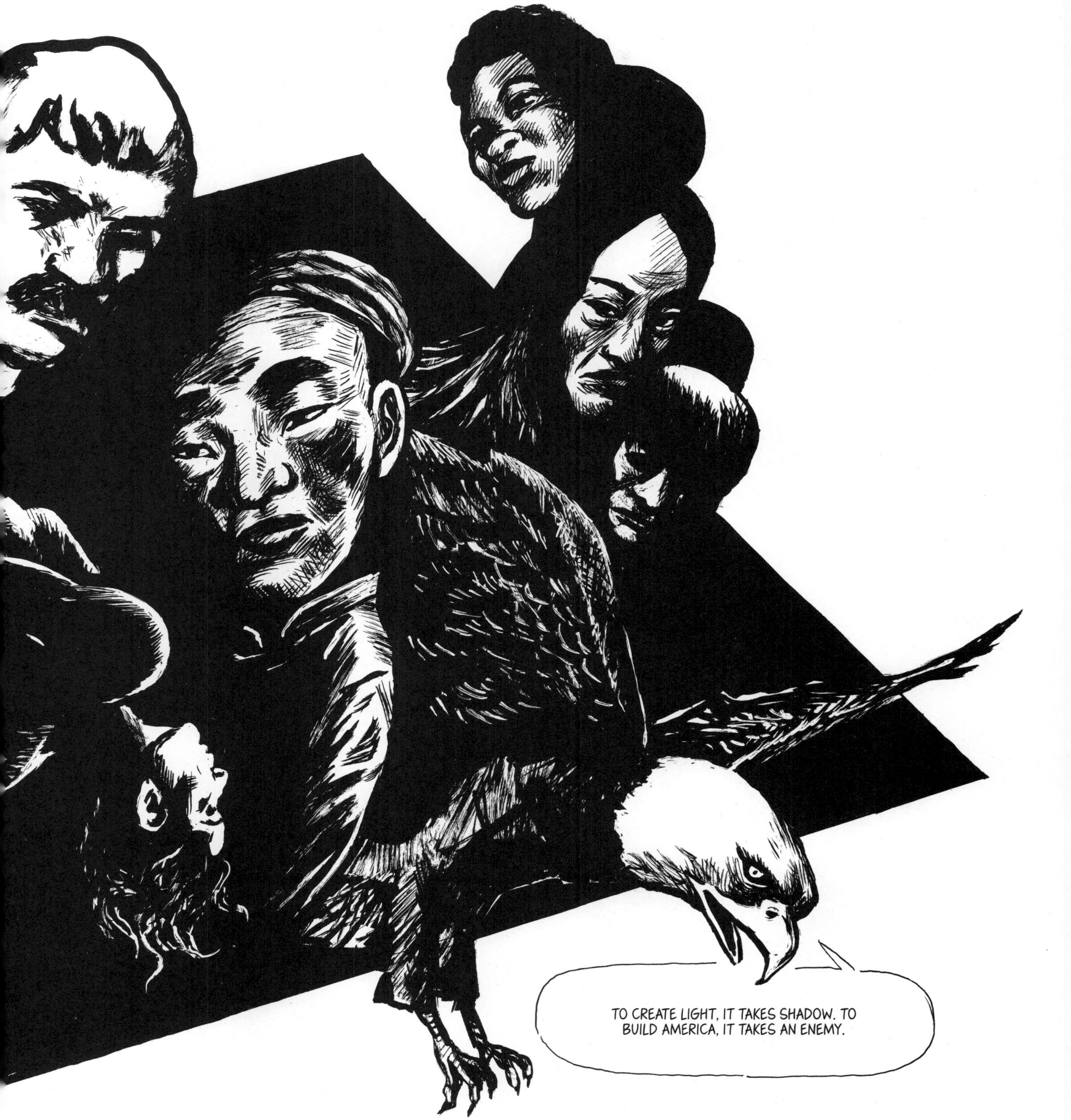
TO CREATE LIGHT, IT TAKES SHADOW. TO BUILD AMERICA, IT TAKES AN ENEMY.

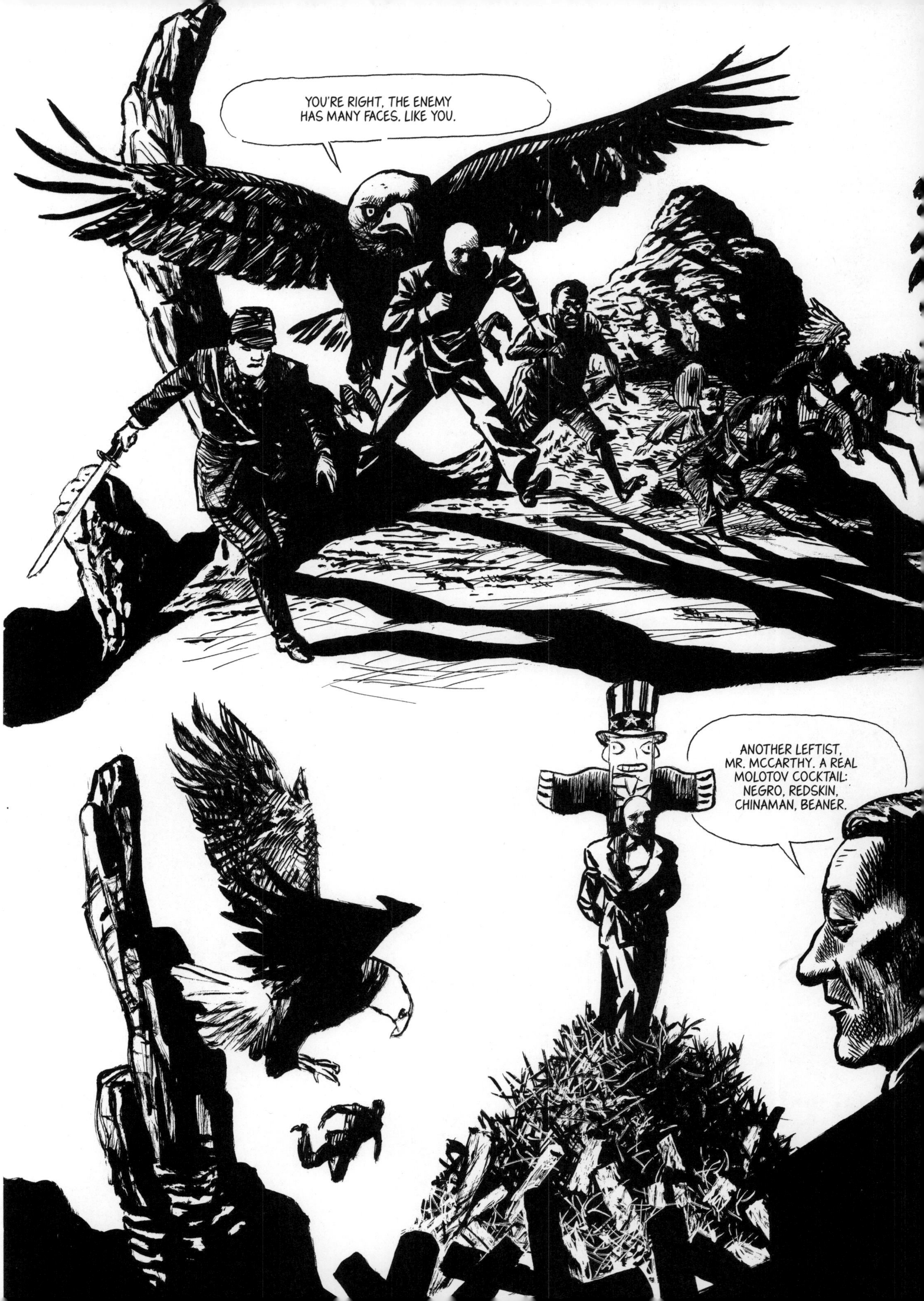
YOU'RE RIGHT, THE ENEMY HAS MANY FACES. LIKE YOU.
ANOTHER LEFTIST, MR. MCCARTHY. A REAL MOLOTOV COCKTAIL: NEGRO, REDSKIN, CHINAMAN, BEANER.

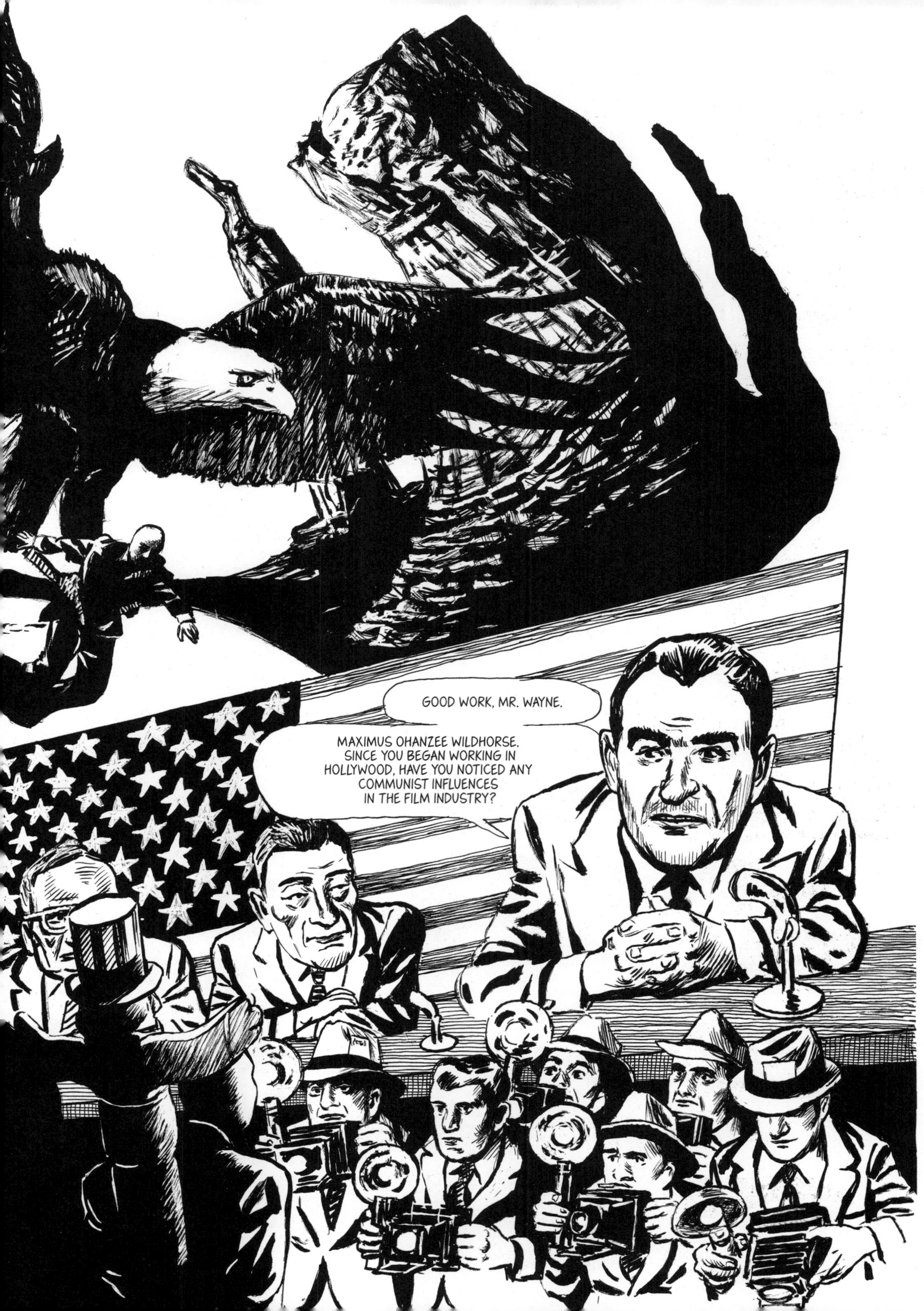
GOOD WORK, MR. WAYNE.
MAXIMUS OHANZEE WILDHORSE. SINCE YOU BEGAN WORKING IN HOLLYWOOD, HAVE YOU NOTICED ANY COMMUNIST INFLUENCES IN THE FILM INDUSTRY?

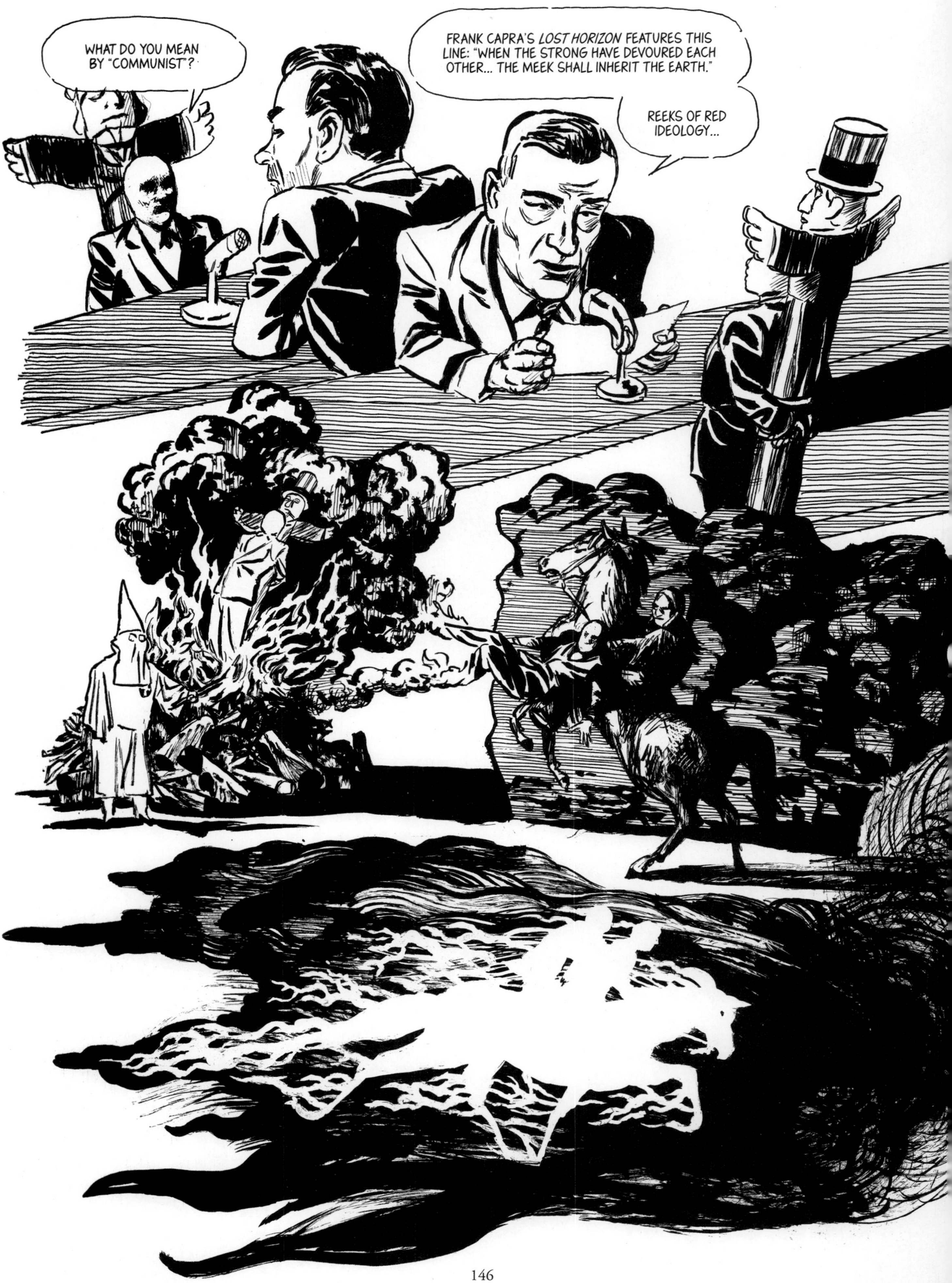
WHAT DO YOU MEAN BY "COMMUNIST"?
FRANK CAPRA'S *LOST HORIZON* FEATURES THIS LINE: "WHEN THE STRONG HAVE DEVOURED EACH OTHER... THE MEEK SHALL INHERIT THE EARTH."
REEKS OF RED IDEOLOGY...

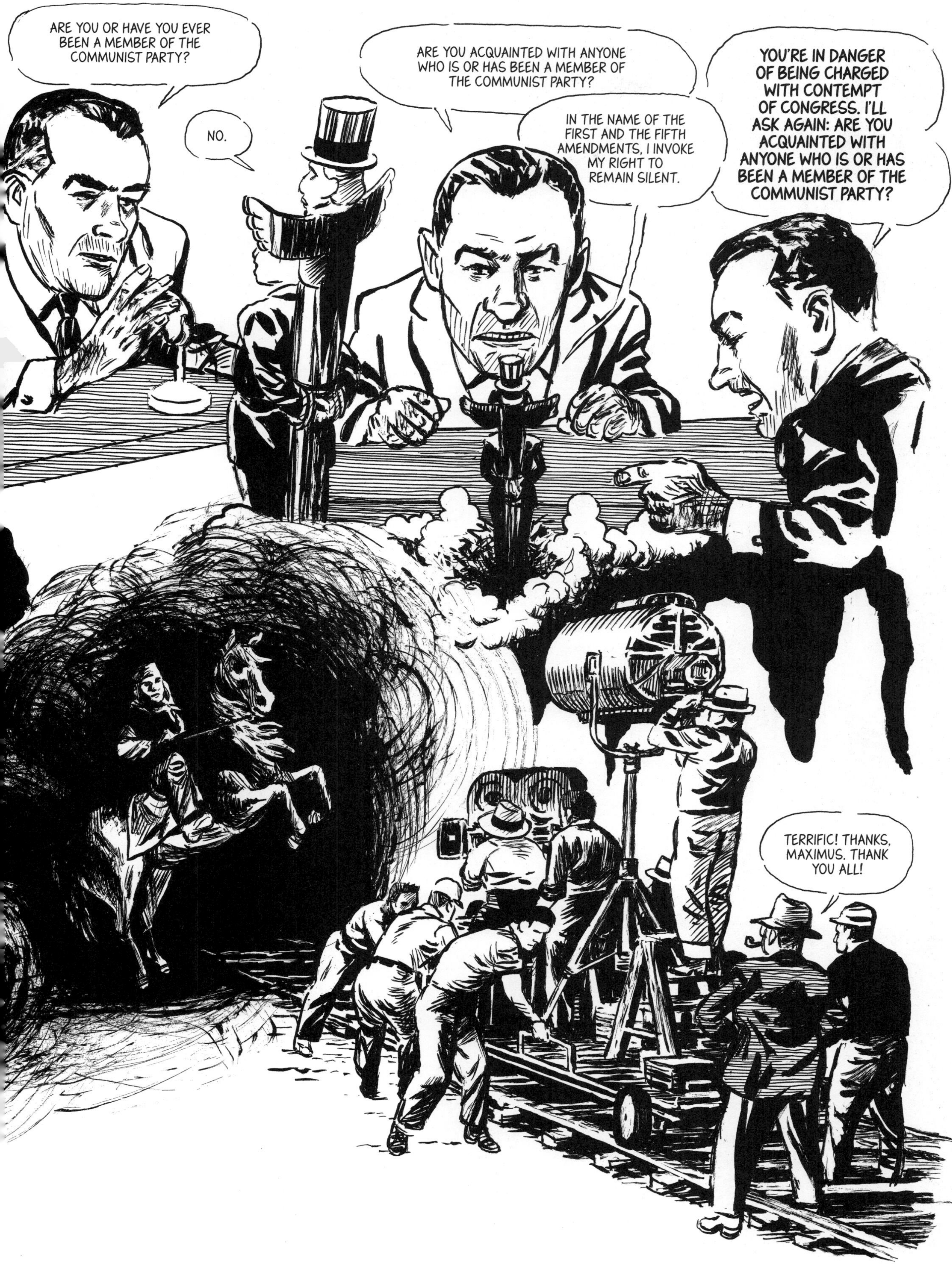
ARE YOU OR HAVE YOU EVER BEEN A MEMBER OF THE COMMUNIST PARTY?
NO.
ARE YOU ACQUAINTED WITH ANYONE WHO IS OR HAS BEEN A MEMBER OF THE COMMUNIST PARTY?
IN THE NAME OF THE FIRST AND THE FIFTH AMENDMENTS, I INVOKE MY RIGHT TO REMAIN SILENT.
YOU'RE IN DANGER OF BEING CHARGED WITH CONTEMPT OF CONGRESS. I'LL ASK AGAIN: ARE YOU ACQUAINTED WITH ANYONE WHO IS OR HAS BEEN A MEMBER OF THE COMMUNIST PARTY?
TERRIFIC! THANKS, MAXIMUS. THANK YOU ALL!

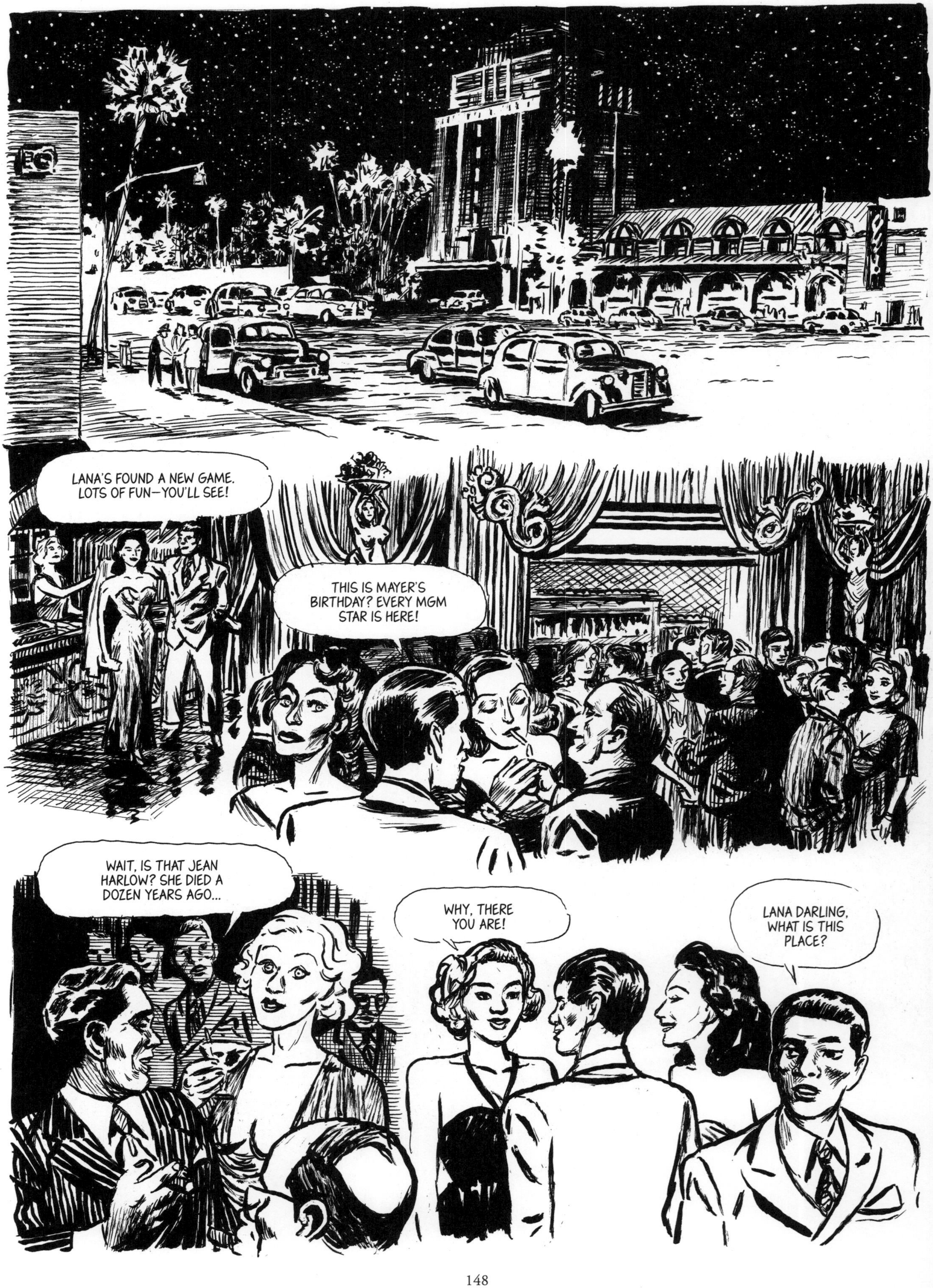
LANA'S FOUND A NEW GAME. LOTS OF FUN—YOU'LL SEE!
THIS IS MAYER'S BIRTHDAY? EVERY MGM STAR IS HERE!
WAIT, IS THAT JEAN HARLOW? SHE DIED A DOZEN YEARS AGO...
WHY, THERE YOU ARE!
LANA DARLING, WHAT IS THIS PLACE?

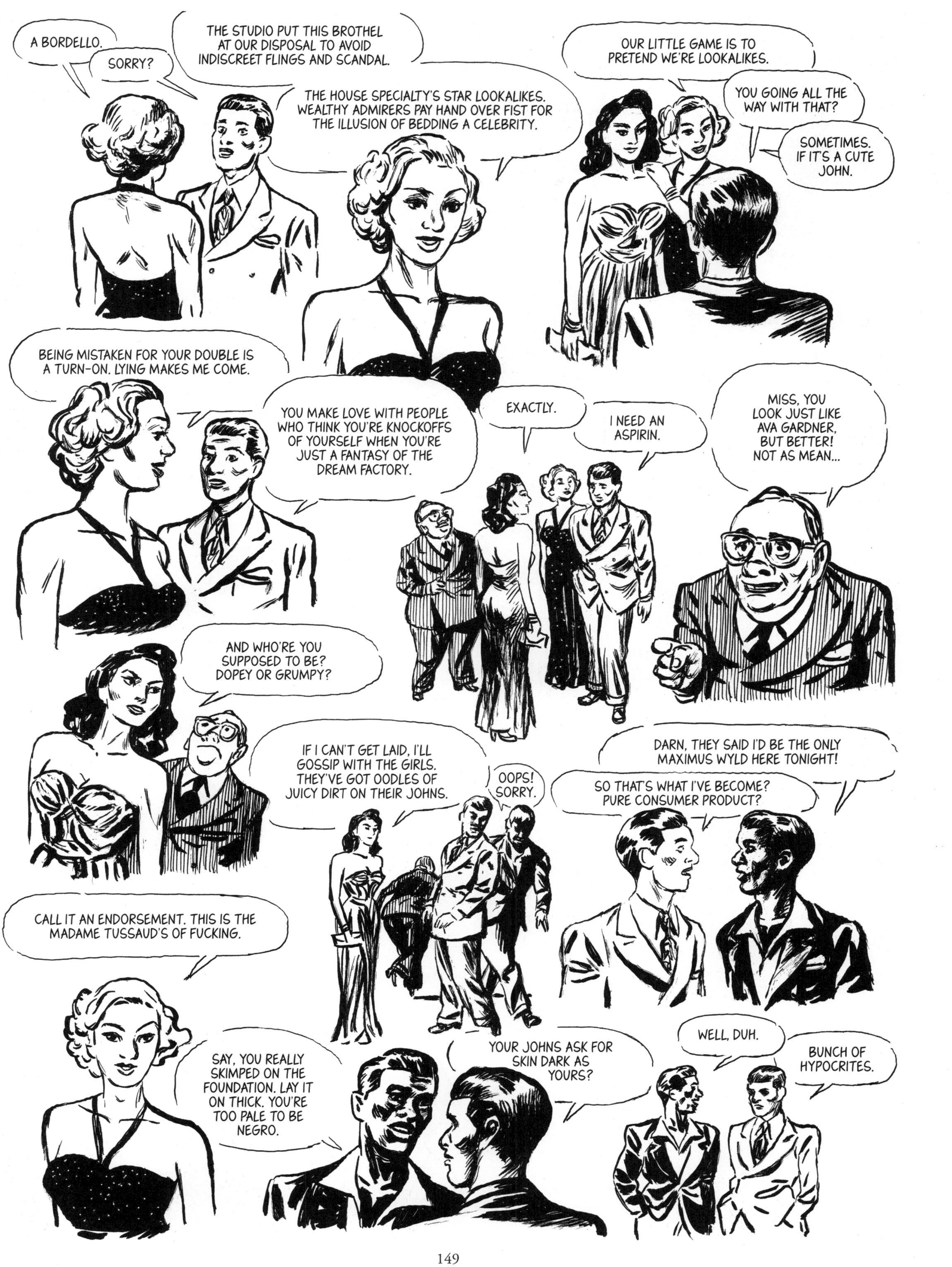

A BORDELLO.
SORRY?
THE STUDIO PUT THIS BROTHEL AT OUR DISPOSAL TO AVOID INDISCREET FLINGS AND SCANDAL.
THE HOUSE SPECIALTY'S STAR LOOKALIKES. WEALTHY ADMIRERS PAY HAND OVER FIST FOR THE ILLUSION OF BEDDING A CELEBRITY.
OUR LITTLE GAME IS TO PRETEND WE'RE LOOKALIKES.
YOU GOING ALL THE WAY WITH THAT?
SOMETIMES. IF IT'S A CUTE JOHN.
BEING MISTAKEN FOR YOUR DOUBLE IS A TURN-ON. LYING MAKES ME COME.
YOU MAKE LOVE WITH PEOPLE WHO THINK YOU'RE KNOCKOFFS OF YOURSELF WHEN YOU'RE JUST A FANTASY OF THE DREAM FACTORY.
EXACTLY.
I NEED AN ASPIRIN.
MISS, YOU LOOK JUST LIKE AVA GARDNER, BUT BETTER! NOT AS MEAN...
AND WHO'RE YOU SUPPOSED TO BE? DOPEY OR GRUMPY?
IF I CAN'T GET LAID, I'LL GOSSIP WITH THE GIRLS. THEY'VE GOT OODLES OF JUICY DIRT ON THEIR JOHNS.
OOPS! SORRY.
DARN, THEY SAID I'D BE THE ONLY MAXIMUS WYLD HERE TONIGHT!
SO THAT'S WHAT I'VE BECOME? PURE CONSUMER PRODUCT?
CALL IT AN ENDORSEMENT. THIS IS THE MADAME TUSSAUD'S OF FUCKING.
SAY, YOU REALLY SKIMPED ON THE FOUNDATION. LAY IT ON THICK. YOU'RE TOO PALE TO BE NEGRO.
YOUR JOHNS ASK FOR SKIN DARK AS YOURS?
WELL, DUH.
BUNCH OF HYPOCRITES.

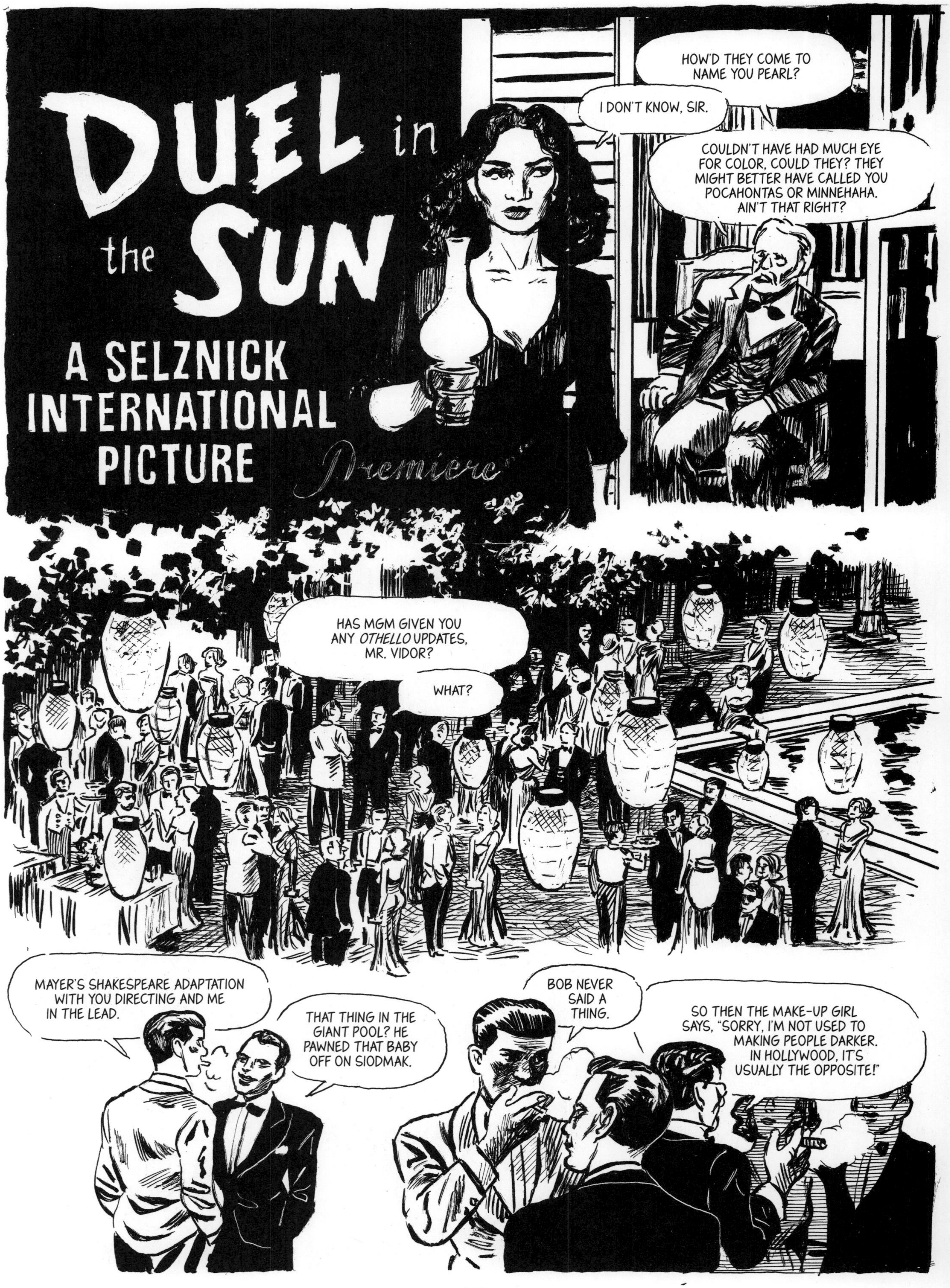

DUEL in the SUN
A SELZNICK INTERNATIONAL PICTURE
Premiere
HOW'D THEY COME TO NAME YOU PEARL?
I DON'T KNOW, SIR.
COULDN'T HAVE HAD MUCH EYE FOR COLOR, COULD THEY? THEY MIGHT BETTER HAVE CALLED YOU POCAHONTAS OR MINNEHAHA. AIN'T THAT RIGHT?
HAS MGM GIVEN YOU ANY *OTHELLO* UPDATES, MR. VIDOR?
WHAT?
MAYER'S SHAKESPEARE ADAPTATION WITH YOU DIRECTING AND ME IN THE LEAD.
THAT THING IN THE GIANT POOL? HE PAWNED THAT BABY OFF ON SIODMAK.
BOB NEVER SAID A THING.
SO THEN THE MAKE-UP GIRL SAYS, "SORRY, I'M NOT USED TO MAKING PEOPLE DARKER. IN HOLLYWOOD, IT'S USUALLY THE OPPOSITE!"

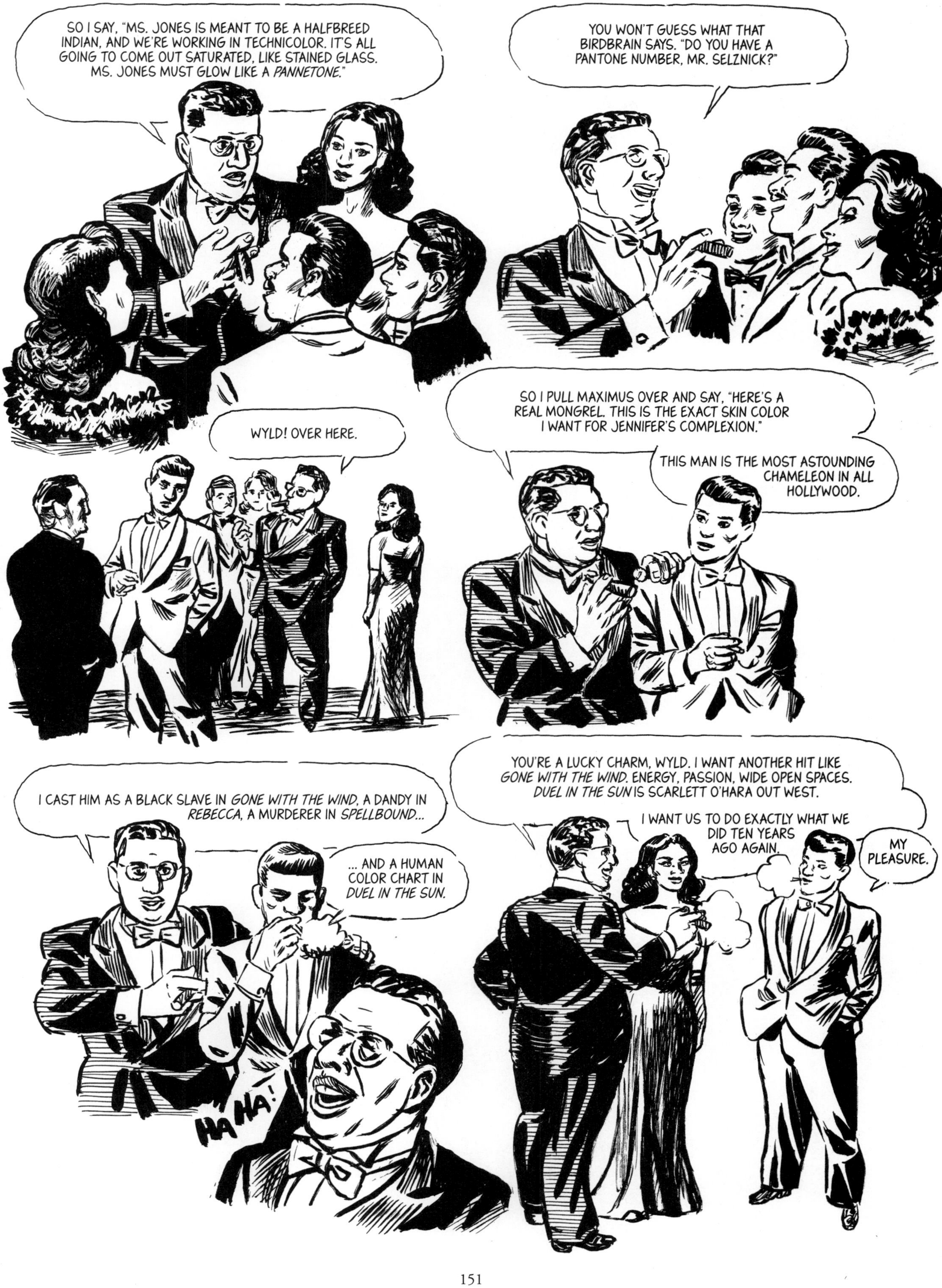
SO I SAY, "MS. JONES IS MEANT TO BE A HALFBREED INDIAN, AND WE'RE WORKING IN TECHNICOLOR. IT'S ALL GOING TO COME OUT SATURATED, LIKE STAINED GLASS. MS. JONES MUST GLOW LIKE A *PANNETONE.*"
YOU WON'T GUESS WHAT THAT BIRDBRAIN SAYS. "DO YOU HAVE A PANTONE NUMBER, MR. SELZNICK?"
WYLD! OVER HERE.
SO I PULL MAXIMUS OVER AND SAY, "HERE'S A REAL MONGREL. THIS IS THE EXACT SKIN COLOR I WANT FOR JENNIFER'S COMPLEXION."
THIS MAN IS THE MOST ASTOUNDING CHAMELEON IN ALL HOLLYWOOD.
I CAST HIM AS A BLACK SLAVE IN *GONE WITH THE WIND*, A DANDY IN *REBECCA*, A MURDERER IN *SPELLBOUND*...
... AND A HUMAN COLOR CHART IN *DUEL IN THE SUN.*
HA HA!
YOU'RE A LUCKY CHARM, WYLD. I WANT ANOTHER HIT LIKE *GONE WITH THE WIND*. ENERGY, PASSION, WIDE OPEN SPACES. *DUEL IN THE SUN* IS SCARLETT O'HARA OUT WEST.
I WANT US TO DO EXACTLY WHAT WE DID TEN YEARS AGO AGAIN.
MY PLEASURE.

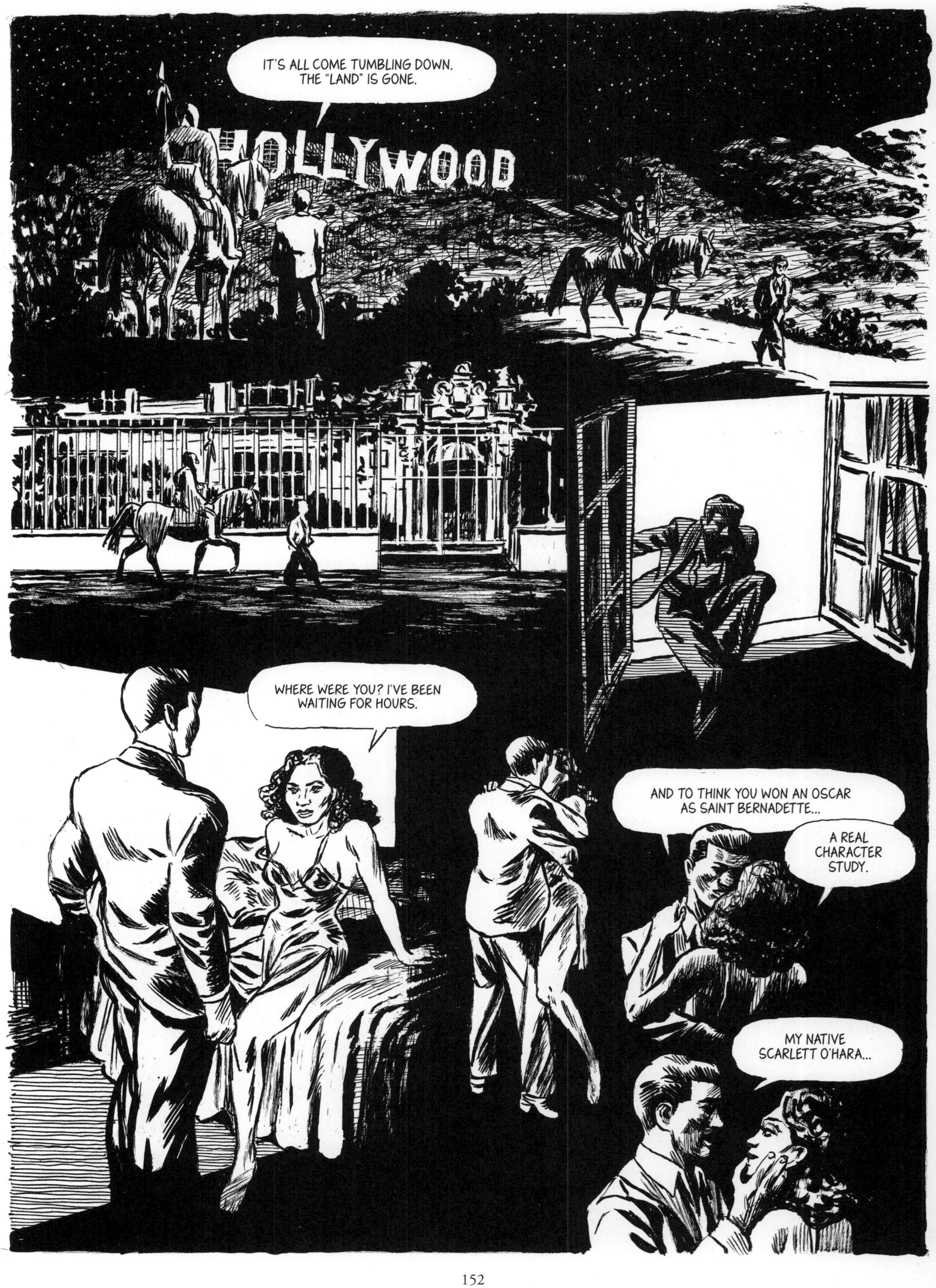
IT'S ALL COME TUMBLING DOWN. THE "LAND" IS GONE.
HOLLYWOOD
WHERE WERE YOU? I'VE BEEN WAITING FOR HOURS.
AND TO THINK YOU WON AN OSCAR AS SAINT BERNADETTE...
A REAL CHARACTER STUDY.
MY NATIVE SCARLETT O'HARA...

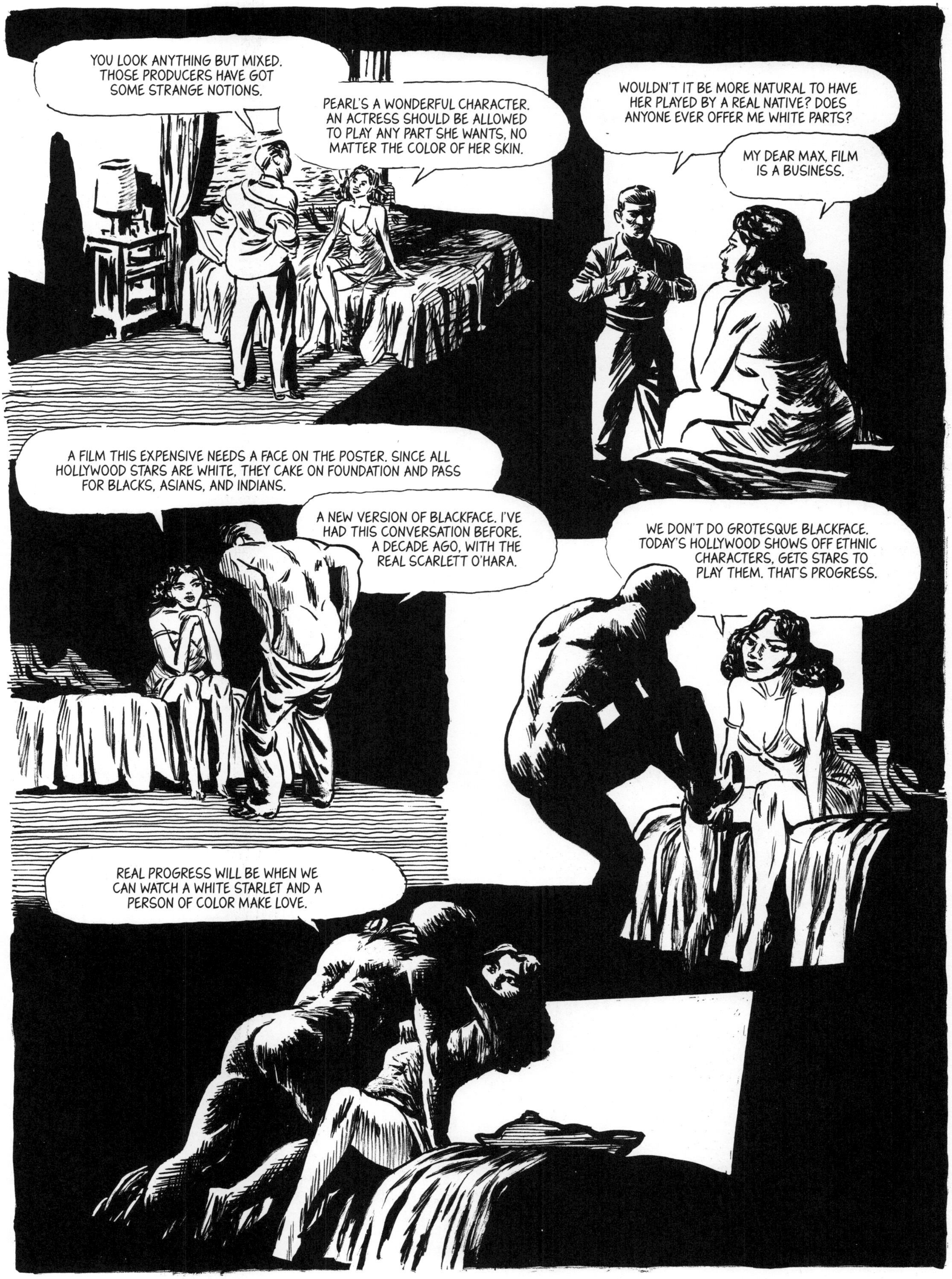
YOU LOOK ANYTHING BUT MIXED. THOSE PRODUCERS HAVE GOT SOME STRANGE NOTIONS.
PEARL'S A WONDERFUL CHARACTER. AN ACTRESS SHOULD BE ALLOWED TO PLAY ANY PART SHE WANTS, NO MATTER THE COLOR OF HER SKIN.
WOULDN'T IT BE MORE NATURAL TO HAVE HER PLAYED BY A REAL NATIVE? DOES ANYONE EVER OFFER ME WHITE PARTS?
MY DEAR MAX, FILM IS A BUSINESS.
A FILM THIS EXPENSIVE NEEDS A FACE ON THE POSTER. SINCE ALL HOLLYWOOD STARS ARE WHITE, THEY CAKE ON FOUNDATION AND PASS FOR BLACKS, ASIANS, AND INDIANS.
A NEW VERSION OF BLACKFACE. I'VE HAD THIS CONVERSATION BEFORE. A DECADE AGO, WITH THE REAL SCARLETT O'HARA.
WE DON'T DO GROTESQUE BLACKFACE. TODAY'S HOLLYWOOD SHOWS OFF ETHNIC CHARACTERS, GETS STARS TO PLAY THEM. THAT'S PROGRESS.
REAL PROGRESS WILL BE WHEN WE CAN WATCH A WHITE STARLET AND A PERSON OF COLOR MAKE LOVE.

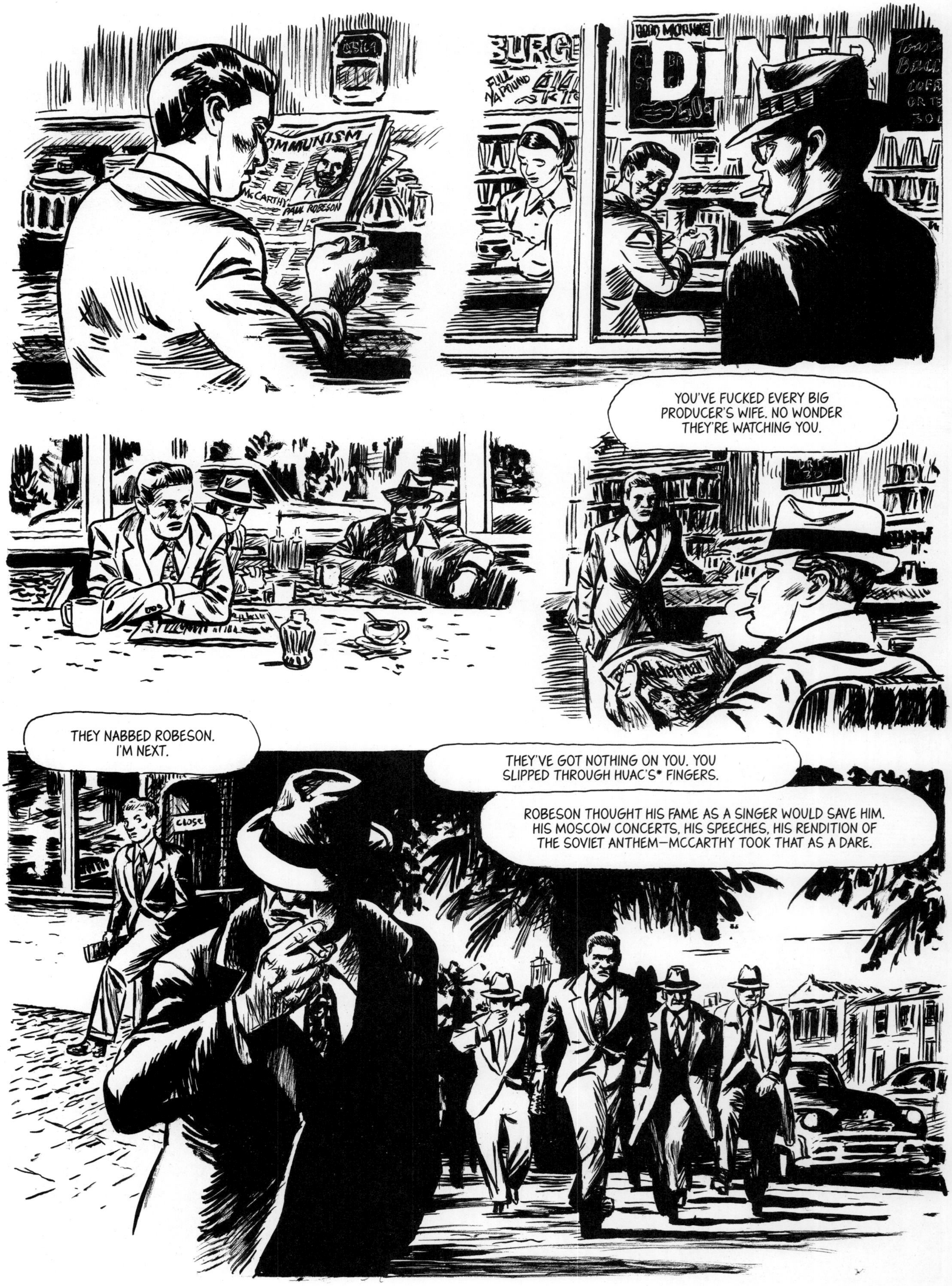
COMMUNISM
McCARTHY
PAUL ROBESON
DINER
YOU'VE FUCKED EVERY BIG PRODUCER'S WIFE. NO WONDER THEY'RE WATCHING YOU.
THEY NABBED ROBESON. I'M NEXT.
THEY'VE GOT NOTHING ON YOU. YOU SLIPPED THROUGH HUAC'S* FINGERS.
ROBESON THOUGHT HIS FAME AS A SINGER WOULD SAVE HIM. HIS MOSCOW CONCERTS, HIS SPEECHES, HIS RENDITION OF THE SOVIET ANTHEM—MCCARTHY TOOK THAT AS A DARE.
CLOSE

* HOUSE UN-AMERICAN ACTIVITIES COMMITTEE

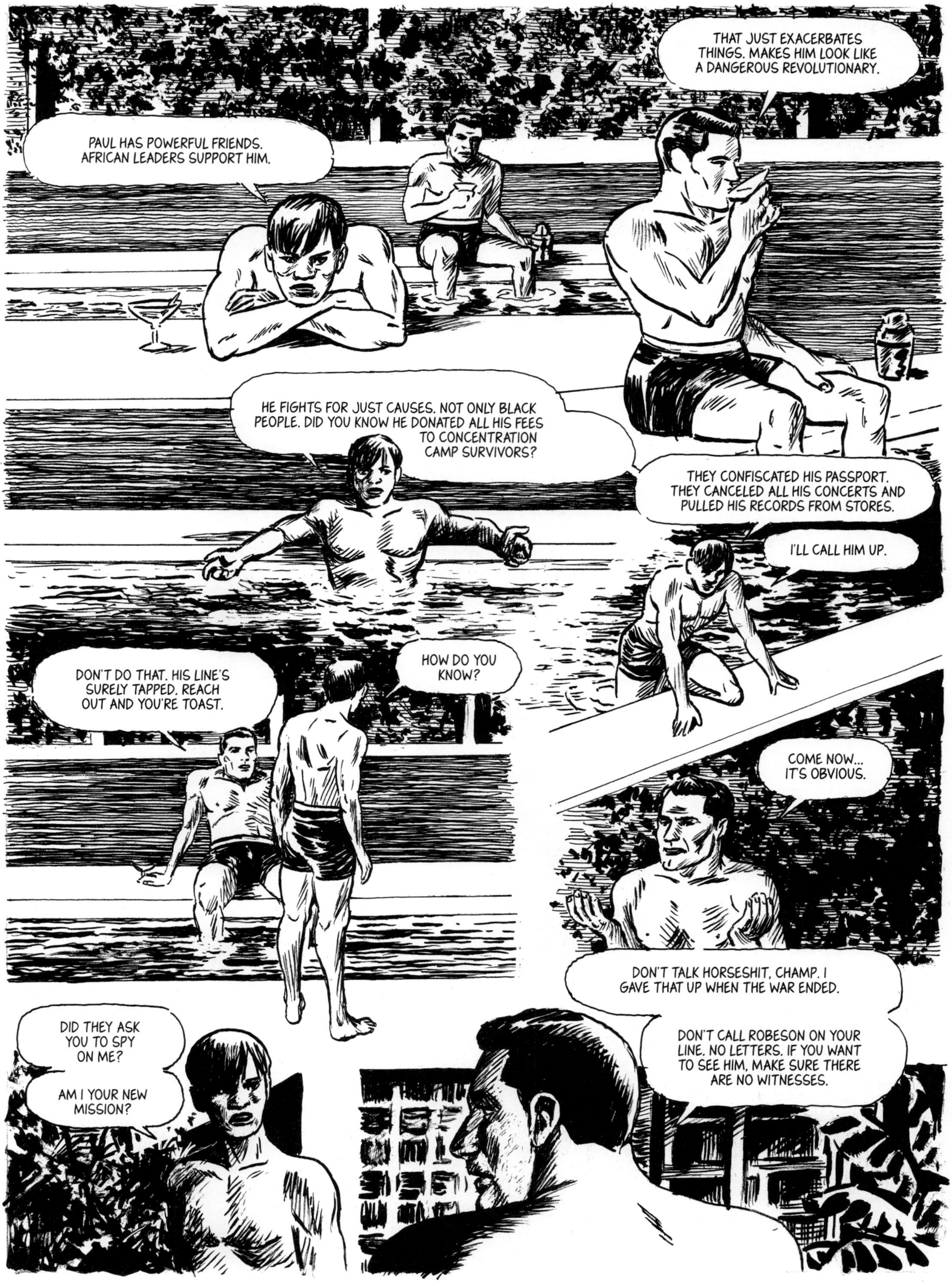
PAUL HAS POWERFUL FRIENDS. AFRICAN LEADERS SUPPORT HIM.
THAT JUST EXACERBATES THINGS. MAKES HIM LOOK LIKE A DANGEROUS REVOLUTIONARY.
HE FIGHTS FOR JUST CAUSES. NOT ONLY BLACK PEOPLE. DID YOU KNOW HE DONATED ALL HIS FEES TO CONCENTRATION CAMP SURVIVORS?
THEY CONFISCATED HIS PASSPORT. THEY CANCELED ALL HIS CONCERTS AND PULLED HIS RECORDS FROM STORES.
I'LL CALL HIM UP.
DON'T DO THAT. HIS LINE'S SURELY TAPPED. REACH OUT AND YOU'RE TOAST.
HOW DO YOU KNOW?
COME NOW... IT'S OBVIOUS.
DID THEY ASK YOU TO SPY ON ME?
AM I YOUR NEW MISSION?
DON'T TALK HORSESHIT, CHAMP. I GAVE THAT UP WHEN THE WAR ENDED.
DON'T CALL ROBESON ON YOUR LINE. NO LETTERS. IF YOU WANT TO SEE HIM, MAKE SURE THERE ARE NO WITNESSES.

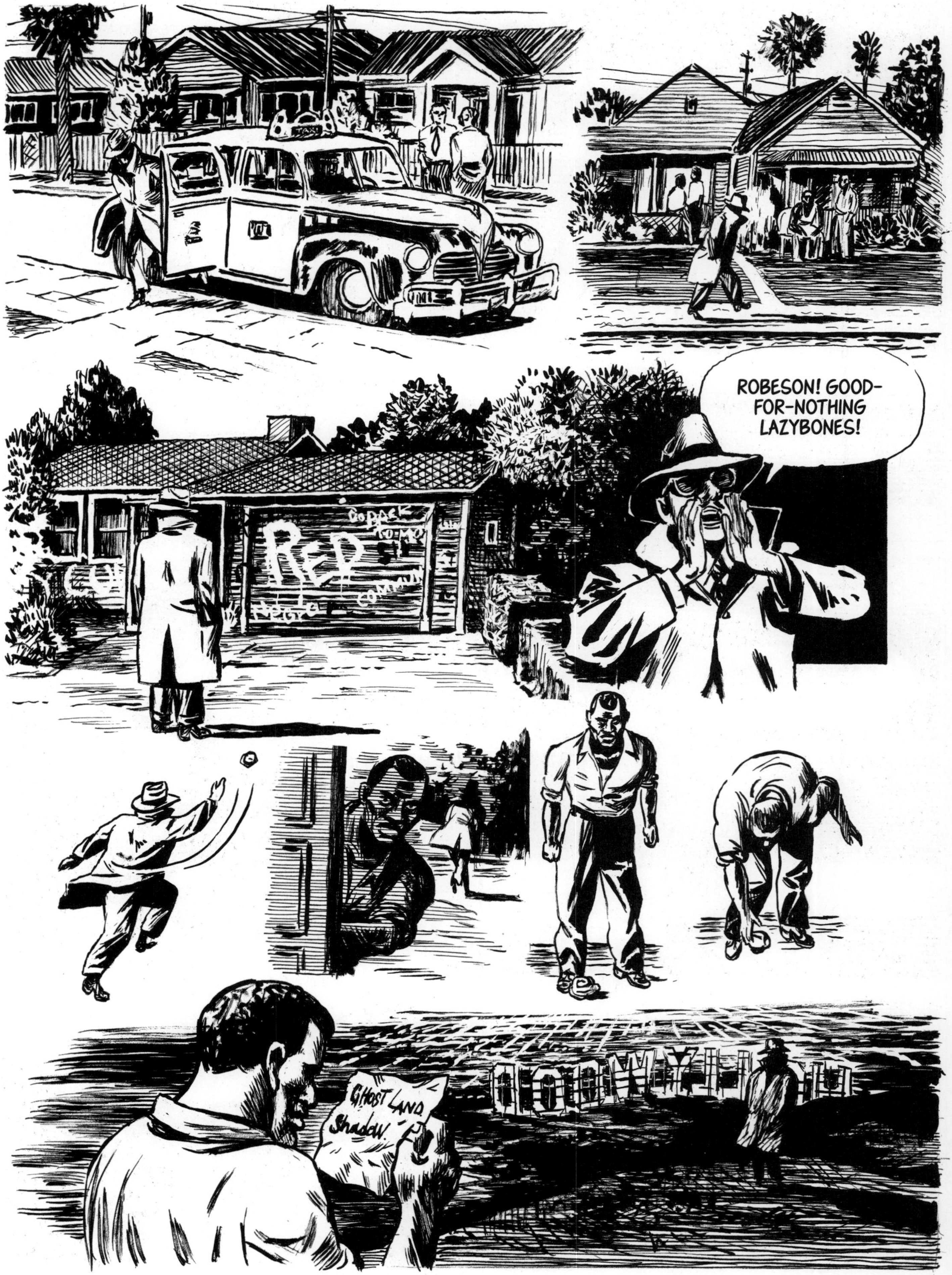
ROBESON! GOOD-FOR-NOTHING LAZYBONES!
RED
GHOST LAND
Shadow

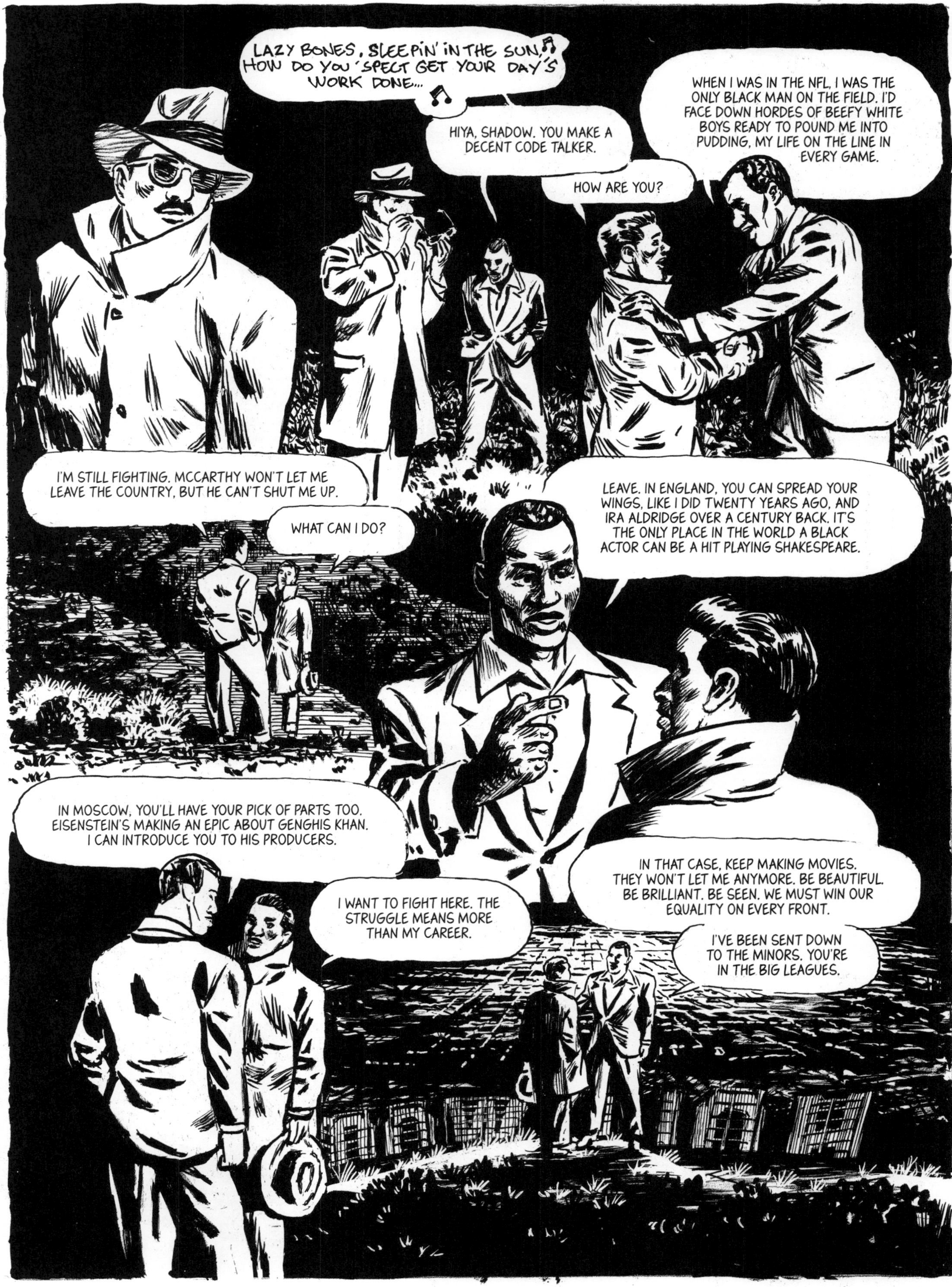
LAZY BONES, SLEEPIN' IN THE SUN, HOW DO YOU 'SPECT GET YOUR DAY'S WORK DONE...
HIYA, SHADOW. YOU MAKE A DECENT CODE TALKER.
HOW ARE YOU?
WHEN I WAS IN THE NFL, I WAS THE ONLY BLACK MAN ON THE FIELD. I'D FACE DOWN HORDES OF BEEFY WHITE BOYS READY TO POUND ME INTO PUDDING, MY LIFE ON THE LINE IN EVERY GAME.
I'M STILL FIGHTING. MCCARTHY WON'T LET ME LEAVE THE COUNTRY, BUT HE CAN'T SHUT ME UP.
WHAT CAN I DO?
LEAVE. IN ENGLAND, YOU CAN SPREAD YOUR WINGS, LIKE I DID TWENTY YEARS AGO, AND IRA ALDRIDGE OVER A CENTURY BACK. IT'S THE ONLY PLACE IN THE WORLD A BLACK ACTOR CAN BE A HIT PLAYING SHAKESPEARE.
IN MOSCOW, YOU'LL HAVE YOUR PICK OF PARTS TOO. EISENSTEIN'S MAKING AN EPIC ABOUT GENGHIS KHAN. I CAN INTRODUCE YOU TO HIS PRODUCERS.
I WANT TO FIGHT HERE. THE STRUGGLE MEANS MORE THAN MY CAREER.
IN THAT CASE, KEEP MAKING MOVIES. THEY WON'T LET ME ANYMORE. BE BEAUTIFUL. BE BRILLIANT. BE SEEN. WE MUST WIN OUR EQUALITY ON EVERY FRONT.
I'VE BEEN SENT DOWN TO THE MINORS. YOU'RE IN THE BIG LEAGUES.

MAXIMUS FOLLOWED ROBESON'S ADVICE, MAKING ONE MOVIE AFTER ANOTHER. IN DEMAND FOR WESTERNS, HE CHOSE CAREFULLY, ONLY CONSENTING TO APPEAR IN PRO-NATIVE FILMS. IN THOSE THAT DEPICTED NATIVES AS THE OUTRIGHT ENEMY, MAXIMUS DETECTED RACISM AND AN ANTI-COMMUNIST SUBTEXT.

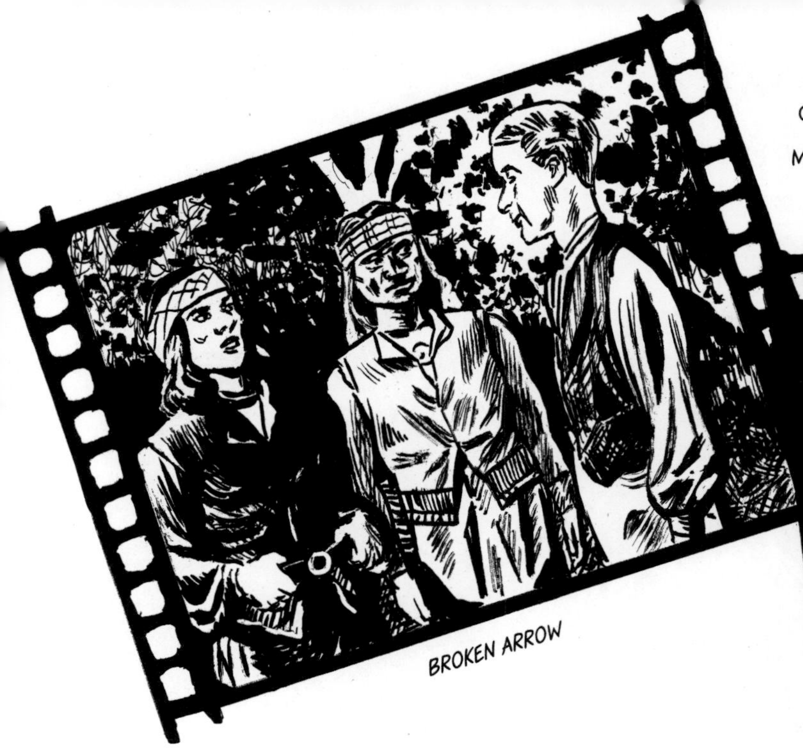

BROKEN ARROW

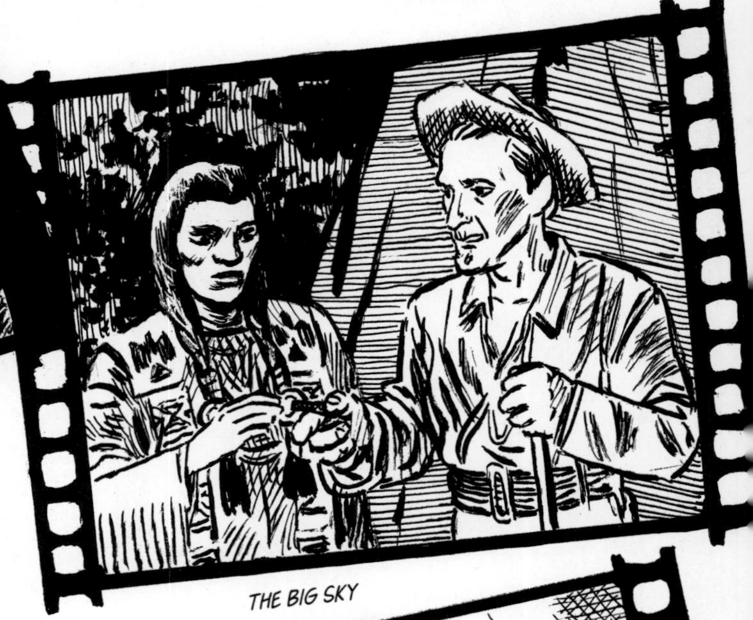

THE BIG SKY

IN THE LATE '40S, THE ONCE OUTMODED SWORD-AND-SANDAL FILM MADE A COMEBACK. GLITTERING, OVER-THE-TOP, MEGALOMANIACAL, POLITICAL, IT BECAME A NEW AND GRATIFYING PLAYING FIELD FOR MAXIMUS.

HIS FILMOGRAPHY REFLECTED IDEOLOGICAL STRATEGY. IT BECAME AN UNDERGROUND MANIFESTO THAT FLOUTED MCCARTHYIST SUSPICIONS AND THE STUDIOS' CONSERVATIVE CONTEMPT.

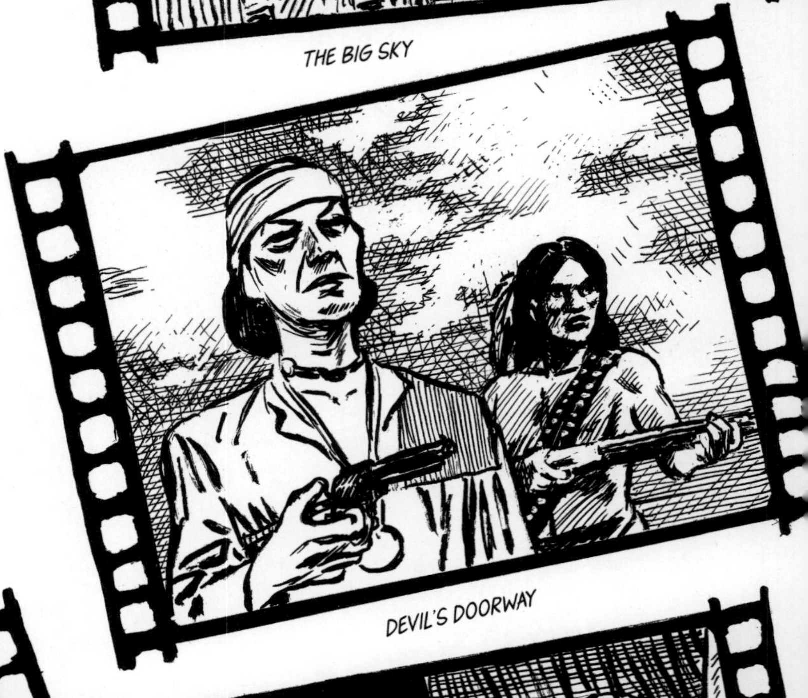

DEVIL'S DOORWAY

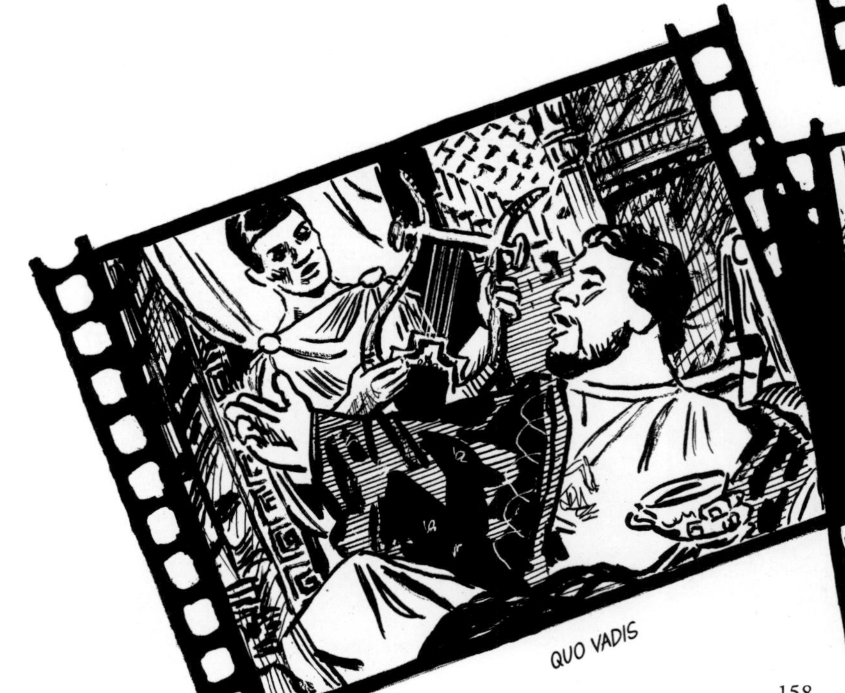

QUO VADIS

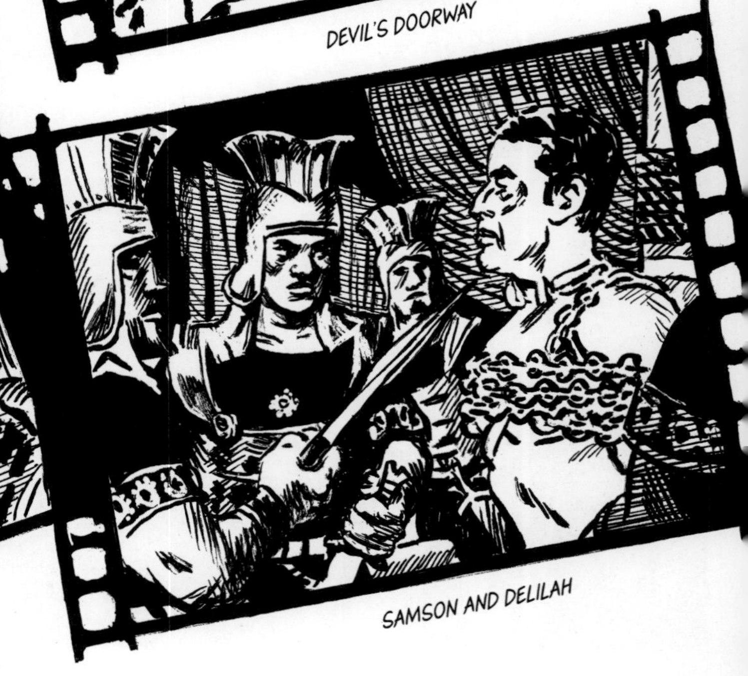

SAMSON AND DELILAH

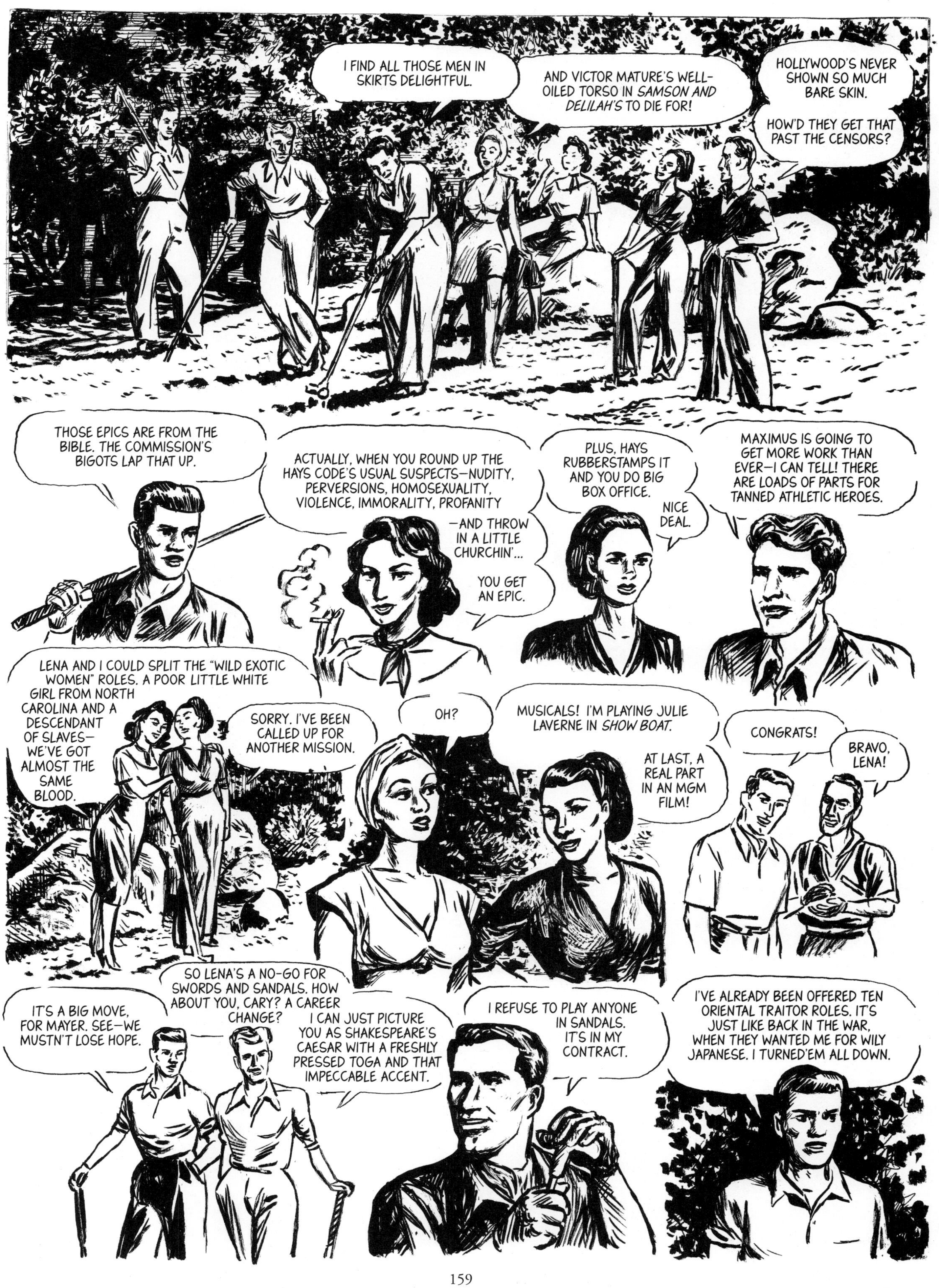
I FIND ALL THOSE MEN IN SKIRTS DELIGHTFUL.
AND VICTOR MATURE'S WELL-OILED TORSO IN *SAMSON AND DELILAH'S* TO DIE FOR!
HOLLYWOOD'S NEVER SHOWN SO MUCH BARE SKIN.
HOW'D THEY GET THAT PAST THE CENSORS?
THOSE EPICS ARE FROM THE BIBLE. THE COMMISSION'S BIGOTS LAP THAT UP.
ACTUALLY, WHEN YOU ROUND UP THE HAYS CODE'S USUAL SUSPECTS—NUDITY, PERVERSIONS, HOMOSEXUALITY, VIOLENCE, IMMORALITY, PROFANITY
—AND THROW IN A LITTLE CHURCHIN'...
YOU GET AN EPIC.
PLUS, HAYS RUBBERSTAMPS IT AND YOU DO BIG BOX OFFICE.
NICE DEAL.
MAXIMUS IS GOING TO GET MORE WORK THAN EVER—I CAN TELL! THERE ARE LOADS OF PARTS FOR TANNED ATHLETIC HEROES.
LENA AND I COULD SPLIT THE "WILD EXOTIC WOMEN" ROLES. A POOR LITTLE WHITE GIRL FROM NORTH CAROLINA AND A DESCENDANT OF SLAVES—WE'VE GOT ALMOST THE SAME BLOOD.
SORRY. I'VE BEEN CALLED UP FOR ANOTHER MISSION.
OH?
MUSICALS! I'M PLAYING JULIE LAVERNE IN *SHOW BOAT.*
AT LAST, A REAL PART IN AN MGM FILM!
CONGRATS!
BRAVO, LENA!
IT'S A BIG MOVE, FOR MAYER. SEE—WE MUSTN'T LOSE HOPE.
SO LENA'S A NO-GO FOR SWORDS AND SANDALS. HOW ABOUT YOU, CARY? A CAREER CHANGE?
I CAN JUST PICTURE YOU AS SHAKESPEARE'S CAESAR WITH A FRESHLY PRESSED TOGA AND THAT IMPECCABLE ACCENT.
I REFUSE TO PLAY ANYONE IN SANDALS. IT'S IN MY CONTRACT.
I'VE ALREADY BEEN OFFERED TEN ORIENTAL TRAITOR ROLES. IT'S JUST LIKE BACK IN THE WAR, WHEN THEY WANTED ME FOR WILY JAPANESE. I TURNED'EM ALL DOWN.

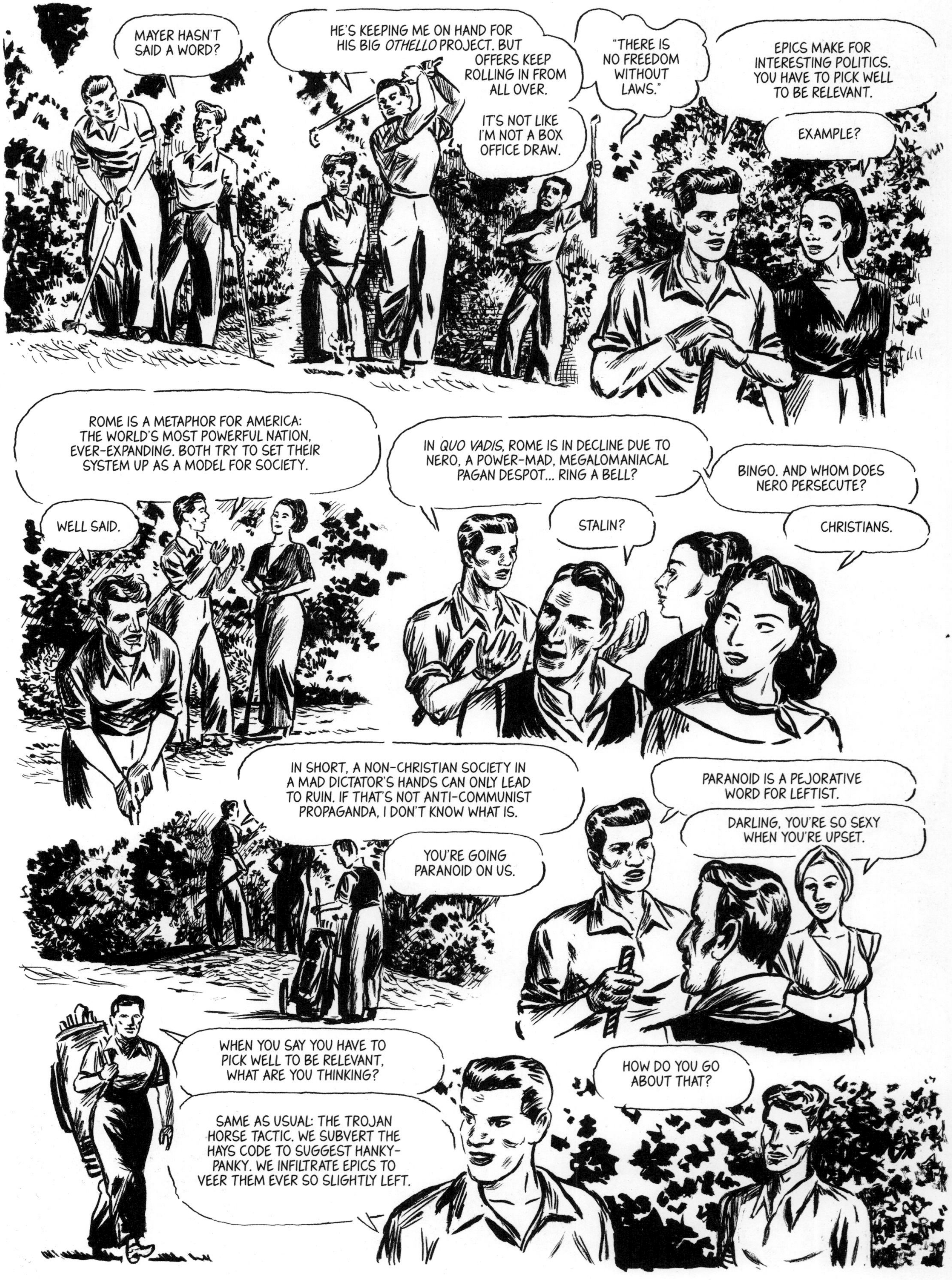
MAYER HASN'T SAID A WORD?
HE'S KEEPING ME ON HAND FOR HIS BIG *OTHELLO* PROJECT. BUT OFFERS KEEP ROLLING IN FROM ALL OVER.
IT'S NOT LIKE I'M NOT A BOX OFFICE DRAW.
"THERE IS NO FREEDOM WITHOUT LAWS."
EPICS MAKE FOR INTERESTING POLITICS. YOU HAVE TO PICK WELL TO BE RELEVANT.
EXAMPLE?
ROME IS A METAPHOR FOR AMERICA: THE WORLD'S MOST POWERFUL NATION, EVER-EXPANDING. BOTH TRY TO SET THEIR SYSTEM UP AS A MODEL FOR SOCIETY.
WELL SAID.
IN *QUO VADIS*, ROME IS IN DECLINE DUE TO NERO, A POWER-MAD, MEGALOMANIACAL PAGAN DESPOT... RING A BELL?
STALIN?
BINGO. AND WHOM DOES NERO PERSECUTE?
CHRISTIANS.
IN SHORT, A NON-CHRISTIAN SOCIETY IN A MAD DICTATOR'S HANDS CAN ONLY LEAD TO RUIN. IF THAT'S NOT ANTI-COMMUNIST PROPAGANDA, I DON'T KNOW WHAT IS.
YOU'RE GOING PARANOID ON US.
PARANOID IS A PEJORATIVE WORD FOR LEFTIST.
DARLING, YOU'RE SO SEXY WHEN YOU'RE UPSET.
WHEN YOU SAY YOU HAVE TO PICK WELL TO BE RELEVANT, WHAT ARE YOU THINKING?
SAME AS USUAL: THE TROJAN HORSE TACTIC. WE SUBVERT THE HAYS CODE TO SUGGEST HANKY-PANKY. WE INFILTRATE EPICS TO VEER THEM EVER SO SLIGHTLY LEFT.
HOW DO YOU GO ABOUT THAT?

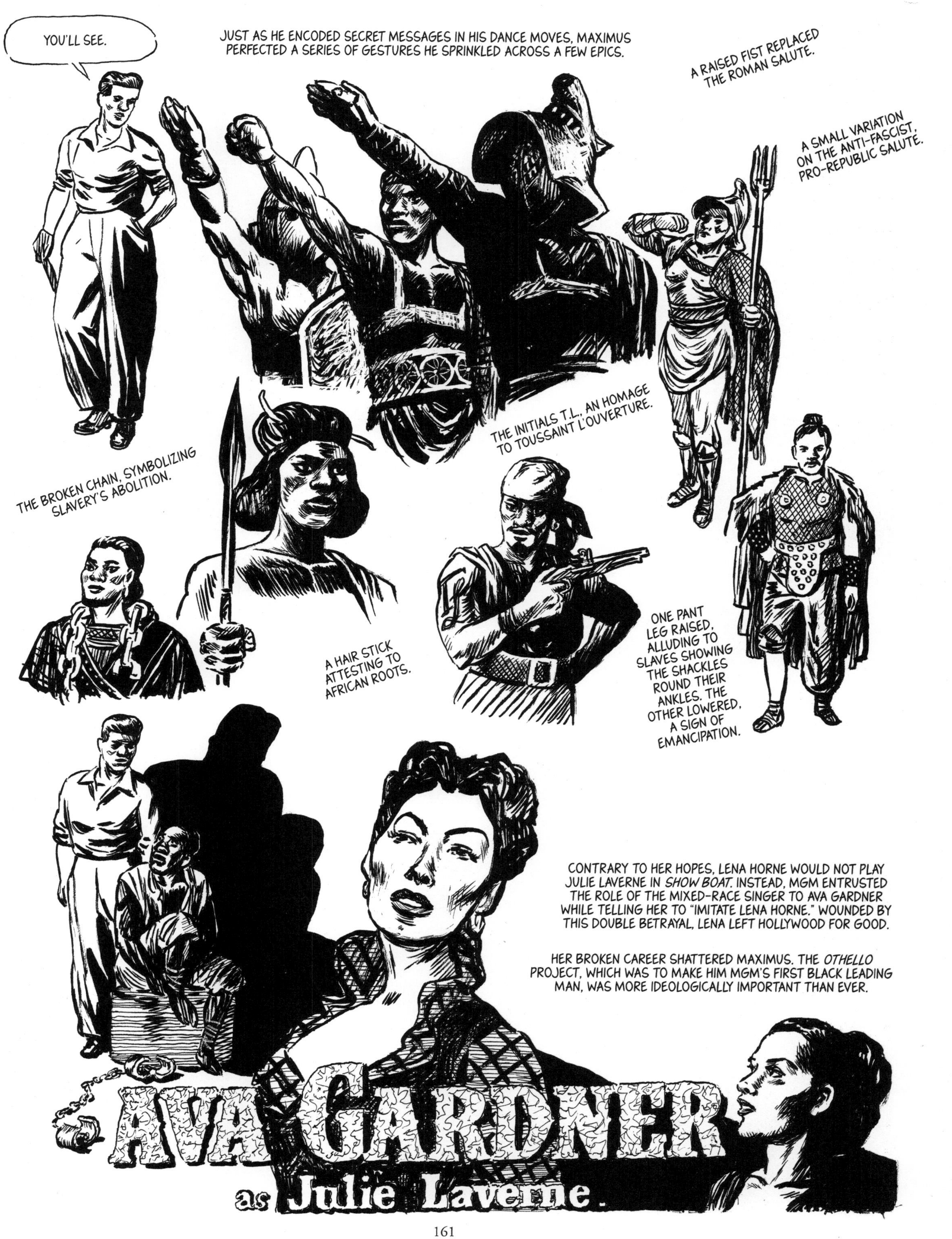

YOU'LL SEE.
JUST AS HE ENCODED SECRET MESSAGES IN HIS DANCE MOVES, MAXIMUS PERFECTED A SERIES OF GESTURES HE SPRINKLED ACROSS A FEW EPICS.
A RAISED FIST REPLACED THE ROMAN SALUTE.
A SMALL VARIATION ON THE ANTI-FASCIST, PRO-REPUBLIC SALUTE.
THE INITIALS T.L., AN HOMAGE TO TOUSSAINT L'OUVERTURE.
THE BROKEN CHAIN, SYMBOLIZING SLAVERY'S ABOLITION.
A HAIR STICK ATTESTING TO AFRICAN ROOTS.
ONE PANT LEG RAISED, ALLUDING TO SLAVES SHOWING THE SHACKLES ROUND THEIR ANKLES. THE OTHER LOWERED, A SIGN OF EMANCIPATION.
CONTRARY TO HER HOPES, LENA HORNE WOULD NOT PLAY JULIE LAVERNE IN *SHOW BOAT*. INSTEAD, MGM ENTRUSTED THE ROLE OF THE MIXED-RACE SINGER TO AVA GARDNER WHILE TELLING HER TO "IMITATE LENA HORNE." WOUNDED BY THIS DOUBLE BETRAYAL, LENA LEFT HOLLYWOOD FOR GOOD.
HER BROKEN CAREER SHATTERED MAXIMUS. THE *OTHELLO* PROJECT, WHICH WAS TO MAKE HIM MGM'S FIRST BLACK LEADING MAN, WAS MORE IDEOLOGICALLY IMPORTANT THAN EVER.
AVA GARDNER
as Julie Laverne

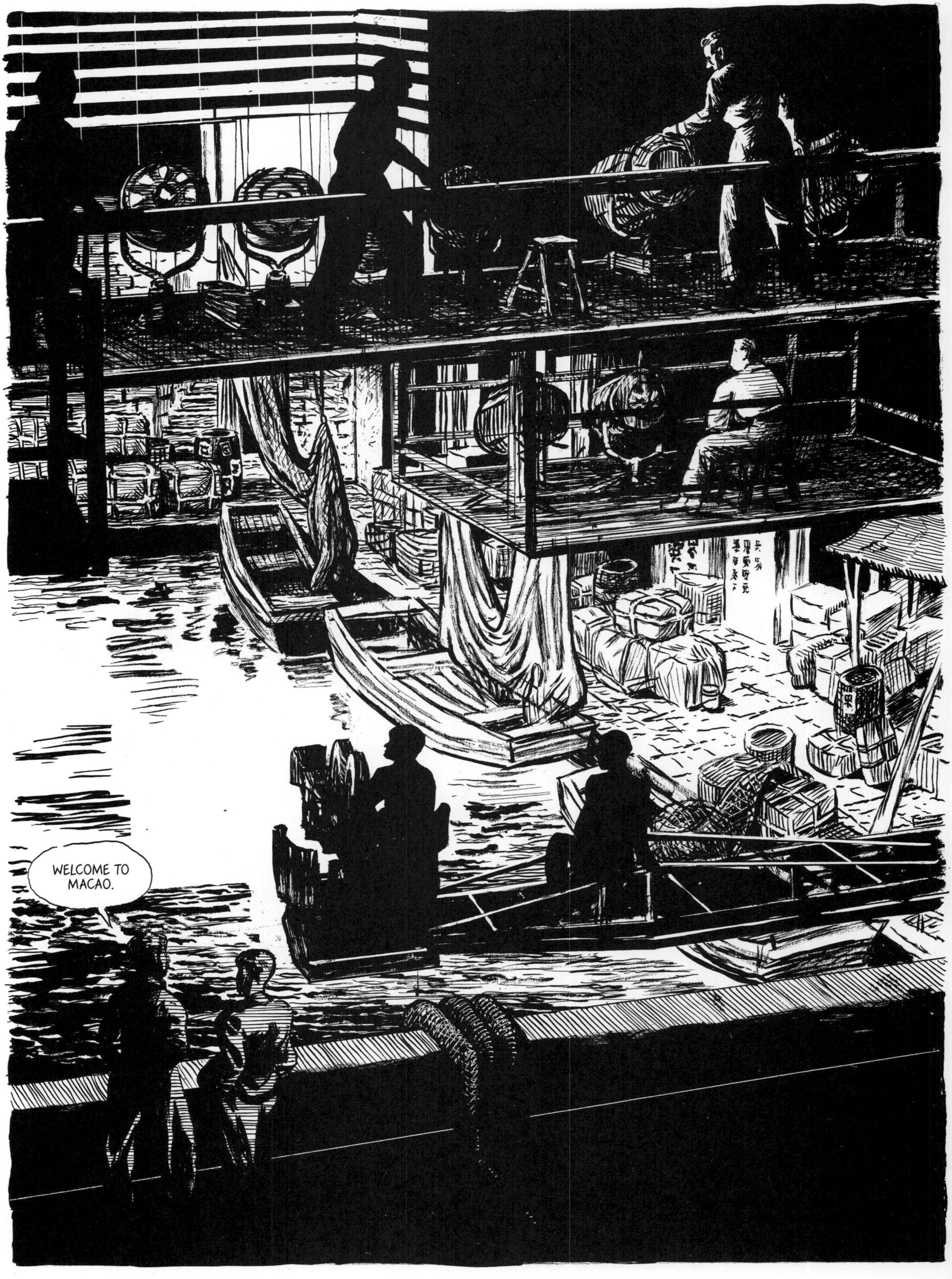
WELCOME TO MACAO.

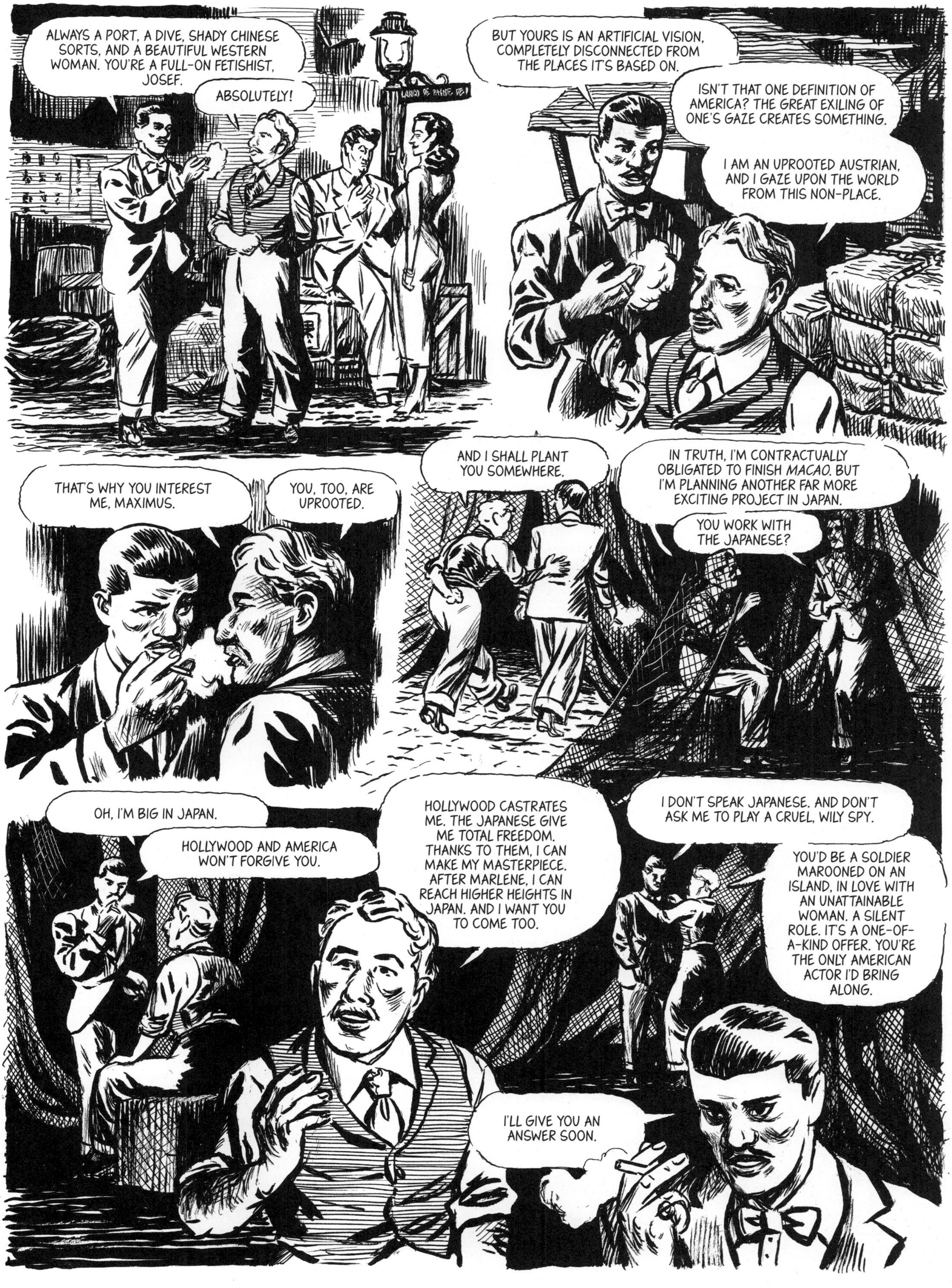

ALWAYS A PORT, A DIVE, SHADY CHINESE SORTS, AND A BEAUTIFUL WESTERN WOMAN. YOU'RE A FULL-ON FETISHIST, JOSEF.
ABSOLUTELY!
BUT YOURS IS AN ARTIFICIAL VISION, COMPLETELY DISCONNECTED FROM THE PLACES IT'S BASED ON.
ISN'T THAT ONE DEFINITION OF AMERICA? THE GREAT EXILING OF ONE'S GAZE CREATES SOMETHING.
I AM AN UPROOTED AUSTRIAN, AND I GAZE UPON THE WORLD FROM THIS NON-PLACE.
THAT'S WHY YOU INTEREST ME, MAXIMUS.
YOU, TOO, ARE UPROOTED.
AND I SHALL PLANT YOU SOMEWHERE.
IN TRUTH, I'M CONTRACTUALLY OBLIGATED TO FINISH *MACAO*. BUT I'M PLANNING ANOTHER FAR MORE EXCITING PROJECT IN JAPAN.
YOU WORK WITH THE JAPANESE?
OH, I'M BIG IN JAPAN.
HOLLYWOOD AND AMERICA WON'T FORGIVE YOU.
HOLLYWOOD CASTRATES ME. THE JAPANESE GIVE ME TOTAL FREEDOM. THANKS TO THEM, I CAN MAKE MY MASTERPIECE. AFTER MARLENE, I CAN REACH HIGHER HEIGHTS IN JAPAN. AND I WANT YOU TO COME TOO.
I DON'T SPEAK JAPANESE. AND DON'T ASK ME TO PLAY A CRUEL, WILY SPY.
YOU'D BE A SOLDIER MAROONED ON AN ISLAND, IN LOVE WITH AN UNATTAINABLE WOMAN. A SILENT ROLE. IT'S A ONE-OF-A-KIND OFFER. YOU'RE THE ONLY AMERICAN ACTOR I'D BRING ALONG.
I'LL GIVE YOU AN ANSWER SOON.

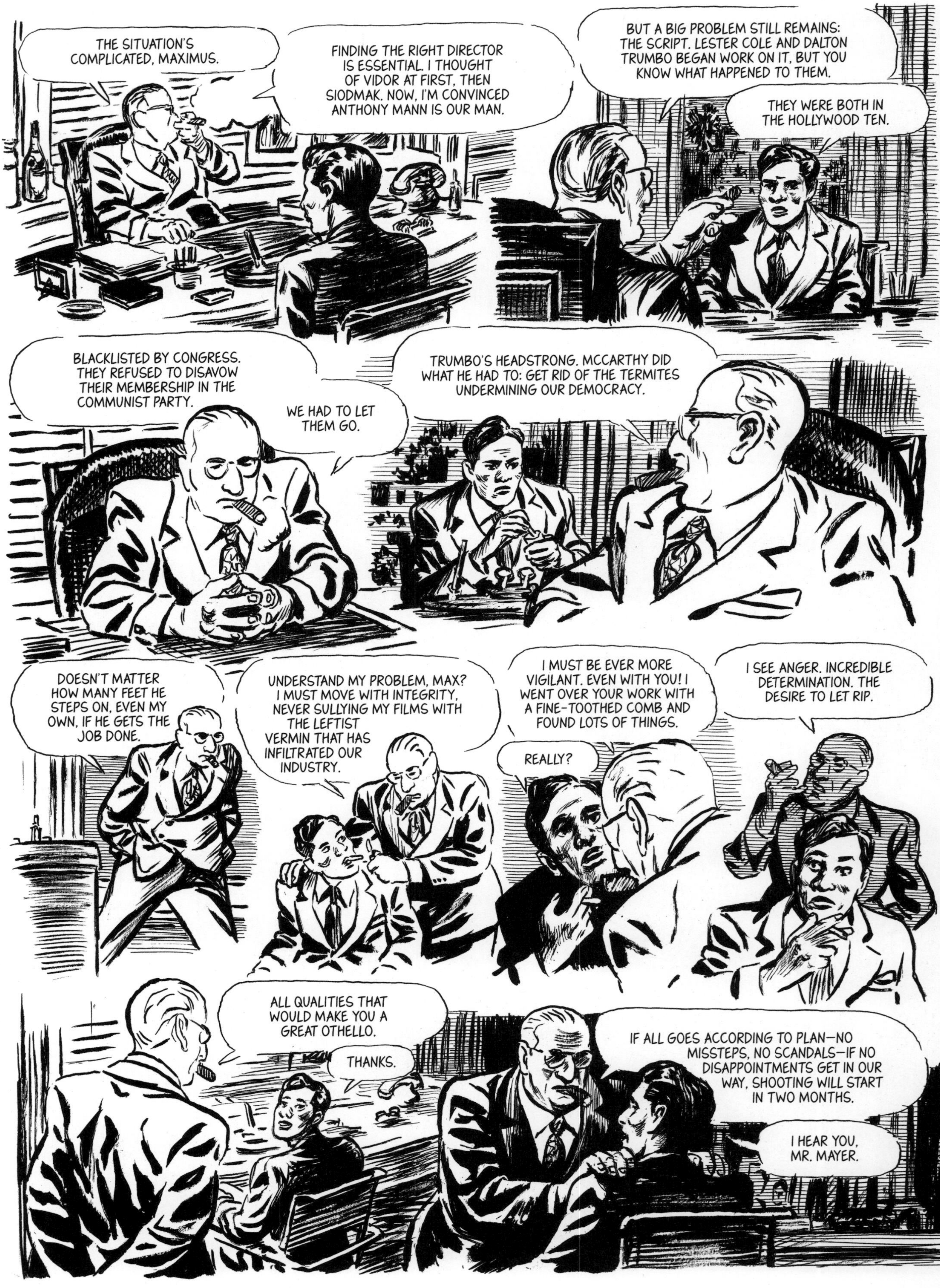
THE SITUATION'S COMPLICATED, MAXIMUS.
FINDING THE RIGHT DIRECTOR IS ESSENTIAL. I THOUGHT OF VIDOR AT FIRST, THEN SIODMAK. NOW, I'M CONVINCED ANTHONY MANN IS OUR MAN.
BUT A BIG PROBLEM STILL REMAINS: THE SCRIPT. LESTER COLE AND DALTON TRUMBO BEGAN WORK ON IT, BUT YOU KNOW WHAT HAPPENED TO THEM.
THEY WERE BOTH IN THE HOLLYWOOD TEN.
BLACKLISTED BY CONGRESS. THEY REFUSED TO DISAVOW THEIR MEMBERSHIP IN THE COMMUNIST PARTY.
WE HAD TO LET THEM GO.
TRUMBO'S HEADSTRONG. MCCARTHY DID WHAT HE HAD TO: GET RID OF THE TERMITES UNDERMINING OUR DEMOCRACY.
DOESN'T MATTER HOW MANY FEET HE STEPS ON, EVEN MY OWN, IF HE GETS THE JOB DONE.
UNDERSTAND MY PROBLEM, MAX? I MUST MOVE WITH INTEGRITY, NEVER SULLYING MY FILMS WITH THE LEFTIST VERMIN THAT HAS INFILTRATED OUR INDUSTRY.
I MUST BE EVER MORE VIGILANT. EVEN WITH YOU! I WENT OVER YOUR WORK WITH A FINE-TOOTHED COMB AND FOUND LOTS OF THINGS.
REALLY?
I SEE ANGER. INCREDIBLE DETERMINATION. THE DESIRE TO LET RIP.
ALL QUALITIES THAT WOULD MAKE YOU A GREAT OTHELLO.
THANKS.
IF ALL GOES ACCORDING TO PLAN—NO MISSTEPS, NO SCANDALS—IF NO DISAPPOINTMENTS GET IN OUR WAY, SHOOTING WILL START IN TWO MONTHS.
I HEAR YOU, MR. MAYER.

DESPITE MAYER'S PROMISES, THE OTHELLO PROJECT WAS PUSHED BACK YET AGAIN. TO ALLAY MAXIMUS' IMPATIENCE, MAYER SENT HIM TO AFRICA WITH JOHN FORD FOR A SUPERPRODUCTION WHOSE SCOPE ALREADY GUARANTEED ADVENTURE.

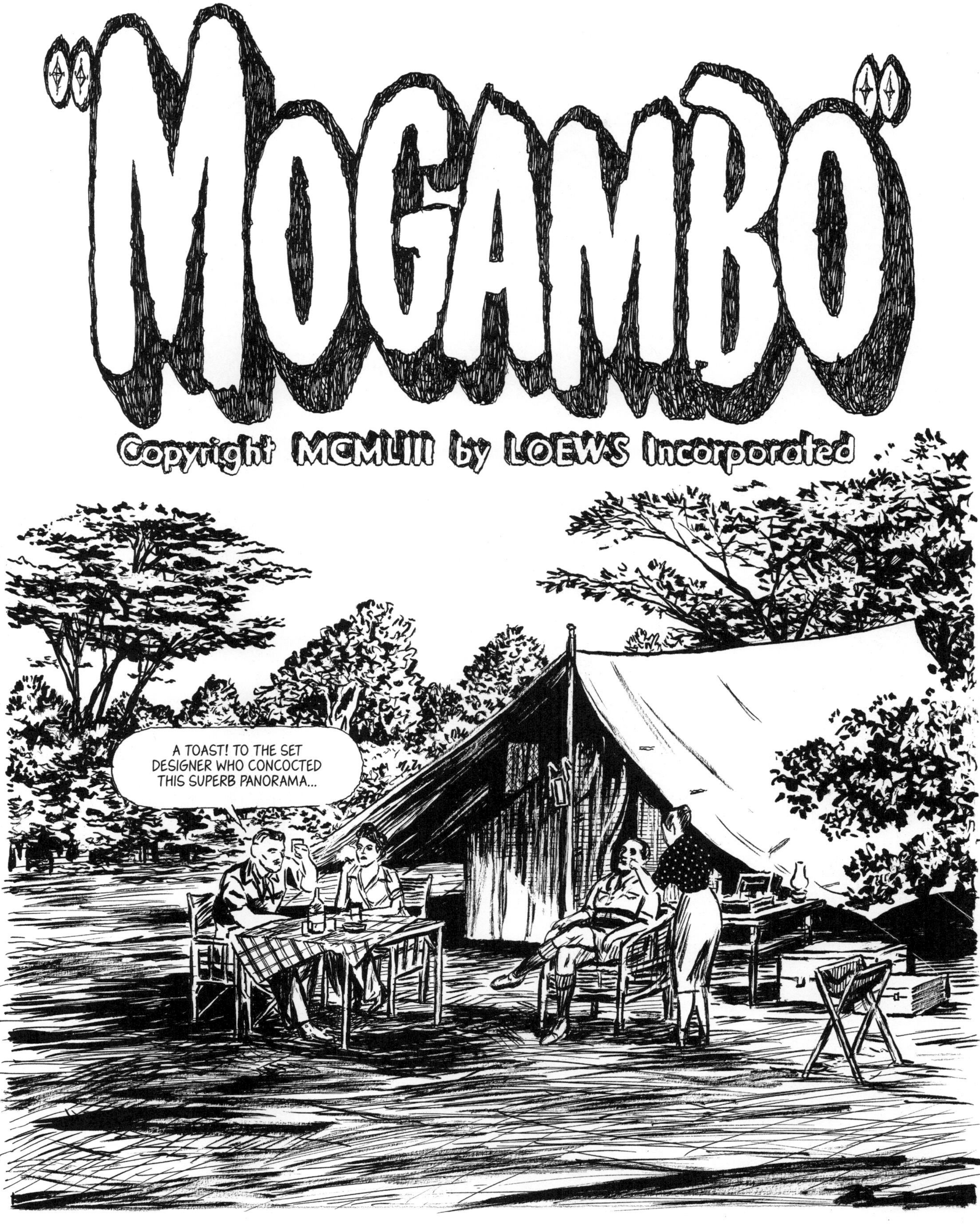
"MOGAMBO"
Copyright MCMLIII by LOEWS Incorporated
A TOAST! TO THE SET DESIGNER WHO CONCOCTED THIS SUPERB PANORAMA...

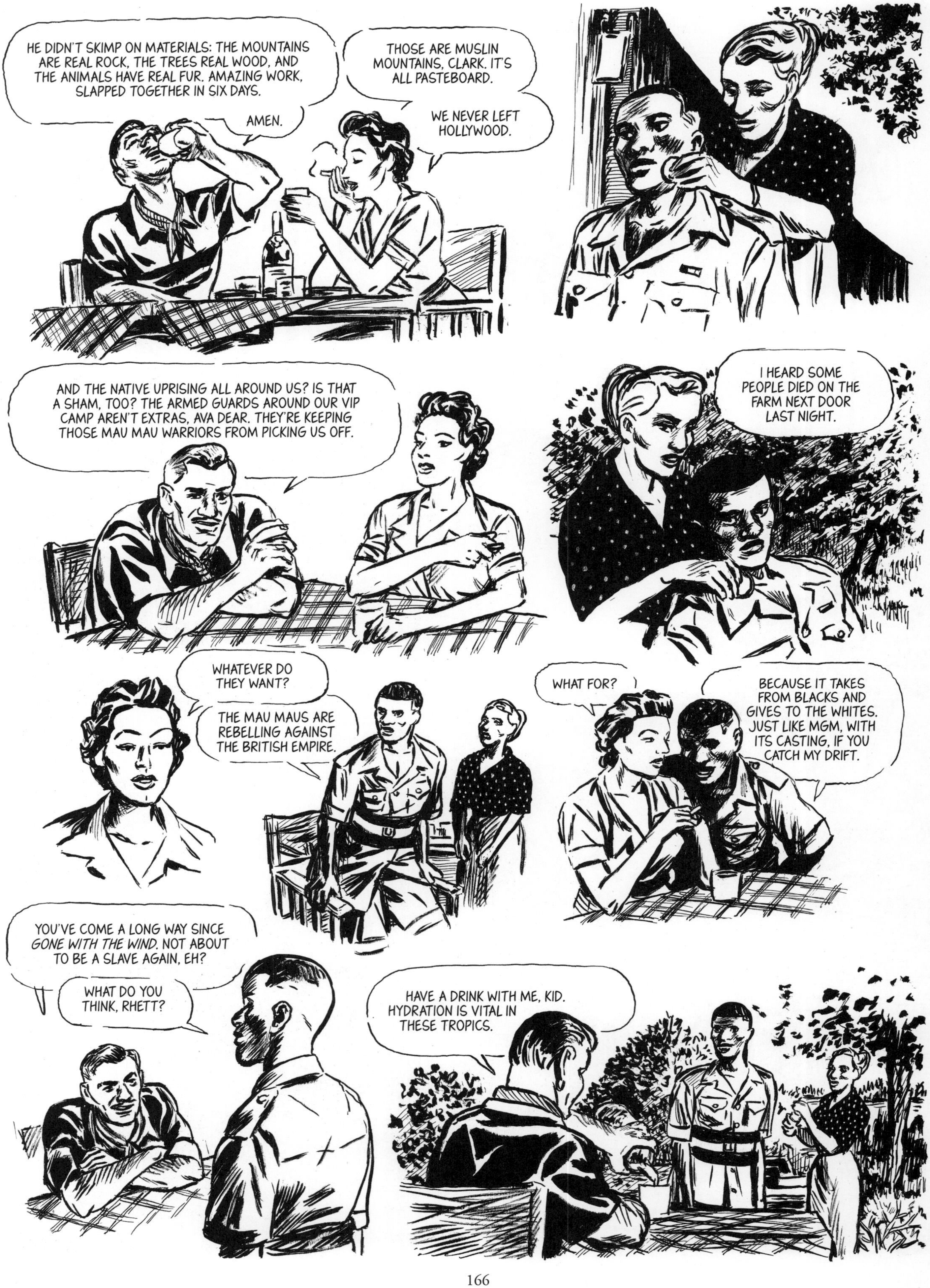
HE DIDN'T SKIMP ON MATERIALS: THE MOUNTAINS ARE REAL ROCK, THE TREES REAL WOOD, AND THE ANIMALS HAVE REAL FUR. AMAZING WORK, SLAPPED TOGETHER IN SIX DAYS.
AMEN.
THOSE ARE MUSLIN MOUNTAINS, CLARK. IT'S ALL PASTEBOARD.
WE NEVER LEFT HOLLYWOOD.
AND THE NATIVE UPRISING ALL AROUND US? IS THAT A SHAM, TOO? THE ARMED GUARDS AROUND OUR VIP CAMP AREN'T EXTRAS, AVA DEAR. THEY'RE KEEPING THOSE MAU MAU WARRIORS FROM PICKING US OFF.
I HEARD SOME PEOPLE DIED ON THE FARM NEXT DOOR LAST NIGHT.
WHATEVER DO THEY WANT?
THE MAU MAUS ARE REBELLING AGAINST THE BRITISH EMPIRE.
WHAT FOR?
BECAUSE IT TAKES FROM BLACKS AND GIVES TO THE WHITES. JUST LIKE MGM, WITH ITS CASTING, IF YOU CATCH MY DRIFT.
YOU'VE COME A LONG WAY SINCE *GONE WITH THE WIND*. NOT ABOUT TO BE A SLAVE AGAIN, EH?
WHAT DO YOU THINK, RHETT?
HAVE A DRINK WITH ME, KID. HYDRATION IS VITAL IN THESE TROPICS.

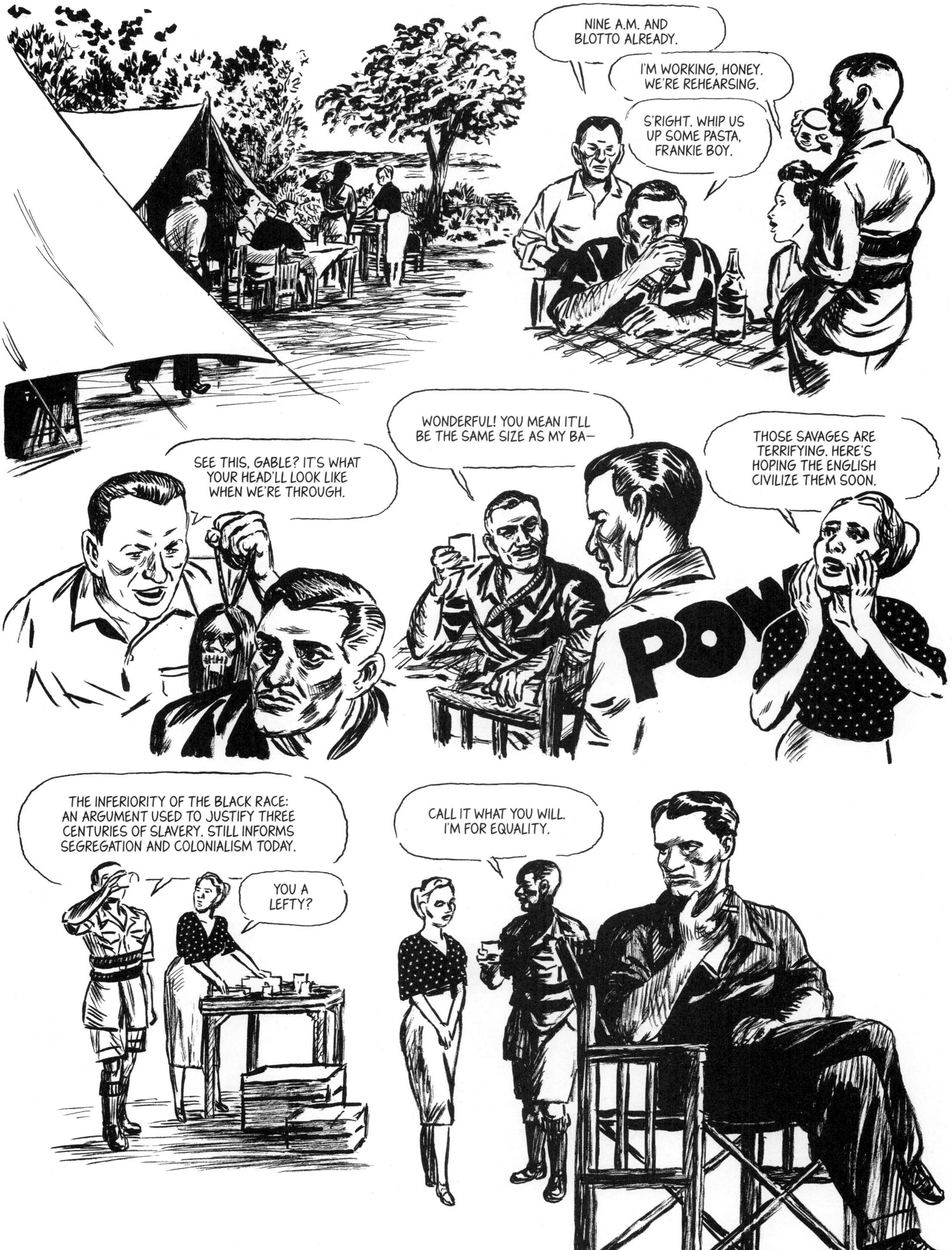
NINE A.M. AND BLOTTO ALREADY.
I'M WORKING, HONEY. WE'RE REHEARSING.
S'RIGHT. WHIP US UP SOME PASTA, FRANKIE BOY.
SEE THIS, GABLE? IT'S WHAT YOUR HEAD'LL LOOK LIKE WHEN WE'RE THROUGH.
WONDERFUL! YOU MEAN IT'LL BE THE SAME SIZE AS MY BA–
POW
THOSE SAVAGES ARE TERRIFYING. HERE'S HOPING THE ENGLISH CIVILIZE THEM SOON.
THE INFERIORITY OF THE BLACK RACE: AN ARGUMENT USED TO JUSTIFY THREE CENTURIES OF SLAVERY. STILL INFORMS SEGREGATION AND COLONIALISM TODAY.
YOU A LEFTY?
CALL IT WHAT YOU WILL. I'M FOR EQUALITY.

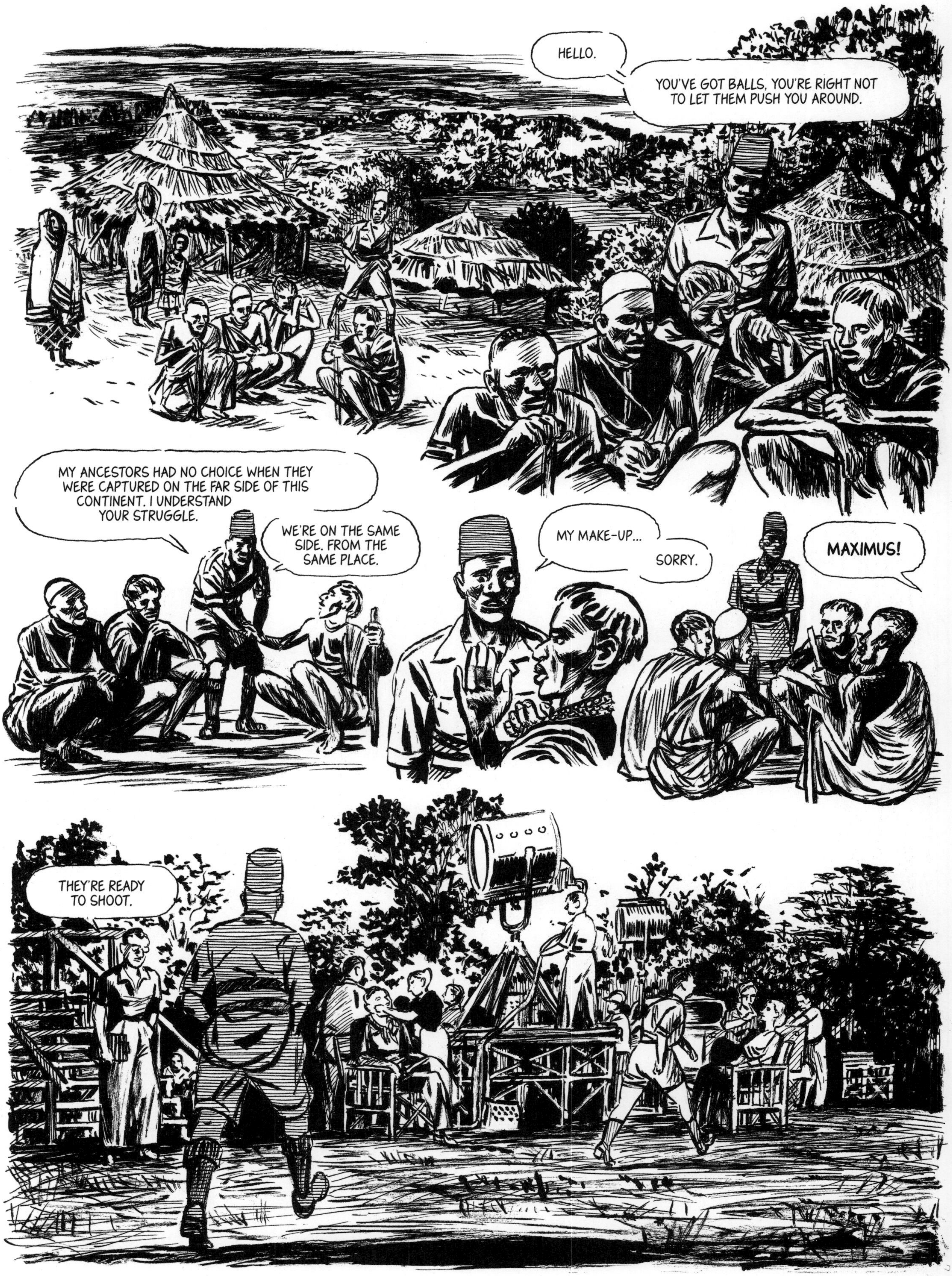
HELLO.
YOU'VE GOT BALLS, YOU'RE RIGHT NOT TO LET THEM PUSH YOU AROUND.
MY ANCESTORS HAD NO CHOICE WHEN THEY WERE CAPTURED ON THE FAR SIDE OF THIS CONTINENT. I UNDERSTAND YOUR STRUGGLE.
WE'RE ON THE SAME SIDE. FROM THE SAME PLACE.
MY MAKE-UP...
SORRY.
MAXIMUS!
THEY'RE READY TO SHOOT.

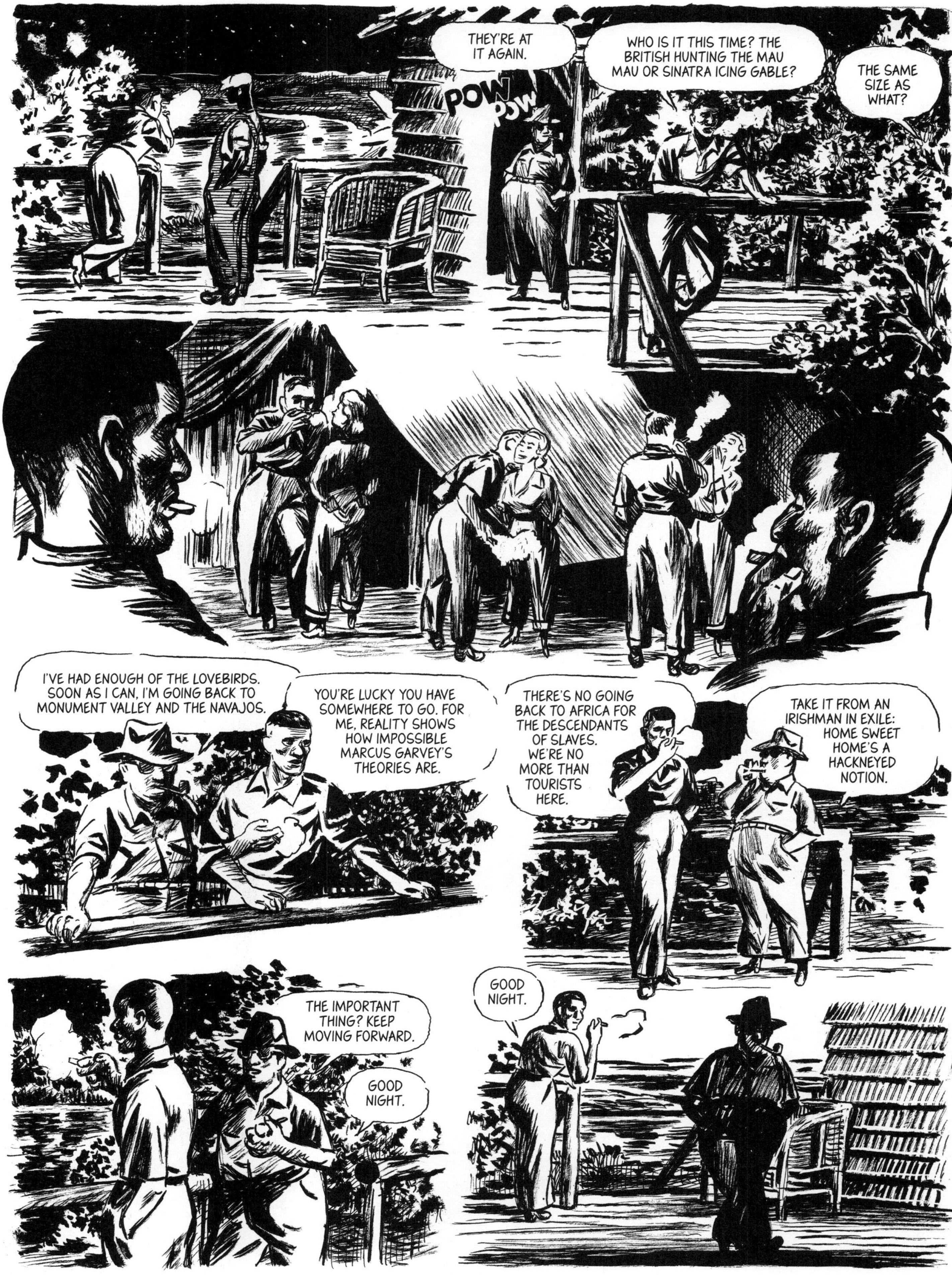

THEY'RE AT IT AGAIN.
POW POW
WHO IS IT THIS TIME? THE BRITISH HUNTING THE MAU MAU OR SINATRA ICING GABLE?
THE SAME SIZE AS WHAT?
I'VE HAD ENOUGH OF THE LOVEBIRDS. SOON AS I CAN, I'M GOING BACK TO MONUMENT VALLEY AND THE NAVAJOS.
YOU'RE LUCKY YOU HAVE SOMEWHERE TO GO. FOR ME, REALITY SHOWS HOW IMPOSSIBLE MARCUS GARVEY'S THEORIES ARE.
THERE'S NO GOING BACK TO AFRICA FOR THE DESCENDANTS OF SLAVES. WE'RE NO MORE THAN TOURISTS HERE.
TAKE IT FROM AN IRISHMAN IN EXILE: HOME SWEET HOME'S A HACKNEYED NOTION.
THE IMPORTANT THING? KEEP MOVING FORWARD.
GOOD NIGHT.
GOOD NIGHT.

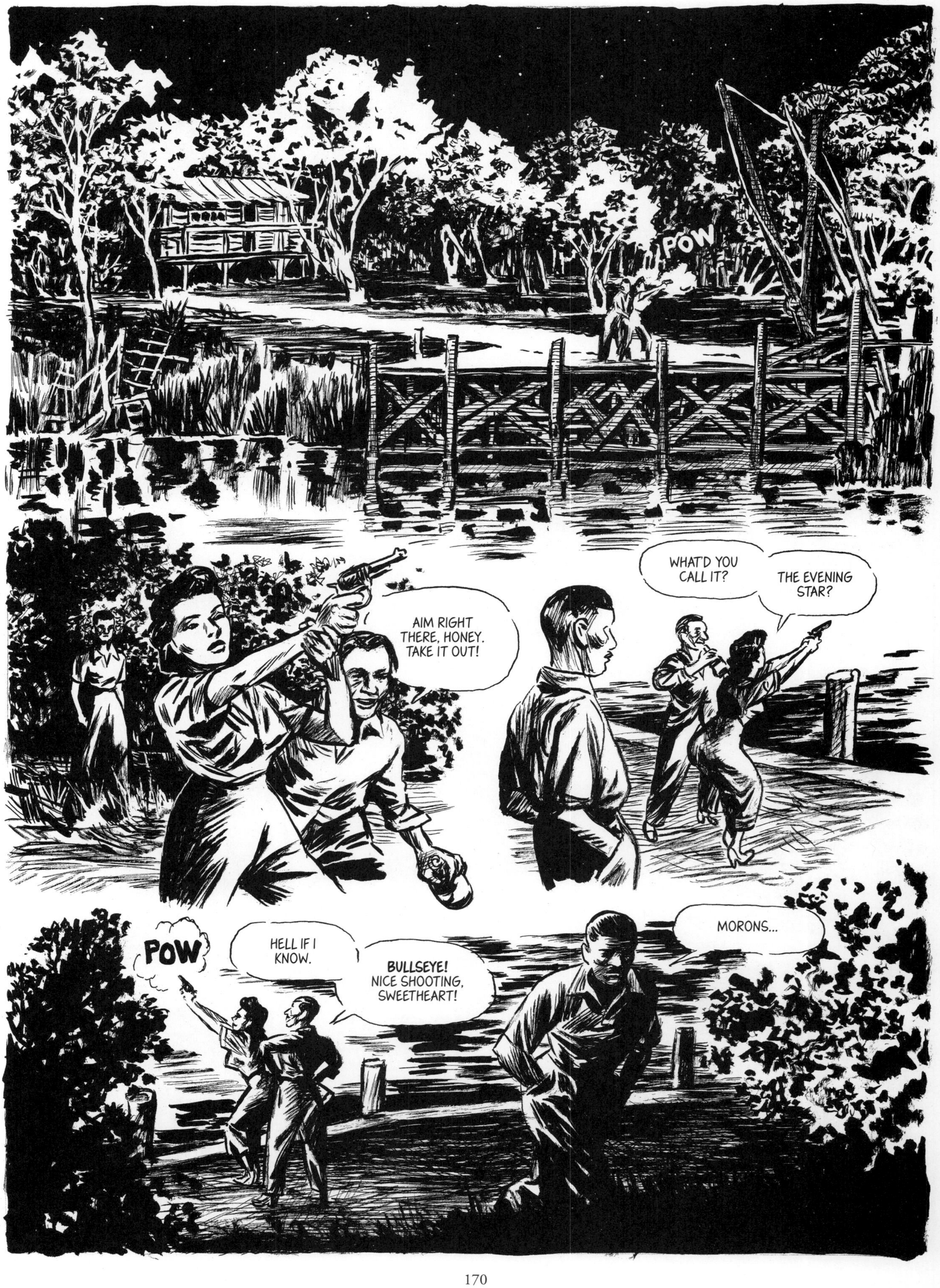
POW
AIM RIGHT THERE, HONEY. TAKE IT OUT!
WHAT'D YOU CALL IT?
THE EVENING STAR?
POW
HELL IF I KNOW.
BULLSEYE! NICE SHOOTING, SWEETHEART!
MORONS...

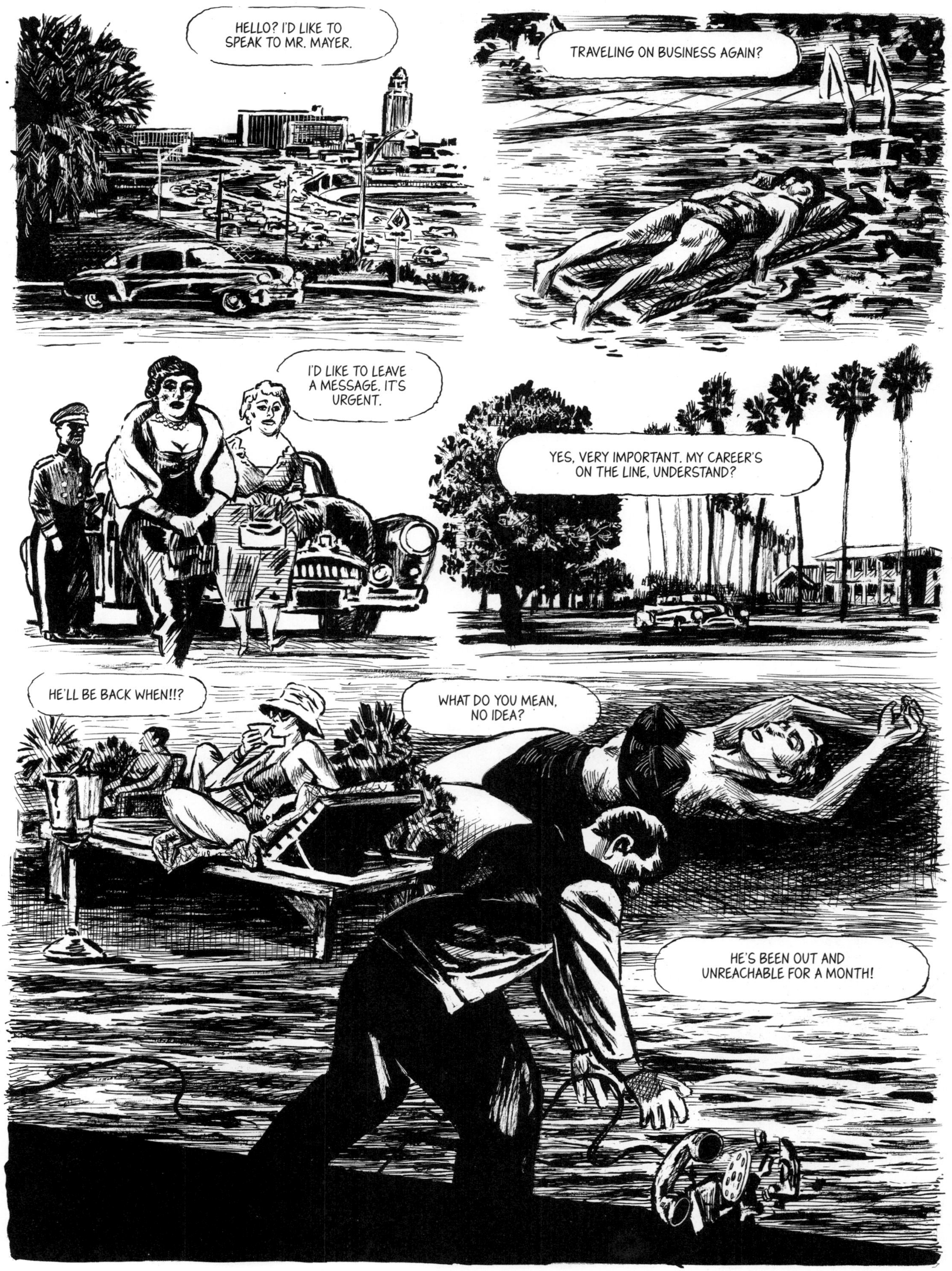
HELLO? I'D LIKE TO SPEAK TO MR. MAYER.
TRAVELING ON BUSINESS AGAIN?
I'D LIKE TO LEAVE A MESSAGE. IT'S URGENT.
YES, VERY IMPORTANT. MY CAREER'S ON THE LINE, UNDERSTAND?
HE'LL BE BACK WHEN!!?
WHAT DO YOU MEAN, NO IDEA?
HE'S BEEN OUT AND UNREACHABLE FOR A MONTH!

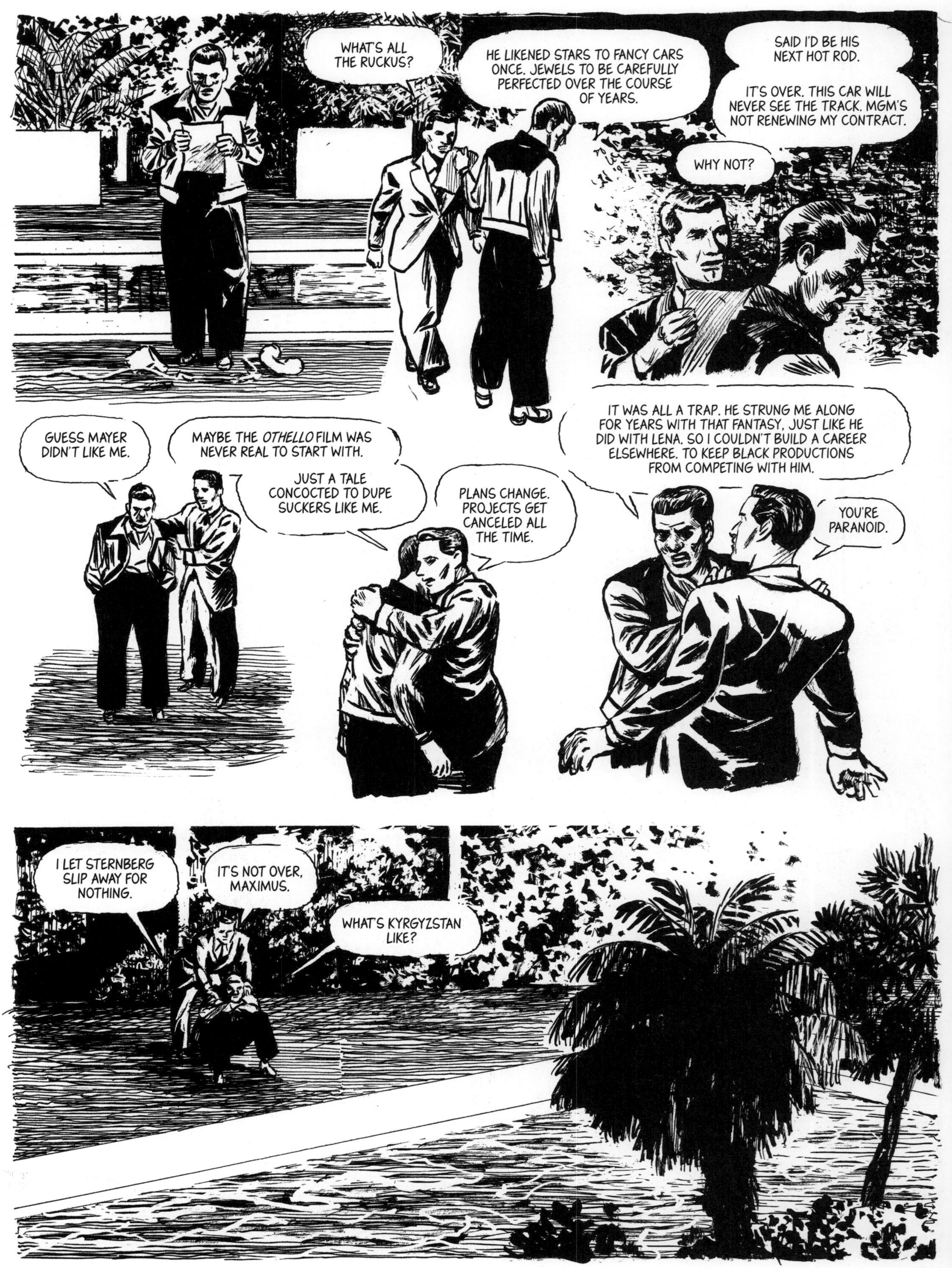
WHAT'S ALL THE RUCKUS?
HE LIKENED STARS TO FANCY CARS ONCE. JEWELS TO BE CAREFULLY PERFECTED OVER THE COURSE OF YEARS.
SAID I'D BE HIS NEXT HOT ROD.
IT'S OVER. THIS CAR WILL NEVER SEE THE TRACK. MGM'S NOT RENEWING MY CONTRACT.
WHY NOT?
GUESS MAYER DIDN'T LIKE ME.
MAYBE THE *OTHELLO* FILM WAS NEVER REAL TO START WITH.
JUST A TALE CONCOCTED TO DUPE SUCKERS LIKE ME.
PLANS CHANGE. PROJECTS GET CANCELED ALL THE TIME.
IT WAS ALL A TRAP. HE STRUNG ME ALONG FOR YEARS WITH THAT FANTASY, JUST LIKE HE DID WITH LENA. SO I COULDN'T BUILD A CAREER ELSEWHERE. TO KEEP BLACK PRODUCTIONS FROM COMPETING WITH HIM.
YOU'RE PARANOID.
I LET STERNBERG SLIP AWAY FOR NOTHING.
IT'S NOT OVER, MAXIMUS.
WHAT'S KYRGYZSTAN LIKE?

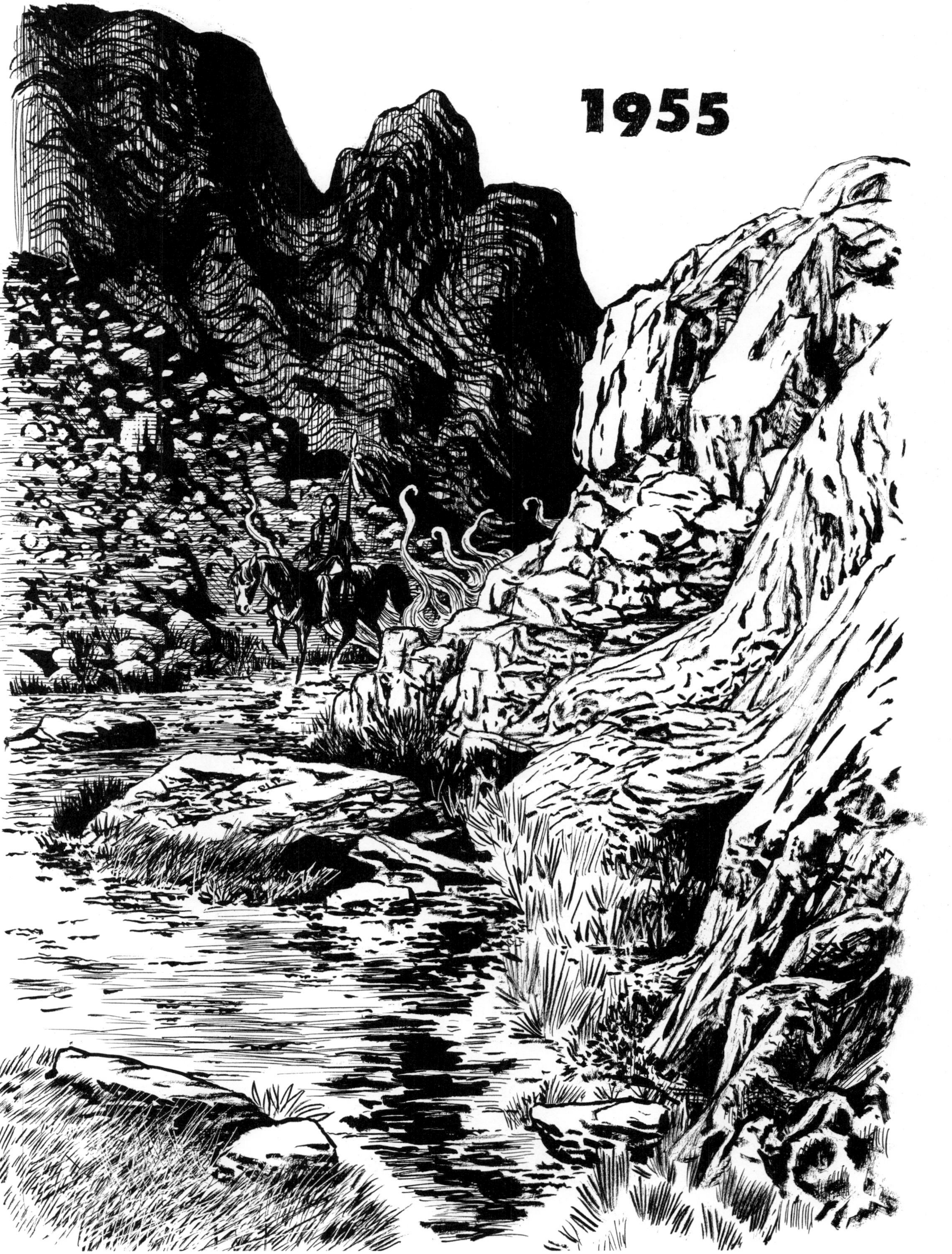
1955

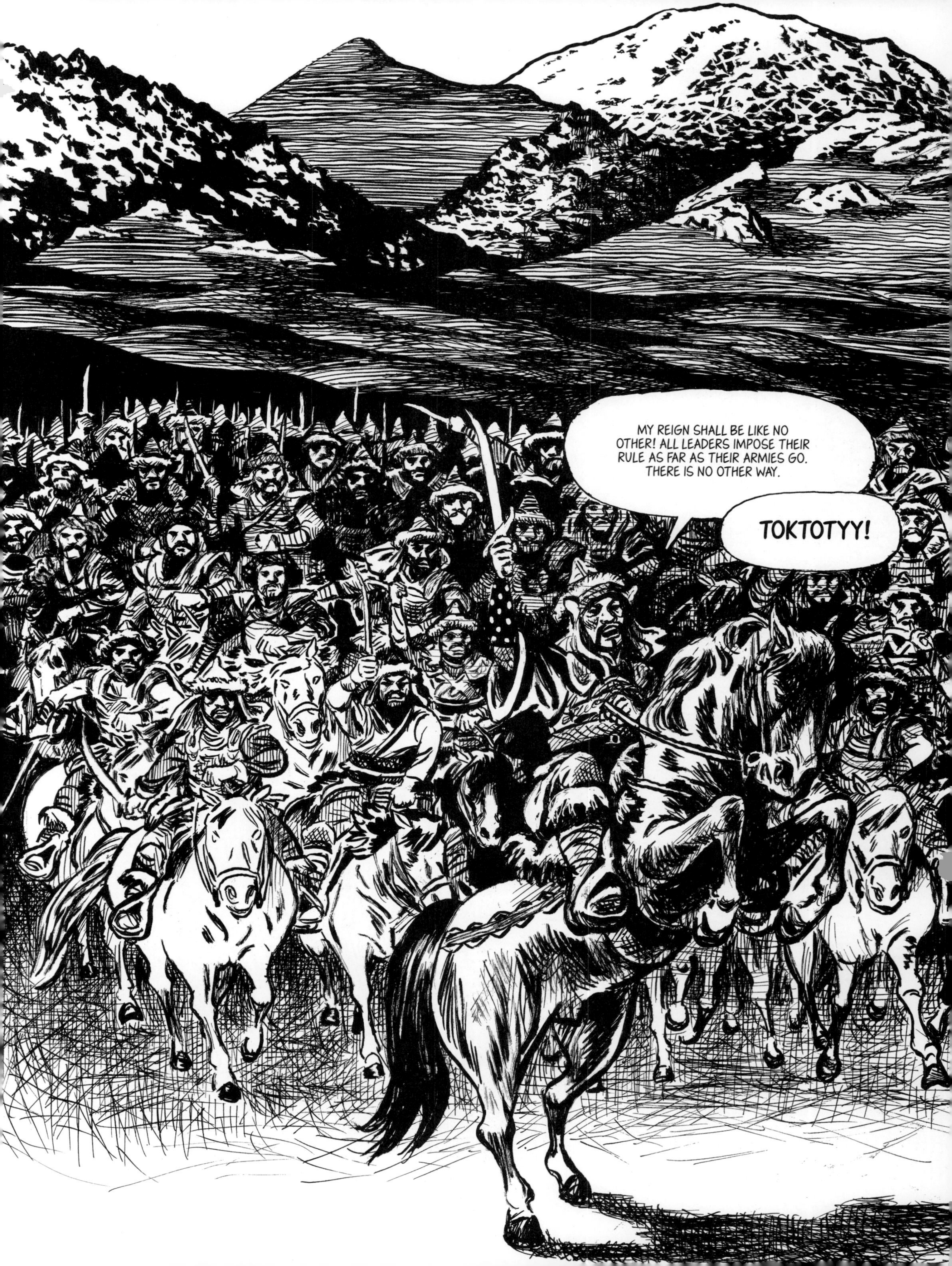
MY REIGN SHALL BE LIKE NO OTHER! ALL LEADERS IMPOSE THEIR RULE AS FAR AS THEIR ARMIES GO. THERE IS NO OTHER WAY.
TOKTOTYY!

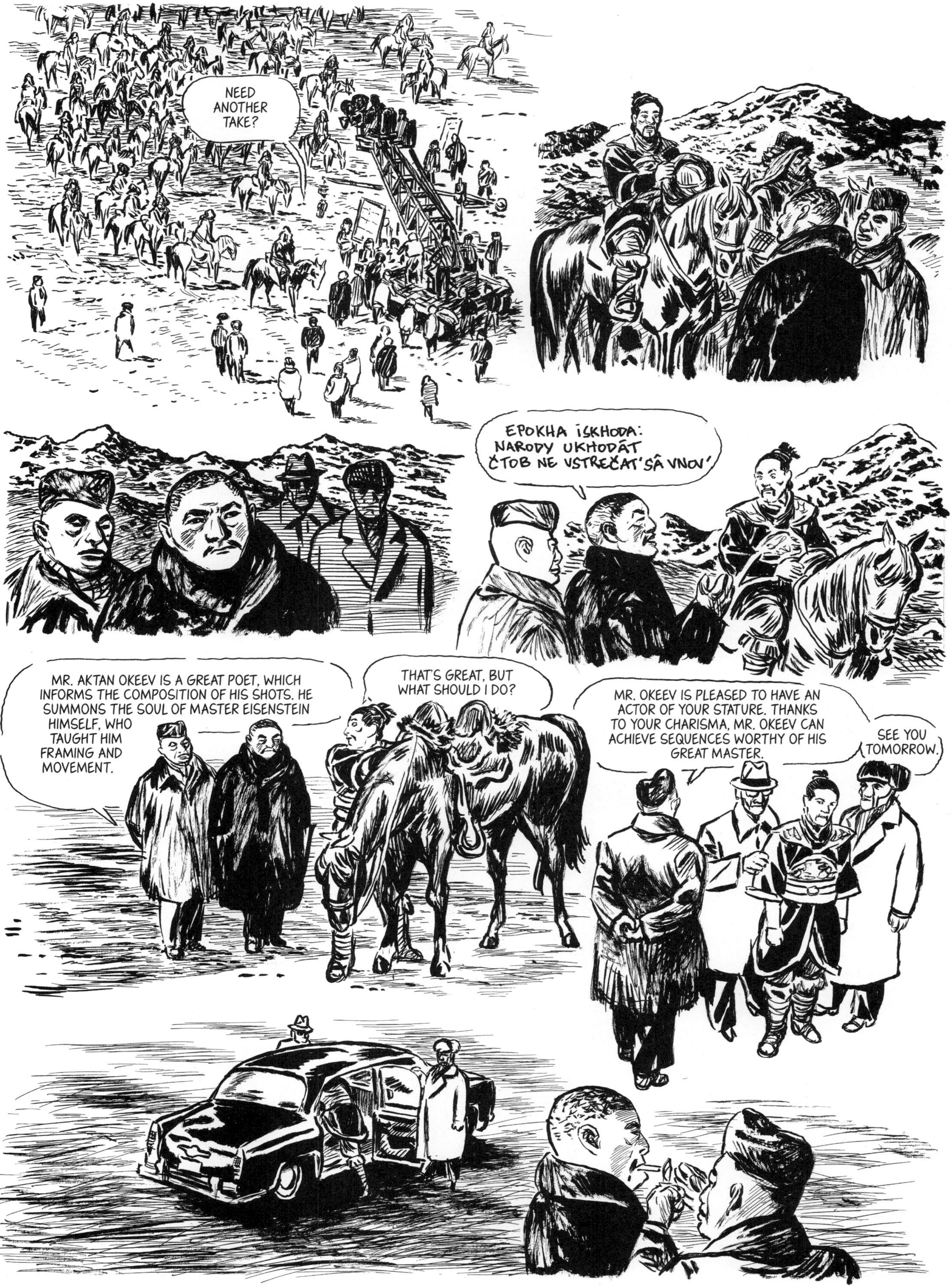
NEED ANOTHER TAKE?
EPOKHA ISKHODA: NARODY UKHODÂT ČTOB NE VSTREČAT'SÂ VNOV'
MR. AKTAN OKEEV IS A GREAT POET, WHICH INFORMS THE COMPOSITION OF HIS SHOTS. HE SUMMONS THE SOUL OF MASTER EISENSTEIN HIMSELF, WHO TAUGHT HIM FRAMING AND MOVEMENT.
THAT'S GREAT, BUT WHAT SHOULD I DO?
MR. OKEEV IS PLEASED TO HAVE AN ACTOR OF YOUR STATURE. THANKS TO YOUR CHARISMA, MR. OKEEV CAN ACHIEVE SEQUENCES WORTHY OF HIS GREAT MASTER.
SEE YOU TOMORROW.

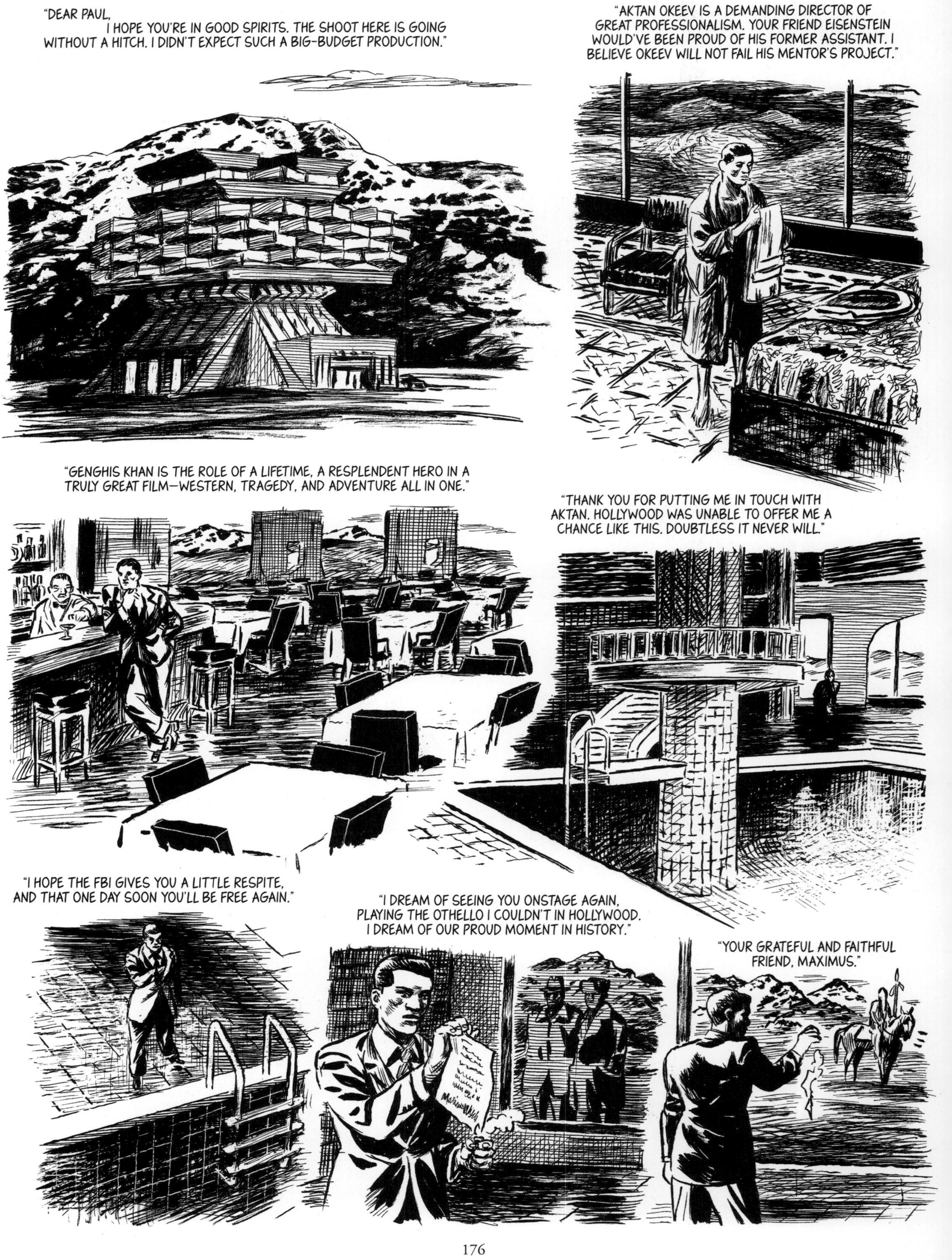
"DEAR PAUL,
I HOPE YOU'RE IN GOOD SPIRITS. THE SHOOT HERE IS GOING WITHOUT A HITCH. I DIDN'T EXPECT SUCH A BIG-BUDGET PRODUCTION."
"AKTAN OKEEV IS A DEMANDING DIRECTOR OF GREAT PROFESSIONALISM. YOUR FRIEND EISENSTEIN WOULD'VE BEEN PROUD OF HIS FORMER ASSISTANT. I BELIEVE OKEEV WILL NOT FAIL HIS MENTOR'S PROJECT."
"GENGHIS KHAN IS THE ROLE OF A LIFETIME, A RESPLENDENT HERO IN A TRULY GREAT FILM—WESTERN, TRAGEDY, AND ADVENTURE ALL IN ONE."
"THANK YOU FOR PUTTING ME IN TOUCH WITH AKTAN. HOLLYWOOD WAS UNABLE TO OFFER ME A CHANCE LIKE THIS. DOUBTLESS IT NEVER WILL."
"I HOPE THE FBI GIVES YOU A LITTLE RESPITE, AND THAT ONE DAY SOON YOU'LL BE FREE AGAIN."
"I DREAM OF SEEING YOU ONSTAGE AGAIN, PLAYING THE OTHELLO I COULDN'T IN HOLLYWOOD. I DREAM OF OUR PROUD MOMENT IN HISTORY."
"YOUR GRATEFUL AND FAITHFUL FRIEND, MAXIMUS."

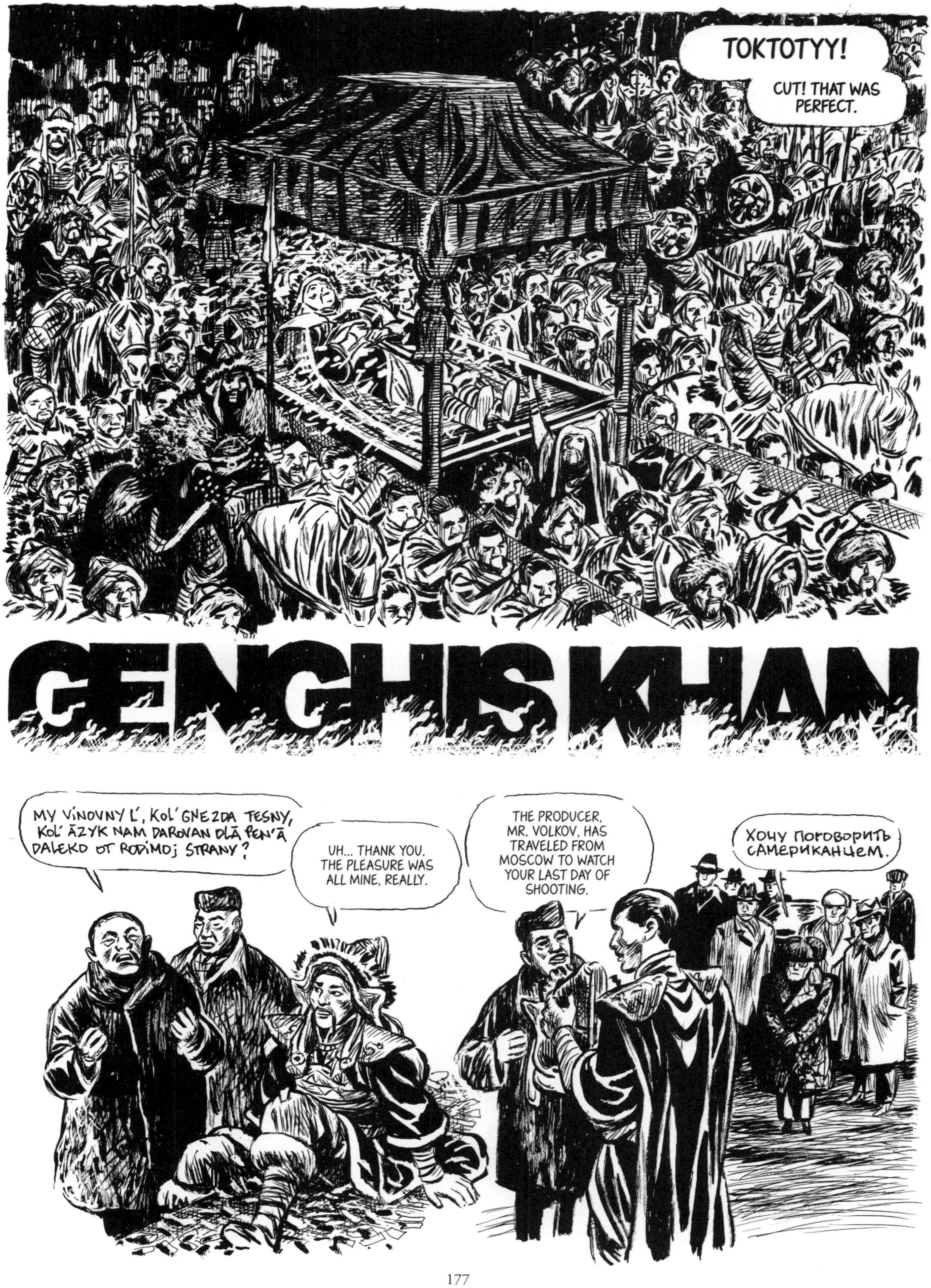

TOKTOTYY!
CUT! THAT WAS PERFECT.
GENGHIS KHAN
MY VINOVNY L', KOL' GNEZDA TESNY, KOL' ĀZYK NAM DAROVAN DLĀ PEN'Ā DALEKO OT RODIMOJ STRANY?
UH... THANK YOU. THE PLEASURE WAS ALL MINE, REALLY.
THE PRODUCER, MR. VOLKOV, HAS TRAVELED FROM MOSCOW TO WATCH YOUR LAST DAY OF SHOOTING.
Хочу поговорить с американцем.

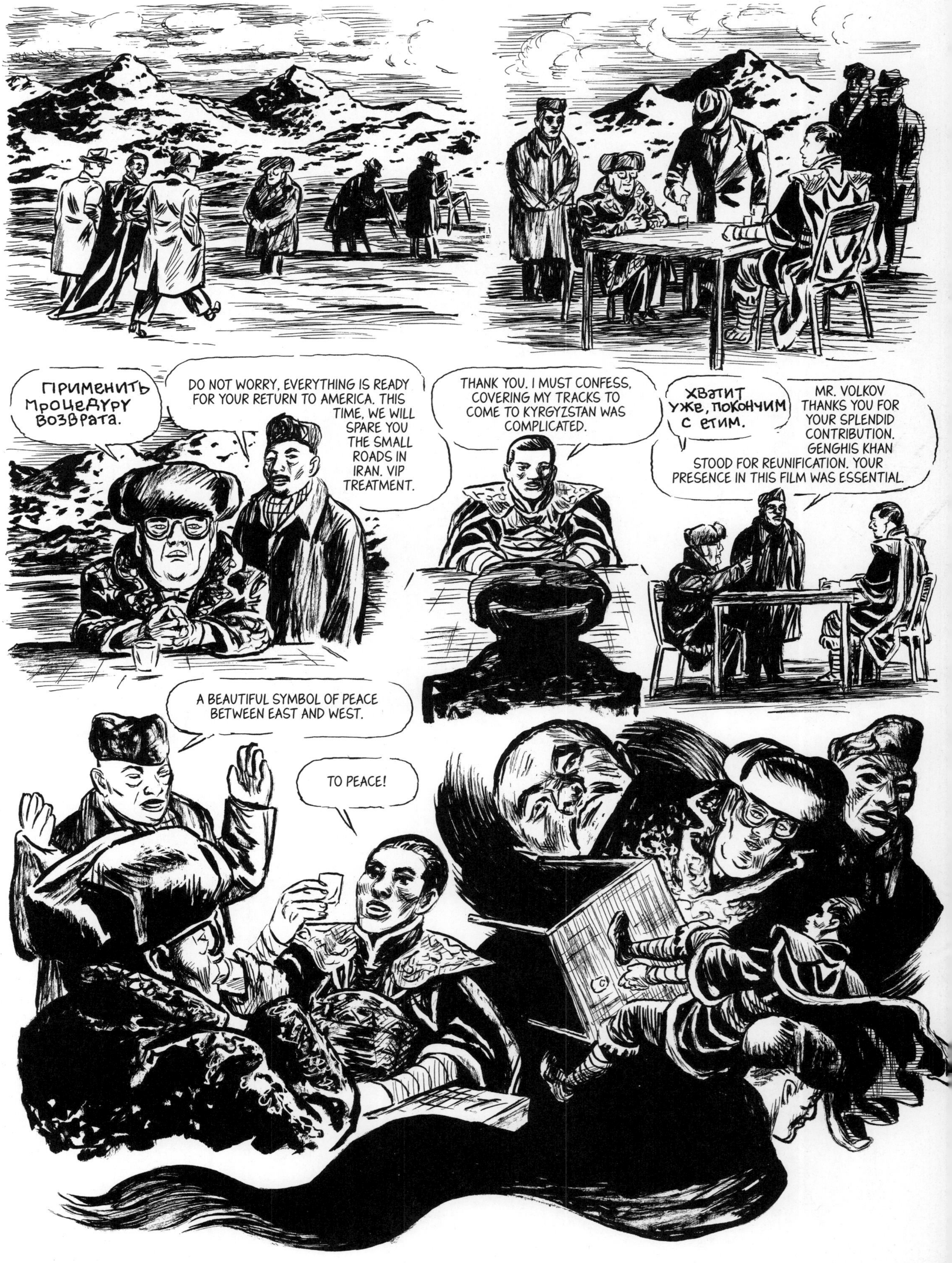
Применить мроцедуру возврата.
DO NOT WORRY, EVERYTHING IS READY FOR YOUR RETURN TO AMERICA. THIS TIME, WE WILL SPARE YOU THE SMALL ROADS IN IRAN. VIP TREATMENT.
THANK YOU. I MUST CONFESS, COVERING MY TRACKS TO COME TO KYRGYZSTAN WAS COMPLICATED.
Хватит уже, покончим с етим.
MR. VOLKOV THANKS YOU FOR YOUR SPLENDID CONTRIBUTION. GENGHIS KHAN STOOD FOR REUNIFICATION. YOUR PRESENCE IN THIS FILM WAS ESSENTIAL.
A BEAUTIFUL SYMBOL OF PEACE BETWEEN EAST AND WEST.
TO PEACE!

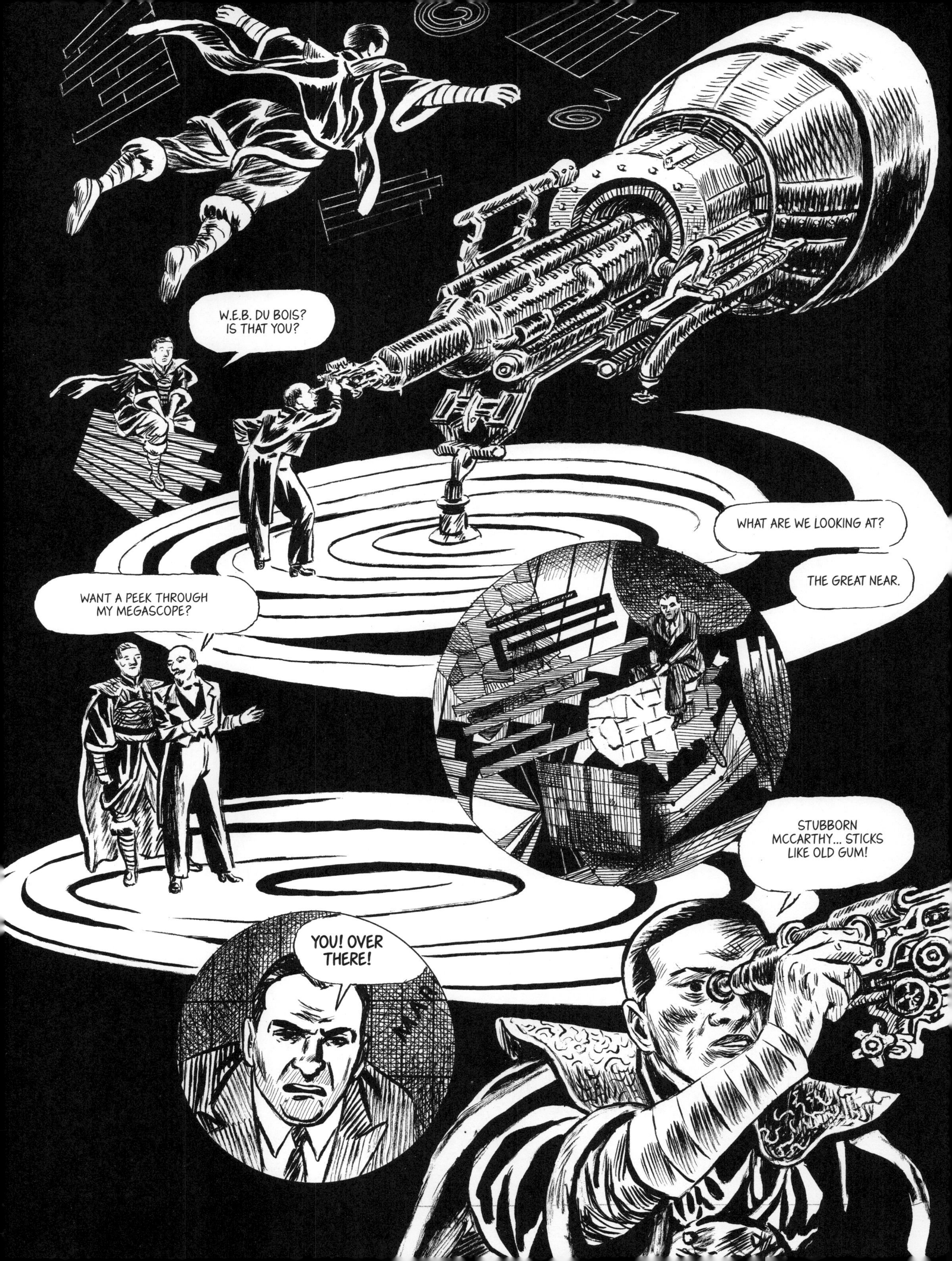
W.E.B. DU BOIS? IS THAT YOU?
WHAT ARE WE LOOKING AT?
THE GREAT NEAR.
WANT A PEEK THROUGH MY MEGASCOPE?
STUBBORN MCCARTHY... STICKS LIKE OLD GUM!
YOU! OVER THERE!

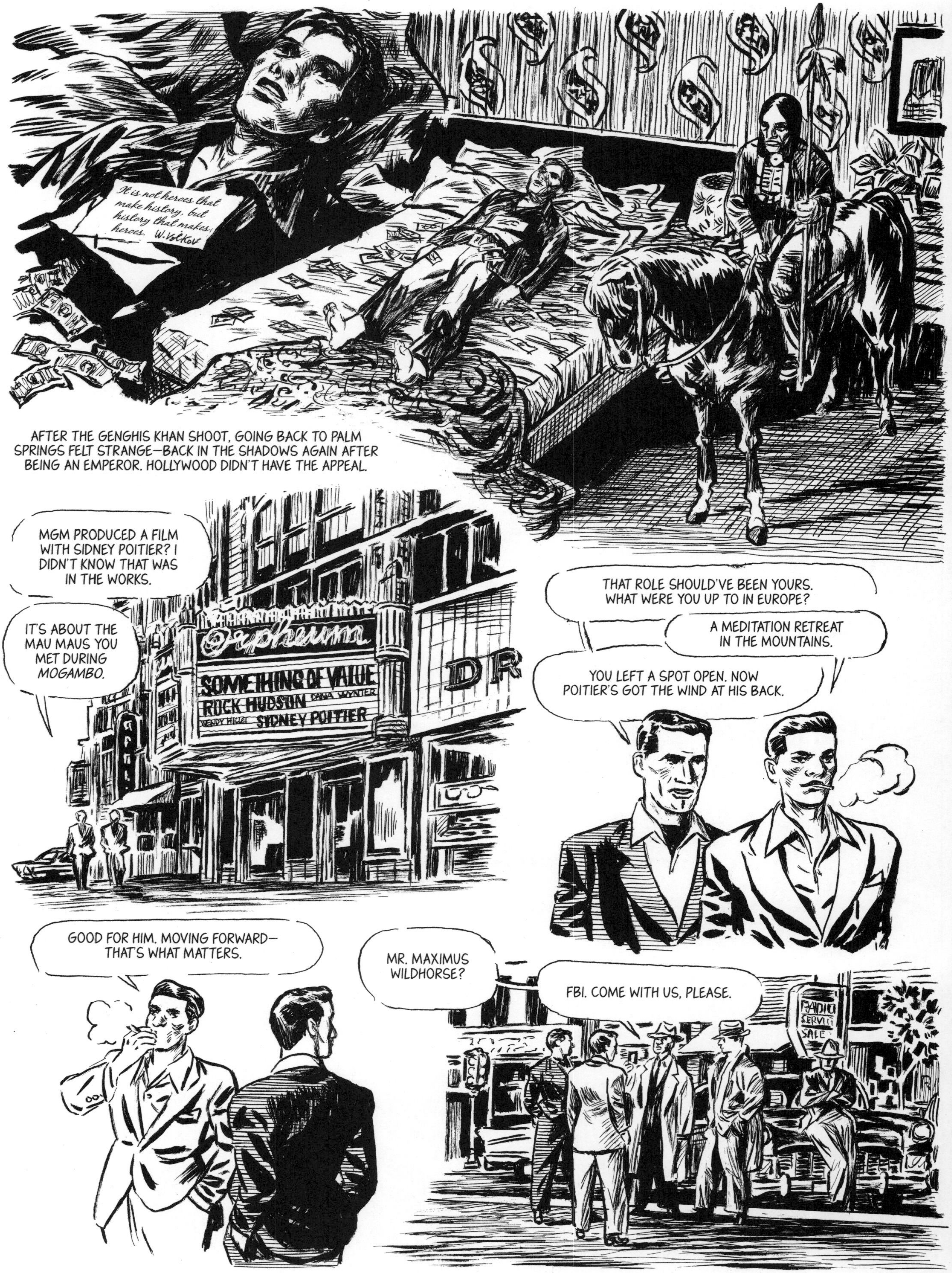
It is not heroes that make history, but history that makes heroes. W.Volkov
AFTER THE GENGHIS KHAN SHOOT, GOING BACK TO PALM SPRINGS FELT STRANGE—BACK IN THE SHADOWS AGAIN AFTER BEING AN EMPEROR. HOLLYWOOD DIDN'T HAVE THE APPEAL.
MGM PRODUCED A FILM WITH SIDNEY POITIER? I DIDN'T KNOW THAT WAS IN THE WORKS.
IT'S ABOUT THE MAU MAUS YOU MET DURING *MOGAMBO*.
Orpheum
SOMETHING OF VALUE
ROCK HUDSON DANA WYNTER
WENDY HILLER SIDNEY POITIER
THAT ROLE SHOULD'VE BEEN YOURS. WHAT WERE YOU UP TO IN EUROPE?
A MEDITATION RETREAT IN THE MOUNTAINS.
YOU LEFT A SPOT OPEN. NOW POITIER'S GOT THE WIND AT HIS BACK.
GOOD FOR HIM. MOVING FORWARD—THAT'S WHAT MATTERS.
MR. MAXIMUS WILDHORSE?
FBI. COME WITH US, PLEASE.
RADIO SERVICE SALE

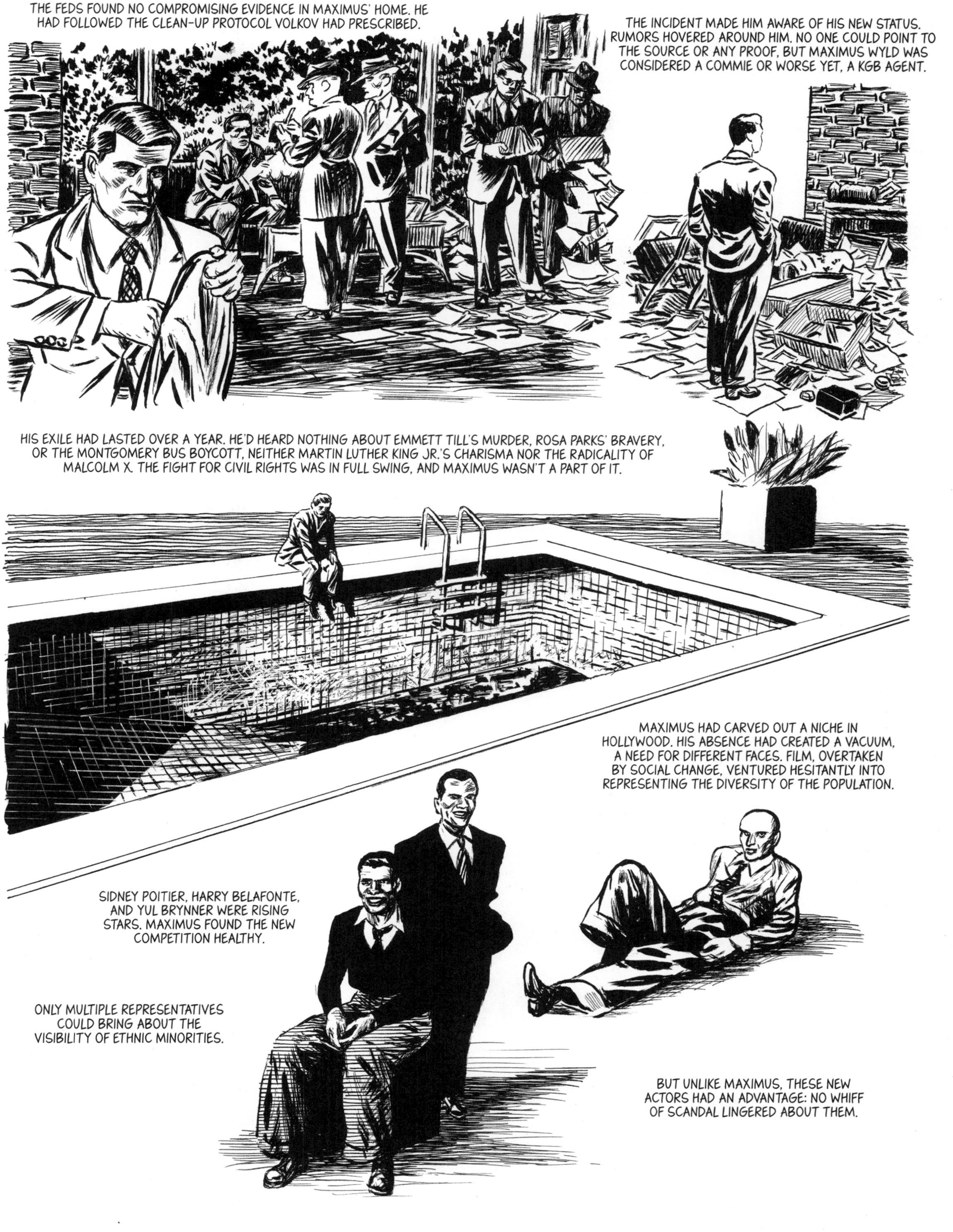
THE FEDS FOUND NO COMPROMISING EVIDENCE IN MAXIMUS' HOME. HE HAD FOLLOWED THE CLEAN-UP PROTOCOL VOLKOV HAD PRESCRIBED.
THE INCIDENT MADE HIM AWARE OF HIS NEW STATUS. RUMORS HOVERED AROUND HIM. NO ONE COULD POINT TO THE SOURCE OR ANY PROOF, BUT MAXIMUS WYLD WAS CONSIDERED A COMMIE OR WORSE YET, A KGB AGENT.
HIS EXILE HAD LASTED OVER A YEAR. HE'D HEARD NOTHING ABOUT EMMETT TILL'S MURDER, ROSA PARKS' BRAVERY, OR THE MONTGOMERY BUS BOYCOTT, NEITHER MARTIN LUTHER KING JR.'S CHARISMA NOR THE RADICALITY OF MALCOLM X. THE FIGHT FOR CIVIL RIGHTS WAS IN FULL SWING, AND MAXIMUS WASN'T A PART OF IT.
MAXIMUS HAD CARVED OUT A NICHE IN HOLLYWOOD. HIS ABSENCE HAD CREATED A VACUUM, A NEED FOR DIFFERENT FACES. FILM, OVERTAKEN BY SOCIAL CHANGE, VENTURED HESITANTLY INTO REPRESENTING THE DIVERSITY OF THE POPULATION.
SIDNEY POITIER, HARRY BELAFONTE, AND YUL BRYNNER WERE RISING STARS. MAXIMUS FOUND THE NEW COMPETITION HEALTHY.
ONLY MULTIPLE REPRESENTATIVES COULD BRING ABOUT THE VISIBILITY OF ETHNIC MINORITIES.
BUT UNLIKE MAXIMUS, THESE NEW ACTORS HAD AN ADVANTAGE: NO WHIFF OF SCANDAL LINGERED ABOUT THEM.

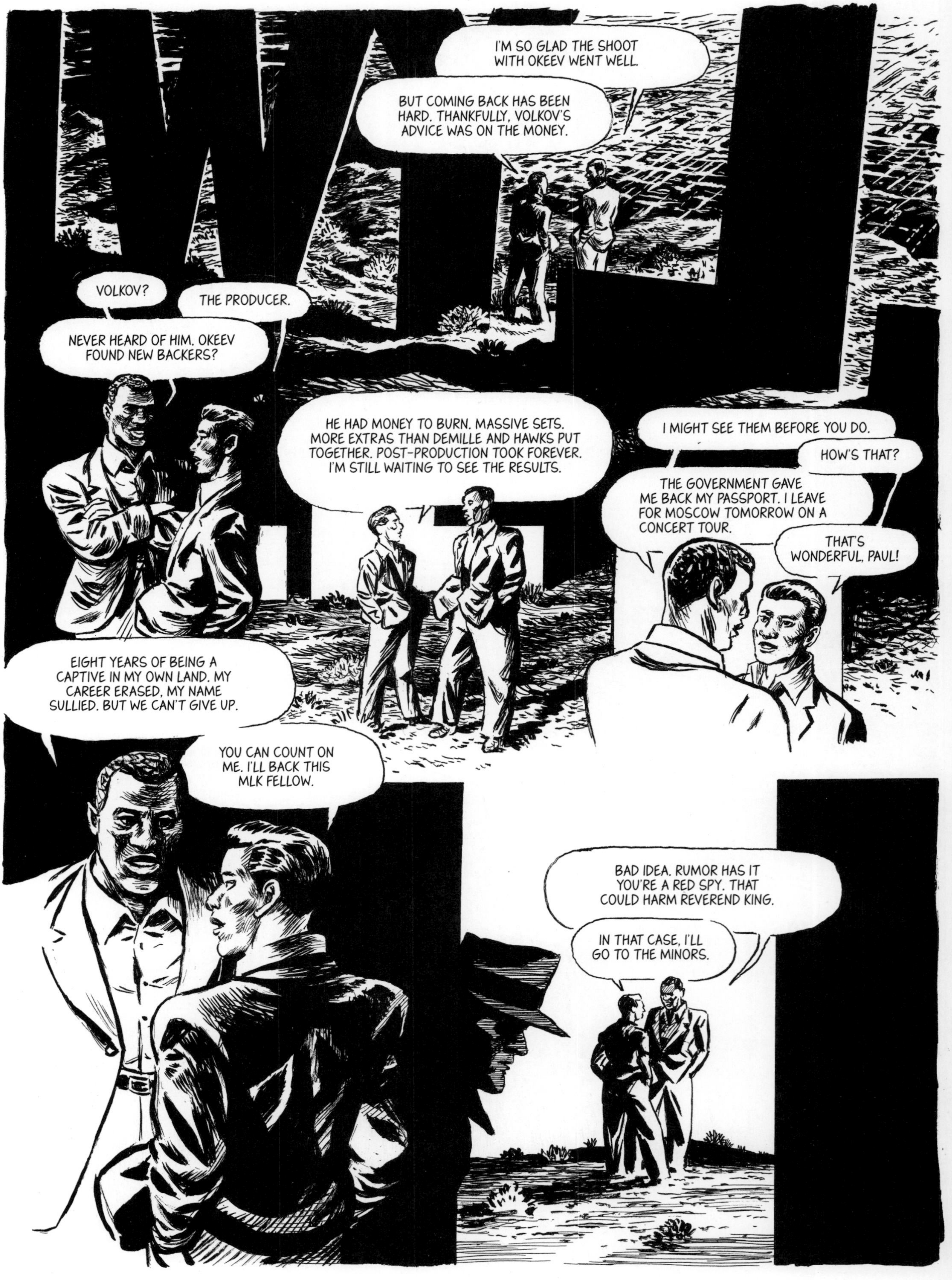
I'M SO GLAD THE SHOOT WITH OKEEV WENT WELL.
BUT COMING BACK HAS BEEN HARD. THANKFULLY, VOLKOV'S ADVICE WAS ON THE MONEY.
VOLKOV?
THE PRODUCER.
NEVER HEARD OF HIM. OKEEV FOUND NEW BACKERS?
HE HAD MONEY TO BURN. MASSIVE SETS. MORE EXTRAS THAN DEMILLE AND HAWKS PUT TOGETHER. POST-PRODUCTION TOOK FOREVER. I'M STILL WAITING TO SEE THE RESULTS.
I MIGHT SEE THEM BEFORE YOU DO.
HOW'S THAT?
THE GOVERNMENT GAVE ME BACK MY PASSPORT. I LEAVE FOR MOSCOW TOMORROW ON A CONCERT TOUR.
THAT'S WONDERFUL, PAUL!
EIGHT YEARS OF BEING A CAPTIVE IN MY OWN LAND. MY CAREER ERASED, MY NAME SULLIED. BUT WE CAN'T GIVE UP.
YOU CAN COUNT ON ME. I'LL BACK THIS MLK FELLOW.
BAD IDEA. RUMOR HAS IT YOU'RE A RED SPY. THAT COULD HARM REVEREND KING.
IN THAT CASE, I'LL GO TO THE MINORS.

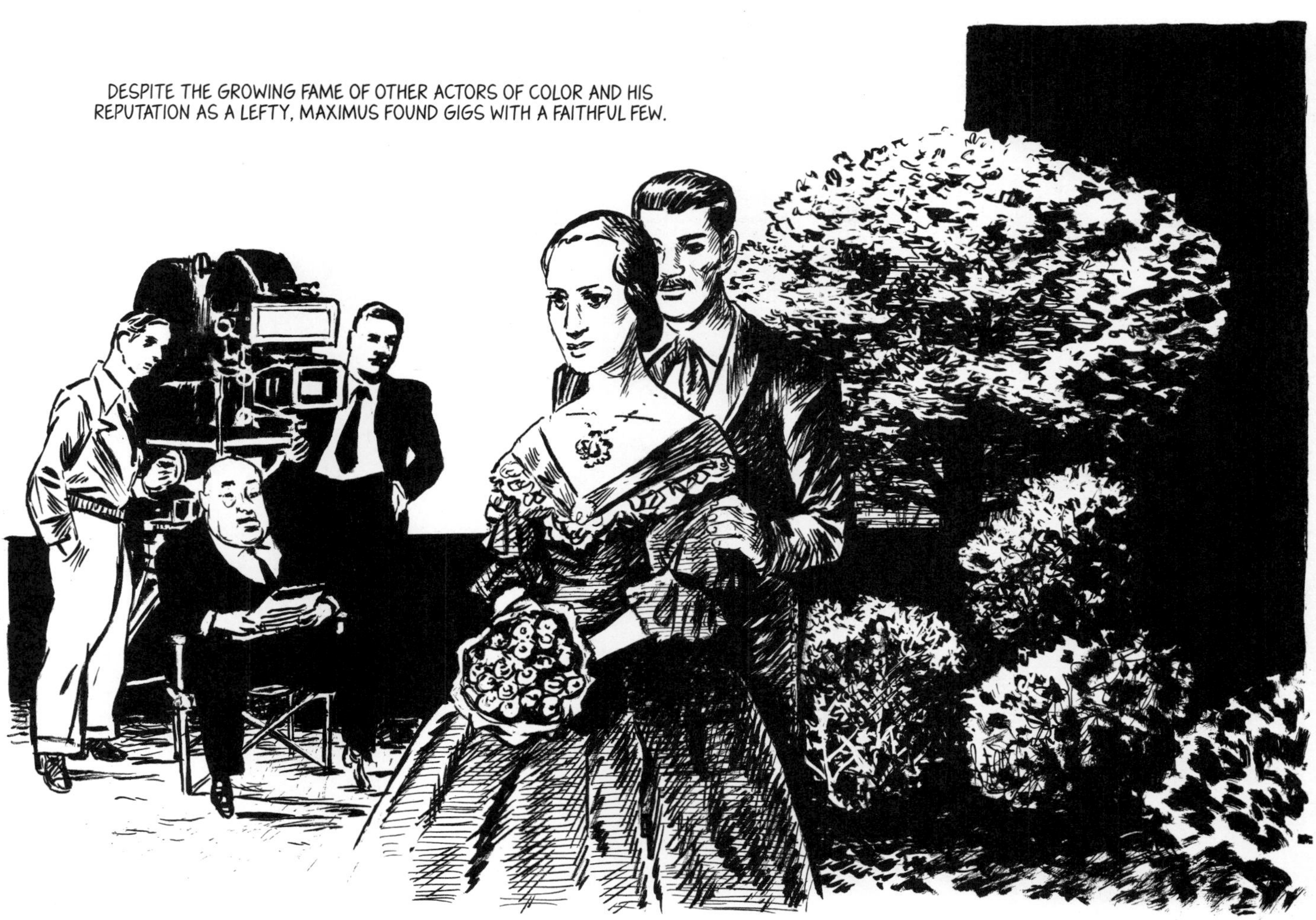
DESPITE THE GROWING FAME OF OTHER ACTORS OF COLOR AND HIS REPUTATION AS A LEFTY, MAXIMUS FOUND GIGS WITH A FAITHFUL FEW.

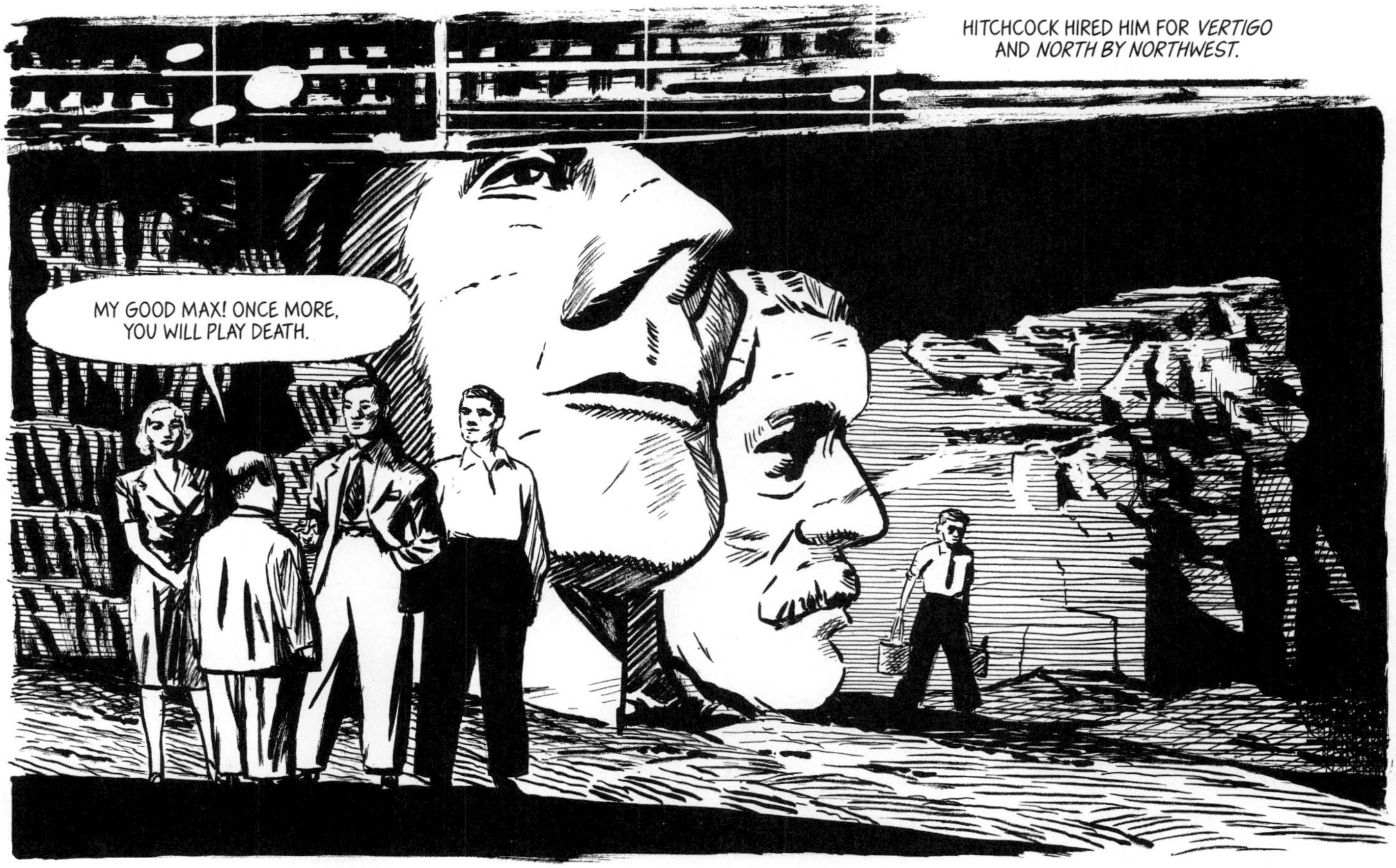
HITCHCOCK HIRED HIM FOR *VERTIGO* AND *NORTH BY NORTHWEST*.
MY GOOD MAX! ONCE MORE, YOU WILL PLAY DEATH.

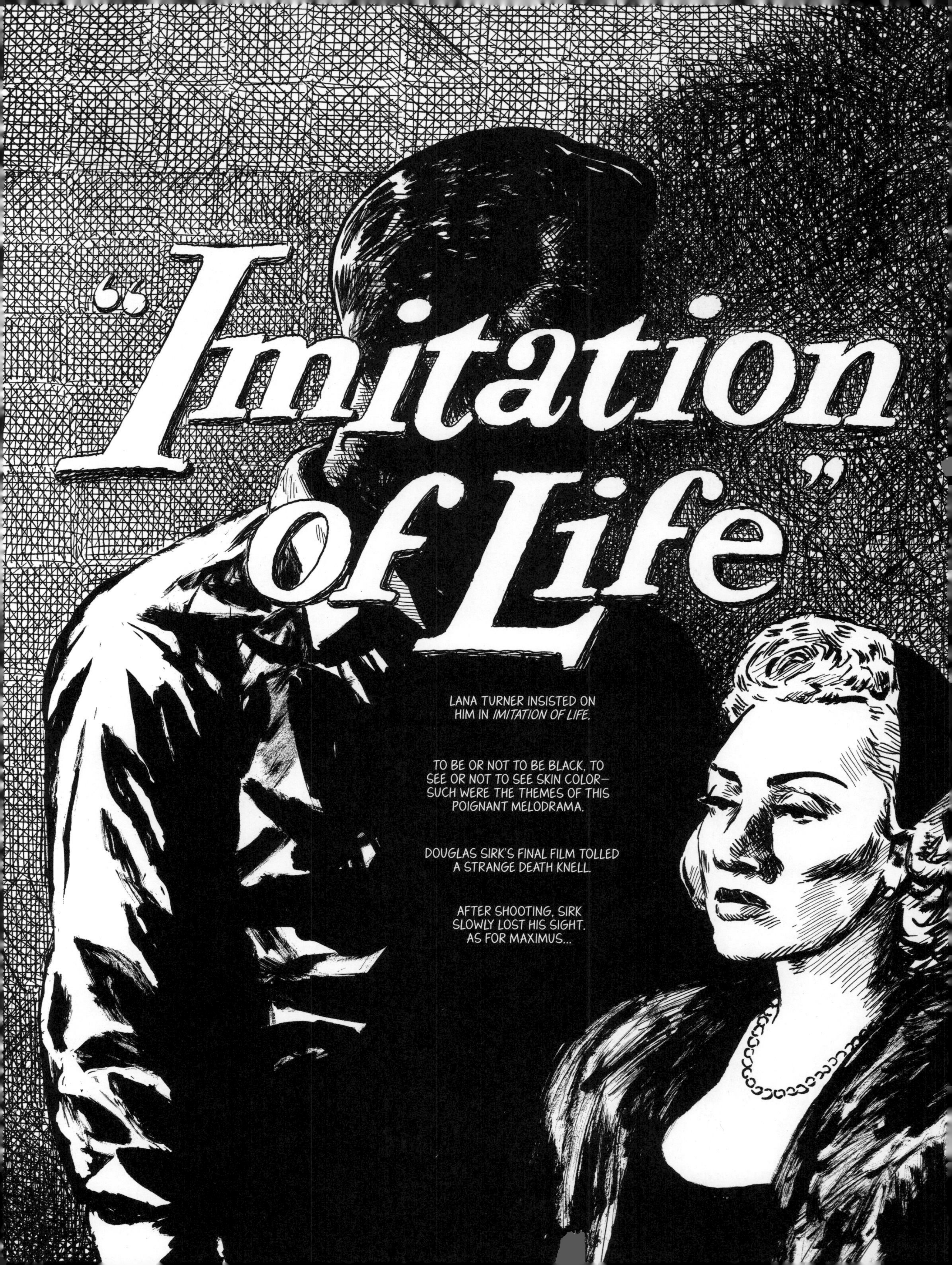

"Imitation of Life"
LANA TURNER INSISTED ON HIM IN *IMITATION OF LIFE*.
TO BE OR NOT TO BE BLACK, TO SEE OR NOT TO SEE SKIN COLOR— SUCH WERE THE THEMES OF THIS POIGNANT MELODRAMA.
DOUGLAS SIRK'S FINAL FILM TOLLED A STRANGE DEATH KNELL.
AFTER SHOOTING, SIRK SLOWLY LOST HIS SIGHT. AS FOR MAXIMUS...

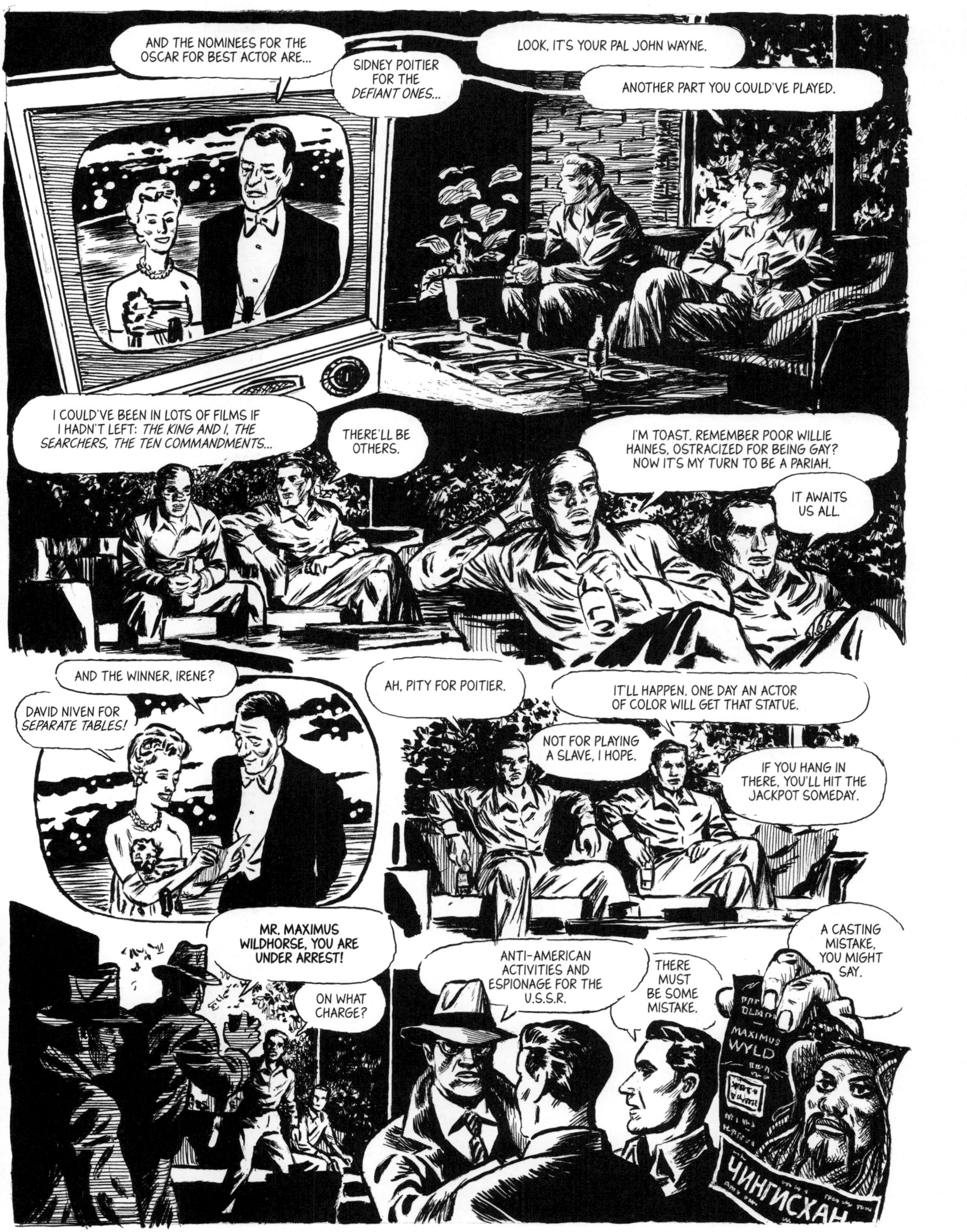
AND THE NOMINEES FOR THE OSCAR FOR BEST ACTOR ARE...
SIDNEY POITIER FOR THE *DEFIANT ONES*...
LOOK, IT'S YOUR PAL JOHN WAYNE.
ANOTHER PART YOU COULD'VE PLAYED.
I COULD'VE BEEN IN LOTS OF FILMS IF I HADN'T LEFT: *THE KING AND I, THE SEARCHERS, THE TEN COMMANDMENTS*...
THERE'LL BE OTHERS.
I'M TOAST. REMEMBER POOR WILLIE HAINES, OSTRACIZED FOR BEING GAY? NOW IT'S MY TURN TO BE A PARIAH.
IT AWAITS US ALL.
AND THE WINNER, IRENE?
DAVID NIVEN FOR *SEPARATE TABLES!*
AH, PITY FOR POITIER.
IT'LL HAPPEN. ONE DAY AN ACTOR OF COLOR WILL GET THAT STATUE.
NOT FOR PLAYING A SLAVE, I HOPE.
IF YOU HANG IN THERE, YOU'LL HIT THE JACKPOT SOMEDAY.
**MR. MAXIMUS WILDHORSE, YOU ARE UNDER ARREST!**
ON WHAT CHARGE?
ANTI-AMERICAN ACTIVITIES AND ESPIONAGE FOR THE U.S.S.R.
THERE MUST BE SOME MISTAKE.
A CASTING MISTAKE, YOU MIGHT SAY.
MAXIMUS WYLD
ЧИНГИСХАН

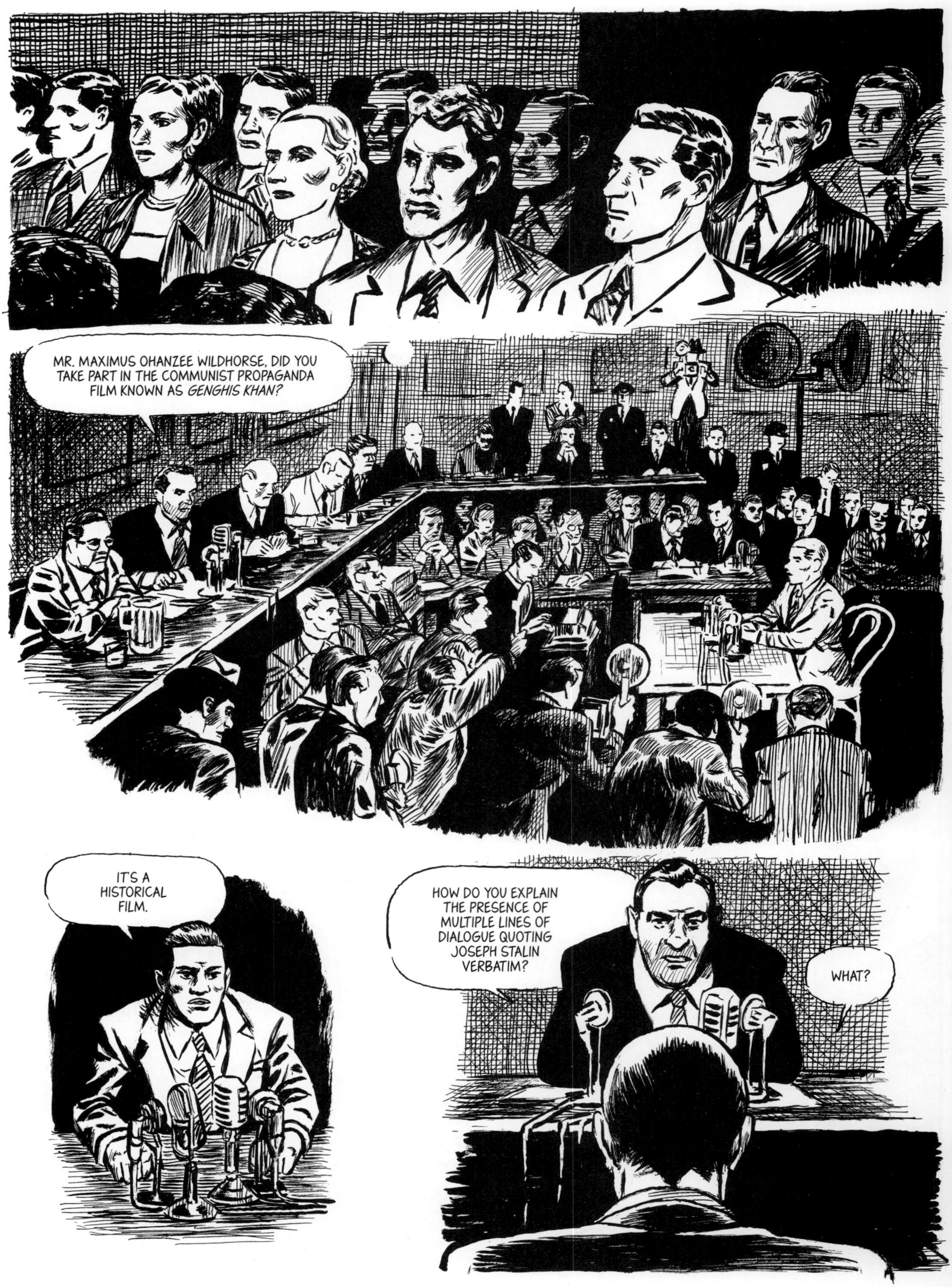

MR. MAXIMUS OHANZEE WILDHORSE, DID YOU TAKE PART IN THE COMMUNIST PROPAGANDA FILM KNOWN AS *GENGHIS KHAN?*
IT'S A HISTORICAL FILM.
HOW DO YOU EXPLAIN THE PRESENCE OF MULTIPLE LINES OF DIALOGUE QUOTING JOSEPH STALIN VERBATIM?
WHAT?

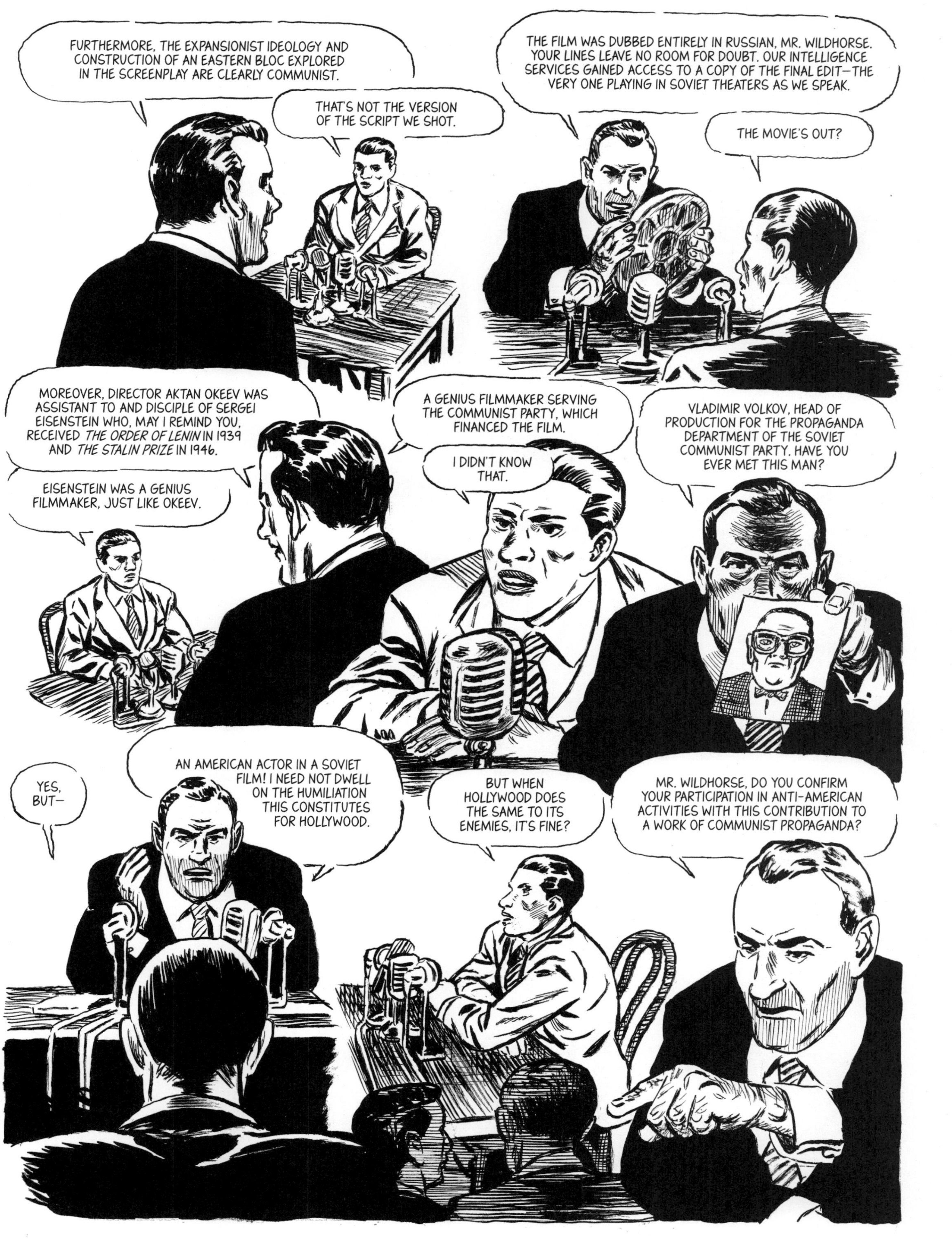
FURTHERMORE, THE EXPANSIONIST IDEOLOGY AND CONSTRUCTION OF AN EASTERN BLOC EXPLORED IN THE SCREENPLAY ARE CLEARLY COMMUNIST.
THAT'S NOT THE VERSION OF THE SCRIPT WE SHOT.
THE FILM WAS DUBBED ENTIRELY IN RUSSIAN, MR. WILDHORSE. YOUR LINES LEAVE NO ROOM FOR DOUBT. OUR INTELLIGENCE SERVICES GAINED ACCESS TO A COPY OF THE FINAL EDIT—THE VERY ONE PLAYING IN SOVIET THEATERS AS WE SPEAK.
THE MOVIE'S OUT?
MOREOVER, DIRECTOR AKTAN OKEEV WAS ASSISTANT TO AND DISCIPLE OF SERGEI EISENSTEIN WHO, MAY I REMIND YOU, RECEIVED *THE ORDER OF LENIN* IN 1939 AND *THE STALIN PRIZE* IN 1946.
EISENSTEIN WAS A GENIUS FILMMAKER, JUST LIKE OKEEV.
A GENIUS FILMMAKER SERVING THE COMMUNIST PARTY, WHICH FINANCED THE FILM.
I DIDN'T KNOW THAT.
VLADIMIR VOLKOV, HEAD OF PRODUCTION FOR THE PROPAGANDA DEPARTMENT OF THE SOVIET COMMUNIST PARTY. HAVE YOU EVER MET THIS MAN?
YES, BUT—
AN AMERICAN ACTOR IN A SOVIET FILM! I NEED NOT DWELL ON THE HUMILIATION THIS CONSTITUTES FOR HOLLYWOOD.
BUT WHEN HOLLYWOOD DOES THE SAME TO ITS ENEMIES, IT'S FINE?
MR. WILDHORSE, DO YOU CONFIRM YOUR PARTICIPATION IN ANTI-AMERICAN ACTIVITIES WITH THIS CONTRIBUTION TO A WORK OF COMMUNIST PROPAGANDA?

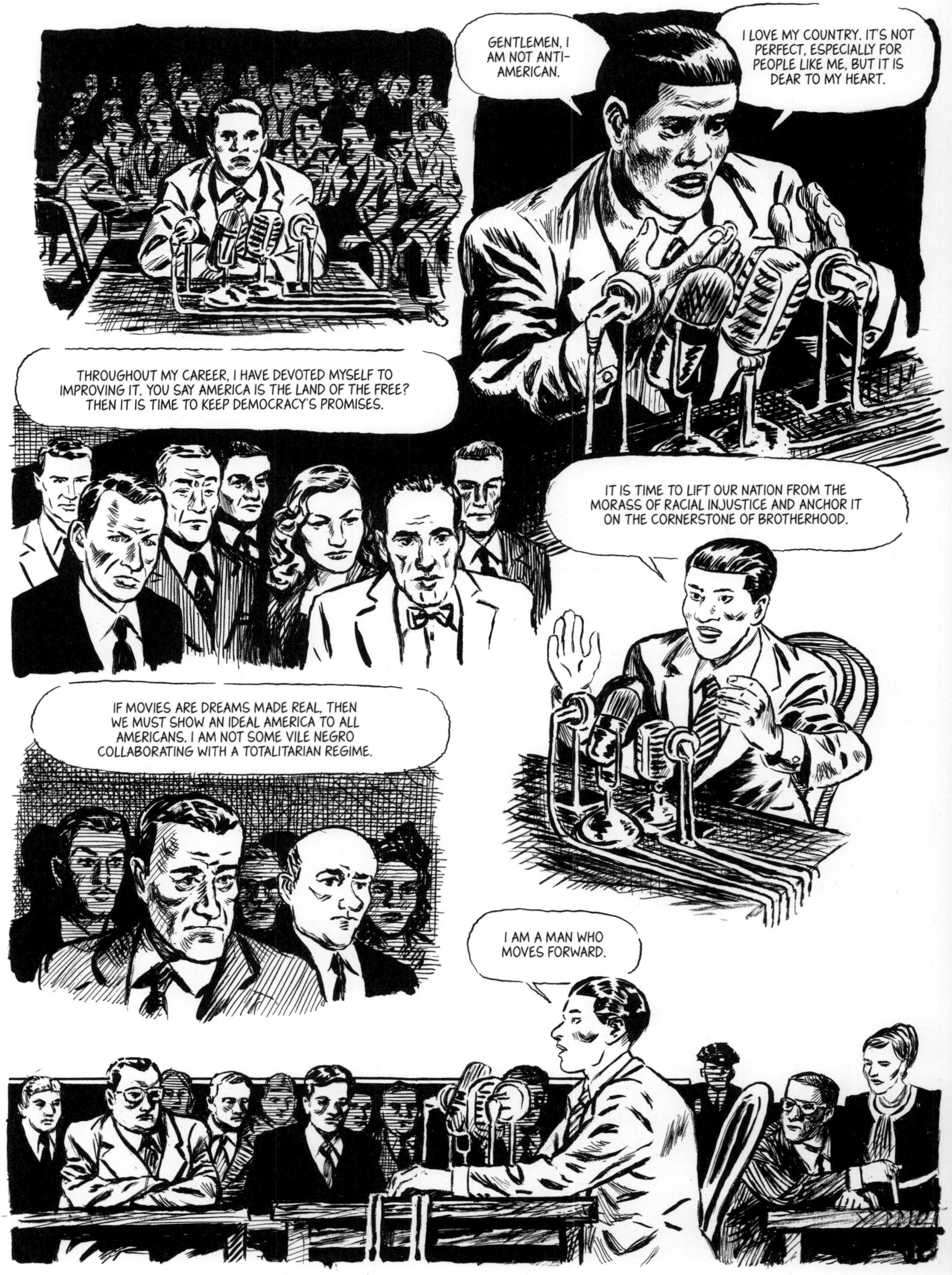
GENTLEMEN, I AM NOT ANTI-AMERICAN.
I LOVE MY COUNTRY. IT'S NOT PERFECT, ESPECIALLY FOR PEOPLE LIKE ME, BUT IT IS DEAR TO MY HEART.
THROUGHOUT MY CAREER, I HAVE DEVOTED MYSELF TO IMPROVING IT. YOU SAY AMERICA IS THE LAND OF THE FREE? THEN IT IS TIME TO KEEP DEMOCRACY'S PROMISES.
IT IS TIME TO LIFT OUR NATION FROM THE MORASS OF RACIAL INJUSTICE AND ANCHOR IT ON THE CORNERSTONE OF BROTHERHOOD.
IF MOVIES ARE DREAMS MADE REAL, THEN WE MUST SHOW AN IDEAL AMERICA TO ALL AMERICANS. I AM NOT SOME VILE NEGRO COLLABORATING WITH A TOTALITARIAN REGIME.
I AM A MAN WHO MOVES FORWARD.

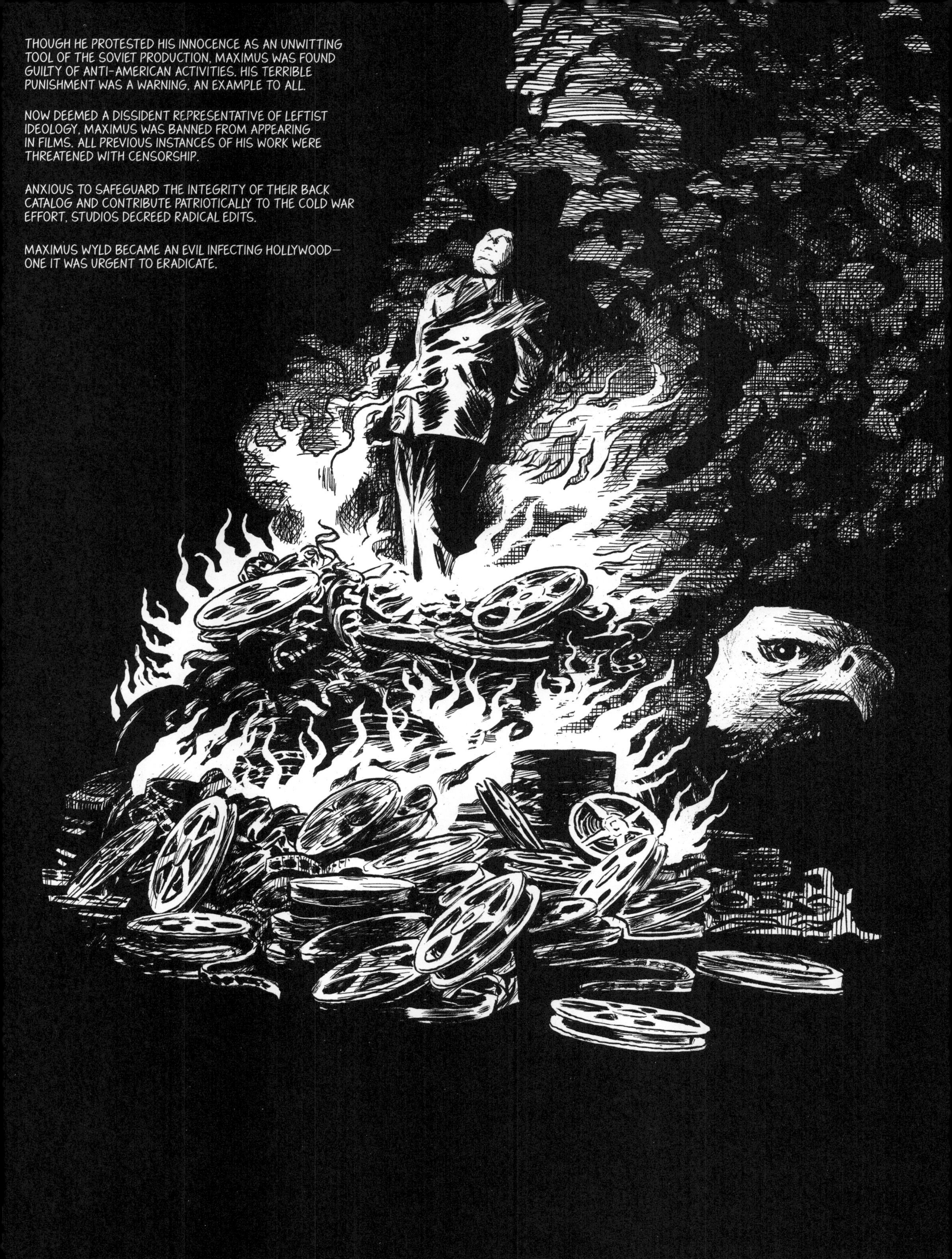
THOUGH HE PROTESTED HIS INNOCENCE AS AN UNWITTING TOOL OF THE SOVIET PRODUCTION, MAXIMUS WAS FOUND GUILTY OF ANTI-AMERICAN ACTIVITIES. HIS TERRIBLE PUNISHMENT WAS A WARNING, AN EXAMPLE TO ALL.
NOW DEEMED A DISSIDENT REPRESENTATIVE OF LEFTIST IDEOLOGY, MAXIMUS WAS BANNED FROM APPEARING IN FILMS. ALL PREVIOUS INSTANCES OF HIS WORK WERE THREATENED WITH CENSORSHIP.
ANXIOUS TO SAFEGUARD THE INTEGRITY OF THEIR BACK CATALOG AND CONTRIBUTE PATRIOTICALLY TO THE COLD WAR EFFORT, STUDIOS DECREED RADICAL EDITS.
MAXIMUS WYLD BECAME AN EVIL INFECTING HOLLYWOOD— ONE IT WAS URGENT TO ERADICATE.

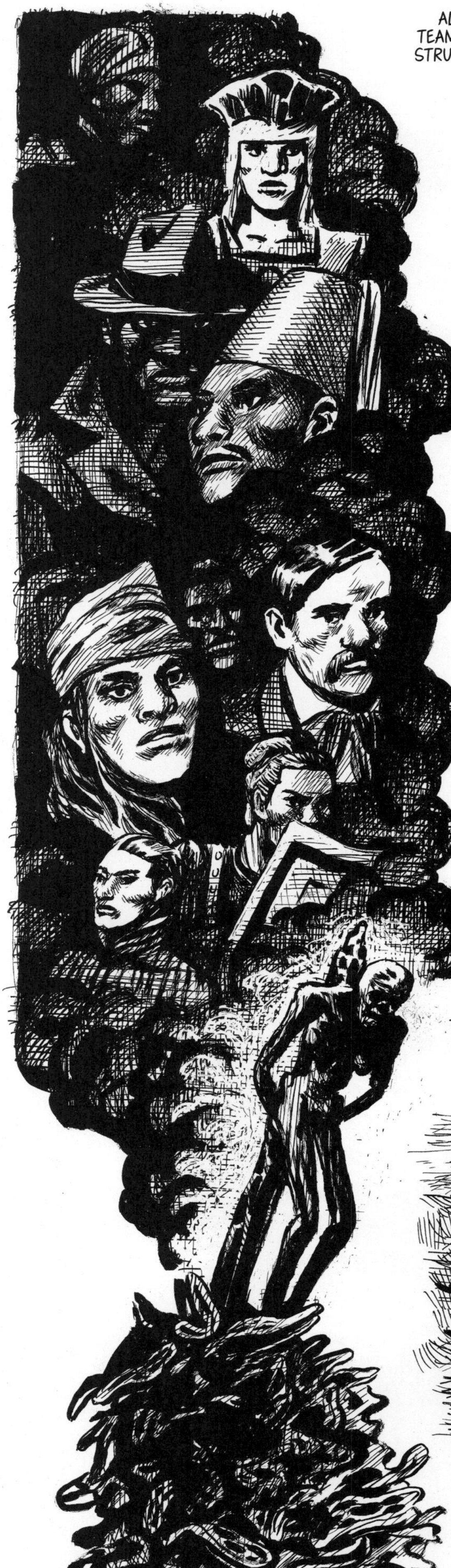

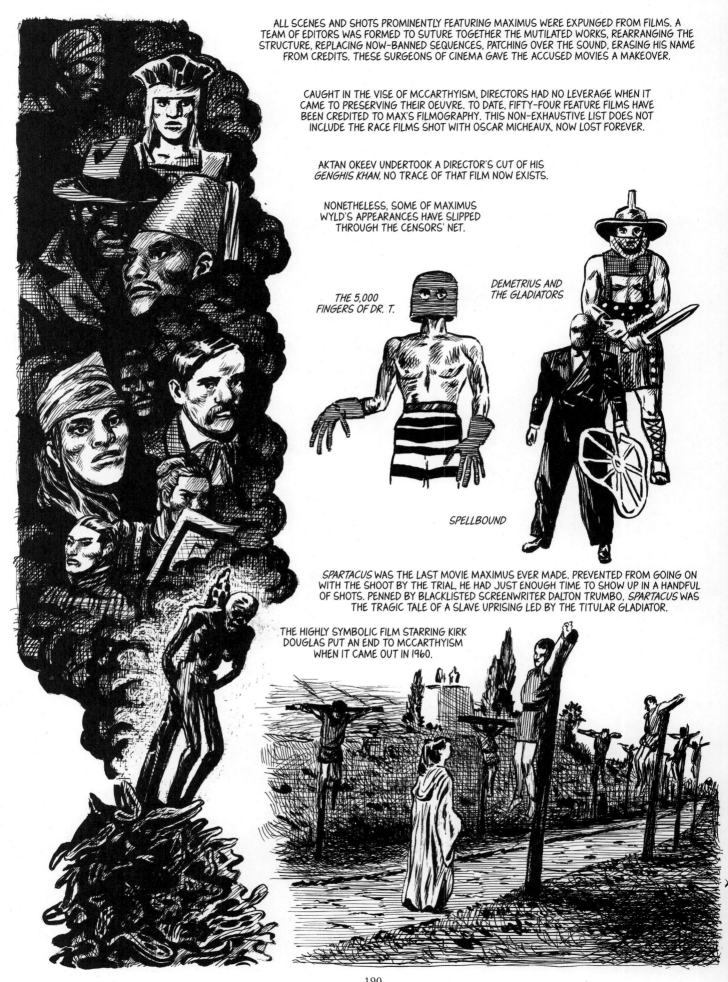

ALL SCENES AND SHOTS PROMINENTLY FEATURING MAXIMUS WERE EXPUNGED FROM FILMS. A TEAM OF EDITORS WAS FORMED TO SUTURE TOGETHER THE MUTILATED WORKS, REARRANGING THE STRUCTURE, REPLACING NOW-BANNED SEQUENCES, PATCHING OVER THE SOUND, ERASING HIS NAME FROM CREDITS. THESE SURGEONS OF CINEMA GAVE THE ACCUSED MOVIES A MAKEOVER.

CAUGHT IN THE VISE OF MCCARTHYISM, DIRECTORS HAD NO LEVERAGE WHEN IT CAME TO PRESERVING THEIR OEUVRE. TO DATE, FIFTY-FOUR FEATURE FILMS HAVE BEEN CREDITED TO MAX'S FILMOGRAPHY. THIS NON-EXHAUSTIVE LIST DOES NOT INCLUDE THE RACE FILMS SHOT WITH OSCAR MICHEAUX, NOW LOST FOREVER.

AKTAN OKEEV UNDERTOOK A DIRECTOR'S CUT OF HIS *GENGHIS KHAN*. NO TRACE OF THAT FILM NOW EXISTS.

NONETHELESS, SOME OF MAXIMUS WYLD'S APPEARANCES HAVE SLIPPED THROUGH THE CENSORS' NET.

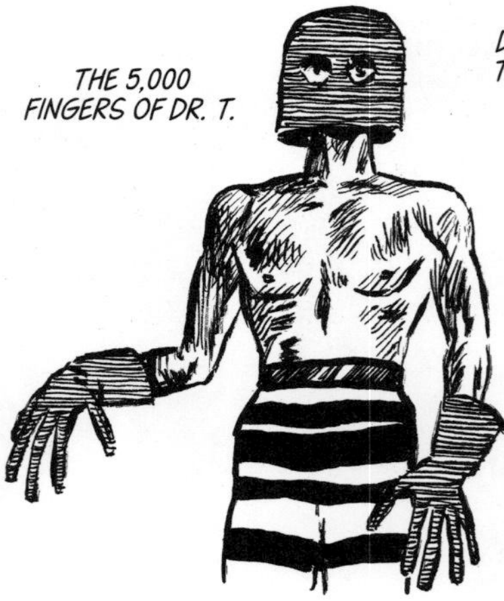

*THE 5,000 FINGERS OF DR. T.*

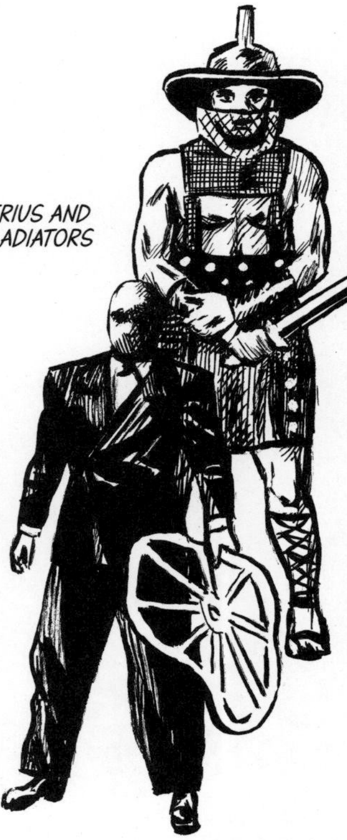

*DEMETRIUS AND THE GLADIATORS*

*SPELLBOUND*

*SPARTACUS* WAS THE LAST MOVIE MAXIMUS EVER MADE. PREVENTED FROM GOING ON WITH THE SHOOT BY THE TRIAL, HE HAD JUST ENOUGH TIME TO SHOW UP IN A HANDFUL OF SHOTS. PENNED BY BLACKLISTED SCREENWRITER DALTON TRUMBO, *SPARTACUS* WAS THE TRAGIC TALE OF A SLAVE UPRISING LED BY THE TITULAR GLADIATOR.

THE HIGHLY SYMBOLIC FILM STARRING KIRK DOUGLAS PUT AN END TO MCCARTHYISM WHEN IT CAME OUT IN 1960.

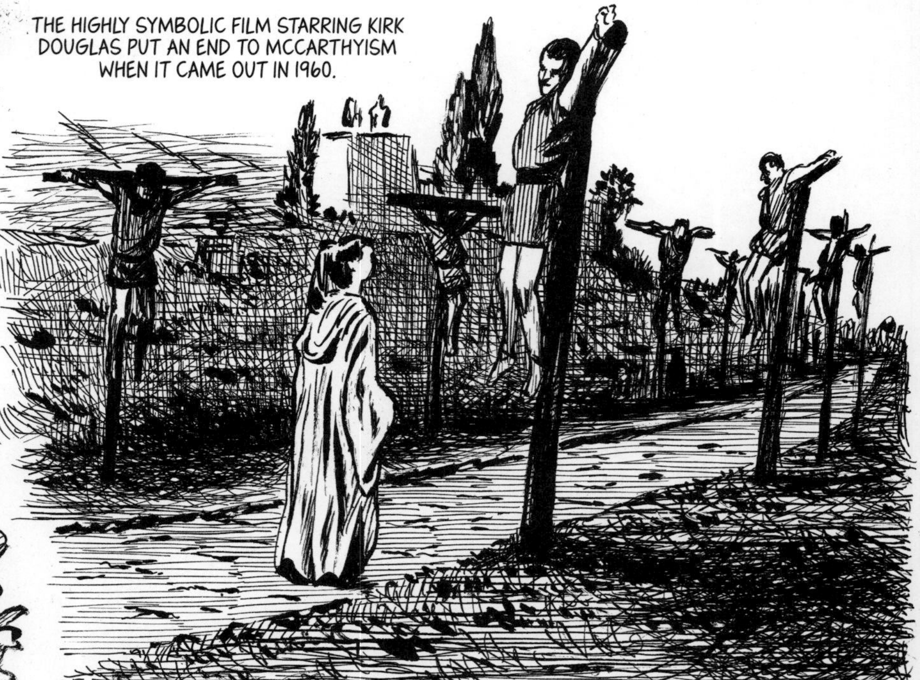

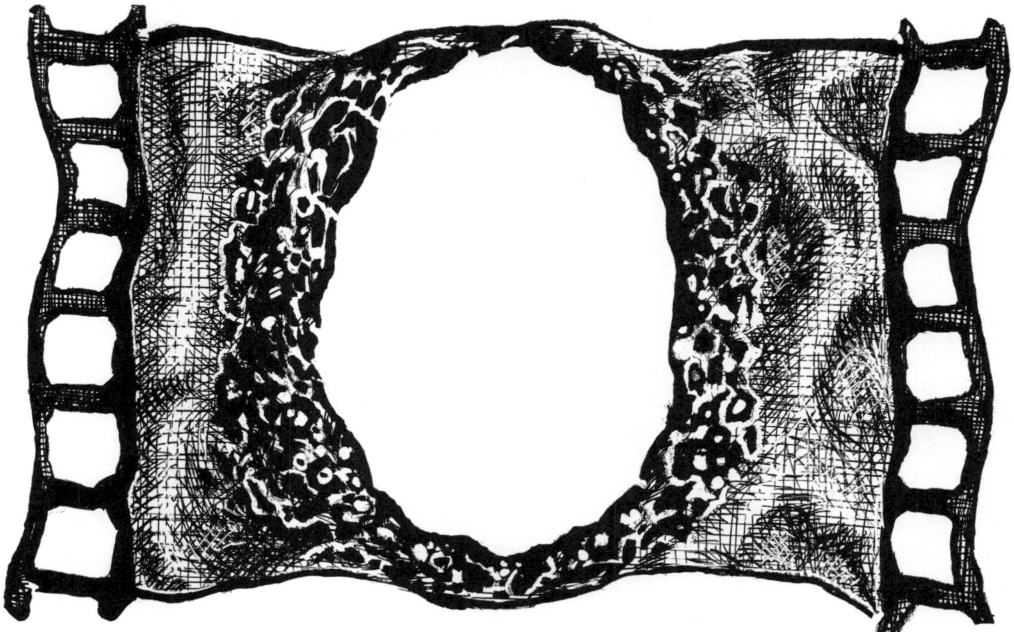

MAXIMUS WYLD SERVED TWO YEARS IN PRISON AND WAS BANNED FROM ANY AND ALL PARTICIPATION IN CINEMA. HIS SENTENCE SENT A SHOCKWAVE THROUGH HOLLYWOOD, LOWERING A CONE OF FEAR AND SILENCE OVER THE INDUSTRY. BY UNSPOKEN AGREEMENT, NO ONE DARED BRING UP THE "MAXIMUS WYLD" AFFAIR.

IN THE '60S, PAUL ROBESON SANK INTO A CRIPPLING DEPRESSION THAT LEFT HIM CONSIDERABLY DIMINISHED, FORCING HIM TO HALT HIS ACTIVITIES UNTIL HIS DEATH IN 1976. HIS SON SUSPECTED AMERICAN INTELLIGENCE AGENCIES OF POISONING HIM. THE CENSORSHIP THAT HELD SWAY IN THE '50S EFFACED HIS REPUTATION, HIS RENOWN, AND THE SCOPE OF HIS FIGHT AGAINST INEQUALITY. A PRECURSOR TO MARTIN LUTHER KING JR.'S ACTIVISM, HE REMAINS LITTLE KNOWN TO AUDIENCES TODAY.

MUCH LIKE ROBESON, W.E.B. DU BOIS—SOCIOLOGIST, HISTORIAN, GREAT DEFENDER OF CIVIL RIGHTS—WAS OFTEN HOUNDED BY THE AMERICAN GOVERNMENT FOR HIS SOCIALIST IDEAS, AND STRIPPED OF HIS PASSPORT DURING THE '50S. IN 1960, HE CHOSE EXILE IN GHANA, WHERE HE PASSED AWAY ON AUGUST 27, 1963.

ON FEBRUARY 21, 1965, MALCOLM X WAS SHOT DOWN BY THREE MEMBERS OF THE NATION OF ISLAM. THE FBI IS SUSPECTED OF HAVING ENCOURAGED THIS SETTLING OF SCORES.

MARTIN LUTHER KING JR. DIED ON APRIL 4, 1968. ALTHOUGH JAMES EARL RAY WAS CONVICTED OF HIS MURDER, SUSPICION REMAINS THAT FEDERAL AGENCIES WERE INVOLVED IN A CONSPIRACY AGAINST HIM.

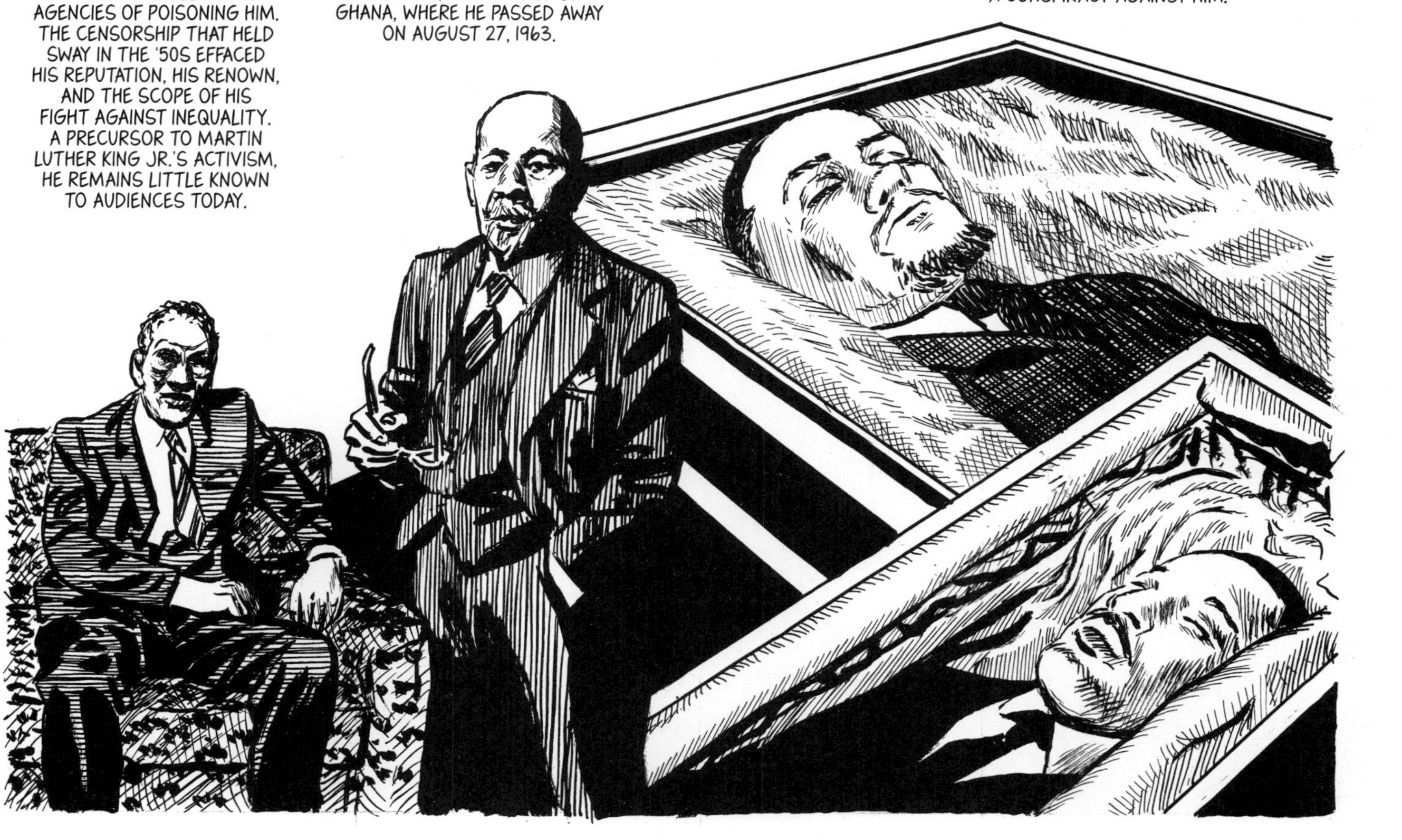

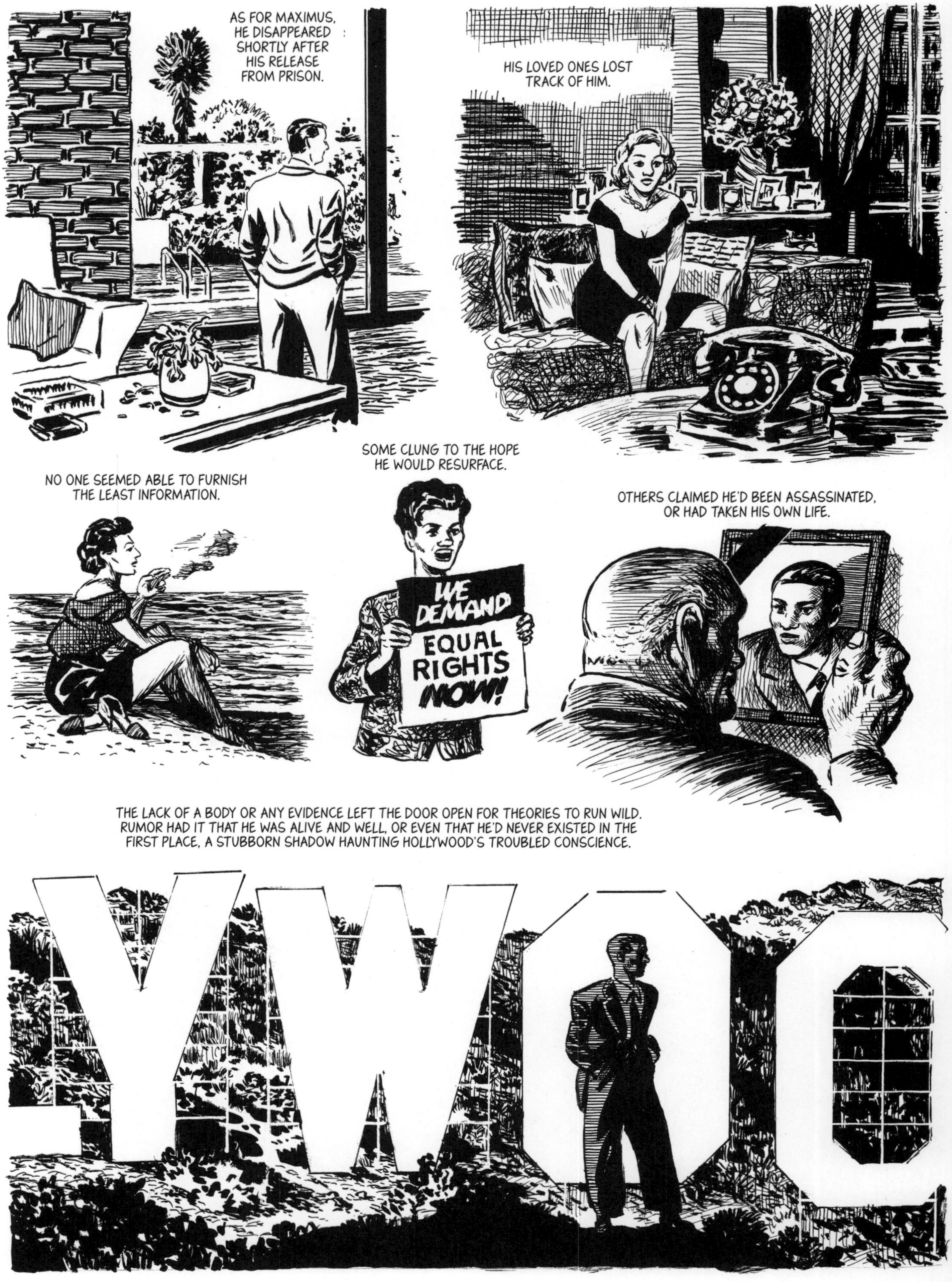
AS FOR MAXIMUS, HE DISAPPEARED SHORTLY AFTER HIS RELEASE FROM PRISON.
HIS LOVED ONES LOST TRACK OF HIM.
NO ONE SEEMED ABLE TO FURNISH THE LEAST INFORMATION.
SOME CLUNG TO THE HOPE HE WOULD RESURFACE.
WE DEMAND EQUAL RIGHTS NOW!
OTHERS CLAIMED HE'D BEEN ASSASSINATED, OR HAD TAKEN HIS OWN LIFE.
THE LACK OF A BODY OR ANY EVIDENCE LEFT THE DOOR OPEN FOR THEORIES TO RUN WILD. RUMOR HAD IT THAT HE WAS ALIVE AND WELL, OR EVEN THAT HE'D NEVER EXISTED IN THE FIRST PLACE, A STUBBORN SHADOW HAUNTING HOLLYWOOD'S TROUBLED CONSCIENCE.

ALL THOSE SCENES THAT FEATURED MAXIMUS WYLD... WHERE ARE THEY NOW? OFFICIALLY, THE EXCISED SEQUENCES WERE FED TO STUDIO INCINERATORS. LEGEND HAS IT THEY WERE MIRACULOUSLY AND SECRETLY PRESERVED IN A CAN LOST DEEP IN A FILM ARCHIVE, AND THAT SPLICING THESE FRAGMENTS TOGETHER WOULD MAKE A MOVIE LIKE NO OTHER: THE COUNTER-HISTORY OF HOLLYWOOD, A VIBRANT VISION OF ABSENCE, THE UNSPOKEN AND THE UNSEEN, AN ANTHOLOGY OF FORBIDDEN CINEMA, OF UNDERSIDES AND MUFFLED GHOSTS.

IN OTHER WORDS, THE ESSENCE OF MYTH.

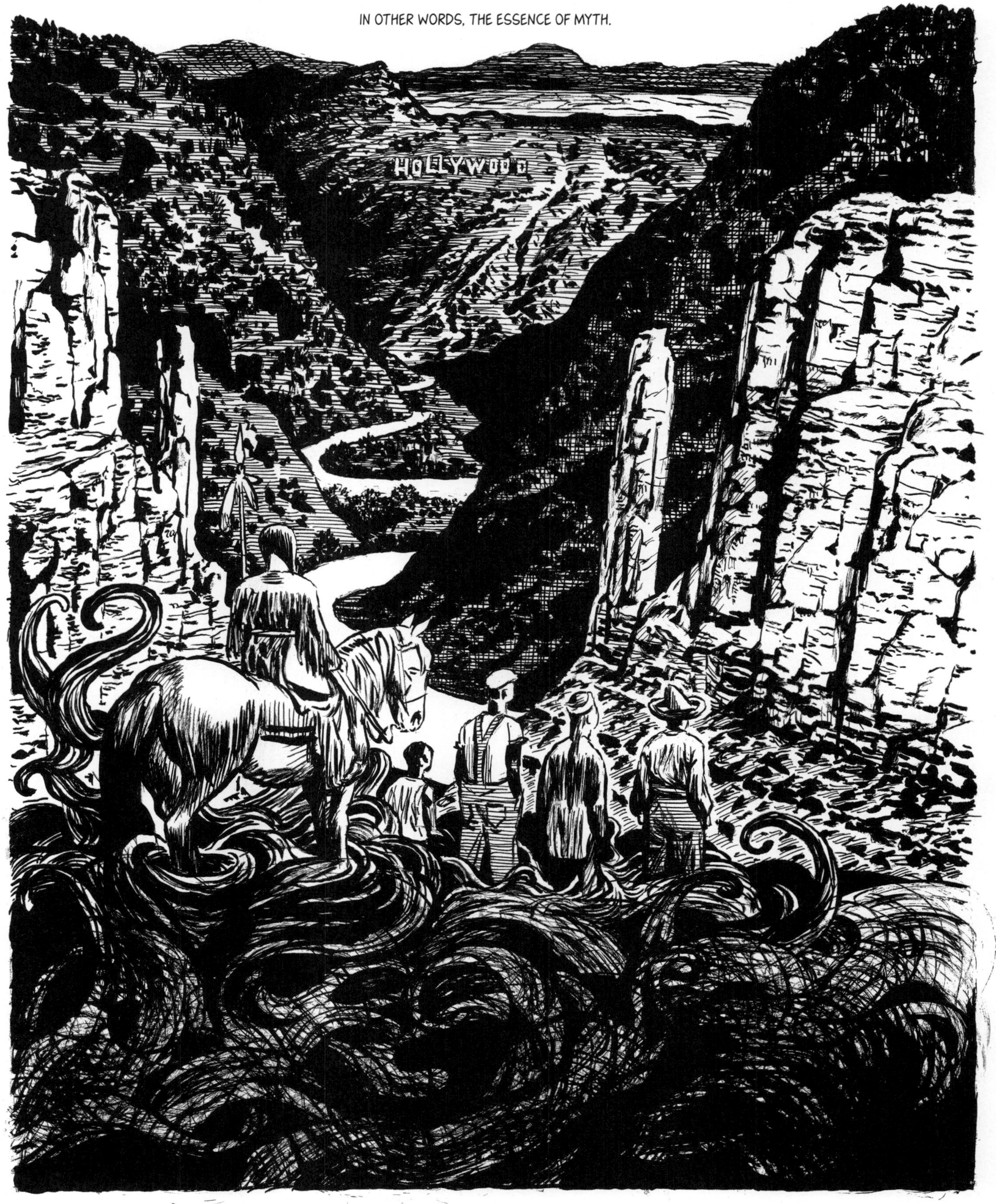
HOLLYWOOD

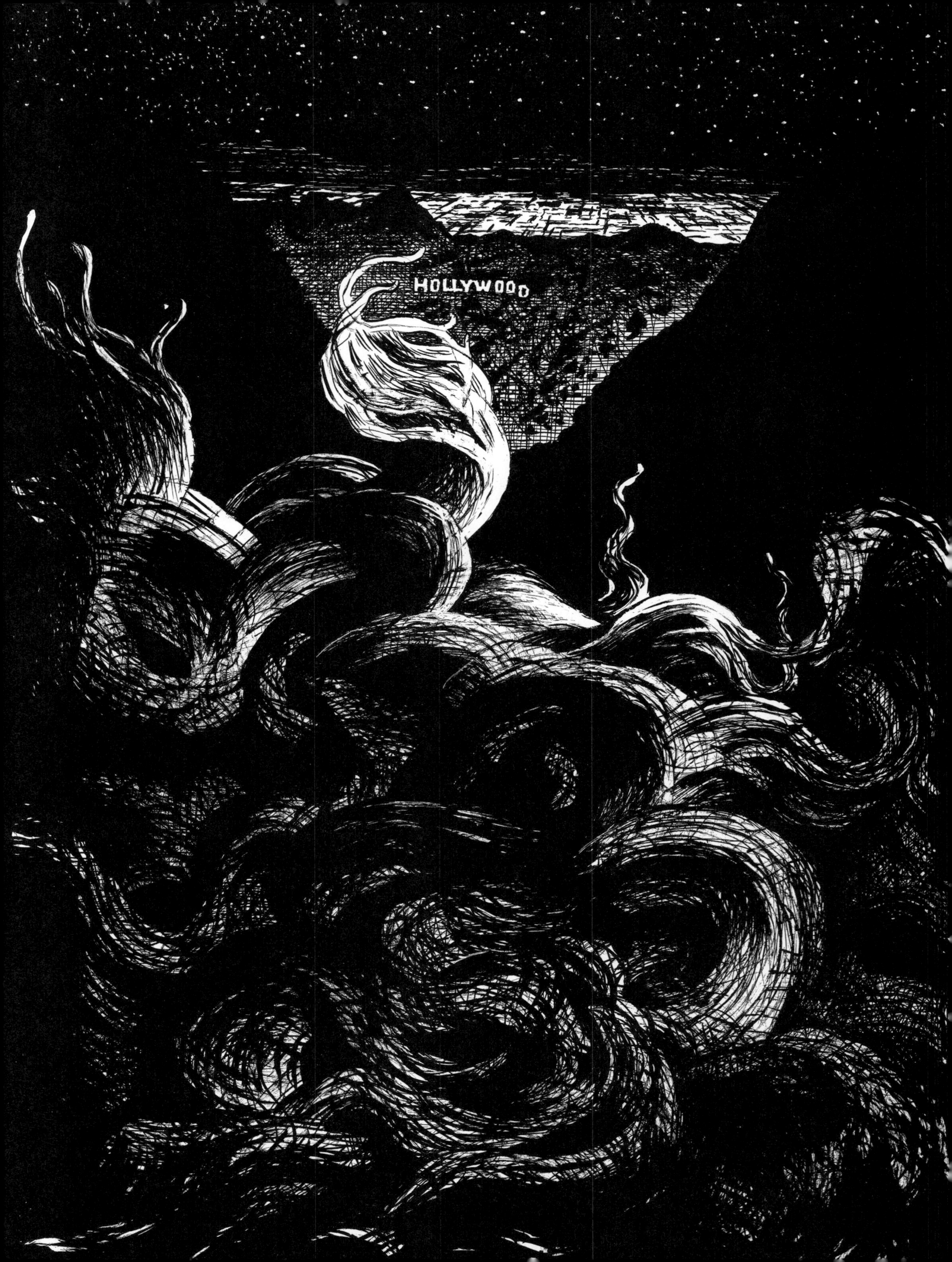
HOLLYWOOD

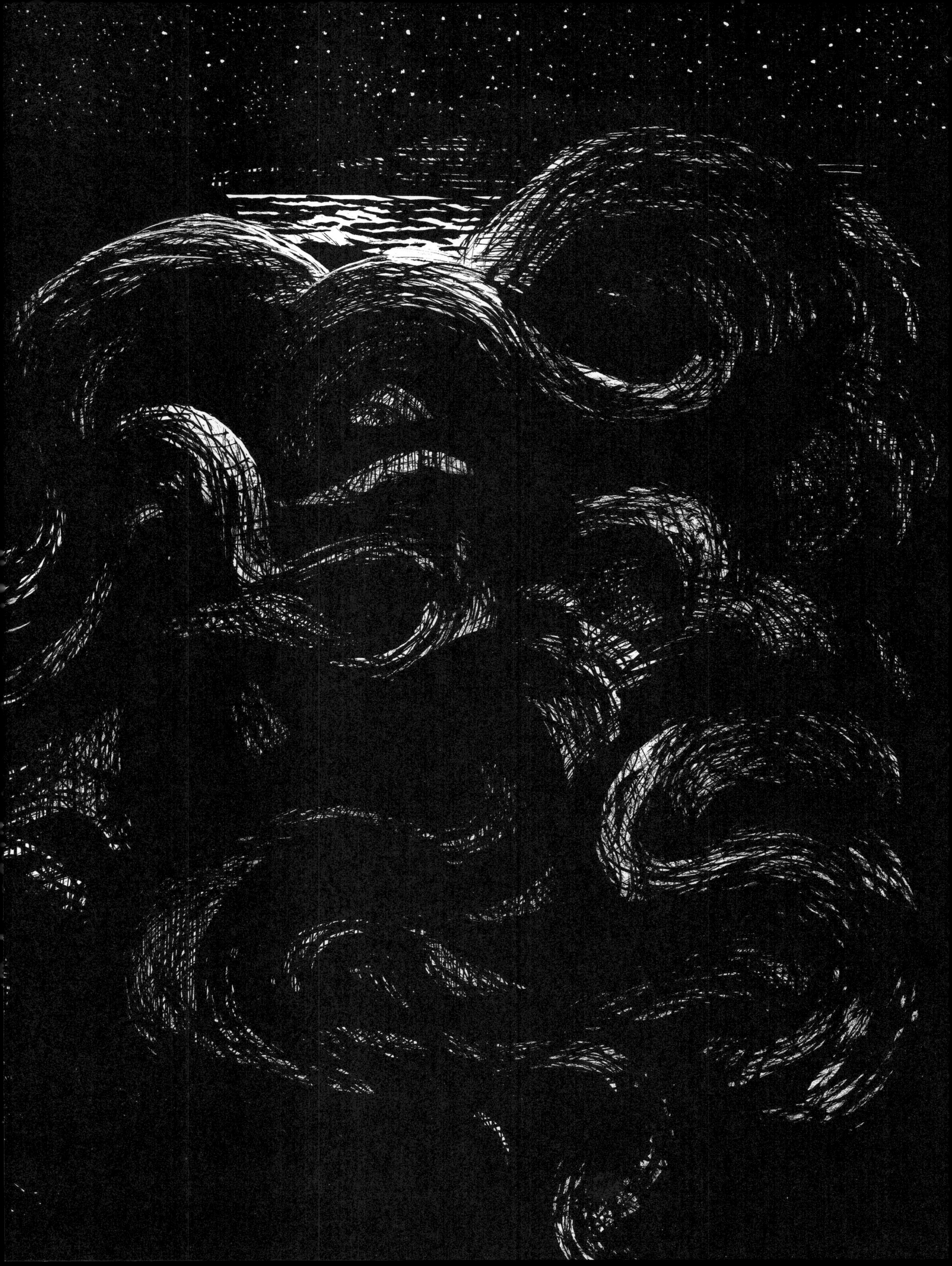

# ÉPILOGUE
# 1986

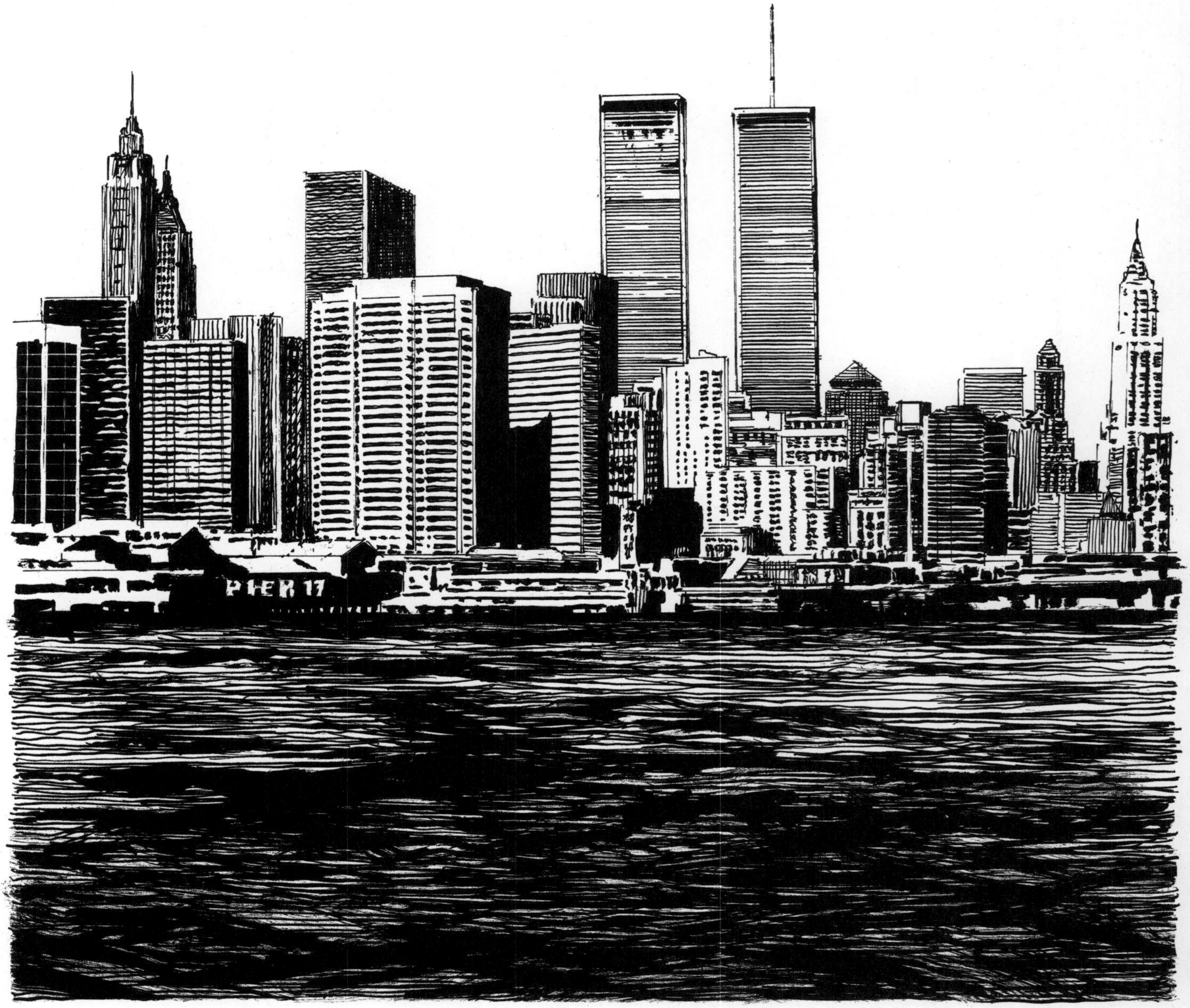

PIER 17

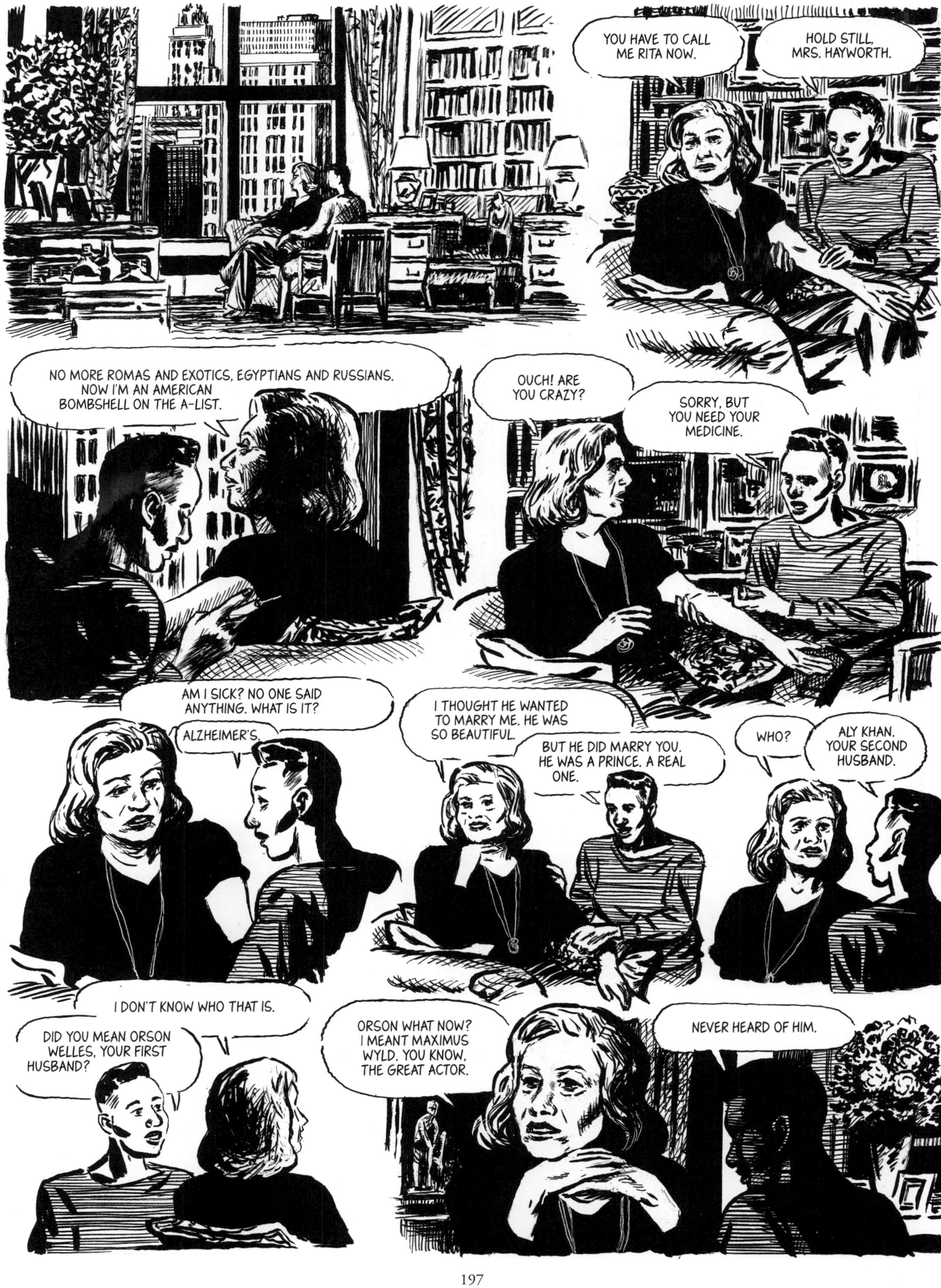
YOU HAVE TO CALL ME RITA NOW.
HOLD STILL, MRS. HAYWORTH.
NO MORE ROMAS AND EXOTICS, EGYPTIANS AND RUSSIANS. NOW I'M AN AMERICAN BOMBSHELL ON THE A-LIST.
OUCH! ARE YOU CRAZY?
SORRY, BUT YOU NEED YOUR MEDICINE.
AM I SICK? NO ONE SAID ANYTHING. WHAT IS IT?
ALZHEIMER'S.
I THOUGHT HE WANTED TO MARRY ME. HE WAS SO BEAUTIFUL.
BUT HE DID MARRY YOU. HE WAS A PRINCE. A REAL ONE.
WHO?
ALY KHAN. YOUR SECOND HUSBAND.
I DON'T KNOW WHO THAT IS.
DID YOU MEAN ORSON WELLES, YOUR FIRST HUSBAND?
ORSON WHAT NOW? I MEANT MAXIMUS WYLD. YOU KNOW, THE GREAT ACTOR.
NEVER HEARD OF HIM.

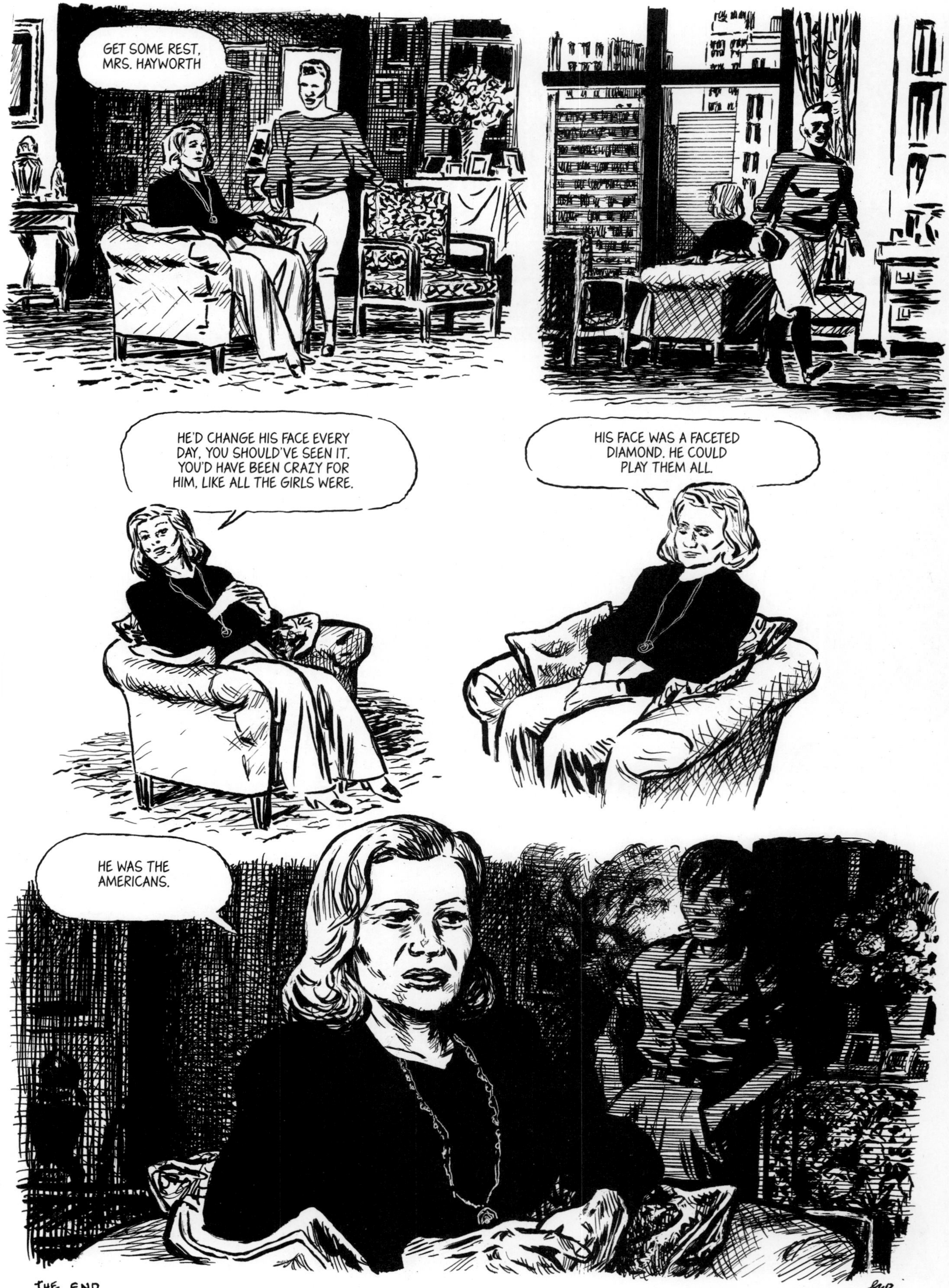
GET SOME REST, MRS. HAYWORTH
HE'D CHANGE HIS FACE EVERY DAY, YOU SHOULD'VE SEEN IT. YOU'D HAVE BEEN CRAZY FOR HIM, LIKE ALL THE GIRLS WERE.
HIS FACE WAS A FACETED DIAMOND. HE COULD PLAY THEM ALL.
HE WAS THE AMERICANS.

THE END

LOO HUI PHANG - HUGUES MICOL

# AFTERWORD

On my first read of *Erased: An Actor of Color's Journey Through the Heyday of Hollywood*, I thought it was nonfiction. I was sure I was learning about a victim of racism during the Golden Age of Hollywood I hadn't heard of. I put the graphic novel's hero Maximus Wyld alongside Anna May Wong, Paul Robeson, Lena Horne, James Hong, and countless other talented performers relegated to a career of supporting roles drenched in racial stereotypes. I even googled "Maximus Wyld" expecting to find encyclopedia entries, documentaries, and photographs.

Fool me once, shame on me, but credit French authors Loo Hui Phang and Hugues Micol for blending fact and fiction so seamlessly in the book's art and dialogue. Erased is a fictive biography of Wyld, a forgotten mixed-race Hollywood actor whose ethnic ambiguity qualifies him to play a range of characters of colors: a Tibetan monk in Frank Capra's *Lost Horizons*, a slave in *Gone With The Wind*, a Turkish gangster in *Maltese Falcon*. One studio exec calls Wyld "the most astounding chameleon in all of Hollywood" and a "human color chart."

This versatility comes at a cost to Wyld, who's marginalized by Tinseltown at every turn. "I'm sick of being left out of frame," he says at opening night of *Stormy Weather*, the iconic 1943 Black musical that starred Fayard and Harold Nicholas, Fats Waller, Lena Horne, Cab Calloway, and Bill "Bojangles" Robinson. (Wyld is in the dance numbers "separate from the main action.") His life becomes one of many compromises. Part-Chinese, he tans himself so he can win Black roles, but Wyld chases "real" progress in Hollywood, a land of make-believe. "What we need is a real colored star who can charm white and colored audiences alike," he says, believing, of course, that he can be one of those stars.

In the Old Hollywood of Erased, Sidney Poitier, Harry Belafonte, and Yul Brynner become the crossover stars Wyld dreams of being. Wyld becomes simply a forgotten predecessor. Erased reminds us that there have always been forgotten predecessors, and that if you look hard enough, no one is ever truly the first. One might remember Simu Liu playing a comic-book superhero in *Shang-Chi and the Legend of the Ten Rings* as a contemporary breakthrough but forget that Bruce Lee's son Brandon played (and died on set) as a comic-book superhero *The Crow* nearly thirty years before.

Today, Hollywood boasts of having evolved past its racist history, and yet, despite all the virtue-signaling hashtags about diversity and representation, it is still primarily as a narrative factory for white protagonists, while actors of color are slotted in as best friends, sassy sidekicks, and stylish but non-verbal villains. *Erased* is a reminder that if "real progress" has been made, there's still a long way to go before actors of color are the heroes and antiheroes in our collective racial imagination.

--Leland Cheuk, author, publisher, book critic

Also available from NBM Graphic Novels:

**NINA SIMONE In Comics**

*"Adriansen skillfully weaves together the highs and lows of Simone's life, portraying her as not just an artist but a symbol of resilience and determination."*

-Amsterdam News

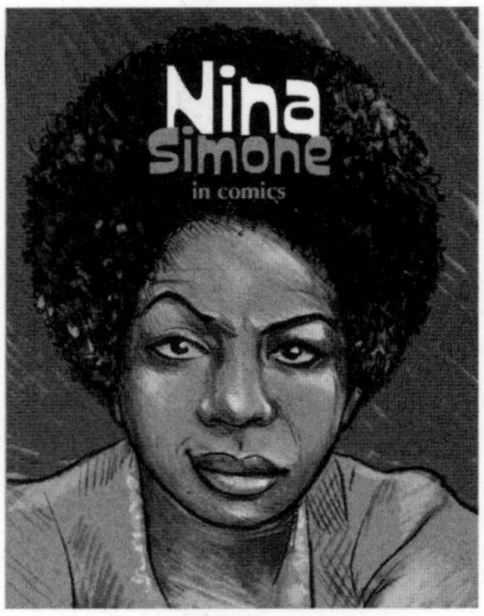
Nina
Simone
in comics

**ROSA PARKS**

*"4 out of 5 stars. The story of Rosa Parks has been told in many ways, but this is a good one."*

-ICv2

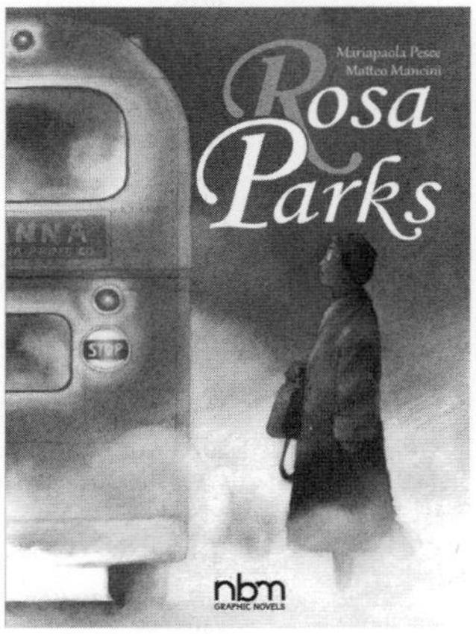
Rosa
Parks
nbm

**MINGUS**

*"The book evokes Mingus's keen intelligence, volatile personality, and virtuoso musicianship, as well as the vicious anti-Black racism of the period..."*

-Calvin Reid, Publishers Weekly

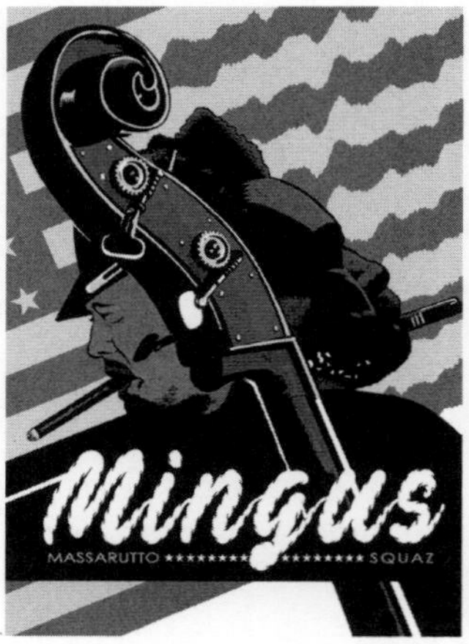
Mingus
MASSARUTTO SQUAZ

**HARLEM**

The story of Queenie, the hard-driving black woman who owned the numbers game in Harlem during the Great Depression.

WINNER OF THE MoCCA 2024
AWARD OF EXCELLENCE

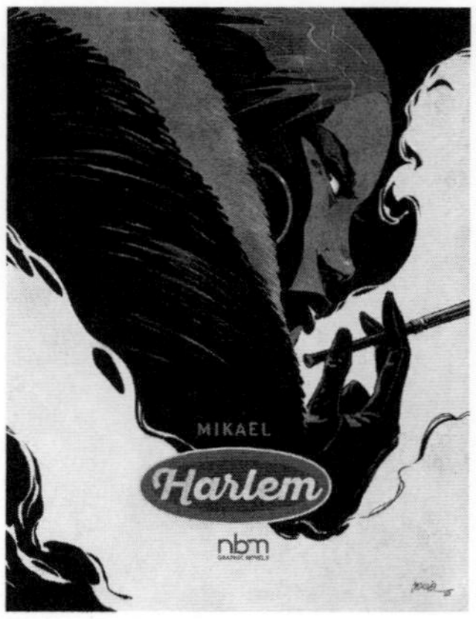
MIKAEL
Harlem
nbm

**See previews, get exclusives and order from:**
**NBMPUB.COM**

We have hundreds of graphic novels available.
Subscribe to our monthly newsletter
Follow us on Facebook & Instagram (nbmgraphicnovels),
X (Twitter, @nbmpub), Blue Sky (@nbmpub.bsky.social)

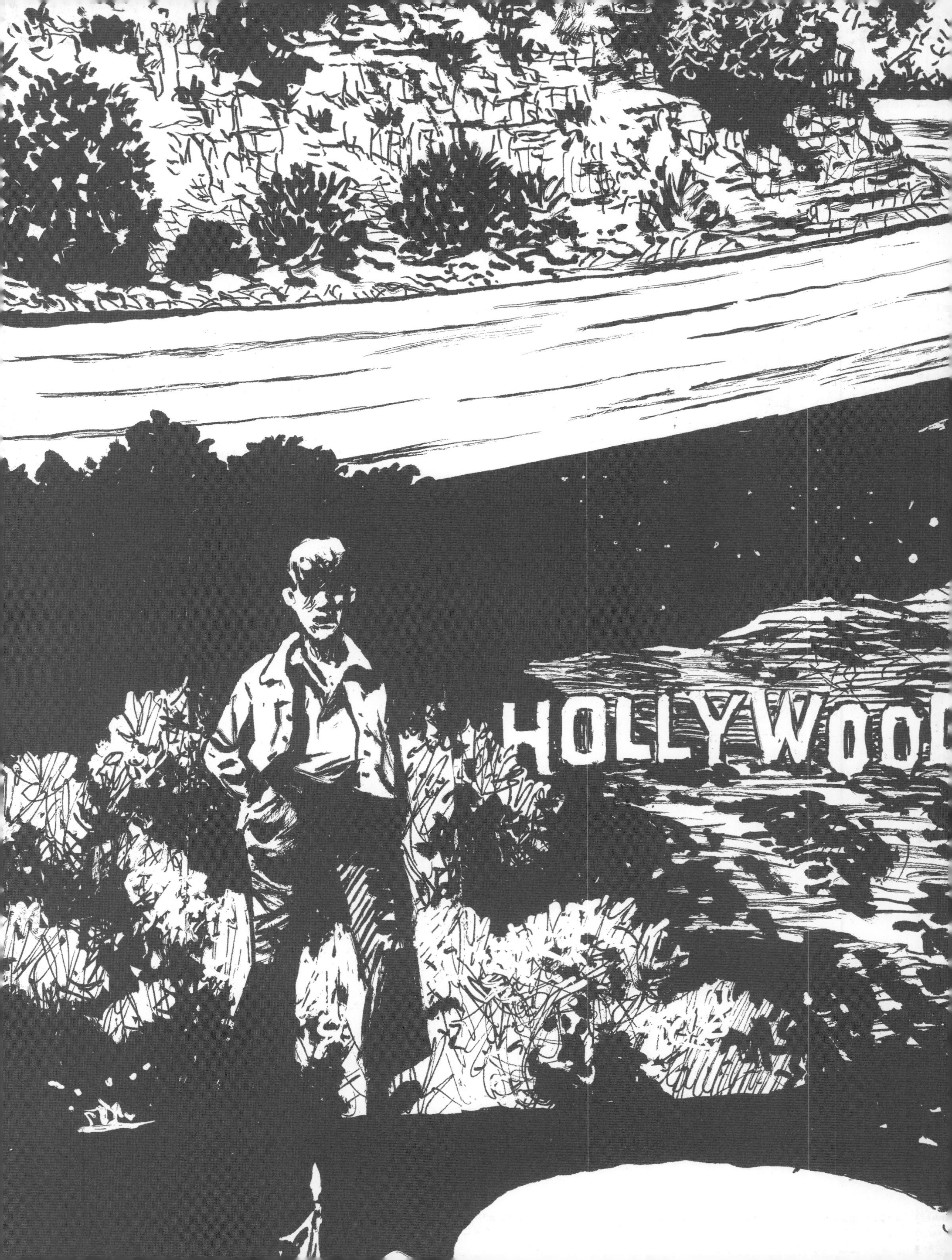
HOLLYWOO